LABOR AND EMPLOYMENT

RELATIONS ASSOCIATION SERIES

No One Size Fits All:
Worker Organization, Policy, and Movement in a New Economic Age

Edited By

Janice Fine
Linda Burnham
Kati Griffith
Minsun Ji
Victor Narro
Steven Pitts

First Edition
ISBN 978-0-913447-16-1
Price: $34.95

LABOR AND EMPLOYMENT RELATIONS ASSOCIATION SERIES
  LERA *Proceedings of the Annual Meeting* (published online annually,
    in the fall)
  LERA *Annual Research Volume* (published annually, in the summer/fall)
  LERA Online Membership Directory (updated daily, member/subscriber
    access only)
  LERA *Labor and Employment Law News* (published online each quarter)
  LERA *Perspectives on Work* (published annually, in the fall)

Information regarding membership, subscriptions, meetings, publications, and general affairs
of the LERA can be found at the Association website at www.leraweb.org. Members can make
changes to their member records, including contact information, affiliations, and preferences,
by accessing the online directory at the website or by contacting the LERA national office.

LABOR AND EMPLOYMENT RELATIONS ASSOCIATION
University of Illinois at Urbana-Champaign
School of Labor and Employment Relations
121 Labor and Employment Relations Building
504 East Armory Ave., MC-504
Champaign, IL 61820
Telephone: 217/333-0072   Fax: 217/265-5130
Website: www.leraweb.org
E-mail: LERAoffice@illinois.edu

Acknowledgments

The editors wish to express their appreciation and gratitude for the extraordinary work of Sonia Szczesna, research assistant at Rutgers, whose smarts, commitment, organization, and tenacity were instrumental in bringing this project to fruition. We also thank Ari Avgar, Editor-in-Chief for the Labor and Employment Relations Association, for the confidence he always expressed in our ability to pull this off, his strong belief in the importance of this project, and his sage advice along the way.

Contents

Section Four: Working Up the Chain

Introduction

Janice Fine
School of Management and Labor Relations, Rutgers University,
and the Center for Innovation in Worker Organization

Kati L. Griffith
School of Industrial and Labor Relations, Cornell University

Victor Narro
UCLA Labor Center

Steven C. Pitts
UC Berkeley Labor Center

Workers and their organizations are facing enormous obstacles today. Corporations wield immense power, not only in the marketplace but also in politics, which has, for many years, effectively blocked the updating of antiquated laws governing labor relations. Instead, unions have been subjected to a steady onslaught of attacks at the state level and growing hostility from the US Supreme Court. They have all but lost basic protections that the legal system once provided—making organizing, bargaining, and striking increasingly difficult. Black workers continue to face a decades-long job crisis characterized by disproportionate unemployment (compared with White workers) and poor job quality. Immigrant workers of all statuses feel the threat of exclusionary immigration policies and heightened xenophobic rhetoric coming from the top echelons of the US government.

Similar to worker organizing in the United States before the New Deal contract, organizations in the late 20th and early 21st centuries have been scrambling to find leverage within an increasingly hostile economic, political, and legal environment. Despite formidable obstacles, this volume shows that vibrant, creative experimentation has never ceased. In lieu of new federal regulation, public and private sector national unions and local affiliates have been actively trying out new approaches that pair organizing with mechanisms that support bargaining. They have doubled down on electoral politics and creative policy fights to raise standards and facilitate organizing, with an unprecedented focus on low-wage workers. They have forged closer, more equal partnerships with community organizations than ever before. Still much more work needs to be done.

New organizational models are also emergent. These experiments, which include worker centers and what some refer to as "alt labor" groups, diverge from traditional labor unions in a number of ways. They aim to represent workers and their workplace interests but do not typically work within the New Deal collective bargaining construct regulated by the government.

Janice Fine's groundbreaking 2006 book, *Worker Centers: Organizing Communities at the Edge of the Dream,* revealed worker centers to be community organizations that use a variety of strategies (including organizing, policy advocacy, and service provision) in their quest to improve the working lives of low-wage workers. Since the publication of Fine's book, organizations have continued to experiment with new ways to change working conditions, even when they cannot effectively influence private sector actors directly. These strategies, as we elaborate on below, include leveraging the government to improve labor standards enforcement, raising minimum wages, and organizing coalitions that can put economic and moral pressure on companies that are at the top of labor and product supply chains.

Given the strength of the forces arrayed against improving working conditions and building worker power, worker organizations cannot simply follow the organizing and collective bargaining trajectories of the past. They must innovate, and they have been doing so, sometimes achieving significant, albeit limited, victories.

This volume brings together a panoply of examples of efforts that are being made to improve working conditions across the country, while acknowledging the structural dynamics that challenge and condition them in 21st-century America. The title of this volume, *No One Size Fits All,* is intended both to capture the diverse strategic repertoire we found and to stand as a corrective to the idea that there is a single organizational model or strategy. There is no magical model that, like Dumbo's magic feather, would allow workers to soar above employers' rejection of the post-war social compact, virulent union busting, generations' worth of anti-union legal developments, dramatic shifts in firm and industry structures and employment relations, globalization, and technological change. No magical model can overcome the country's reliance on the exploitation of workers who are marked by their racial, gender, and citizenship status. Our view is that the future for workers' organizations is plural rather than singular—containing a multiplicity of organizational forms and strategies.

Several chapters in the volume address macro-level challenges to the movement of worker organizations. They set forth critical information about the labor market and demographic trends underlying the experimentation that has been taking place. Jacobs, Smiley, and Theodore all invoke the decline of the vertically integrated firm and the rise of global supply chains. Poo and Shah describe the aging of the population and concomitant spike in demand for care work, along with the promise and perils of the new on-demand economy platforms. Rhomberg cites the fast food industry as the quintessential example of the precarious and low-paid work that characterizes fissured employment relations. Pitts provides an overview of the dimensions of the Black jobs crisis and the main causal factors underlying it. Fine,

Narro, and Barnes as well as Bada, Gleeson, and de Graauw present immigration demographics and a troubling immigration/labor policy history. McCartin reviews the political and juridical assault on unions of the past half century along with the deregulation and financialization that further weakened them. Taken together, these chapters provide an overview of the key external variables that have shaped the rough terrain on which worker organizations are taking action.

Another set of chapters delves into some of the internal organizational characteristics and dynamics that are shaping the strategic choices unions and worker centers are making. McAlevey explores the reasons for the decline of the strike as a central power-building strategy on the part of most unions. She illuminates the fundamental organizing techniques that have enabled certain unions in strategic sectors of the economy, such as health care and education, to strike and win through the construction and consolidation of powerful workplace committees involved in actions that test the strategic capacity of leaders and depth of member commitment. Fine, Han, Sparks, and Yu present the results of a large survey of job satisfaction and occupational challenges among professional union organizers. Their chapter suggests that while organizers have cited similar difficulties and challenges for many years, unions have not fundamentally altered the model. Gates, Griffith, Kim, Mokhiber, Bazler, and Case find that worker centers' funding strategies look more like those of nonprofit organizations than of unions: overwhelmingly dependent on external funding streams (foundation grants, government grants, and individual donations) rather than those internally generated (membership dues). They also find that a few "giants" skew the average revenue of worker centers, as the vast majority of centers take in less than $100,000 a year. Fine, Narro, and Barnes conclude that the formation of national worker center networks and the expansion of large centers can help explain the main growth spurts in the movement over time. They argue that the 501(c)(3) nonprofit structure, which enabled foundation and government funding, has facilitated the organization of low-wage workers. Nonetheless, this funding model, they contend, also means that centers have less incentive to build a base of dues-paying members. They predict that centers, based on this structure, will continue to limit themselves to public policy campaigns that can be won without the economic power required for strikes and other economic actions.

The chapters, considered together, paint a picture of the variety of change strategies organizations are engaging in. McCartin provides an overview and typology of the strategic repertoire of unions, worker centers, and economic justice coalitions over the past generation, including efforts to organize and bargain beyond the individual employer, to align organizing and bargaining with broader community interests, to use investment strategies to advance organizing and bargaining, to seek alternative union recognition strategies, to engage in creative militancy to revive and redefine strikes and related work actions, and to develop alternative worker organizations. Rhomberg recounts the historical development of the Fight for $15 movement and the central role of the Service Employees International Union in providing financing, organizing, and communications capacity.

Several chapters focus on how unions and community organizations are redefining the meaning of "bargaining" and striking. Smiley posits bargaining as the central conceptual framework for modern worker movements, arguing that non-union workers are building a vibrant movement that is shaping the future of bargaining in ways that could engage large numbers through broadening the scope of traditional bargaining, bargaining with what she calls the "ultimate profiteer" and engaging in community-driven bargaining. In a similar vein, Sneiderman and McCartin propose "Bargaining for the Common Good" as a new model that unites labor and community organizations across issue areas in the struggle against a common target.

Four chapters describe the tremendous accomplishments as well as the limits of organizing for policy change at the state and local levels. Burnham and Mercado compare the two campaigns that led to passage of a Domestic Worker Bill of Rights in New York and in California, highlighting key contextual and tactical differences and acknowledging the indispensable role of unions and state labor federations to both successes. Bada, Gleeson, and de Graauw's chapter highlights the importance of political context and strong labor/immigrant advocacy coalitions to advance pro-immigrant local legislation. Jacobs presents a broad range of creative and successful state and local policy campaigns, such as fair scheduling and paid sick days legislation as well as the promise of sectoral wage setting and efforts to broaden the definition of employee. He warns, however, that there are "major challenges" to enforcing these laws and to turning policy wins into "sustainable worker organization" over time, as well as the counterattack by business that has resulted in legislation preempting cities from adopting higher minimum wages and other employment protections in 25 states. Rhomberg lifts up the extraordinary accomplishments of the Fight for $15 but cautions that policy successes alone cannot offset the power low-wage workers still need to gain through institutional forms of workers' associational power.

Two chapters delve into efforts that have succeeded in holding the corporation that has the most economic power in a given supply chain accountable for the wages and working conditions of workers on the ground. Theodore argues that the shifting geographies of labor organizing require a global response, profiling the Asia Floor Wage campaign to compel major brands to remove wage differentials as a competitive strategy in the garment industry among countries in Asia, and the C.J.'s Seafood campaign, mount-ed by the National Guestworker Alliance, which highlighted the egregious violations of workplace laws that were endemic to the Walmart seafood supply chain and held Walmart accountable for them. Asbed, Albisa, and Sellers describe the failure of corporate social responsibility and multistakeholder initiatives to address the human rights crisis in global supply chains, arguing for worker-driven social responsibility that places workers at the center of developing and enforcing solutions to the problem. The chapter profiles the remarkably effective Fair Food Program of the Coalition of Immokalee Workers and Fair Food Standards Council, which enforces a binding legal agreement between farmworkers at the bottom of a supply chain and retail brands at the top to condition the brands' purchases from the workers' employers on human rights compliance in the workplace, as well as the Accord on Fire and Building Safety in Bangladesh, which was developed by the Worker Rights Consortium and several labor federations and requires signatory companies to compel their supplier factories to undergo fire, building, and electrical inspections and carry out the renovations and repairs necessary to make their factories safe. The signatories also required them to terminate business with any factory that fails to comply with the terms of the agreement.

Pitts' chapter provides the history of Black worker centers and the development of the National Black Worker Center Project and recounts the ways the centers are mounting policy campaigns that leverage public contracts to confront structural racism in the labor market and address what he calls the "power-building imperative." Narro and Fine provide an assessment of the state of union/worker center collaborations based on surveys of the 30 worker centers that have been issued certificates of affiliation with local central labor councils.

Finally, two chapters elucidate the promise and the pitfalls of online employment platforms, efforts to build alliances with "high road" businesses, and those that turn workers into owners through union–cooperatives alliances. Poo and Shah explore the ways in which online platforms have radically disrupted work processes and obscured employment relationships. They ask, "Who are we working for when work is assigned by an algorithm for a customer we don't have a direct relationship with, and who is responsible for the safety and well-being of workers when there is no manager or even a phone number to call when workers need assistance?" They recount the efforts of the National Domestic Workers Alliance innovation hub to intervene in the tech-based care and cleaning marketplace through the promulgation of a good work code that they could negotiate with online companies to adopt, along with a fair care pledge for individual employers. Ji finds inspiring examples across the United States but concludes that the economic scale and impact of unionized worker cooperatives remains quite small.

While there is a great deal of experimentation we have not covered, we hope that what is documented in these pages demonstrates the breadth and depth of the creative search for leverage that has been taking place across space and time. We hope that this volume does justice to the continual crafting, testing, and recrafting of strategy and tactics that is being enacted by unions, worker centers, economic justice coalitions, community organizing groups, and partner research, legal advocacy, policy organizations, and allied elected officials.

Our fondest hope is that *No One Size Fits All* will stand as a corrective to those who have been blithely insisting that the labor movement and worker organizers ran out of ideas and died 40 years ago. As the pages that follow will reveal, they're wrong.

Section One:
Building Organization

CHAPTER 1

Understanding Worker Center Trajectories

JANICE FINE
*School of Management and Labor Relations, Rutgers University
and the Center for Innovation in Worker Organization*

VICTOR NARRO
UCLA Labor Center

JACOB BARNES
School of Management and Labor Relations, Rutgers University

INTRODUCTION

This chapter presents findings based on an updated data set of worker centers. We seek to specify the trajectory of worker center growth over time and account for growth spurts; to explain the geographic distribution of centers and why most are modest in size; and to understand the choices, norms, and practices of the groups themselves and the role of the state and philanthropic foundations in conditioning organizational forms.

We begin by providing a brief introduction to worker centers and the context in which they have emerged, which include, among other things, increased immigration, stalled immigration policy reform, low rates of private sector unionism among low-wage workers, and high rates of exploitation on the job. We then turn to the growth of new centers, finding largely incremental growth in the 1980s and 1990s and then an exceptional spurt between 2000 and 2014. We find that many of the new centers were tied to the emergence of national federations, as well as to expansion by a few individual centers.

Next, we look at the reasons that the model of a nonprofit engaging in service, advocacy, and organizing took hold across the worker center domain rather than, for example, a union or community organizing model. In doing so, we argue that worker centers were drawing on earlier hybrid models that emerged during the 1960s among feminist, civil rights, and Chicano activists, which fused identity-based service provision with organizing (Minkoff 2002). While many theorists of community organizing view service provision as problematic—placing emphasis on the individual and rendering constituents as clients—worker centers saw service as a means of prefiguring social change. In fact, the largest worker centers in politically supportive states have been able to use services to grow and to support their work.

In charting the evolution of worker centers as a field, we find that centers exhibit a common set of structural features in conformity with normative and regulative requirements of the larger organizational field (DiMaggio and Powell 1983). But we argue that focusing on structure alone elides significant differences between centers along industry, strategy, programmatic, and cultural lines.

While characteristics of the low-wage labor market—such as exclusion from National Labor Relations Act or Fair Labor Standards Act coverage, or high proportions of undocumented workers—have limited the structural power of worker center constituents and made construction of mass membership-based worker organizations difficult, worker centers have compensated for this lack of structural and associational power by focusing on public policy change and government administrative action (Fine 2005, 2006, 2011; Gumbrell-McCormick and Hyman 2013; Rhomberg 2012; Wright 2000). Despite their lack of direct economic action, worker centers have been instrumental in state and local policy campaigns, including raising the minimum wage, enacting wage theft laws, adopting paid sick and safe time laws (Jacobs, this volume), and passing the domestic workers' bills of rights (Burnham and Mercado, this volume).

BACKGROUND

Worker centers are hybrid organizations that combine the service provision of traditional voluntary organizations with political advocacy focused on labor and immigrant rights and often focus on gender, race, and broad critiques of neoliberalism (Fine 2006; Jayaraman and Ness 2005; Louie 2001; Milkman, Bloom, and Narro 2010; Milkman and Ott 2014). The cornerstone of centers is the organization of a strong base of workers at the local level, who often play a key role in organizational decision making. Some have increasingly focused on mobilizing consumers and high-road employers to support their efforts.

The organizational repertoire of worker centers builds on a form that emerged in the 1960s, combining the traditional service provision that had long been carried out by voluntary organizations, particularly among women, immigrants, and African Americans, with an emphasis on political advocacy for civil and social rights (Minkoff 2002). These organizations borrowed from both traditional as well as newly emergent social movement organizational forms. Minkoff argues that in establishing these hybrids, movement groups imported models of organization that were already culturally legitimate—but not previously recognized as political.

Currently, there are 226 worker centers in operation. Some of the larger cities, such as Chicago, Los Angeles, New York, and San Francisco, have multiple centers based in specific neighborhoods and sectors, but in many other cities and suburban areas there are just one or two centers, often based in an ethnic enclave, that tend to address the needs of workers in multiple sectors with large immigrant workforces. Over 90 centers focus their work on a particular sector: construction, domestic and home health care, taxi driving, restaurants, food processing, warehousing, and car washes, among others. Several others hold a particular focus on two or three sectors; the rest support workers across a broad range of sectors.

Although there is a strong focus on worker issues, worker centers are not unions (Naduris-Weissman 2009). They do not organize workplaces for ongoing representation. Although they engage in collective action, they do not negotiate collective bargaining agreements. By and large, workers are not required to become dues-paying members in order to receive services or to participate in other ways.

The emergence of new actors in US industrial relations who are not enmeshed in collective bargaining structures has paralleled the decline of traditional unions, the decentering of firm and industry structures, and the dramatic increase in immigration during the final decades of the 20th century. During the late 1970s and 1980s, the decline of unions sharply reduced the quality of jobs in manufacturing and service industries, leading to an exodus of native workers and an influx of immigrants to fill vacancies in the lowest-paying occupations with the worst working conditions (Milkman 2006). Unionization among low-wage workers had always been low, and during the 1980s, unionization among the bottom quintile of wage earners flatlined at about 6% in the private sector and remained there.[1] At the same time, heightened imperatives to cut costs and limit liability contributed to more widespread "fissuring" of employment relationships (Weil 2014) through subcontracting, franchising, and increased use of fixed-term contracts, temporary staffing agencies, and independent contracting arrangements, normalizing "low-road" employment practices across industries.

A ground-breaking study of low-wage occupations in three metropolitan cities found that almost 26% of workers in the bottom 15% of the labor market failed to receive the legally required minimum wage; 70% did not receive legally required documentation of earnings; and of those eligible for overtime, a whopping 75% did not receive the pay they were entitled to (Bernhardt, Spiller, and Theodore 2013: 817–818). Many of the industries most prone to violations such as wage theft and unpaid overtime are also industries that are most heavily populated by immigrant workers (Bobo 2011; Capps, Fortuny, and Fix 2007; Waldinger 1996).

Immigration policy and politics are also instrumental to the story of worker centers. The total foreign-born population in the United States more than tripled from 14.1 million in 1980 to 43.7 million in 2016 (Figure 1). By 2009, foreign-born workers accounted for 15.7% of the civilian labor force; eight million of them were undocumented immigrants accounting

FIGURE 1
Number of Worker Centers, Total Foreign-Born Population

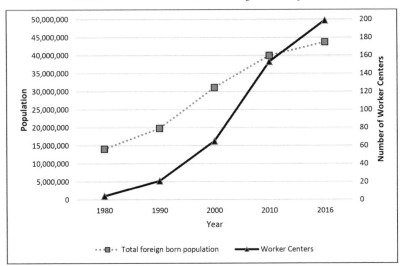

for over 5% of the labor force (Kochhar, Espinoza, and Hinze-Pifer 2010). While there had been a sharp decline in the size of the undocumented population from 12.2 million in 2007 to 11.3 million in 2009, presumably caused by the Great Recession, the number of undocumented residents by 2012 had risen to 11.7 million (Passel, Cohn, and Gonzalez-Barrera 2013).

The number of worker centers founded since 1980 has grown alongside the foreign-born population. The number of active worker centers by state is significantly correlated, at 0.699, with the percentage of the state's population that is foreign born. The correlation between the undocumented immigrant share of the labor force and worker centers by state is also significant, at 0.496.

Several waves of immigration are particularly relevant to the rise of worker centers. The growth of the Mexican-born population—especially those who are undocumented—has catalyzed the worker center movement in California, Illinois, New York, and Texas (Alba and Nee 2005). Proportionally one of the least skilled and lowest-paid foreign-born populations (Alba and Nee 2005), Mexican immigrants entered the United States in large numbers for "3-D" work (dirty, dangerous, and demeaning) until 2007 (Passel, Cohn, and Gonzalez-Barrera et al. 2012).

Similarly, Salvadoran immigration during the 1980s and early 1990s shaped the growth of worker centers in Los Angeles, New York City, and Long Island (Alba and Nee 2005). Increases in Chinese and Filipino immigrants from 1980 to 2000 also played an important role in catalyzing the worker center movement (Asis 2017; Zong and Batalova 2017).

Over the close to five decades since the first worker centers emerged we have been able to identify a total of 286 that have been operational at some point. Despite extensive research, we have been unable to find information for 29 centers and have concluded that 31 are no longer in operation. By our estimates, at least 226 are currently operational. When compared with the number of union locals (still over 40,000) that sounds rather small. But if we think of them as more akin to settlement houses—community-based organizations that connect immigrant workers to services while advocating strongly for factory reforms and supporting worker-organizing efforts—another picture emerges. In 1913, at the height of their prominence, *The Handbook of Settlements* listed 413 settlement houses in 32 states. Like worker centers, settlement houses were in part a response to rising immigration levels and largely held a dual focus on social service and social reform (Koerin 2003). Despite their comparatively modest numbers, these organizations have had an outsized influence on industrial relations and labor regulation in their cities and states as well as nationally.

ORIGINS AND GROWTH TRENDS

Economist Richard Freeman has found that unionism has generally grown in discontinuous upticks or spurts rather than through gradual accretion. He defines a spurt as a concentrated episode of union growth that occurs under a specific set of conditions and when there is an appropriate vehicle through which workers can organize. In the case of US unions, Freeman finds that the uptick that occurred in the 1930s and 1940s was undergirded by high rates of employer–employee conflict over organization and the existence of industrial unions through which large numbers of factory workers could come together across traditional dividing lines of jurisdiction, skill, or occupation (Freeman 1997).

At a much smaller scale, we find a similar spurt in the growth trajectory of worker centers. As can be seen in Figure 2, although worker centers were being founded throughout the 1980s and 1990s, growth was modest until the year 2000. Since then, there were significant upticks between the years 2000 and 2002, 2006 and 2009, and 2012 and 2014. During these periods, an average of 10.8 worker centers was founded each year, compared to an overall average of 4.7 centers per year.

During the 1980s, in response to the massive flow of political refugees fleeing the wars in El Salvador and Guatemala, the Reagan administration instituted a process of expedited deportation proceedings, which sparked organizing efforts and advocacy campaigns in the United States. These efforts were furthered by a coalition of church-based organizations such as the Unitarian church and the Quaker-led Sanctuary Movement, solidarity groups such as the Committee In Solidarity with the People of El Salvador (CISPES), and

FIGURE 2
Number of Worker Centers Founded by Year

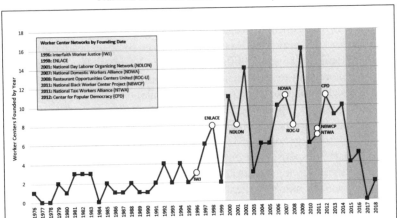

networks created by immigrants themselves such as the Central American Resource Center (CARECEN), El Rescate, Centro Presente, and CASA de Maryland.

Within this wave of migration from Central America were labor and community organizers who fled political persecution, particularly from El Salvador and Guatemala. They would later transform the immigrant worker movements across the country—especially in Los Angeles, by participating in campaigns such as Justice for Janitors (Waldinger et al. 1996). The uptick of migration during the 1980s led to a sharp increase in day laborers looking for work. The increase in day laborers at street corners led to a concerted effort among municipalities to limit their rights to look for work in public areas. Law enforcement agencies began to selectively target them for overzealous enforcement, while businesses and residents' groups led local efforts to rid their communities of day laborers through a process of attrition.

These types of repressive responses resulted in the first effort by advocacy groups to organize day laborers. Efforts to educate these workers about their rights transformed into organizing efforts to include the recovery of unpaid wages, prevention of labor rights abuses, and advocacy on behalf of day laborers with police and other key community stakeholders. The effort to fight back the local attacks of day laborers through political and legal strategies allowed these organizers the opportunity to formulate organizing strategies to empower day laborers based on popular education methodologies. Popular education is a method most widely attributed to Paulo Freire, a Brazilian teacher and activist. The California city of Agoura Hills, for example, has a long history of day laborer organizing, led by refugees from Guatemala who fled persecution for their community activism work (Narro and Shadduck-Hernández 2014).

The Immigration Reform and Control Act (IRCA) of 1986 created the need to implement outreach programs to ensure that undocumented immigrants who qualified for the legalization program would apply within the short amnesty time period, as well as provided government funding for community organizations to assist immigrants in filling out applications and educate them about the anti-discrimination provisions of the act. CARECEN and El Rescate shifted focus to assisting with the amnesty applications. Advocates in Los Angeles also came together to create a project—affiliated with the United Way until 1995—called the Coalition for Humane Immigrant Rights of Los Angeles (CHIRLA), which used its federal grant to create the Workers' Rights Project.

After the IRCA application process period ended, CHIRLA became an education and outreach project. As CHIRLA began reaching out to the day laborers and domestic workers—employment categories that were not eligible for the amnesty under IRCA—they returned with cases of police harassment and abuses by employers. Consequently, in 1989, CHIRLA created the Day Laborer Project and Domestic Workers Project. During the same period in Pasadena, the Institute of Popular Education of Southern California (Instituto de Educacion Popular del Sur de California, IDEPSCA) began to receive request for assistance from many of the students from its ESL classes who were day laborers and domestic workers, which led to creation of the Pasadena Day Laborer Association and the Mujeres en Movimiento project.

From 1997 through 2001, CHIRLA and IDEPSCA created an innovative strategy to use City of Los Angeles funding to open up new day labor worker centers throughout the city. CHIRLA also began to organize corners and create designated areas in parts of Los Angeles where they developed strong leadership among the workers. With legal support from the Mexican American Legal Defense and Educational Fund, the Day Laborer Association filed a lawsuit in 1998 against Los Angeles County, challenging its anti-day laborer solicitation ordinance. This case resulted in a major federal court victory when the judge struck down the ordinance as unconstitutional in violation of the First Amendment rights of day laborers (Narro 2010; Patler 2010).

From 1998 through 2000, CHIRLA and IDEPSCA began to connect with groups around the country that were organizing day laborers and dealing with stakeholders who were trying to remove day laborers from their communities. This process of sharing information and experiences became a key motivation for the founding of the National Day Laborer Organizing Network (NDLON) in 2001.

Other centers had faith-based beginnings in churches and shelters and evolved from being strictly service providers to advocacy and organizing. Many were connected to Interfaith Worker Justice (IWJ), including the Chicago Interfaith Worker Rights Center (now called ARISE), Workers Defense Project in Texas, Voces de la Frontera in Wisconsin, Northwest Arkansas Worker Center, and Western North Carolina Worker Center. As IWJ set about creating and strengthening labor–faith coalitions, it began to encounter nascent immigrant worker rights projects and helped transform them into established worker centers.

IWJ became a central resource for newly emergent worker centers in cities and towns in the US Midwest, Northeast, and South. IWJ tried to pioneer a model of matching the workers who came into centers with unions, but this met with mixed results (Fine 2006, 2007). Over the years, IWJ has had a dedicated organizer who focuses on the worker center network, helping with fund-raising and organizing trainings and conferences specific to their interests and needs, in particular pioneering work on wage theft (Bobo 2011).

A number of the worker centers that emerged in this period had connections to the labor movement. After years of supporting employer sanctions, in 2000 the AFL-CIO reversed course and called for repeal of the employer sanctions provision that it had strongly supported as part of IRCA. The AFL-CIO had come to the conclusion that employer sanctions were a failed strategy that was empowering employers to retaliate against workers involved in organizing drives. The same Executive Council resolution that foreswore opposition to employer sanctions also called for expanding the organizing rights of immigrant workers, a broad amnesty for the undocumented, and immigrant admissions based on family reunification.

The comprehensiveness of this approach represented the culmination of a shift in the AFL-CIO's outlook and strategy, which had begun in the 1970s when it provided strong support for farmworker organizing and later in that decade came out in support of a broad amnesty program. It also reflected efforts by important international unions such as the Service Employees International Union (SEIU) and UNITE HERE throughout the 1990s to organize the undocumented workers while disavowing employer sanctions. It was a gradual but ultimately decisive shift from viewing unskilled foreign-born Latino and largely undocumented workers as "unorganizable" and pursuing policies to exclude them to seeing these workers as instrumental to building the membership of the labor movement and pursuing policies to extend them legal status (Fine and Tichenor 2009).

NDLON was established in 2001 by day labor organizers in Los Angeles, who were connected to CHIRLA and IDEPSCA. The creation of NDLON gave national attention to the rise of worker centers in major cities throughout the country.

During the mid-2000s, 45 new worker centers were founded. In the winter of 2005, HB 4437 narrowly passed the Republican-controlled House of

Representatives. It proposed, for the first time, to make illegal presence in the United States a felony and a crime for any people or organizations to lend support to undocumented immigrants. For three months—between March 10 and May 1, 2006—five million immigrants (most of whom were Latino) and their supporters demonstrated in over 100 cities throughout the United States. On March 25 in Los Angeles, close to one million immigrants responded on their own to announcements on Spanish-language television and radio and in newspapers, without the guidance of community leaders, labor, or community groups and participated in one of the largest mobilizations in history. This mobilization was a major wake-up call for the immigrant rights and labor movements. More specifically, the immigrant rights and labor movements "missed the boat" with the March 25 march.

Soon thereafter, labor and immigrant rights groups joined grassroots, immigrant-based organizations throughout the country to launch a series of mobilizations and protests that culminated in the largest International Workers' Day demonstration in US history.[2] The irony is that this historic May 1 mobilization was not led by the US labor movement but by immigrant workers themselves. For many of the marchers throughout the three months, it was their first time participating in public demonstrations in this country. NDLON members and many other worker centers were in the center of much of the organized resistance to HB 4437 (Voss and Bloemraad 2011).

During this period, the failure to pass comprehensive immigration reform in Congress culminated in immigration enforcement policies that had significant impact on the members of many worker centers, especially those working with day laborers. Day laborers became the front line of the immigration reform debate and were the focus of attacks by the Federation for American Immigration Reform (FAIR), a national organization that seeks to reduce immigration; the Minutemen Project, a group that was recruiting armed volunteers to patrol the border; and other right-wing forces. Additionally, day laborers became major targets of cities and states that were enacting their own anti-immigrant policies. Sheriff Joe Arpaio in Maricopa County, Arizona, became the most visible leader of this effort with his local policies of rounding up immigrants and turning them over to US Immigration and Customs Enforcement (ICE) for processing or placing them in tent cities.

In 2007, NDLON abandoned the comprehensive immigration reform strategy framework that was, by then, considered by many immigrant rights advocates to be a failure because of the stalemate in Congress. Immediately thereafter, NDLON and other worker center networks joined to create the Turning the Tides movement. This new movement sought to establish a progressive parallel to the right-wing strategy of taking the immigrant rights fight to the local level. It would become the groundswell that would push back against and cause the Obama administration to end its Secure Communities

Program (S-Comm), the federal program that emerged in 2008 and led to the deportation of close to three million undocumented immigrants during his two terms as US president. In jurisdictions where S-Comm was activated, any time an individual was arrested and booked into a local jail for any reason, his or her fingerprints were electronically run through ICE's immigration database, allowing ICE to identify noncitizens and potentially initiate deportation proceedings against them.

During this period, six centers, including Fe y Justicia in Houston and Centro de Trabajadores Unidos en La Lucha (CTUL) in Minneapolis, were initially connected to faith-based organizations and IWJ; and five, including two day laborer centers in Florida and two in Arizona, were connected to NDLON. Four new centers were the product of an expansion by an existing worker center—CASA de Maryland—opening offices in new locations in that state. Seven centers were connected in some way to unions, central labor councils, or individual labor activists, including Warehouse Workers for Justice in Chicago, Warehouse Worker Resource Center in California, Lynn Worker Center in Massachusetts, MassCOSH Immigrant Worker Center in Boston, and Brandworkers in New York City. Three were domestic worker organizations.

In the immediate aftermath of the 2006 marches, the AFL-CIO became a major supporter of worker centers and initiated partnerships with the national federations. NDLON and the AFL-CIO announced a national partnership agreement in August 2006. In a formal resolution passed by the AFL-CIO Executive Council, the federation explicitly recognized the role of worker centers:

> Many of these centers are important to the immigrant community and play an essential role in helping immigrant workers understand and enforce their workplace rights. In doing so, they also play a critical role for all workers—immigrant and US-born alike—by fighting unscrupulous employers who try to use the immigrant workforce to lower wage and other benefit standards that protect the entire workforce. (AFL-CIO 2006)

The AFL-CIO has been committed to working with NDLON to defeat anti-day laborer center bills in Congress and to support immigration reforms that include legalization and a pathway to citizenship. Institutionally, the AFL-CIO president was authorized to issue certificates of affiliation to worker centers interested in joining state federations and central labor councils (Narro and Fine, this volume). In 2007, the AFL-CIO announced a similar partnership with IWJ and its network of 18 interfaith worker centers and Enlace, a network of worker centers and unions organizing low-wage workers in the United States and Mexico.

Over this period, two additional federations emerged. First, the National Domestic Workers Alliance (NDWA) was formed in 2007 at the US Social Forum in Detroit. Thirteen organizations, including CHIRLA, Andolan, Unity Housecleaners Cooperative of the Workplace Project, Haitian Women for Haitian Refugees, Damayan Migrant Workers Association, CASA de Maryland, Mujeres Unidas y Activas, and Domestic Workers United, convened to establish a national organization of domestic workers. It was the first national organization of domestic workers to be attempted in 30 years (Boris and Nadasen 2008).

Second, the Restaurant Opportunities Center United (ROC-United) was formed in Chicago by the leaders of ROC-New York. ROC-United was formed with a goal of establishing affiliates in the top ten restaurant markets in the United States and pursuing new state and federal tipped minimum-wage and paid sick-time policies. ROC-United has a three-pronged strategy for local affiliates: a worker-led approach to organizing for workplace justice, labor–management partnerships to promote a high-road approach that includes training programs, along with research and policy work, to highlight problems in the industry and set forth solutions. Today, ROC is leading One Fair Wage, a national campaign to eliminate the federal tipped minimum wage for restaurant workers. ROC has also become a leading voice for restaurant workers in the #MeToo movement through its efforts to bring public attention to the rampant sexual harassment and gender discrimination taking place every day in the restaurant industry.

In 2010, with the strong support of the UC Berkeley and UCLA labor centers, the Los Angeles Black Worker Center (LABWC) was created to address the three-dimensional jobs crisis of unemployment, underemployment, and low-wage work. LABWC's work with the Los Angeles County Metropolitan Transportation Authority's five-year master project labor agreement led to a major victory for black workers in Los Angeles. More recently, LABWC has been at the forefront in pushing for state and local policies to combat discrimination against black workers in many industries. LABWC became the impetus for the creation of new black worker centers throughout the country (Fine 2017a, 2017b; Pitts, this volume).

In 2012 through 2014, 30 more worker centers were established. Twelve were connected to worker center networks:

- Domesticas Unidas in San Antonio and MISMA in Austin were connected to NDWA.
- The Center for Worker Justice of Eastern Iowa, Indianapolis Justice Center, Greater Minnesota Worker Center, and Micah Worker Center in Grand Rapids, Michigan, were connected to IWJ.
- Trajabadoras Unidos in Washington, D.C., and Adelante Alabama Worker Center were connected to NDLON.

- ROC-Houston was established by ROC.
- Two taxi worker–organizing projects, in San Francisco and Montgomery County, Maryland, were affiliated with the National Taxi Workers Alliance.
- Six centers were founded by unions, central labor councils, or individual labor activists, and four were connected to community organizing groups and social justice organizations.

Three more national networks were formed during this period: the National Taxi Workers Alliance in 2011 and the Center for Popular Democracy in 2012 joined forces with the network of local and state organizations that had formerly been affiliates of the Association of Community Organizations for Reform Now (ACORN). In 2011, the AFL-CIO announced partnership agreements—similar to the ones it had with NDLON and IWJ—with NDWA and the National Guestworker Alliance (NGA), the national organization that had emerged in the aftermath of Hurricane Katrina through the organizing efforts of the New Orleans Workers' Center for Racial Justice. The National Black Worker Center Project was founded in 2014.

In 2012, the "Gang of Eight," a bipartisan group in the Senate, began working on the development of a comprehensive immigration reform proposal that could move through Congress. The Border Security, Economic Opportunity, and Immigration Modernization Act (S.744) passed the Senate in summer 2013, but the House of Representatives refused to consider any other form of immigration reform. In the following Congress, the only pieces of immigration legislation debated were enforcement-only bills. With this federal impasse, the fight for immigrant rights moved away from Washington, D.C., to the local and state levels.

In Arizona, Governor Jan Brewer signed into law SB 1070, the most sweeping and restrictive immigration bill in the nation. The bill gave police the power to detain anyone suspected of being in the country illegally and made failure to carry immigration documents a crime rather than a civil offense. NDLON and local worker centers led efforts to fight back against SB 1070 and other similar measures at the state level.

THE ROLE OF FEDERATIONS, FEDERATION FUNDING, AND LARGE WORKER CENTER EXPANSION

As explained above, a set of national federations—many operating in specific sectors—has been instrumental to worker center growth. Each of these federations engages in its own significant program development and advocacy at the national level, leading policy campaigns and forming alliances with other national advocacy organizations. Isomorphic with individual centers, they are also structured as 501(c)(3) organizations and funded by foundations. While all of the federations provide organizational support to their affiliates, the form and extent of that support vary.

In research on worker centers between 1998 and 2006, Fine found that worker centers were under-networked at every level, preventing them from aggregating their power to bring pressure to bear on employers and industries and achieve more legislatively as well as inhibiting their access to higher levels of foundation support and recognition from the labor movement (Fine 2006). At the national level at that time, there were three promising but under-financed networks bringing together collections of worker centers: NDLON, National Interfaith Justice (NIF), and Enlace. In 2006, 64% of worker centers were unaffiliated with any national network, but by 2018, only 26% are now unaffiliated with any networks (Figure 3).

Federations and large worker center expansions have been facilitated, in large part, through foundation funding. In the 1990s, this funding was linked to a small group of national social justice funders (e.g., New World, Discount, Solidago, Veatch, Jewish Funds for Justice) and city- or regionally based funders (e.g., New York Foundation, Liberty Hill Foundation in Los Angeles).

In the early 2000s, searching for a way to have impact on the labor market conditions of an increasing population of low-wage workers, a set of funders affiliated with the Labor and Community Working Group—now called Funders for a Just Economy—of the Neighborhood Funders Group supported research on the rising numbers of day laborers and on worker centers as a phenomenon. These foundations focused on worker centers as a promising strategy and followed recommendations regarding the important role that national federations could play in building capacity and strengthening impact (Fine 2006). As the national networks emerged over the next few years, foundations including Ford, Rockefeller, Kellogg, Surdna, Nathan Cummings,

FIGURE 3
Worker Center Federation Affiliations

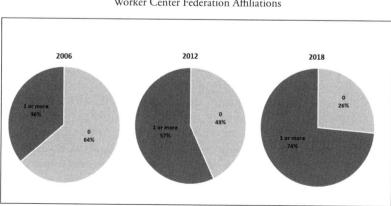

Public Welfare, and Marguerite Casey began providing major financial support to their initiatives. By aggregating local affiliated organizations, the national networks facilitated funding from these large national foundations that typically eschew becoming involved with funding at the local level.

Between the years 2013 and 2016, NDWA received approximately $14.4 million from foundations. During this same period, ROC-United received approximately $9.6 million from foundations, and NDLON received about $3.4 million (Manheim 2017). A few large centers that were expanding to other cities or states also received significant foundation funding during this time, including CASA de Maryland, the Workers Defense Project in Texas, and Make the Road New York.

UNDERSTANDING THE EXPANSION OF THE WORKER CENTER MODEL

Because worker centers receive the vast majority of their funds from philanthropic foundations, they developed great expertise in writing grants, tailoring their programmatic work to foundation priorities, engaging and cultivating foundation program officers, and satisfying ongoing reporting requirements. Additionally, they have incorporated themselves as 501(c)(3) charitable organizations. The widespread adoption of this structure supports Meyer and Rowan's argument that, as modern administrative states expanded their dominance over social life, organizational structures increasingly came to reflect the rules institutionalized and legitimated by the state (Meyer and Rowan 1977).

What explains the pattern of worker center growth? We find that it is consistent with DiMaggio and Powell's theory that organizations tend to model themselves after similar organizations that they perceive to be successful and that reliance on established procedures enhances organizational legitimacy and chances of survival. That so many organizations used the same model also supports their finding that the fewer the number of visible alternative organizational models, the faster the rate of isomorphism in the field (DiMaggio and Powell 1983). Our findings also point to the importance of an organizational accelerant—in this case, that centers formed federations, which could then help new centers get off the ground and implement program, as well as the rise of entrepreneurial centers that have spun off new affiliates.

Worker center strategy and structure has been influenced by these organizational conditions. The majority of worker centers do not hold formal elections to choose their leaders; they have to couch what they do in terms of "education" and limit their lobbying activities—and most have shied away from forming 501(c)(5) organizations (i.e., unions) because they fear doing so will limit the tactics they can employ and impose onerous reporting requirements. To avoid alienating foundations with rhetoric that is too anti-business, worker centers have learned to walk a careful line when they talk about their work. All of this comports with McCarthy and his co-authors' notion of "institutional channeling"—that the consequence of the normative adoption of the 501(c)(3) structure for social movement organizations is the narrowing of "the range of structures, tactics and substantive goals of organizations which choose to become legitimate organizations in the eyes of the state," but only to a degree (McCarthy, Britt, and Wolfson 1991: 48). In the view of many centers with whom we have spoken, foundation funding has not directly conditioned the goals, strategies or educational programs of worker centers. Rhetoric aside, it has not, for example, prevented them from campaigning for major immigration and labor policy reforms or mounting aggressive campaigns against specific corporate targets.

Both Meyer and Rowan and DiMaggio and Powell conclude that reliance on similar sources of financial support lead to the homogenization of organizational models (DiMaggio and Powell 1983; Meyer and Rowan 1977). We find strong supporting evidence for this in the case of how worker center reliance on foundations and, secondarily, government funding, has shaped the field. DiMaggio and Powell further argue that, once an organizational field becomes well established, there is an inexorable push toward homogenization because the adoption of common structural features makes organizations *recognizable* and *legitimate* as part of the common norms and culture of that field. Certainly, common structural features have been important as a signal to funders that a particular center is within the bounds of the worker center model and organizational field they are already supporting.

Nevertheless, there is significant variation between centers in terms of their scope and programmatic focus. There are worker centers that organize in specific neighborhoods in a city (e.g., Korean Immigrant Worker Advocates in Koreatown in Los Angeles), some that are citywide (e.g., CTUL in Minneapolis, and Workers Defense Project organizations in Austin, Dallas, and Houston), others that are countywide, and some that are functionally statewide (e.g., Voces de la Frontera in Wisconsin and Make the Road New Jersey). Some concentrate their work on one industry, such as the New York Taxi Workers Alliance, the day laborer centers that are part of NDLON, the ROC affiliates, and domestic worker organizations such as Damayan and Adhikaar in New York. Others operate in more than one sector. For example, many of the day laborer centers also have domestic worker projects.

Many worker centers have taken root from within specific ethnic, racial, or country of origin communities such as the Chinese Staff and Workers' Association in New York, the Chinese Progressive Association worker centers in Boston and San Francisco, and the Pilipino Workers Center in Los Angeles, and sister organizations in San Francisco and Chicago. Some organizations, such as ROC, OUR Walmart, CTUL, NGA, and the Coalition of Immokalee Workers have targeted specific companies and employer associations, while other organizations, such as NDWA, IWJ, and NDLON, have focused more on supporting or opposing passage of specific public policies.

As discussed previously, while some of the earliest worker centers engaged solely in advocacy and organizing, most saw the need for service provision from the very beginning in order to help workers recover unpaid wages and, in the case of day laborer centers, facilitate fair pay (Fine 2006; Theodore, Valenzuela and Meléndez 2006). Thus, the 501(c)(3) structure has facilitated service provision but was not the main reason that centers first began to engage in that activity.

In embracing service provision along with organizing, worker centers were tapping into a hybrid model that had already been in the repertoire of social movements. Hybrid models that fused identity-based service provision with organizing were forged during the 1960s by feminist and black power groups. Hybridity is a common element of the worker center model; however, the ratio of service to organizing or organizing to advocacy still varies significantly across centers. In an extensive study of the survival rates of organizations that were established in the 1960s, Minkoff found that hybrid organizations, by combining service and organizing, were able to "ride free" on the resources and legitimacy available to their parent forms and were thus able to hedge their bets against environmental shocks by establishing "multiple competences" and avenues for bringing in funding (Minkoff 2002: 384). This seems to be the case with worker centers as well: those that are able to diversify their funding base have been most likely to survive. However, it is important to distinguish between diversification of external funding sources and internal sources that come from the base.

The research of Gates et al. (this volume) into the funding trends of 104 worker centers confirms that more than 80% of worker center funding comes from external sources, with membership dues playing a very small role in the funding portfolios of these groups. Based on their research on worker organizations and civic organizations, respectively, both Stinchcombe (1965) and Clemens (1993) reached similar conclusions that organizations founded at particular moments construct their models with the resources that are available to them. We would qualify this claim: organizations construct their models with the resources they *perceive* to be available for their use.

In the case of worker centers, the resources they perceive to be available are derived from philanthropic foundations, government agencies, and individual donors. Diversification has involved seeking out additional foundations but not radically altering the mode of organizational funding. This can be attributed to three factors: the difficulty of collecting dues outside of the workplace, long-term trends in civil society, and the organizational culture of worker centers.

Fundamentally, most worker centers have limited structural power because of the weak labor market power of the workforces with which they engage. Union organizational models are tied to labor market structures, but worker center constituents are often distributed across many small workplaces, work for contractors and subcontractors or as temporary workers, and are frequently misclassified as independent contractors. While they may have connections to large companies, these workers are most likely to be found marooned at the bottom of supply chains. Most are employed in industries that have had low levels of unionization where government enforcement of labor standards has been weak, including retail, restaurant, hospitality, and other service sectors. While garment workers were once able to build significant structural power despite their position at the bottom of multilevel labor and product supply chains, we have few contemporary models of widespread successful unionization among unskilled private sector workers beyond construction laborers, janitors and security guards. Among low-wage public sector workers such as homecare, recent advances in unionism were made possible through public policy campaigns advanced by powerful unions.

In our view, the ability to access foundation funding is a major factor that has kept worker centers from having to do the very difficult work of locking in a dues-paying membership base outside of the workplace, and this has had implications for power building. The lack of a financial incentive to place recruitment at the heart of the organizing and leadership models has limited the size of the base of workers and consequently has limited the power they have been able to exercise.

While the lack of structural power of many of the workers who are constituents of centers, in conjunction with the logistical difficulty of collecting dues outside of the workplace, drives worker center leaders' belief that collecting dues at a scale large enough to make a difference is just too hard, it is worth noting that these organizations also emerged during a period in which the very idea of membership had been withering away. Traditional membership associations of the 19th and early to mid-20th centuries required recruitment of "civic entrepreneurs" across many states and towns to lead local chapters and recruit members. Members developed strong organizational identity, participating in meetings and club events, running for chapter office, representing the organization in meetings with local elected officials, and the like. The national organizations relied on local leaders to keep chapters vibrant and on local members paying dues to support them, much like community organizing groups of the 1970s such as ACORN, Citizen Action, and National People's Action. The decline of these organizations shifted the focus away from a dues-paying membership model; the "new" model of professionally managed associations that emerged was based on foundation grants, direct-mail techniques, and getting their message out through the mass media (Skocpol 2003: 210).

Of particular importance in this shift were changes in electoral regulations in the late 1980s. Many organizations decided that the safest way to stay within the law was to consider anyone who signed a petition a member because the law at that time allowed political communication only between organizations and their members (Kendall, personal communication, 2015). With the advent of Internet-based organizations beginning with MoveOn in 1998, this trend became more pronounced. As Karpf writes in the *MoveOn Effect*, "Membership in MoveOn is the singular most disruptive feature of the group's model. Much as the direct-mail pioneers redefined organizational membership from 'participant' to 'small donor,' MoveOn redefines membership from 'small donor' to 'message recipient.'... As a result, many of the organization's members remain unaware that they merit such classification" (Karpf 2012: 31).

Worker center notions of membership have been formed in this context. Like MoveOn, most centers and national federations do not distinguish between "members" and "dues-paying members."

A final contributing factor for their decisions regarding dues relates to organizational culture. Many directors and organizers express concerns that workers are either too poor or suspicious of organizations that ask for money. Most are resistant to making dues a requirement, and even when some say that they are not resistant, implementation of the culture changes and procedures required in order to regularly collect dues from members has not been a priority. We also find evidence that, for some centers, service provision—and the requirement on the part of government funders that services be available to all—likely reinforces an essential discomfort with asking for dues.

There are a few low-wage worker organizations that, despite the lack of structural power, have implemented models of member-based funding. The United Farm Workers famously required its very-low-income members to pay dues even before achieving collective bargaining rights that locked in a membership-based income stream (Chavez 1971), and Pineros y Campesinos Unidos del Noroeste (PCUN), the farmworker organization in Oregon, also has insisted on membership dues (Kleinman 2011; Stephen 2012). Members of SEIU's 32BJ building services local are overwhelmingly immigrants, people of color, low-income, and working for subcontractors at the bottom of supply chains, yet they have figured out how to lock in associational power in this setting, repeatedly voting in favor of significant dues increases.

Likewise, a few centers have focused on dues, including New Labor in New Jersey, the Pilipino Worker Center in Los Angeles, and the New York Taxi Workers Alliance. Make the Road and CASA de Maryland have very large numbers of workers contributing nominal dues to their organizations, and CASA has been experimenting with ESL classes as a potential mass membership draw and income generating program. NDWA has set a goal of 200,000 members, and its Fair Care Labs has been systematically testing the appeal of various services, benefits, and training to their constituents.

Ultimately, the question is whether the 501(c)(3) form of organization, despite the absence of collective bargaining and the ability to collect dues in the workplace, is a sufficiently effective mechanism to be able to maintain an activist cadre and implement and safeguard policy victories over time.

PLACING WORKER CENTER FUNDING IN CONTEXT

While the worker center model is not state specific, the concentration of centers in certain cities and states does follow certain patterns. Most are small. Gates et al. (this volume) find most worker center revenues tend to be low, with a quarter of all centers in their sample claiming yearly revenue of less than $179,163. Of the 22 worker centers in the modal revenue range of $100,000 to $200,000, 12 had revenue below $150,000. Furthermore, the median revenue level for their sample was only $410,010 (Figure 4).

Many worker centers have small budgets because their local political opportunity structures—the combination of political institutions and traditions, as well as public policy, political discourse, and elite alignment including

FIGURE 4
Worker Center Revenues, 2012

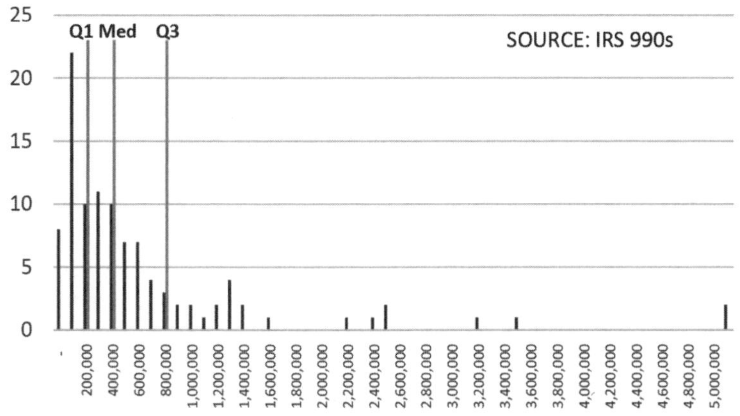

N	Mean	StdDv	Min	Q1	Median	Q3	Max
104	747,431	1,186,875	10,808	179,163	410,010	779,036	8,366,068

Source: Gates et al. (this volume).

philanthropic support—are limited (Gamson and Meyer 1996; Meyer and Staggenborg 1996; Tarrow 1993; Tilly 1978). They have limited access to local foundation and government money and are not located in states that are viewed as strategically important to national funders. In addition, while mutual-aid societies were able to generate income to their organizations through the provision of life insurance (Beito 2000; Murray 2013), worker centers have not yet succeeded in delivering a benefit or service that is as essential to their constituencies. Two projects that seem to have the greatest promise of generating revenue for worker centers and networks are Better Builders, a worksite monitoring program incubated at the Workers Defense Project, and OUR Walmart's WorkIT app, a peer-to-peer digital tool that enables workers to access critical information about their company's HR policies.

Nevertheless, there are some small worker centers that are located in major cities and Democratic states where there is access to foundation and government funding and where there are worker centers that are much larger. In many of these cases, we suspect that smallness may be a consequence of choice. Certain organization theorists have argued that structural change attends growth and that an organization cannot grow indefinitely and maintain its original character and form (Boulding 1953; Haire 1959). For organizations that pride themselves on the depth of relationships that exist between and among staff, leaders, and members, there is real concern that growth in the number of members could reduce their ability to carry on face-to-face interactions. In other cases, smallness may be a consequence of limited strategic capacity or an inability to inspire the confidence of area government officials or foundations to invest in their work (Ganz 2000).

A minority of worker centers have made a conscious choice not to engage in service delivery in order to focus their work exclusively on organizing and advocacy. Community and union organizing philosophies have long discouraged organizers from getting caught up in service provision. Service delivery is extremely labor intensive, can end up monopolizing an organizations' staff time, places the emphasis on individual versus collective solutions to problems, and often leads organizations to see their base as clients rather than members and leaders.

Interestingly, the decision to focus purely on organizing may actually be leading those organizations to have fewer resources with which to do so. The hybridity of organizations like Make the Road and CASA de Maryland generates an income stream from services that allows them to build a larger infrastructure and therefore to funnel greater financial resources into organizing.

Our research on worker centers over many years leads us to conclude that the scale of centers, measured through the size of their budgets, depends on both internal strategic choices and political opportunity structures. Greater amounts of foundation and government funding for worker centers are available in the more highly Democratic cities and states (Table 1). The seven states

TABLE 1
Political Partisanship History; States with Most Worker Centers

Partisan Composition of State Legislatures

State	Worker Centers, 2018	Rank, % of State Population, Foreign Born, 2016	1980	1986	1992	1998	2004	2010	Senate and House Seats, Democrat, 2017	Senate and House Seats, Republican, 2017	% of Seats Held by Party in Control, 2017	Governor
California	42	1	D	D	D	D	D	D	82	38	68.3	D
New York	41	2	S	S	S	S	S	D	139	74	65.3	D
Texas	14	7	D	D	D	S	R	R	67	114	63.0	R
Massachusetts	14	8	D	D	D	D	D	D	159	41	79.5	R
Illinois	12	12	S	D	S	S	D	D	104	73	58.8	R
Florida	11	4	D	D	S	R	R	R	55	104	65.0	R
Maryland	9	9	D	D	D	D	D	D	123	65	65.4	R

D = Democrat
R = Republican
S = Split

with the largest concentrations of worker centers—California, New York, Texas, Massachusetts, Illinois, Florida, and Maryland, with the exception of Florida and Texas—have had primarily Democratic-controlled legislatures since 1980 (although some now have Republican governors), and several of them also have a strong set of locally based foundations that support the work. In Florida and Texas, it is likely that the higher number of centers there is due to strong support from national funders, who perceive them to be strategically important to national social change efforts and elections as well as local funders in more cosmopolitan regions of the state.

The research by Gates et al. (this volume) confirms that California, Florida, Maryland, and New York are states where total worker center revenue is the highest. According to their findings, these four states were in the top five of total worker center revenue by state each year between 2008 and 2014.

Make the Road New York and CASA de Maryland are the two largest individual centers. Make the Road New York, which actually comprises five centers in New York City and Long Island, has a total 2017 budget of $13.35 million; CASA de Maryland, which also comprises multiple centers, has a total 2017 budget of $9.37 million. They are located in strongly Democratic cities and states where political systems are permeable, there is foundation and government funding available to support the work, and staff and leaders have the strategic capacity to leverage foundation and government funding. Additionally, size begets support: funders looking to have an impact in an area are likely to favor scale and gravitate toward organizations that are larger and well established rather than having to do the research required to identify and evaluate multiple smaller organizations.

Both CASA de Maryland and Make the Road New York are raising high percentages of their total budgets from government grants to provide services and support. CASA received very large grants from Montgomery and Prince Georges Counties to operate welcome centers. Make the Road received government grants in 2017 for the provision of a range of services, including over $4 million for legal and support services, $1.1 million for adult literacy programs, and $547,000 for school-based programs. Providing a range of services opens a broad array of potential resource streams, potentially increasing an organization's chance of survival in an unstable environment (Hannan and Freeman 1977; Minkoff 2002).

Despite their similarities today, Make the Road and CASA had disparate organizational trajectories. CASA started out solely as a service providing organization. In 1985, some US citizens and a group of immigrants who had been activists in their home countries came together to create CASA in the basement of the Presbyterian Church in Tacoma Park, in order to provide basic services for immigrants fleeing the civil wars in El Salvador, Guatemala, and Honduras. It was not until six years later, in 1991, when the organization made a decision to become involved in defending the rights of day laborers, that it began to engage in organizing those workers and advocating for their rights. Worker centers grew out of that effort and became central to CASA's identity.

In 2000, the organization made another set of momentous decisions—first, to move away from identifying solely as a Central American organization and to open its doors to all immigrants and refugees and, relatedly, to recreate and rebrand their worker centers as welcome centers. According to Gustavo Torres, CASA's executive director,

> We wanted to make sure people saw CASA's centers not as a day laborer center but as a community center where people are welcome and can organize. A lot of our members are not just day laborers and domestics, but also people fighting for drivers' licenses, minimum wage increases, and immigration reform. Others just came for services. That is how we grew our membership: people fighting for justice and people coming for services. (Torres, personal communication)

In 2010, CASA created a 501(c)(4) organization, CASA in Action, to endorse candidates and engage in voter education and get out the vote activities. It also decided to expand into Pennsylvania and Maryland. CASA now has 180 different sources of funding including private foundations, individuals, the federal government, and state, local, and county governments. It also claims the largest dues-paying membership base in the worker center world: about 100,000 members who are paying $40 per year.

In contrast, Make the Road New York was formed out of a merger of two organizations in 2007 that had, from the outset, combined legal services with education and multi-issue community organizing. The Latin American Immigration Center (LAIC) was founded in 1992 in Jackson Heights, Queens, by a group of Colombians forced to emigrate by the political violence of the 1980s and 1990s. Like many worker centers where highly educated people found themselves on the bottom rungs of the labor market after they emigrated, LAIC was founded by a human rights attorney in Colombia who worked as a housecleaner in the United States. The organization advocated for the rights of Latino immigrants and encouraged their civic participation in New York City.

Make the Road was founded in 1997 in Bushwick, Brooklyn, by two Georgetown University Law School students looking to support immigrant welfare recipients subjected to illegal disruptions in their public benefits in the wake of 1995 federal welfare reform. It won equal access to public services for all New York City residents. The organization always integrated education, organizing, and leadership development with legal aid and other support services.

Post-merger, Make the Road grew into a major force for immigrant rights in New York City, looked to by government agencies as a prime vehicle for providing services to vulnerable, hard-to-reach immigrant workers. Government funding grew enormously and is now 65% of the organization's overall budget (Figure 5). CASA's revised budget for fiscal year 2017 is shown in Figure 6.

Neither CASA nor Make the Road sees itself as solely a worker center. While the organizations carry out the functions of worker centers, they consider themselves multi-purpose immigrant organizations that deal with multiple issues and organize multiple constituencies.

CONCLUSION

In this chapter, we have brought data and theory to bear on several key questions: What has been the trajectory of worker center growth and what accounts for growth spurts? What explains the geographic distribution of centers? Why are most of modest size? What accounts for the outliers? We also analyze the choices, norms, and practices of the groups themselves in the context of legal requirements and political opportunity structures in conditioning organizational forms.

We find that organizers turned to the worker center model as immigration was surging, pathways to legalization were contracting, employment was becoming more precarious, and unionization in the bottom quintile of wage earners had been flat for some time. Growth spurts are connected to the emergence of national federations as well as the expansion of large centers. There are higher concentrations of centers in Democratic cities and states where there are favorable political opportunity structures such as greater funding opportunities through foundations and government. We argue that while worker centers share a common legal structure and funding base, they are not homogeneous—they differ widely in terms of constituency and programmatic focus.

We also argue that while service provision has traditionally been viewed by labor and community organizers as a distraction (a view shared by some worker centers), the largest worker centers have been able to use services to grow and subsidize the overall work, including organizing.[3] In taking this approach to service and organizing, we argue that worker centers were adopting a hybrid model that had its contemporary expression during the 1960s among feminists and black power activists (Minkoff 2002), and even earlier in the century by Settlement House pioneers and mutual aid–society leaders (Addams 1990; Koerin 2003).

As long-time observers of the worker center phenomenon, we have found that most worker center founders have never had a union model in their heads and (whether they have articulated it this way or not) have not seen themselves or their constituents as capable of building and exercising significant structural power or associational power in the workplace. This

FIGURE 5
Make the Road 2017 Revenue (Committed Only)

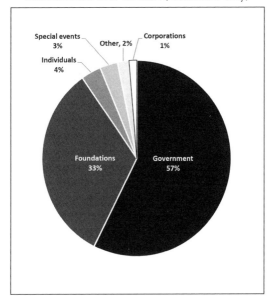

FIGURE 6
CASA de Maryland Revised FY2017 Budget

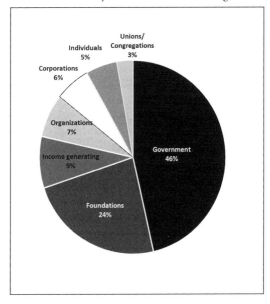

perception has had important implications for the organizing campaigns and strategies centers have pursued. The vast majority of organizations have focused on ensuring that employers actually obey existing laws and workers are able to recover wages owed when they do not. Most successful worker center campaigns for improvements have focused on winning policy change rather than pressuring companies directly through strikes or consumer boycotts. This focus on policy campaigns has enabled them to succeed through the exercise of symbolic power (Chun 2009; Clemens 1993; Rozado Marzán 2017) rather than associational or structural power (Gumbrell-McCormick and Hyman 2013; Rhomberg 2012; Wright 2000), which would have required the action of a mass base in a workplace or industry rather than a smaller base of activists (Fine 2005; McAlevey 2016). Reliance on foundation funding and civil society or state-based solutions is conditioning worker centers' associational power, but it has its roots in the limited structural power they wield within firms, supply chains, industries, and labor markets.

In the end, it is our view that the 501(c)(3) structure, which has enabled foundation and government funding, has facilitated the organization of low-wage workers rather than preventing more-powerful, large-scale organizations from emerging. But it is also likely that, as long as worker centers are able to rely on foundation funding, they will not be compelled to build mass bases of dues-paying members and, as long as this is the case, they are likely to limit themselves to public policy campaigns and corporate shaming strategies that can be won without the associational and structural power required for strikes and other economic actions.

ACKNOWLEDGMENTS

The authors would like to thank Deborah Axt of Make the Road New York and Gustavo Torres of CASA de Maryland for generously sharing their expertise and budget information, Heidi Shierholz and John Schmitt of the Economic Policy Institute for providing the data on unionization rates in the bottom quintile, Chris Rhomberg and Ruth Milkman for providing extensive and invaluable feedback on the draft, and Kati Griffith and her colleagues (see Gates et al., this volume) for sharing their data, serving as important thought partners, and providing feedback on the draft.

ENDNOTES

[1] John Schmitt, Economic Policy Institute data.
[2] Two million marched through the streets of Los Angeles between the March 25 and May 1 mobilizations, close to half a million in Chicago on March 10 and May 1, and 350,000 in New York on May 1. Other cities throughout the country held the largest demonstrations in their city's history—10,000 in Oklahoma City, Oklahoma; 25,000 in Madison, Wisconsin; 5,000 in Charlotte, North Carolina; and 6,000 in Des Moines, Iowa, to name a few.

[3] There are limits, however, to what can be done with this funding. It often comes with restrictions on its use, including that organizations cannot require clients to join in order to receive services, and the funding is strongly impacted by shifts in political direction. The election of Donald Trump has resulted in less federal money, for example, for navigator services connected to the Affordable Care Act and for citizenship services.

REFERENCES

Addams, Jane. 1990. *Twenty Years at Hull-House*. Champaign, IL: University of Illinois Press.

AFL-CIO. 2006 (Aug. 9). "A National Worker Center–AFL-CIO Partnership." http://bit.ly.2vxWsya

Alba, Richard, and Victor Nee. 2005. *Remaking the American Mainstream: Assimilation and Contemporary Immigration*. Cambridge, MA: Harvard University Press.

Asis, Maruja M.B. 2017 (Jul. 12). "The Philippines: Beyond Labor Migration, Toward Development and (Possibly) Return." Migration Policy Institute. http://bit.ly/2xVr7DA

Beito, David T. 2000. *From Mutual Aid to the Welfare State: Fraternal Societies and Social Services, 1890–1967*. Chapel Hill, NC: University of North Carolina Press.

Bernhardt, Annette, Michael W. Spiller, and Nik Theodore. 2013. "Employers Gone Rogue: Explaining Industry Variation in Violations of Workplace Laws." *ILR Review* 66 (4): 808–832.

Bobo, Kim. 2011. *Wage Theft in America: Why Millions of Working Americans Are Not Getting Paid—And What We Can Do About It*. New York: The New Press.

Boris, Eileen, and Premilla Nadasen. 2008. "DOMESTIC WORKERS ORGANIZE!" *WorkingUSA: The Journal of Labor and Society* 11: 413–437.

Boulding, Kenneth. 1953. "Toward a General Theory of Growth." *Canadian Journal of Economics and Political Science* 19: 326–340.

Capps, Randy, Karina Fortuny, and Michael Fix. 2007. "Trends in the Low-Wage Immigrant Labor Force, 2000–2005." Washington, DC: The Urban Institute.

Chavez, Cesar. 1971. "On Money and Organizing," United Farm Worker Digital Archives. San Diego, CA: University of California at San Diego.

Chun, Jennifer Jihye. 2009. *Organizing at the Margins: The Symbolic Politics of Labor in South Korea and the United States*. Ithaca, NY: ILR Press.

Clemens, Elisabeth S. 1993. "Organizational Repertoires and Institutional change: Women's Groups and the Transformation of U.S. Politics, 1890–1920." *American Journal of Sociology* 98 (4): 755–798.

DiMaggio, Paul J., and Walter W. Powell. 1983. "The Iron Cage Revisited: Institutional Isomorphism and Collective Rationality in Organizational Fields." *American Sociological Review* 48 (2): 147–160.

Fine, Janice. 2005. "Community Unions and the Revival of the American Labor Movement." *Politics & Society* 33(1): 153-199.

Fine, Janice. 2006. *Worker Centers: Organizing Communities at the Edge of the Dream*. Ithaca, NY: ILR Press.

Fine, Janice. 2007. "A Marriage Made in Heaven? Mismatches and Misunderstandings Between Worker Centres and Unions." *British Journal of Industrial Relations* 45 (2): 335–360.

Fine, Janice. 2011. "New Forms to Settle Old Scores: Updating the Worker Centre Story in the United States." *Relations Industrielles* 66 (4): 604–630.

Fine, Janice. 2017a. Enforcing Labor Standards in Partnership with Civil Society: Can Co-Enforcement Succeed Where the State Alone Has Failed?. *Politics & Society* 45 (3): 359–388.

Fine, Janice. 2017b. "New Approaches to Enforcing Labor Standards: How Co-Enforcement Partnerships Between Government and Civil Society Are Showing the Way Forward." *University of Chicago Legal Forum* Vol. 2017, Article 7: 143–176.

Fine, Janice, and Daniel J. Tichenor. 2009. "A Movement Wrestling: American Labor's Enduring Struggle with Immigration, 1866–2007." *Studies in American Political Development* 23: 84–113.

Freeman, Richard B. 1997. "Spurts in Union Growth: Defining Moments and Social Processes." Working Paper 6012. Washington, DC: National Bureau of Economic Research.

Gamson, William A., and David S. Meyer. 1996. "Framing Political Opportunity." In *Comparative Perspectives on Social Movements: Political Opportunities, Mobilizing Structures, and Cultural Framings*, edited by Doug McAdam, John D. McCarthy, and Mayer N. Zald, pp. 275–290. Cambridge, UK: Cambridge University Press.

Ganz, Marshall. 2000. "Resources and Resourcefulness: Strategic Capacity in the Unionization of California Agriculture, 1959–1966. *American Journal of Sociology* 105 (4): 1003–1062.

Gumbrell-McCormick, Rebecca, and Richard Hyman. 2013. *Trade Unions in Western Europe: Hard Times, Hard Choices.* New York, NY: Oxford University Press.

Haire, Mason. 1959. "Biological Models and Empirical Histories of the Growth of Organizations." In *Modern Organization Theory*, edited by Mason Haire, pp. 272–306. New York, NY: Wiley.

Hannan, Michael T., and John Freeman. 1977. "The Population Ecology of Organizations." *American Journal of Sociology* 82 (5): 929–964.

Jayaraman, Sarumathi, and Immanuel Ness. 2005. "Models of Worker Organizing." In *The New Urban Immigrant Workforce: Innovative Models for Labor Organizing,* edited by Sarumathi Jayaraman and Immanuel Ness, pp. 71–84. Armonk, NY: M.E. Sharpe.

Karpf, David. 2012. *The MoveOn Effect: The Unexpected Transformation of American Political Advocacy.* New York, NY: Oxford University Press.

Kleinman, Larry. 2011 (Sep.). "Dues Worth Paying." *Grassroots Fundraising Journal*, 30th Anniversary Issue.

Kochhar, Rakesh, C. Soledad Espinoza, and Rebecca Hinze-Pifer. 2010 (Oct. 29). "After the Great Recession: Foreign Born Gain Jobs; Native Born Lose Jobs." Pew Research Center. https://pewrsr.ch/2xT7DPT

Koerin, Beverly. 2003. "The Settlement House Tradition: Current Trends and Future Concerns." *Journal of Sociology & Social Welfare* 30 (2): 53–68.

Louie, Miriam Ching Yoon. 2001. *Sweatshop Warriors: Immigrant Women Workers Take on the Global Factory.* Cambridge, MA: South End Press.

Manheim, Jarol B. 2017. *The Emerging Role of Worker Centers in Union Organizing: An Update and Supplement.* Washington, DC: U.S. Chamber of Commerce Workforce Freedom Initiative.

McAlevey, Jane F. 2016. *No Shortcuts: Organizing for Power in the New Gilded Age.* New York, NY: Oxford University Press.

McCarthy, John D., David W. Britt, and Mark Wolfson. 1991. "The Institutional Channeling of Social Movements by the State in the United States." In *Research in Social Movements, Conflicts and Change*, Vol. 13, edited by Metta Spencer, pp. 45–76. Greenwich, CT: JAI Press.

Meyer, David S., and Suzanne Staggenborg. 1996. "Movements, Countermovements, and the Structure of Political Opportunity." *American Journal of Sociology* 101 (6): 1628–1660.

Meyer, John W., and Brian Rowan. 1977. "Institutionalized Organizations: Formal Structure as Myth and Ceremony." *American Journal of Sociology* 83 (2): 340–363.

Milkman, Ruth. 2006. *LA Story: Immigrant Workers and the Future of the US Labor Movement.* New York, NY: Russell Sage.

Milkman, Ruth, Joshua Bloom, and Victor Narro. 2010. *Working for Justice: The L.A. Model of Organizing and Advocacy.* Ithaca, NY: ILR Press.

Milkman, Ruth, and Ed Ott. 2014. *New Labor in New York: Precarious Workers and the Future of the Labor Movement.* Ithaca, NY: ILR Press.

Minkoff, Debra C. 2002. "The Emergence of Hybrid Organizational Forms: Combining Identity-Based Service Provision and Political Action." *Nonprofit and Voluntary Sector Quarterly* 31 (3): 377–401.

Murray, Peter. 2013 (Fall). "The Secret of Scale." *Stanford Social Innovation Review.* http://bit.ly/2xQh2rt

Naduris-Weissman, Eli. 2009. "The Worker Center Movement and Traditional Labor Law: A Contextual Analysis." *Berkeley Journal of Employment and Labor Law* 30: 232–335.

Narro, Victor. 2010. "Afterword." In *Working for Justice: The L.A. Model of Organizing and Advocacy,* edited by Ruth Milkman, Joshua Bloom, and Victor Narro, pp. 233–244. Ithaca, NY: LR Press.

Narro, Victor, and Janna Shadduck-Hernández. 2014. "The Informality of Day Labor Work: Challenges and Approaches to Addressing Working Conditions of Day Laborers." In *Hidden Lives and Human Rights in the United States: Understanding the Controversies and Tragedies of Undocumented Immigration,* Vol. 3, edited by Lois Ann Lorentzen, pp. 141–166. Santa Barbara, CA: Praeger.

Passel, Jeffrey S., D'Vera Cohn, and Ana Gonzalez-Barrera. 2012 (Apr. 23). "Net Migration from Mexico Falls to Zero—and Perhaps Less." Washington, DC: Pew Research Center. https://pewrsr.ch/2xSEu7v

Passel, Jeffrey S., D'Vera Cohn, and Ana Gonzalez-Barrera. 2013 (Sep. 23). "Population Decline of Unauthorized Immigrants Stalls, May Have Reversed." Washington, DC: Pew Research Center. https://pewrsr.ch/2R0t5Lx

Patler, Caitlin C. 2010. "Alliance-Building and Organizing for Immigrant Rights: The Case of the Coalition for Humane Immigrant Rights of Los Angeles." In *Working for Justice: The L.A. Model of Organizing and Advocacy,* edited by Ruth Milkman, Joshua Bloom, and Victor Narro, pp. 71–88. Ithaca, NY: LR Press.

Rhomberg, Chris. 2012. *The Broken Table: The Detroit Newspaper Strike and the State of American Labor.* New York, NY: Russell Sage Foundation.

Rozado Marzán, César F. 2017. "Worker Centers and the Moral Economy: Disrupting Through Brokerage, Prestige, and Moral Framing." *University of Chicago Legal Forum,* Vol. 2017, Article 16: 409–434.

Skocpol, Theda. 2003. *Diminished Democracy: From Membership to Management in American Civic Life.* Norman, OK: University of Oklahoma Press.

Stephen, Lynn. 2012. *The Story of PCUN and the Farmworker Movement in Oregon,* Revised Edition. Eugene, OR: Center for Latino/a and Latin American Studies (CLLAS), University of Oregon.

Stinchcombe, Arthur L. 1965. "Social Structure and Organizations." In *Handbook of Organizations,* edited by James G. March, pp. 142–193. New York, NY: Rand McNally.

Tarrow, Sidney. 1993. "Cycles of Collective Action: Between Moments of Madness and the Repertoire of Contention." *Social Science History* 17 (2): 281–307.

Theodore, Nik, Abel Valenzuela Jr., and Edwin Meléndez. 2006. "La Esquina (The Corner): Day Laborers on the Margins of New York's Formal Economy." *WorkingUSA: The Journal of Labor and Society* 9: 407–423.

Tilly, Charles. 1978. *From Mobilization to Revolution.* New York, NY: McGraw-Hill College.

Voss, Kim, and Irene Bloemraad. 2011. *Rallying for Immigrant Rights: The Fight for Inclusion in 21st Century America.* Oakland, CA: University of California Press.

Waldinger, Roger. 1996. "From Ellis Island to LAX: Immigrant Prospects in the American City." *International Migration Review* 30 (4): 1078–1086.

Waldinger, Roger D., Chris Erickson, Ruth Milkman, Daniel Mitchell, Abel Valenzuela, Kent Wong, and Maurice Zeitlan. 1996. *Helots No More: A Case Study of the Justice for Janitors Campaign in Los Angeles.* Working Paper #15. Los Angeles, CA: UCLA Lewis Center for Regional Policy Studies.

Weil, David. 2014. *The Fissured Workplace: Why Work Became So Bad for So Many and What Can Be Done to Improve It.* Cambridge, MA: Harvard University Press.

Wright, Erik Olin. 2000. "Working-Class Power, Capitalist-Class Interests, and Class Compromise." *American Journal of Sociology* 105 (4): 957–1002.

Zong, Jie, and Jeanne Batalova. 2017 (Sep 29). "Chinese Immigrants in the United States." Washington, DC: Migration Policy Institute. http://bit.ly/2R27AtR

Sizing Up Worker Center Income (2008–2014): A Study of Revenue Size, Stability, and Streams

Leslie C. Gates
Binghamton University

Kati L. Griffith
Jonathan Kim
School of Industrial and Labor Relations, Cornell University

Zane Mokhiber
Economic Policy Institute

Joseph C. Bazler
Austin Case
School of Industrial and Labor Relations, Cornell University

INTRODUCTION

Since the publication of Janice Fine's path-breaking book, *Worker Centers: Communities at the Edge of the Dream* in 2006, scholars and commentators on the left and the right of the political spectrum have grappled with how to characterize these emergent worker organizations on the US labor relations scene. This chapter deepens our understanding of the nature of worker centers by examining the funding trends that underlay the wide range of experimental organizing and advocacy strategies highlighted in other chapters of this volume. Undoubtedly, to emerge and survive, these organizations need money (Bobo and Pabellón 2016). But how financially stable are worker centers? How big are they? Where does the funding come from? How do they compare to labor unions? To address some of these questions, we compiled a large collection of available data to complete the first systematic empirical analysis of worker center funding across multiple years (2008 through 2014).

Our analysis includes the amounts and sources of revenue for more than 100 worker centers over a seven-year period (2008 through 2014). We drew from three main sources of available information to construct funding profiles for each worker center in our sample. First, we incorporated the nonprofit organizations' required annual filings to the US Internal Revenue Service (IRS)—a filing required of any organization that has nonprofit tax-exempt status under Section 501(c)(3) of the US Internal Revenue Code. Most worker centers have nonprofit status, which enables them to access foundation, individual donor, and government funding to support their initiatives to improve the living and working conditions of low-wage workers (Fine 2011). Second, we used labor organizations' required annual filings to the US Department of Labor. Third, we gathered data from the Foundation Directory Online's compilation of foundation donations.

Our "size up" of worker center income from 2008 through 2014 complicates the dominant portrayal of worker centers as small and unstable. Most worker centers are indeed organizations with little revenue. Nevertheless, there is a wide range of revenue size among worker centers. There are even a few "giants," with revenue so high that they were statistical outliers. Worker center budgets are somewhat unstable: the past growth of a worker center's revenue typically has no bearing on its future growth. There also seemed to be no advantage for large-revenue organizations. Worker centers with large budgets were typically just as unstable as centers operating on a shoestring budget and were more susceptible to shrinking in times of economic downturn.

Our inquiry into the streams of funding that worker centers receive tells a "no one size fits all" story of diversity. Unlike labor unions, whose revenue relies almost exclusively on dues from members, worker centers craft diverse funding portfolios and get almost no funding from membership dues. Much like those of other nonprofit organizations, worker centers' revenue streams are diverse. The most common funding streams of worker centers are monies from providing program services, charitable foundation grants, and government funding. In terms of reliance, worker centers overwhelmingly depend on funding streams that are external to the organization (foundation grants, government grants, and individual donations) rather than funding streams that are internally generated, such as membership dues. Despite increased strategic collaborations between some labor unions and worker centers reported elsewhere in this volume, we find that funding from labor unions serves as a minuscule portion of worker center revenue overall.

OUR SAMPLE OF WORKER CENTERS

We derive the population of worker centers in our sample from Fine and Theodore's infographic of worker centers from 2012 (Fine and Theodore 2013). We sought to collect data on each of these worker centers from the forms they are required to submit annually to the IRS, specifically the IRS 990 form (hereafter referred to as IRS 990). We did this for each worker center in every year from 2008 through 2014. Thus, the IRS 990 is both the primary source of data and the primary delimiter of our sample. The IRS 990 offers a trove of data. It includes an organization's address, the names of officers/leaders, and other demographic information, as well as a breakdown of revenue and expenses. While there are limitations to the IRS 990 (Grønbjerg 2002), it is used widely as an adequate source of data on nonprofit revenue and sources of income (Froelich, Knoepfle, and Pollak 2000; Powell and Steinberg 2006).

Table 1 illustrates that for 2012, we obtained IRS 990s for 60% (104) of the 172 worker centers on the 2012 list.[1] Our analysis of those worker centers for which we could not obtain IRS 990s, and therefore could not include in our sample, leads us to conclude that our sample likely over-represents larger and more stable worker centers. First, a substantial portion of worker centers, 15% of the total in 2012, were not stand-alone organizations. Instead, they were "parented" by another larger organization.[2] Because they are a program or part of a larger nonprofit that deals with issues beyond workplace justice, we could not isolate the size and funding sources of the worker centers within the parents' overall budgets.

Second, we confirmed that another roughly 5% of all worker centers were not required to file an IRS 990 because their revenue was so small. Organizations with 501(c)(3) status who have revenue of $50,000 or below are not required to report financial information to the IRS.[3] Third, we know that relying on IRS 990s as a source of data "carries an important undercount bias" more generally (Culleton Colwell 1997; Gleeson and Bloemraad 2012; Grønbjerg 1993). Gleeson and Bloemraad (2012) have shown that some groups may not have enough resources to even register for 501(c)(3) nonprofit status in the first place, while others may simply not file the 990 even though they are obligated to do so. Thus, relying on

TABLE 1
Percentage of Worker Centers by Rationale for Availability of Data

	2008	2009	2010	2011	2012	2013	2014
% in sample (with IRS 990 data)	62	61	59	60	60	59	62
% not in sample (known rationale)	22	23	23	23	23	23	23
% parented	13	15	15	15	15	15	15
% too small	6	5	5	5	5	5	5
% religious or other exempt	3	3	3	3	3	3	3
% don't know why not in sample	16	16	17	17	16	17	15
Total %	100	100	100	100	100	100	100
Total number of worker centers	152	162	166	169	172	172	172

IRS 990s carries a bias toward under-representing resource-poor organizations.

Finally, because our data collection strategy focused on a list of worker centers created in 2012, our sample of worker centers in earlier years (2008 through 2011) likely missed some worker centers that existed in these years but did not survive until 2012. For those years, our sample over-represents organizations with stable-enough funding sources to survive until 2012. For 2013 and 2014, we collected data on worker centers that existed in 2012. Therefore, our sample does not include organizations that emerged in those two later years. To minimize these effects, we report analyses based on the 2012 data, even though parallel analyses of other years confirm the trends reported for 2012.

FINDINGS ON THE SIZE AND STABILITY OF WORKER CENTER REVENUE

Some scholars and commentators suggest that worker centers are powerful players on the labor relations scene (Manheim 2013; US Chamber of Commerce 2014; Wong 2015). Cordero-Guzmán, Izvănariu, and Narro (2013) highlight some centers have formed sector-based networks that serve as labor market intermediaries. Others question whether most worker centers are even large enough to have a demonstrable impact beyond the individual level (Compa 2015; Eidelson 2013; Fine 2006; Rosenfeld 2006).

Here we consider just how big and stable worker center revenue is. Our data does not allow us to look at all aspects of worker center size, which would entail a more holistic consideration of factors such as membership size, numbers of individuals served, and other measures of organizational impact. Nevertheless, revenue size can undoubtedly help us understand the scope of a worker center's reach. The literature on nonprofit organizations, for instance, suggests that larger revenue can lead to increased political visibility, which increases the likelihood of evoking positive responses from policy makers (de Graauw 2016).

Revenue Size?

Figure 1's histogram shows that worker center revenue tend to be low. This is true even though our sample of worker centers is likely to over-represent larger worker centers. As Figure 1 demonstrates, the modal worker center (the one with the greatest frequency) has a revenue of between $100,000 and $200,000. Of the worker centers in this modal range, more than half of them (12 of the 22) had revenue below $150,000. The concentration of worker centers in this lower revenue range is further affirmed when we consider that a quarter of all worker centers in our sample had yearly revenue of less than $179,163. Furthermore, the median revenue level for our

FIGURE 1

Distribution of Worker Centers by Total Revenue, 2012

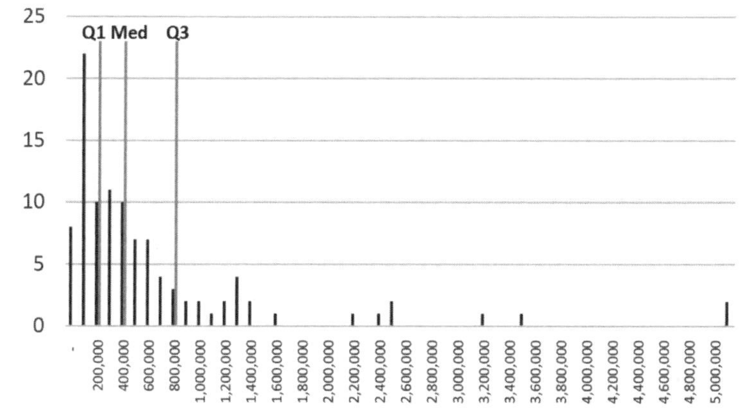

N	Mean	StdDv	Min	Q1	Median	Q3	Max
104	747,431	1,186,875	10,808	179,163	410,010	779,036	8,366,068

Source: IRS 990s.

sample was only $410,010. These observations about the revenue streams of worker centers are consistent with Fine's 2005 study, which showed that more than half of worker centers were small organizations with annual revenue of $250,000 or less (Fine 2006). Low revenue is a trait worker centers share with other nonprofits, which have been characterized as "small and cash-poor" (Grønbjerg 1993: 53).

A brief comparison with revenue among more traditional labor organizations further highlights the relatively small revenue levels of the worker centers in our sample. In 2012, for instance, UNITE HERE's Chicago Local 1 had a revenue of $9 million, and UNITE HERE's San Francisco Local 2 reported a revenue of $6.4 million. A smaller UNITE HERE local in Washington, D.C., Local 25, reported approximately $4 million in revenue for 2012 (DOL LM-2 filings for Local 1, Local 2, and Local 25; US DOL 2012a, 2012b, 2012c). If we look beyond local unions to international unions such as the Service Employees International Union (SEIU), the small revenue sizes of worker centers are put into even more stark relief. In 2012, SEIU's reported revenue was $307 million (US DOL 2012d). In contrast, the combined total revenue of all 104 worker centers in our 2012 sample was equal to just under $78 million.

And yet Figure 1 also reveals how widely worker center revenue ranges. A quarter of worker centers in our sample (26) had revenue greater than $779,036. In this largest quartile, six worker centers had revenue of less than $1 million per year, 12 had revenue between $1 and $2 million per year, and eight had revenue larger than $2 million.[4] These eight worker centers had impressive revenue levels: two of them had revenue of just over $3 million, one had revenue just over $7 million, and one's revenue exceeded $8 million. It is these eight high-revenue cases that pull up the average revenue of worker centers in our sample to $747,431, way above the median or mode. The identification of eight outliers is consistent with Fine's analysis, elsewhere in this volume, that some worker centers have grown into giants that still have some work that fits the definition of a "worker center" but also do organizing and advocacy work that goes well beyond service provision, organizing, and advocacy at the local level.

Revenue Stability?

Worker centers' funding strategies are often characterized as unstable and unsustainable (Compa 2015; Fine 2011; Fisk 2016). Indeed, worker centers are often described as surviving on "shoestring" budgets (Estlund 2015; Greenhouse 2014; Griffith 2015), with highly unstable levels of funding year to year (Cordero-Guzmán 2015). Our multi-year panel data offers a rare opportunity to assess the stability of individual worker center revenue over time, albeit with data that over-represents those worker centers stable enough to have existed before and after 2012. We assess the stability of revenue by measuring each worker center's annual rate of change in total revenue, as other studies of nonprofits have done (Grønbjerg 1993). Worker centers with stable revenue would be those with zero to positive rates of growth from one year to the next. Furthermore, we can assess the relative stability in worker center funding by examining how well a worker center's annual revenue growth in one year predicts that of subsequent years. Table 2 presents a series of multivariate analyses that assess whether the prior year's rate of growth, adjusted for inflation, predicts the subsequent year's rate of growth, controlling for the worker center's total revenue.

The results presented in Table 2 affirm the idea that worker center revenue is unstable. In three of the five years (from 2012 through 2014, represented in columns 3, 4, and 5), the annual rates of growth do not predict the subsequent year's rates of growth. It would seem that worker centers rarely repeat fund-raising success from one year to the next. Additionally, the results for 2010 and 2011 suggest that even when there is a significant relationship between a worker center's rate of growth in a prior year and that of the following year, the effect is not in the direction of stability. For example, column 1 portrays that for every 1% increase in

TABLE 2
The Effects of Worker Center Prior Growth on Subsequent Year's Growth
(Adjusted for Inflation), 2010–2014

Variables	(1) 2010 Growth in Real Revenue	(2) 2011 Growth in Real Revenue	(3) 2012 Growth in Real Revenue	(4) 2013 Growth in Real Revenue	(5) 2014 Growth in Real Revenue
2009 real rate of growth	−0.248* (0.139)				
2009 revenue (adjusted to 2008)	−4.38e-06 (4.33e-06)				
2010 real rate of growth		−0.166** (0.0812)			
2010 revenue (adjusted to 2008)		−3.50e-06 (4.68e-06)			
2011 real rate of growth			0.0935 (0.0856)		
2011 revenue (adjusted to 2008)			−6.48e-06* (3.52e-06)		
2012 real rate of growth				−0.0622 (0.116)	
2012 revenue (adjusted to 2008)				−3.93e-06 (4.44e-06)	
2013 real rate of growth					0.0943 (0.0756)
2013 revenue (adjusted to 2008)					1.32e-06 (3.02e-06)
Constant	15.09** (7.477)	12.53* (6.426)	15.32*** (5.188)	14.88** (6.141)	7.170 (4.475)
Observations	91	94	94	97	99
R-squared	0.053	0.051	0.044	0.012	0.019

Standard errors in parentheses.
***p < 0.01, **p < 0.05, *p < 0.1

worker center revenue from 2008 to 2009, there was a 0.25% decrease in worker center growth from 2009 to 2010, regardless of a worker center's size; that is, it is precisely those that experienced revenue growth in a prior year that tended to experience less growth in subsequent years. It would seem that no good deed—in this case, that of successful fund-raising—goes unpunished at worker centers.

The results for 2010 and 2011 also raise questions about how worker center stability may relate to political or economic shocks, such as the economic recession. An economic crisis unfolded over the course of 18 months that stretched from December 2007 through June 2009 (National Bureau of Economic Research 2010). We know that the crisis affected both government and charitable foundations' ability to support nonprofit agencies like worker centers. Thus, we might anticipate an across-the-board loss of revenue for worker centers. What these results suggest, however, is that this effect was not equally felt. In fact, the recession exacted its toll on precisely those worker centers that had been flourishing at the time the recession hit. The results also raise the question of sustainability of grants. It may be that these organizations benefited from nonrenewable government or foundation grants, or that they were affected by other shocks, such as a loss of political will.

Relationship Between Revenue Size and Stability?

We find little support for the idea that worker centers with smaller revenue were more vulnerable to shrinking than larger-revenue worker centers. Figure 2 characterizes the relationship between a group's size of revenue (in 2012) and its revenue stability in the two successive years (2013 and

FIGURE 2
Average Annual Growth Rate (2012–2014) by Total Revenue

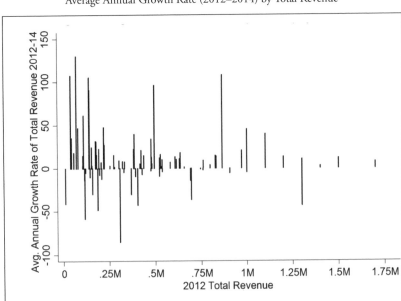

Note: Annual growth rate is calculated after adjusting total revenue for inflation.

2014). Here, we follow prior studies of nonprofit finances (Grønbjerg 1993: 83) in avoiding "unwarranted conclusions about the magnitude and direction of changes" by looking instead at the "average revenues from two adjacent years." Each spike on Figure 2 represents the average percentage change in revenue of a given worker center from 2012 to 2014, arrayed according to total revenue in 2012. Bars that spike up represent worker centers that tended to grow (positive average rate of growth between 2012 and 2014); bars that spike down represent worker centers that tended to contract (negative two-year average rate of growth).

Figure 2 demonstrates that plenty of smaller worker centers experienced significant average growth. Some of the worker centers with the smallest revenue—ones with revenue of less than a quarter of a million dollars—experienced the most dramatic average growth, represented by the cluster of tall spikes close to the vertical axis. All of the organizations that, on average, doubled in size had revenue of less than a million dollars. At the same time, there were groups that had revenue of more than $1 million—double the median size of worker centers—that shrank by more than half. Furthermore, three of the large outliers shrank—ones with revenue well over $2 million for which we could also calculate a two-year average annual rate of change. One even shrank, on average, by a quarter.

We further confirmed the substantive findings illustrated by Figure 2 in our analyses presented in Table 2. In all but one of the years (2012), a worker center's total revenue, adjusted for inflation, did not predict its subsequent annual rate of growth. Moreover, the analysis predicting growth in 2012 (column 3) suggests a counter-intuitive effect of the economic recession on the stability of larger worker centers. We might expect that worker centers that survive on shoestring budgets are the most vulnerable in times of economic downturn. And yet, in 2012, it was larger worker centers that tended to shrink.[5] We can interpret the coefficient in Table 2 as indicating that for every dollar more in a worker center's total revenue, its total revenue decreased by 6%. While there are reasons to be cautious about reading too much into this effect, it is intriguing that larger- rather than smaller-revenue worker centers appear to be the most vulnerable when the economic tides turn against fund-raisers.[6] Once again, it would seem that no good deed—in the case the ability of an organization to exceed the revenue of other worker centers—goes unpunished. Future research could help us unpack what explains this unexpected finding.

DATA STRATEGY FOR BREAKING DOWN WORKER CENTER FUNDING STREAMS

Table 3 illustrates that we were able to identify the funding streams equal to about 60% of the total revenue reported. We cannot disaggregate the

TABLE 3
Percentage of Revenue Identified by Type of Source

	2008	2009	2010	2011	2012	2013	2014	Overall Average
Identified sources	53	58	58	65	57	62	66	59
IRS	37	44	41	43	35	41	43	40
Non-IRS	16	14	17	23	22	21	22	19
Unidentified sources	48	42	42	34	43	38	35	41
Total percentage	100	100	100	100	100	100	100	100
Number of worker centers	94	99	98	102	104	101	105	

remaining 40% of worker center income by stream. Nevertheless, we know this funding comes from sources external to the organizations because it constitutes the income the worker centers placed in the catch-all "all other contributions" portion of the IRS 990.

Table 3 shows that we were able to identify the sources of about 40% of worker centers' overall revenue using the IRS 990s. These forms allowed us to report the specific funding streams of income from program services, membership dues, and government grants with considerable confidence. Nonetheless, the IRS 990 did not indicate how much of "all other contributions" came from two sources that some have alleged are significant: labor unions and charitable foundations. We were able to account for nearly another 20% of a worker center's average funding streams by examining two non-IRS sources.

We sought to uncover union funding to worker centers from the US Department of Labor's Office of Labor Management and Standards (DOL OLMS). Unions must file yearly spending reports with the DOL OLMS that include the receiving organization's name, the date of payment, and the purpose of payment.[7] Unfortunately, there were no unique identifiers for each worker center in the DOL OLMS data. This made the data vulnerable to entries that were spelled differently or incorrectly, and as such may undercount levels of union funding. Nevertheless, we are confident that our efforts yielded a robust list of union contributions to worker centers.

To identify funding to worker centers from charitable foundations, we consulted the Foundation Directory Online, which is self-described as a research tool for nonprofits to find funders. A significant limitation of this source is the coverage of the Foundation Directory itself. It is likely to have missing data because it may pull from different sources year to year. Indeed, its website states that it is "not designed for statistical or aggregate research."[8] Moreover, the Foundation Directory reports grants in the year they are allocated, regardless of whether the grant was actually dispersed over multiple years. Thus, our data collection method is vulnerable to undercounting as well as overcounting foundation funding in a particular year.

Given the work of Fine (2006) and Frantz and Fernandes (2016) and the limitations of the non-IRS data sources on union and foundation revenue streams, we generally consider our estimates on these two streams to be minimum amounts. It is likely that a portion of the roughly 40% of worker center "all other contributions" revenue that remains unidentified may in fact come from foundations and unions, but a substantial portion of it certainly comes from individual donors as well. Thus, the following analysis focuses mainly on what we *can* say about the varied streams of funding using the strengths of our data set.

FINDINGS ON WORKER CENTER FUNDING STREAMS

As scholars of nonprofit funding have noted (Grønbjerg 1993), it is useful to look at the whole group of worker centers because macrolevel patterns affect the field the individual organizations operate within, and they can influence how groups compete and collaborate with one another. Figure 3 gives us a bird's-eye view of the relative size of various funding streams

FIGURE 3
Worker Center Funding Streams, 2012

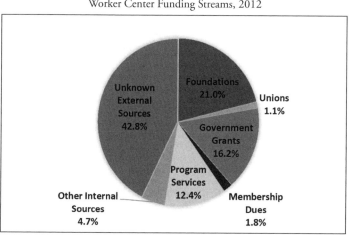

Note: Other internal sources include fund-raising events, investments, and federated campaigns.
Sources: Calculated based on IRS 990s, Foundation Directory Online, and US DOL.

in the total pie of income that worker centers collect. It reveals that worker centers rely on a diverse set of funding streams. As we might expect for any nonprofit, we found that worker centers rely to a significant degree on external, as opposed to internal, sources of funding. Internal revenue streams include membership dues, as well as less significant sources such as fund-raising events and investments. All told, the external sources add up to more than 80% of the overall pool of worker center funding for 2012. This percentage is even higher given that some "program services" income comes from government contracts rather than fees from partici-pants. The relative insignificance of internal sources of funding underscores the degree to which worker centers look beyond their immediate commu-nity to make ends meet. This reliance on external funding sources brings to mind important questions about the extent to which reliance on exter-nal funders affects worker centers' programmatic priorities, questions we take up below in our Directions for Future Research section.

Our analysis also suggested trends about the relative importance of various funding streams to worker center income. Here we drew on Grønbjerg's definition of importance (1993) as an assessment of both how commonly a particular source is used (funding stream prevalence) and how dependent an organization was on a particular source (funding stream dependence).

Member Dues

Our research confirms the predominant wisdom that worker centers find it challenging to receive member dues from their low-wage constituencies (Fine 2006; Gordon 2005). As Figure 3 illustrates, worker centers as a whole obtained merely 1.8% of their total revenue from membership dues in 2012. The dearth of resources obtained from membership dues is even more apparent if we consider the relative prevalence of dues—how this total pot of membership dues is distributed across worker centers. As the "Dues" column of Table 4 shows, the vast majority (68%) of worker cen-ters did not receive any funds from dues. Furthermore, worker centers that did obtain money from dues were not dependent on them. Of the 34 worker centers that reported receiving any money from dues, the vast ma-jority obtained less than 5% of their revenue from membership dues. Only seven worker centers obtained more than 5% of their revenue from dues.

Furthermore, higher-revenue worker centers were not more likely than their smaller counterparts to raise money from dues.[9] Figure 4 gives us a visual snapshot of how dependence on dues relates to revenue size. It confirms that the percentage of revenue that worker centers received from dues was consistently low across each of these sizes.[10] The first bar of Figure 4 represents the smallest quartile of worker centers.[11] The last two groups,

TABLE 4
Frequency Distribution of the Revenue Percent by Funding Stream, 2012

Range	Foundation	Program	Government	Dues	Union
0	38	41	56	68	86
0.1–0.99	3	13	0	15	2
1–4	5	15	6	11	6
5–9	10	5	4	0	3
10–19	14	7	11	3	3
20–29	8	3	9	1	1
30–39	7	6	1	1	0
40–49	8	4	1	1	0
50–74	5	2	8	0	0
75–100	3	4	4	0	0
Mean	16	11	13	2	1
Minimum	1	0	2	0	1
Maximum	112	99	89	41	20
	100	100	100	100	100

FIGURE 4
Mean Percentage of Revenue by Source and Size

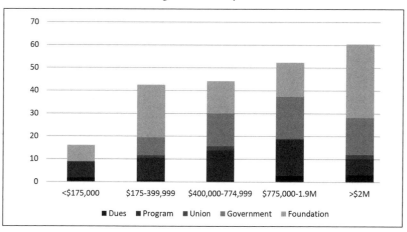

represented in the last two bars, split the largest quartile of worker centers between outliers (those that report revenue in excess of $2 million) and those that fall within the normal distribution.[12]

Program Services

Overall, worker centers benefited much more from income for program services than from the receipt of membership dues. As Figure 3 represents, program services accounted for 12.4% of the total pie of funding received by worker centers in 2012. This finding is not that surprising given that worker centers' nonprofit status is reliant to some extent on their provision of services (although this does not require them to charge fees). The IRS 990 defines "program services" as monies received for activities that accomplish the organization's "exempt purposes" of providing relief to the "poor," "distressed," and "underprivileged."

Program service income was a prevalent source of funding among worker centers. Table 4 shows just 41% of worker centers reported no revenue from program services in 2012. This makes income from program services the second most common stream of revenue for worker centers, second only to foundations. Nonetheless, worker centers' relative dependence on program services varies widely. Table 4 illustrates that nearly 30% of worker centers received less than 5% of their revenue from program services (13% receiving less than 1%, and 15% receiving between 1% and 4.9% of their revenue). However, on average, worker centers received 11% of their revenue from program services, with six worker centers receiving more than half of their funding from program services. There were even two groups that received 99% of their overall funding from program services they provide, such as legal services and trainings.

We might expect that larger worker centers would receive a greater portion of their revenue from program services because they have more organizational capacity to provide larger-scale services. Some authors suggest that direct services can be more difficult for small worker centers (Milkman, Bloom, and Narro 2010: 11). However, it does not seem that size was a predictor of reliance on program services for our sample.[13] Figure 4's stacked bar chart illustrates that program services were an important source of funding across all size groupings. The top quarter (excluding the biggest eight) did receive the highest average percentage from program services (15.6%), and the percentage of revenue received from program services descends in each of the next smaller subgroupings. Nevertheless, the smallest quarter and the largest eight worker centers received a similar average amount from program services (about 7%). The evidence points to an across-the-board, albeit widely ranging, reliance on program services.[14]

GOVERNMENT GRANTS

Unlike labor unions, which are not eligible for many government grants because they are not 501(c)(3) organizations, worker centers receive government grants to engage in a wide range of activities. These activities include tax preparation assistance, citizenship education and training, homelessness alleviation efforts, worker rights education, and efforts to combat labor trafficking.[15] Similar to funding streams of other nonprofits (Grønbjerg 1993), government grants are a relatively common funding stream for worker centers. As Figure 3 represents, we could confirm that more than 16% of worker center revenue in 2012 came from government grants. This is largely consistent with Fine's study (2006), which found that 21% of worker center income came from government sources.

Owing to limitations in the IRS data, the actual percentage of revenue from government grants in our sample is also likely to be higher. The monies worker centers report under the "government contributions" portion of the IRS 990 cannot include those government grants designated for program services that primarily benefit a governmental unit, as opposed to the public as a whole. Worker centers must report such government grants under "program services" rather than "government contributions." This limitation notwithstanding, 44% of the 80 worker centers that had to report whether they received government contributions obtained some type of government grant.[16]

The "Government" column of Table 4 illustrates how difficult it is to characterize the typical degree to which worker centers depend on government grants. The average percentage of revenue that worker centers obtained from government contributions was 13.2%, but the percentage for any given worker center ranged from 2% to 89%. Worker centers that did receive government contributions, though, tended to be more dependent on them than they were on dues or program services. Only 6% of these worker centers obtained less than 5% of their revenue from government contributions. Meanwhile, 12% of the 80 reporting worker centers (nine worker centers) received more than half of their funding from government contributions.[17]

Worker center dependence on this funding stream varies widely regardless of size. Even though they may have more institutional resources, higher-revenue worker centers were not more likely than smaller groups to receive government grants. Figure 4 gives us a visual representation of how the percentage of revenue worker centers obtained from government grants varied across differently sized worker centers.[18] The three bars representing the three largest groupings obtained a roughly similar percentage of their revenue from government, ranging from 14% for the middle group and

peaking in the next highest group at 18%.[19] Those worker centers with
revenue from $175,000 to $400,000 tended to receive just under 8% of
their revenue from government grants, a difference that was, nonetheless,
not significant from the overall average of 15.6% for the remaining groups.[20]
Indeed, it is a relatively small worker center in this group, with revenue of
just under $250,000, that received the highest proportion of its revenue
from government grants. Thus, while government grants are an important
source of funding for worker centers, the prevalence and the relative
dependence of worker centers on such government grants varies tremendously.

Foundations

Our limited evidence on foundation funding confirms what others have
claimed: worker centers would not be able to exist, let alone flourish, were
it not for grants from charitable foundations (Fine 2006; Greenhouse 2014).
As Figure 3 indicates, foundation grants listed in the Foundation Directory
equaled roughly a fifth (21%) of the pooled revenue for all worker centers
in 2012. The true percentage is likely to be much higher given Fine's finding (2006) that 61% of worker center funding came from charitable foundations.

Furthermore, as the first column of Table 4 shows, foundation grants
were the most prevalent stream of funding for worker centers. A minority
of worker centers (just 38%) received no funding from foundations. Given
that we suspect there were foundation grants that we could not track, we
believe that deriving funding from foundations is even more common than
we can show here. We would not want to read too much into the figures
we have on the relative dependence of worker centers on foundation funding because we know foundations may report a multi-year grant in a single
year and that the fiscal years of foundations may differ from those of worker
centers. Nevertheless, a glance down the last column of Table 4 suggests
that the degree to which worker centers rely on foundation grants varies
just as much as their reliance on government grants.[21]

Unions

Several chapters in this volume illustrate ways that worker centers and labor
unions have partnered in recent years to advance such things as minimum-
wage legislation, paid sick leave, and campaigns against large retailers. The
US Chamber of Commerce and other worker center critics have alleged
that some worker centers rely so heavily on union funding that they are
essentially "union fronts" (Manheim 2013).[22] Nonetheless, our research
suggests that worker centers are generally not financially dependent on
labor unions.

Our research shows that the vast majority of worker centers do not
receive significant funding from labor unions. Figure 3, based on DOL

OLMS data, confirmed just a tiny fraction (1%) of the overall pool of worker center funds came from unions. Table 4 confirms how rare receiving funds from unions really is: the vast majority of worker centers (85%) receive no funds from unions. Those that do are not very dependent on union funds. In 2012, just seven worker centers received 5% or more of their funding from unions, with the highest being 20%. Furthermore, between 2008 and 2014, there were just six worker centers that received more than 20% of their revenue from unions in any given year.[23] Neither did it seem that a worker center's size affected its likelihood of obtaining funds from unions.[24] Indeed, as Figure 4 shows, the worker centers that received funds from unions were spread across each of our five subgroupings. In short, union funding was neither common, nor that significant, for the worker centers in our sample.

DIRECTIONS FOR FUTURE RESEARCH ON FUNDING STREAMS

What can funding streams tell us about worker centers? We know that sources of funding and an organization's tax-exempt status can affect an organization's programming choices (de Graauw 2015). Indeed, there are ongoing debates about how different sources of funding might directly affect the programmatic focus and social-change strategies of worker centers in particular. Finding out more about the relationship between funding and programming can tell us more about the nature of this emerging subset of nonprofit organizations, whose diverse funding portfolios are in stark contrast to labor unions' overwhelming reliance on member dues. While it is beyond the scope of this chapter to address all of these issues here, our findings and review of the relevant debates regarding worker center funding strategies to date suggest several fruitful avenues for future empirical inquiry in this area.

More Research on External Funders' Effects on Worker Center Programming

Our finding that 80% of worker center income comes from external sources raises several questions for future research. First, future research could consider the extent to which reliance on external funders takes energy away from organizing and other organization building, given the time it takes to please and report to external funders. External funders range widely in the requirements they impose on their grantees (Grønbjerg 1993). Fine (2006) and others argue that these requirements can tax worker center staff and can encourage the organization to build organizational capacity around fund-raising. This dynamic, Fine argues, can take the organization away from the project of building a dues-paying and fund-raising membership base. Similarly, Grønbjerg (1993: 53) contends that nonprofit reliance on external funders sets up "demanding exchange relationships that restrict organizational choice." These concerns notwithstanding, it is possible that some external grants foster the creation of new program services, which in turn can become somewhat self-sustaining internal sources of funding after the external grant runs out.

Second, future research could consider how external funders may influence organizational priorities more directly (Estey 2006; Fisk 2016). Grønbjerg's study of nonprofits (1993: 53) characterizes many nonprofits as having "limited ability to resist efforts by funders to exert influence" because of low revenue. Others note that some external entities are not interested in nonprofits' efforts to achieve deeper, systemwide change through organizing and agitation (Eidelson 2013). In a similar vein, Franz and Fernandes (2016) argue that some foundations place restraints on larger national worker centers that alter their ability to challenge neoliberal rationalities. They contend that, instead, these grants encourage worker centers to promote program services that foster employer alliances, workforce skills training, and business ventures. In this way, these authors portray some program services as moving organizations away from the more controversial organizing efforts designed to challenge policies and structures that hurt low-wage workers (Eidelson 2013; Franz and Fernandes 2016).

However, disagreement between nonprofit scholars on the question of how government funding affects political advocacy (de Graauw 2016) highlights the need for future research into the extent to which external funders inhibit worker centers from economic agitation and policy advocacy. In contrast to critics of external funding sources, some nonprofit scholars see reliance on government funding as boosting many organizations' ability to engage in political advocacy effectively. For these authors, because government-dependent nonprofits need to advocate for continued government support of their efforts, they constantly build organizational resources around political advocacy that they can capitalize on (Chaves, Stephens, and Galaskiewicz 2004).

In light of the ongoing debates about worker centers' ability to foster structural changes in the low-wage labor market, and the role of bottom-up worker voices in these organizations, future research should continue to unpack the relationship between reliance on external funding and worker centers' financial sustainability and programmatic choices.

More Research on the Nature of Government Grants

Given our finding that government grants provide an important source of funding for many (although certainly not all) worker centers, future research should endeavor to unpack what kinds of activities federal, state, and local government entities fund. Further research, for example, could identify the types of state and local government funding worker centers receive because these state and local sources provide the majority of government funding (Umel 2006). Moreover, prior research shows that local government officials play a key and varied role in filtering money to non-profits (de Graauw, Gleeson, and Bloemraad 2013).[25]

New research could also examine how government funding interacts with the social-change strategies of worker centers. Scholars, for instance, could continue to tease out how government grants relate to public–private efforts to improve the enforcement of labor standards in low-wage labor markets. The executive agencies in charge of enforcing these laws, including the US DOL, cannot ensure full enforcement of the laws on the books (Bernhardt et al. 2009; Weil 2016).[26] Moreover, they often do not have access to the communities that are most at risk of suffering violations (Fine 2017; Gleeson 2009). There is a growing body of literature that considers the role of community groups in labor and employment law "co-enforcement" (Amengual and Fine 2016; Demers and Sylvester 2016; Elmore 2018; Fine 2017; Fine and Gordon 2010; Gleeson 2009; Lesniewski and Canon 2016). Luce's work, for instance, describes the ways that community organizations improved the implementation of city-level living-wage ordinances (2004). In this way, worker centers help keep government agencies accountable to the process of "making rights real" by facilitating their implementation (de Graauw 2016). Co-enforcement, of course, does not require a resource transfer between the government and a nonprofit, but, undoubtedly, funding helps facilitate these collaborations.

Scholars have identified worker center–facilitated connections between government enforcers and workers in such contexts as health and safety initiatives (Fine 2015) and the National Labor Relations Board (Lesniewski and Canon 2016). While we do not know the exact purpose of the majority of government funding, our data confirms that some worker centers obtained federal money to improve the enforcement of worker rights during the period of our study (2008 through 2014). Of the three federal grants that would enable worker centers to assist in the enforcement of worker rights (and which we could confirm on USAspending.gov), the largest was the Susan Harwood Training Grant from the US DOL's Occupational Safety and Health Administration. Susan Harwood grants are intended to provide training and education for employers and workers in an effort to reduce health and safety hazards in the workplace.[27] Other workers' rights enforcement grants from federal sources include the Environmental Justice Small Grant[28] and the Services for Trafficking Victims Program Grant.[29] Future research should comprehensively document, as some have already started to do (Amengual and Fine 2016), the nature and effects of these public–private efforts to patrol the low-wage labor market.[30]

More Research on the Nature of Program Services

Our research revealed that revenue from program services is the most common funding stream for worker centers, but it did little to elaborate on the nature of the services offered to low-wage workers who participate in worker centers. What kinds of services are provided and which are the most common? Future research could deepen our understanding of the variety and nature of program services provided. Here, we propose one area of future inquiry, but there are many more.

Because member dues in the traditional labor union context are seen as a way to connect workers to the organization's decision making and accountability structure, one question our findings raise is the extent to which program services may be an alternative way to give workers a voice in their organizations. Do the worker centers' program service offerings result from participant requests? Do they encourage ongoing participation, or membership, in the day-to-day activities of the organization? More specifically, to what extent do program services hold the organization accountable to the community it serves? A cursory review of select worker center websites suggests that the sorts of program services range from legal help to trainings and professional development—from education about individual rights to community organizing. It is certainly feasible to imagine that some of these classes could result in strong, membership-like connections between workers and worker centers. Moreover, some income from program services comes directly from fees, which are internally generated sources of funding that could help to insulate the organization from the interference and influence of external funding sources.

Relatedly, some recent scholarship contends that worker centers should tie member dues to the program services provided. Fisk's recent work on worker centers (2016) is one example. She argues that worker centers should move toward a dues model, at least in part to increase the organization's accountability to its members rather than to external funders such as charitable foundations and government agencies. In developing her argument for the increased use of member dues by worker centers, she proposes that worker centers tie the amount of dues to the approximate value of program services the worker center is providing to the participant.

Future research, perhaps through the development of in-depth case studies, could consider the ways that worker centers' program services may, in fact, already enhance a worker center's accountability to the communities it serves, or act as a means of encouraging membership.

CONCLUSION

In this chapter, we "sized" up worker center income and found that, literally, no one size fits all worker centers. While most worker centers did indeed have little revenue, worker centers ranged widely in their revenue sizes. Indeed, our sample included a handful of giant worker centers that towered over the pack. Unfortunately, instability in their revenue size is a characteristic that fits all worker centers, big and small. Worker centers with bigger revenue seemed just as unstable as their poorer counterparts. They were also more susceptible to shrinking in times of economic downturn.

With revenue streams, we again found that worker centers cannot be characterized by one story or funding profile. Rather, our picture of diverse funding streams aligns with others who have characterized worker centers as exhibiting organizational "hybridity" (Cordero-Guzmán et al. 2013; Fine 2006). We find worker centers' funding strategies to be as diverse as their organizing strategies discussed elsewhere in this volume. Unlike traditional labor unions, worker centers do not typically use or rely very much on membership dues. Rather, our research confirms that the lion's share of worker center revenue comes from external sources, especially from government and foundation grants. These findings raise important questions about the relationship between funding strategies and programmatic choices at worker centers. Learning more about funding and its effects can tell us about the nature of these emergent organizations on the labor relations scene. Future research should continue to examine the evolving nature of these diverse organizations that seek justice and dignity for workers in the low-wage labor market.

ACKNOWLEDGMENTS

This research benefited enormously from the able assistance of Aliqae Geraci from Cornell's Catherwood Library and would not have been possible without the financial support of the Worker Institute at Cornell, the ILR Dean's office, and the Rawlings Cornell Presidential Research Scholarship program. It would also not have been possible without Janice Fine and Nik Theodore's foundational work mapping worker centers and Janice Fine's continued feedback and generous provision of relevant resources over the past three years. The authors appreciate the invaluable contributions of Caro Achar, Ben Hollander, and Nick Rasch and the students in the Worker Institute's Seminar on Precarious Work during the spring of 2015 who participated in this research as undergraduates at Cornell's ILR School. The authors also benefited from feedback from Hector Cordero-Guzmán, Els de Graauw, Samuel Estreicher, Janice Fine, Courtney Frantz, Shannon Gleeson, and Wilma Liebman, as well as from presentations sponsored by the Worker Institute at Cornell, the New York University School of Law's Center for Labor and Employment Law, the NYU Review of Law & Social Change, the Rawlings Senior Expo at Cornell, Harvard's Engaged Scholarship and Undergraduate Research Conference, and the State University of New York's Undergraduate Research Conference. All errors or omissions are the sole responsibility of the authors.

ENDNOTES

[1] Our sample of worker centers includes every worker center from the Fine/Theodore 2012 list for which we could obtain an IRS 990 for at least one year between 2008 and 2014. The IRS 990 categorized revenue streams differently before 2008, so we were not able to collect data for 2007 or earlier. Our data set ends in 2014 because it is the most recent year for which reliable data was available.

[2] Examples of nonprofits that parented worker centers include Catholic Charities, the Empire Justice Center, Community Partners, the Human Services Council, and the American Friends Service Committee.

[3] A worker center with less than $50,000 annual revenue, for instance, needs to file only an "ePostcard."

[4] These eight cases are defined as outliers by the Tukey method of using the interquartile range to determine mild outliers. They are all above the cutoff for mild outliers—equal to the upper 75 percentile + 1.5 × the interquartile range of 1,678,846. Furthermore, four of these cases would constitute what Tukey called "severe outliers"—those that are larger than the upper 75 percentile + 3 × the interquartile range of $2,578,655.

[5] We confirm this finding with a series of bivariate ordinary least squares (OLS) regression analyses. In all but one of the five years (2011), a worker center's size could not predict the subsequent year's growth.

[6] If we remove the five largest worker centers (those with revenue larger than $3 million) from the 2012 analysis in column 3, the relationship is no longer significant. It is these largest organizations, all but one of which shrank or experienced slower growth in 2012, that appear to be driving the effects.

[7] These reports are publicly available either via the DOL OLMS website's "Payer/Payee" search portal or via a direct download of all union spending records for a given year. The DOL OLMS data was only available through downloading the entire yearly database. This made it extremely onerous to sift through manually, so we ran a search query using Microsoft Access.

[8] Foundation Center, no date. Foundation Directory Online (http://bit.ly/2twfyjM).

[9] There is no significant correlation between revenue in 2012 and the percentage of revenue derived from dues.

[10] There was no statistical difference in the mean percentage of revenue from dues between any single size subgroup of worker centers compared with the overall mean of the remainder of worker centers.

[11] The size groupings are roughly equivalent to the 2012 quartiles as represented in Figure 1 and the inner Tukey fence for identifying outliers.

[12] While the percentages are small, two of the outlier organizations, with revenue above $2 million per year, collect a half million dollars in member dues each year.

[13] There is no significant correlation between revenue in 2012 and the percentage of revenue a worker center received from program services.

[14] We tested for whether the mean proportion of revenue received from program services in each of the subgroups differed significantly from the mean percentage of revenue coming from program services for the remainder of worker centers. None of these t-tests for significant difference in means were significant.

[15] To take a very preliminary look at the nature of the federal government grants worker centers receive, we used the USAspending.gov database. Mandated by the Federal Funding Accountability and Transparency Act of 2006, USAspending.gov is a searchable website "to give the American public access to information on how their tax dollars are spent" (http://bit.ly/2rdZiUs). We identified nine types of federal-level government grants to worker centers for service and education initiatives to address the myriad needs of low-income communities. These were the Susan Harwood Training Grant; Environmental Justice Small Grant; Culturally and Linguistically Specific Services Program Grant; Services for Trafficking Victims Program Grant; Fund for the Improvement of Education Grant; Low Income Taxpayer Clinics Project Grant; Citizenship Education and Training Project Grant; Supportive Housing Project Grant; and Volunteer Income Tax Assistance (VITA) Matching Grant. USAspending.gov is, however, a limited data source and does not have any information on state and local government grants.

[16] Out of our total 104 worker centers for which we could obtain the IRS 990s in 2012, only 80 met the revenue threshold that required they report how much they received from government grants. Organizations with revenue above $50,000, but below $200,000, are required to file only an IRS EZ form, which does not separate the government contributions. Some critique the IRS 990s as having potential inputting errors related to government grants (Froelich, Knoepfle, and Pollak 2000).

[17] These worker centers constitute outliers falling above the inner Tukey fence (here = 44%) for determining outliers from what should be the normal distribution.

[18] The first bar reports no government grants because this grouping includes all those too small to have to report government sources to the IRS.

[19] There was no significant difference in the mean of each of these three subgroups compared with the mean of the remaining worker centers.

[20] The t-test for significant difference revealed that the mean of 7.8% for this subgroup was significantly lower (t = 1.4185, with a p value > 0.10) than the mean received by all other larger revenue worker centers. There was also no significant correlation between total revenue in 2012 and a worker center's relative dependence on government grants. The Pearson's correlation coefficient is 0.1160, which, with 80 observations, does not meet the threshold of significance. This makes sense intuitively when we consider that some of the largest worker centers, those with revenue over $2 million, did not necessarily receive the highest proportion of their revenue from government grants. The largest, for instance, received just over a quarter of their resources from government grants. There were even some in this group that received no government grants.

[21] Similarly, we do not feel confident about coming to any conclusions on whether a worker center's size has much to do with its ability to secure foundation grants. Our research does reveal that the largest eight worker centers obtained a significantly higher percentage of their revenue from foundations (32%), and the smallest worker centers relied much less on foundations (7%). However, the group with the second highest average percentage of revenue that came from foundations, at 23%, was the group of small-to-medium-sized worker

centers (with revenue from $175,000 to $400,000). Furthermore, the correlation between revenue in 2012 and the percentage of a center's revenue reported from foundations was also not significant.

[22] Similarly, Worker Center Watch "aims to expose the direct operational linkages and funding between unions and worker centers by highlighting their tactics" (http://bit.ly/2tBGT4n).

[23] Most of these received around 30% from unions, but there was one small worker center (with a revenue that ranged from roughly $70,000 to $150,000 during the period) that received 65% of its revenue from unions in a single year.

[24] There is no significant correlation between the 2012 revenue and the percentage of revenue obtained from unions.

[25] These are sometimes Community Development Block Grants (CDBG), which are federally funded but locally decided (de Graauw, Gleeson, and Bloemraad 2013). de Graauw, Gleeson, and Bloemraad also show that location, and local officials, matter. Their research compares how local officials managed CDBG grant allocations in three different cities. They expose how immigrant organizations are incorporated differently depending on whether they are in a traditional immigrant gateway, a 21st-century gateway, or a new suburban destination.

[26] There are, for example, only about 1,000 US DOL investigators to enforce federal wage and hour law in the more than seven million establishments covered by such laws across the country (Weil 2016).

[27] Susan Harwood Training Grants are OSHA grants "to provide training and education programs for employers and workers on the recognition, avoidance, and prevention of safety and health hazards in their workplaces and to inform workers of their rights and employers of their responsibilities" (http://bit.ly/2rga9NF). For 2012, the Susan Harwood grant accounted for 10 out of 18 grants, which constitute more than half of the total federal government grant money that we were able to confirm on USAspending.gov.

[28] The Environmental Justice Small Grant program (http://bit.ly/2rfL8lw) "supports and empowers communities working on solutions to local environmental and public health issues. The program is designed to help communities understand and address exposure to multiple environmental harms and risks."

[29] Services for Trafficking Victims Program Grant: State and Local Law Enforcement Assistance (http://bit.ly/2yzeb9X): "The primary goal of this solicitation is to provide timely, high-quality services to victims of human trafficking. … Funding also will support efforts to increase the capacity of communities to respond to victims through the development of interagency partnerships and professional training, public outreach, and awareness campaigns."

[30] While funding for worker centers to enforce worker rights is not without controversy, Gleeson (2009) shows that nonprofits play key roles in helping individuals learn about and mobilize their rights in the workplace. They can provide education in vulnerable communities and provide accessible space, which builds a relationship of trust with labor standards enforcement officials (Fine 2017; Gleeson 2009; Gordon 2005; Weil and Pyles 2005). They can also play a key information-gathering role that can help government agency personnel make decisions about their outreach efforts and enforcement targets (Bernhardt et al. 2009; Delp and Riley 2015; Fine and Gordon 2010).

REFERENCES

Amengual, Matthew, and Janice Fine. 2016. "Co-Enforcing Labor Standards: The Unique Contributions of State and Worker Organizations in Argentina and the United States." *Regulation & Governance.* doi:10.1111/rego.12122

Bernhardt, Annette, Ruth Milkman, Nik Theodore, Douglas Heckathorn, Mirabai Auer, James DeFilippis, and Ana Luz González. 2009. "Broken Laws, Unprotected Workers: Violations of Employment and Labor Laws in America's Cities." Washington, DC: National Employment Law Project. http://bit.ly/2rhaIXp

Bobo, Kimberley A., and Marién Casillas Pabellón. 2016. *The Worker Center Handbook: A Practical Guide to Starting and Building the New Labor Movement.* Ithaca, NY: ILR Press. http://bit.ly/2JJvLZq

Chaves, Mark, Laura Stephens, and Joseph Galaskiewicz. 2004. "Does Government Funding Suppress Nonprofits' Political Activity?" *American Sociological Review* 69 (April): 292–316.

Compa, Lance. 2015. "Careful What You Wish For." *New Labor Forum* 24 (3): 11–16.

Cordero-Guzmán, H.R. 2015. "Worker Centers, Worker Center Networks, and the Promise of Protections for Low-Wage Workers." *WorkingUSA* 18 (1): 31–57. doi:10.1111/wusa.12152

Cordero-Guzmán, H.R., Pamela A. Izvănariu, and Victor Narro. 2013. "The Development of Sectoral Worker Center Networks." *Annals of the American Academy of Political and Social Science* 647 (1): 102–123.

Culleton Colwell, M.A. . 1997. "The Potential for Bias When Research on Voluntary Associations Is Limited to 501(c)3 Organizations." Nonprofit Sector Research Fund Working Paper No. 22. Washington, DC: The Aspen Institute.

de Graauw, E. 2015. "Nonprofits and Cross-Organizational Collaborations to Promote Local Labor Rights Policies." *WorkingUSA* 18: 103–126. doi:10.1111/wusa.12155

de Graauw, E. 2016. *Making Immigrant Rights Real: Nonprofits and the Politics of Integration in San Francisco.* Ithaca, NY: Cornell University Press.

de Graauw, Els, Shannon Gleeson, and Irene Bloemraad. 2013. "Funding Immigrant Organizations: Suburban Free Riding and Local Civic Presence." *American Journal of Sociology* 119 (1): 75–130.

Delp, Linda, and Kevin Riley. 2015. "Worker Engagement in the Health and Safety Regulatory Arena Under Changing Models of Worker Representation." *Labor Studies Journal* 40 (1): 54–83. doi:10.1177/0160449X15569387

Demers, Christoph, and Laura Sylvester. 2016. "MotherWoman and the Massachusetts Pregnant Workers Fairness Act: The Role of Community Organizations in Education and Outreach for State Employment Laws." Amherst, MA: University of Massachusetts School of Public Policy Capstones. http://bit.ly/2JJwee8

Eidelson, Josh. 2013 (Jul. 17). "Who Should Fund Alt-Labor?" *Nation.* Blog. http://bit.ly/2JHUBsL

Elmore, Andrew. 2018. "Collaborative Enforcement." *Northeastern University Law Review* 10 (1): 72–140.

Estey, Ken. 2006. "Worker Centers: Organizing Communities at the Edge of the Dream—Janice Fine." *WorkingUSA* 9 (3): 374–377. doi:10.1111/j.1743-4580.2006.00119.x

Estlund, Cynthia. 2015. "Are Unions a Constitutional Anomaly?" *Michigan Law Review* 114: 169–234.

Fine, Janice. 2006. *Worker Centers: Organizing Communities at the Edge of the Dream*. Ithaca, NY: ILR Press/Cornell University Press. http://bit.ly/2JLVxfG

Fine, Janice. 2011. "Worker Centers: Entering a New Stage of Growth and Development." *New Labor Forum* 20 (3): 44–53.

Fine, Janice. 2015. "Co-Production: Bringing Together the Unique Capabilities of Government and Society for Labor Standards Enforcement." Northampton, MA: LIFT Fund. http://bit.ly/2JOtOeu

Fine, Janice. 2017. "Enforcing Labor Standards in Partnership with Civil Society: Can Co-Enforcement Succeed Where the State Alone Has Failed?" *Politics & Society* 45 (3): 359–388. doi:10.1177/0032329217702603

Fine, Janice, and Jennifer Gordon. 2010. "Strengthening Labor Standards Enforcement Through Partnerships with Workers' Organizations." *Politics & Society* 38: 552–585.

Fine, Janice, and Nik Theodore. 2013 (Jan. 2). "Worker Centers 2012—Community Based and Worker Led Organizations." Infographic. New Brunswick, NJ: Rutgers University Center for Remote Sensing and Spatial Awareness. http://bit.ly/2JLVQXS

Fisk, Catherine L. 2016. "Workplace Democracy and Democratic Worker Organizations: Notes on Worker Centers." *Theoretical Inquiries in Law* 17 (1): 101–130.

Frantz, Courtney, and Sujatha Fernandes. 2016. "Whose Movement Is It? Strategic Philanthropy and Worker Centers." *Critical Sociology* 44 (4–5): 645–660. doi:10.1177/0896920516661857

Froelich, Karen A., Terry W. Knoepfle, and Thomas H. Pollak. 2000. "Financial Measures in Nonprofit Organization Research: Comparing IRS 990 Return and Audited Financial Statement Data." *Nonprofit and Voluntary Sector Quarterly* 29 (2): 232–254.

Gleeson, Shannon. 2009. "From Rights to Claims: The Role of Civil Society in Making Rights Real for Vulnerable Workers." *Law & Society Review* 43 (3): 669–700. http://bit.ly/2JNprA9

Gleeson, Shannon, and Irene Bloemraad. 2012. "Assessing the Scope of Immigrant Organizations: Official Undercounts and Actual Underrepresentation." *Nonprofit and Voluntary Sector Quarterly* 42 (2): 344–368.

Gordon, Jennifer. 2005. *Suburban Sweatshops*. Cambridge, MA: Harvard University Press.

Greenhouse, Steven. 2014 (Jan. 16). "Advocates for Workers Raise the Ire from Business." *New York Times*. https://nyti.ms/2JGU0rd

Griffith, Kati L. 2015. "Worker Centers and Labor Law Protections: Why Aren't They Having Their Cake?" *Berkeley Journal of Employment and Labor Law* 36 (2): 331–349. http://bit.ly/2JHW02v

Grønbjerg, Kirsten A. 1993. *Understanding Nonprofit Funding*. San Francisco, CA: Jossey-Bass.

Grønbjerg, Kirsten A. 2002. "Evaluating Nonprofit Databases." *American Behavioral Scientist* 45 (11): 1741–1777.

Lesniewski, Jacob, and Ramsin Canon. 2016. "Worker Centres, Cities and Grassroots Regulation of the Labour Market." *Community Development Journal* 15 (1): 114–131. doi:10.1093/cdj/bsv059

Luce, Stephanie. 2004. *Fighting for a Living Wage.* Ithaca, NY: ILR/Cornell University Press.

Manheim, Jarol. 2013. "The Emerging Role of Worker Centers in Union Organizing: A Strategic Assessment." Working Paper. Washington, DC: US Chamber of Commerce. https://uscham.com/2I7ujTG

Milkman, R., Joshua Bloom, and Victor Narro. 2010. *Working for Justice: The L.A. Model of Organizing and Advocacy.* Ithaca, NY: ILR Press/Cornell University Press. http://bit.ly/2IcxKZm

National Bureau of Economic Research. 2010. (Sep. 20). Business Cycle Dating Committee. Washington, DC: National Bureau of Economic Research. http://bit.ly/2JNrqoe

Powell, W.W., and R. Steinberg. 2006. *The Nonprofit Sector: A Research Handbook.* New Haven. CT: Yale University Press.

Rosenfeld, David. 2006. "Worker Centers: Emerging Labor Organizations—Until They Confront the National Labor Relations Act." *Berkeley Journal of Employment and Labor Law* 27 (2): 469–513.

Umel, Iryll Sue. 2006. "Cultivating Strength: The Role of the Philipino Workers' Center COURAGE Campaign in Addressing Labor Violations Committed Against Filipinos in the Los Angeles Private Home Care Industry." *UCLA Asian Pacific American Law Journal* 12 (1): 35.

US Chamber of Commerce. 2014. "The New Model of Representation: An Overview of Leading Worker Centers." Washington, DC: US Chamber of Commerce. https://uscham.com/2JL5t95

US Department of Labor. 2012a. "Labor Organization Annual Report, Form LM-2, UNITE HERE Local 1." Washington, DC: US Department of Labor.

US Department of Labor. 2012b. "Labor Organization Annual Report, Form LM-2, UNITE HERE Local 2." Washington, DC: US Department of Labor.

US Department of Labor. 2012c. "Labor Organization Annual Report, Form LM-2, UNITE HERE Local 25." Washington, DC: US Department of Labor.

US Department of Labor. 2012d. "Labor Organization Annual Report, Form LM-2, SEIU." Washington, DC: US Department of Labor.

Weil, David. 2016. "Strategic Enforcement in the Fissured Workplace." In *Who Is an Employee and Who Is the Employer? Proceedings of the New York University 68th Annual Conference on Labor,* edited by Kati L. Griffith and Samuel Estreicher, pp. 19–27. New York, NY: LexisNexis.

Weil, David, and Amanda Pyles. 2005. "Why Complain—Complaints, Compliance, and the Problem of Enforcement in the US Workplace." *Comparative Labor Law & Policy Journal* 27 (1): 59–92.

Wong, Kent. 2015. "A New Labor Movement for a New Working Class: Unions, Worker Centers, and Immigrants." *Berkeley Journal of Employment & Labor Law* 36 (1): 205–213. doi:10.15779/Z38WC57

Chapter 3

Labor Unions/Worker Center Relationships, Joint Efforts, Experiences

Victor Narro
UCLA Labor Center

Janice Fine
*School of Management and Labor Relations, Rutgers University,
and the Center for Innovation in Worker Organization*

INTRODUCTION

During the 1980s, deindustrialization and the decline of unions led to a sharp reduction in the quality of jobs in manufacturing and service industries—and a subsequent exodus of native workers. As a consequence of these shifts, employers increasingly turned to immigrants to fill vacancies in the lowest-paying occupations with the worst working conditions. The employer sanction sections of the Immigration Reform and Control Act of 1986 (IRCA) (Chishti 2004; Passel 2005: 27) added to an environment of exploitation of undocumented workers in many low-wage industries because they feared employers had been given the tools not only to fire workers for taking a stand but also to have them deported. Despite these perils, some took action. Many immigrant workers were no strangers to collective action, having participated in organizations and political movements in their home countries. There were many instances in which they engaged in workplace actions and community organizing, and when unions or worker centers reached out to them, they often responded favorably (Bloom, Milkman, and Narro 2010: 4–5; Erickson et al. 2002; Fine 2006, 2007; Milkman and Ott 2014; Milkman 2006; Ness 2005).

The demographic transformation of key industries by immigrant workers, their willingness to organize, labor's need for new recruits, and pressure from key national unions led by UNITE HERE, which represents workers in the hotel, gaming, food service, airport, textile, manufacturing, distribution, laundry, and transportation industries; and the Service Employees International Union (SEIU), resulted in major shifts in policy within the AFL-CIO. In February 2000, the federation made a historic policy announcement to champion a new legalization program and increased labor protections for immigrant workers and also to withdraw its long-standing support for employer sanctions (Fine 2007; Fine and Tichenor 2009).

Six years later, the federation took another major step in the direction of support for immigrant worker organizing, when it entered into a series of partnerships with national worker center networks. In August 2006, the AFL-CIO's Executive Council unanimously passed a resolution, creating the AFL-CIO Worker Center Partnership, which called on organized labor at all levels to build and strengthen ties with worker centers in their communities. The resolution acknowledged worker centers as a vibrant and important part of today's labor movement.

Many low-wage immigrant workers in the United States today function within industries in which there have been few or no unions through which they can speak and act to effect improvements. Worker centers emerged in response to the increasing exploitation of low-wage immigrant workers, persistent racism, and xenophobia in labor markets and society in general; the narrowing of channels for legalization of immigration status; and the decline of the labor movement. While varying in organizational structure, the centers mainly serve low-wage workers in efforts to improve workplace conditions through direct action, policy advocacy, research, and legal strategies. They engage in policy campaigns to improve the laws and policies that impact these workers, many of whom are excluded from basic legal protections, including those in the National Labor Relations Act (NLRA).

While they often target particular employers as well as industries within local labor markets, worker centers are not worksite based. Unlike the traditional American union, most do not focus on organizing for majority representation in individual worksites or on negotiating collective bargaining agreements for individual groups of workers. Worker centers are hybrids that combine elements of different types of organizations from political parties, settlement houses, immigrant civic organizations, community organizing, and social movement groups to unions, feminist consciousness-raising organizations and producer cooperatives. In many centers, ethnicity and language, rather than occupation or industry, are the primary identities through which workers come to participate in the organizations, and ethnic identity and the experience of prejudice are central analytical lenses through which experiences in and the organization of the labor market as a whole are understood. They are largely community-based organizations, most often with an Internal Revenue Service 501(c)(3) tax status that makes them tax exempt and allows them to take in charitable contributions that are deductible for the donors. Most have relatively small budgets (well under $1 million) and a very informal membership structure. Typically, over 80% of their resources come from private foundations. The rest comes from government funding, membership fees, and other donations (Fine 2006; Gates et al., this volume).

The number of worker centers in the United States has been growing steadily. In 1992, there were five centers nationwide; by 2005, there were

142 organizations; by 2012, there were 214 centers; and today there are an estimated 266 of them. As of 2013, 33 states had worker centers—California (36) and New York (43) have the most, followed by Texas (20), Massachusetts (12), Florida (11), Illinois (10), New Jersey (9) Michigan (5), Pennsylvania (5) and Virginia (5). All other states have four or fewer (Fine, Narro, and Barnes, this volume; Fine and Theodore 2013).

This chapter focuses on recent efforts by the AFL-CIO to relate to the growing movement of worker centers and to establish alliances with them. The first places worker centers in historical context. The second provides a narrative of events that led to the creation of the AFL-CIO Worker Center Partnership. The third provides an analysis of the components of the partnership and their implementation. The last section evaluates the partnerships, and our conclusion discusses considerations and opportunities for continued collaboration and next steps.

WORKER CENTERS, UNIONS, AND THE LOW-WAGE ECONOMY

A discussion of how partnerships have played out on the ground must be placed within the larger conceptual framework of these two radically different organizations. While unions and worker centers have a common mission of worker uplift, there is a sharp divergence in structure, culture, and ideology. Unionization in the United States has been built on achieving exclusive bargaining rights, controlling access to skilled labor, and taking wages out of competition across labor markets of various types. With this model, unions institutionalized themselves, evolving into complex organizations with highly established internal structures and methods of operation. They are labor market institutions mapped to craft and industrial work via firms, industries, and the state in stable and predictable ways; structure, culture, and ideology are based on narrow but robust worker identities revolving around the production of goods and services as commodities in the economy. While at the federal level, national federations have been central to the enactment of broader wage and hour, occupational health and safety, and social insurance legislation, individual national unions and their local affiliates often operate from a narrower perspective.

Worker centers are the inverse of prototypical American unions. While they play an important role in teaching low-wage immigrant workers about their rights under federal and state labor and employment laws and working to enforce them, they have mostly not sought to formalize their roles as labor market actors, even though they are defending workers' rights, filing wage claims, intervening on behalf of workers with employers, and, in the case of day laborer centers, operating quasi-hiring halls. They are social movement organizations bent on raising labor standards community-wide largely through policy rather than economic action. They are nonbureaucratic, grassroots organizations with small budgets, loose membership structures, improvisational cultures, and strategies that are funded by foundation grants rather than member dues. Worker centers are "local movement centers" that focus on issues of work because employment is such a central area of exploitation for immigrants and native-born workers of color. Rather than focus on the narrow relations of production, centers concern themselves with the much broader issues of social reproduction and economic and political incorporation. Most have viewed organizing a union not as an end in itself but as a means to improving labor standards and establishing a societal social wage while building a grassroots social movement that can transform society. Their structure, culture, and ideology are reflective of this larger agenda.

Worker centers advocate for workers' rights generally through policy campaigns, research, communication, and community organizing. They have been at the forefront of campaigns for increases in the minimum wage, creation of policies to combat wage theft and reductions of the tip credit, provision of paid sick days, labor standards for domestic workers, and other policies that improve conditions for low-wage workers. The centers also work with federal and state government agencies to improve labor standards enforcement. Increasingly, worker centers are directly engaging employers or groups of employers to effectuate change in the wages, hours, and terms and conditions of employment for their members, sometimes in partnership with unions.

Even though they don't engage in unionization and collective bargaining, worker centers are able to engage in organizing strategies where they are not forced into the "straitjacket" of the NLRA. The legal framework under the NLRA, originally intended to support unionization efforts and promote collective bargaining, is now used by many employers to limit union growth and worker power. For example, there are no restrictions on worker centers engaging in secondary boycotts and similar actions against employers as there are with unions under the NLRA. This is particularly important in the context of widespread subcontracting, where the real power to change conditions lies not with the immediate employer but with corporations at the top of the supply chain that are setting prices that contractors must accept. Moreover, worker centers do not have to accommodate to the extensive regulations that cover union organizations.

There is little doubt that workers in low-wage industries benefit substantially from unionization. An empirical analysis of 15 low-wage occupations found that unionized workers in low-wage industries earn 16% or more than their non-union counterparts and are significantly more likely to receive additional benefits (Schmitt, Walker, Fremstad, and Zipperer 2008). Unions have historically played a central role in setting and defending labor standards, but private sector union coverage is at 7.3% (US Bureau of Labor Statistics 2017). Likewise, there is nothing inherent in these jobs that requires them to be low paid. In a comprehensive empirical analysis of low-wage work in the United States and Europe, Gautié and Schmitt (2010) find vast differences in labor market conditions across countries. Likewise, Mason and Salverda (2010: 39) find that in the United States, 25% of workers are engaged in low-wage work (defined as earning two thirds of the national median wage), whereas in France the percentage is 11.1%, and in Denmark it is even lower at 8.5%. Furthermore, greater numbers of immigrants do not result in larger proportions of low-wage workers.

Today, the AFL-CIO's highest concentration of union members is in "professionalized" jobs requiring professional certification and/or training, though most job growth in the United States is in low-wage industries. A recent report by the National Employment Law Project showed that nearly 60% of job gains since the recession have been in low-wage sectors, even though low-wage jobs represented only roughly 20% of recession job losses—an acceleration of a long-term trend in the US job market (National Employment Law Project 2014).

Many workers in low-wage industries find themselves in contracting arrangements that make it impossible to exercise many of the workplace protections that are afforded to them under the law. Likewise, this restructuring of the low-wage economy has hampered unions' ability to make inroads into organizing workers. Worker centers, on the other hand, because they don't engage in traditional union organizing, are able to target the companies that are setting conditions at the bottom of their supply chains. Their organizing approaches provide flexibility to adapt to changes in the restructuring of employment dynamics, such as subcontracting.

Affiliating with sectoral worker center networks became a key growth strategy as worker centers continued to develop tools to build their low-wage worker movement; share organizing and advocacy strategies; support their social service, workforce, and labor market programs; and increase opportunities for funding and organizational development. Worker centers came together to form organizational networks around certain sectors and segments of the low-wage labor market where workers were concentrated. The key national worker center networks that have developed over the past 15 years include the National Day Laborer Organizing Network (NDLON) in the construction, landscaping, demolition and laborer sectors; the Restaurant Opportunities Center (ROC) with workers in the large restaurant industry; the National Domestic Workers Alliance (NDWA) with domestic and some childcare workers; the National Taxi Workers Alliance (NTWA) with workers in the taxi industry; the National Black Worker Center Project focusing on Black workers across different industries; and the National

Guestworker Alliance (NGA) with guestworkers and other temporary workers from various industry sectors. Interfaith Worker Justice, the only faith-based national network, also has a thriving alliance of worker centers (Interfaith Worker Justice 2018). Today, close to half of all worker centers are affiliated with one or more of the national worker center networks. Organizations in the other half are not as sectorally specific, and some tend to be ethnic based—providing services to a particular ethnic community within a geographic area.

HISTORY LEADING UP TO THE AFL-CIO/WORKER CENTER PARTNERSHIP

The creation of NDLON in August 2001 gave national attention to the rise of worker centers in major cities throughout the country. NDLON's founding convention in 2001 created a platform for NDLON member groups to identify areas of work it wanted the national organization to focus on. The two chief priorities that came out of this platform were (1) the right under the First Amendment of day laborers to seek work in public places, and (2) a new legalization program that would include day laborers. "Looking for Work Is Not a Crime" and "Somos Un Pueblo Sin Fronteras" became the major themes of NDLON's work for the future. NDLON became one of the main avenues through which the AFL-CIO expressed its support for immigrant workers and worker centers. NDLON also became a major stakeholder in the immigrant rights debate in Washington, D.C., asserting a different perspective and sometimes adopting opposing positions from the more mainstream immigrant rights groups such as the National Immigration Forum and UnidosUS (formerly known as the National Council of La Raza). NDLON's on-the-ground experience and legal expertise and its willingness to make frequent forays to the District of Columbia to represent its point of view resulted in day laborers having a seat at the table when discussing proposals and legislation relating to comprehensive immigration reform (CIR).

The tragic events of 9/11 took place the month after the founding of NDLON. The post-9/11 national security hysteria promoted by the right wing led to wholesale roundups and deportations of Muslim immigrants and to the passage in 2005 of House Bill 4437, proposed by Congress member James Sensenbrenner. Among the bill's many draconian provisions was one that would, for the first time in American history, make it a felony for a noncitizen to be in the United States without proper documents or for an individual or organization to knowingly provide services or assistance to such a person in any way (Narro and Shadduck-Hernández 2014; Narro, Shadduck-Hernández, and Wong 2007). The threat of this new law propelled millions of immigrants into the streets in 2006. The notion of being labeled a criminal for contributing to the economy was an insult to immigrant communities. With the passage in the House of Representatives of HR 4437, NDLON began to respond to the attacks on day laborers by the by the right wing and their allies (Narro and Shadduck-Hernández 2014).

Public comments depicting immigrants as criminals and stereotyping them as "un-American" created a hostile environment in many parts of the country, and there was a need for advocates to respond. This became most notable among day laborers and their advocates because of their high visibility in local communities and the ongoing crusades of anti-immigrant groups such as the Minutemen to target them. The political climate brought out hundreds of thousands who had never marched before. They found a new sense of dignity and pride through their activism (Narro and Shadduck-Hernández 2014). NDLON made unique contributions to the growing groundswell of activism that led to major mobilizations during the spring of 2006, when over four million immigrants took to the streets to denounce HR 4437, beginning with a huge march in Los Angeles on March 26 in which over half a million immigrant families participated. The march was the largest ever in Los Angeles and one of the largest in the history of the immigrant and civil rights movements (Narro and Shadduck-Hernández 2014).

Following the 2006 marches, however, right-wing anti-immigrant right groups commenced a war of attrition on immigrant communities (Narro and Shadduck-Hernández 2014). Their strategy was to promote policies—such as the anti-immigrant legislation SB 1070 in Arizona—in states and cities throughout the country, calculating that the quality of life for immigrants would deteriorate to the level that many undocumented immigrants would "self-deport." As discussed below, this right-wing strategy caused NDLON and other groups to shift away from comprehensive immigration reform efforts and instead focus on fighting back at the state and local levels (Narro and Shadduck-Hernández 2014).

Secure Communities (S-Comm) emerged in 2008 under the Obama administration as the mechanism from which to implement a policy that led to the deportation of close to three million undocumented immigrants during Obama's two terms as U.S. president. S-Comm was a federal immigration enforcement program that was implemented by U.S. Immigration and Customs Enforcement (ICE) in 2009. In jurisdictions where S-Comm was activated, any time an individual was arrested and booked into a local jail for any reason, his or her fingerprints are electronically run through ICE's immigration database. This allowed ICE to identify people who may be noncitizens—including lawful immigrants and permanent residents—and potentially to initiate deportation proceedings against them.

Because it targeted people at the time of arrest, not conviction, S-Comm captured people who will never be charged with a state crime—including crime victims (such as victims of domestic violence), witnesses, and individuals who were wrongly arrested. S-Comm also caused the unlawful detention of U.S. citizens. NDLON and other immigrant advocates took on the Obama administration in an effort to eliminate S-Comm. They argued that the program eroded immigrants' trust in police and resulted in the deportations of people who had committed no crime or only minor infractions. At the same time, hundreds of local and state governments, including in California, enacted policies to limit law enforcement from cooperating with the program. NDLON was a leader in the effort for the passage of the TRUST Act, which placed restrictions on the S-Comm program in California. These challenges appeared to pay off when Obama announced he was ending Secure Communities as part of his larger immigration strategy in November 2014.

Day laborers became the human face and the frontline of the immigration reform debate. They became the poster children for attacks by the Federation for American Immigration Reform (FAIR), a national organization that seeks to reduce immigration; the Minutemen Project, a group that was recruiting armed volunteers to patrol the border; and other right-wing forces. Additionally, day laborers became major targets of cities and states that were enacting their own anti-immigrant policies. In 2007, NDLON left the CIR strategy framework, which was by then considered by many immigrant rights advocates to be a failure as a result of the polarized stalemate in Congress to pass a comprehensive immigration reform legislation. Immediately thereafter, NDLON and other worker center networks joined together to create the Turning the Tides movement. This new movement was intended to establish a progressive parallel front to the right-wing strategy of taking the immigrant rights fight to the local level. Since then, NDLON and local worker centers have led efforts to fight back against SB 1070 and other similar measures at the state level. They have adopted a model of local community organizing to fight back against these measures and others like S-Comm in order to turn the tide in the fight for immigrant rights. They have increasingly become the model for a new strategy for pursuing immigrant rights because it has become increasingly clear that CIR is no longer a realistic goal in Congress.

During this same period, a 2005 national study on day laborers by Abel Valenzuela, Nik Theodore, Edwin Meléndez, and Ana Luz Gonzalez (2006) lent credence to NDLON's efforts to fight back against the growing attacks on day laborers. It placed national attention on day laborers as a viable, growing, and legitimate part of the low-wage economy. The report captured the attention of key stakeholders such as the AFL-CIO and policy makers. The following year, Janice Fine's book (2006) on worker centers and accompanying map was also a significant development; it helped to educate the AFL-CIO, foundations, and other key stakeholders about the important role that worker centers were playing in reaching out to and organizing immigrant workers in sectors where the traditional labor organizing model was not successful.

At the same time, union density continued its steep decline. Close observers of the labor movement noted that even if every campaign presently undertaken were successful, the number of new workers organized would still fall far short of the mark in terms of what would be required for a gain in union density or even to maintain current levels. Some suggested that until local communities identified more directly with the labor movement, and perceived unions as organizations of their own and not just (at best) external allies, labor organizing at significant scale would be impossible. In 2005, seven AFL-CIO member unions—SEIU, UNITE HERE, Laborers' Union (LIUNA), Teamsters, United Food and Commercial Workers International Union (UFCW), United Farm Workers (UFW), and United Brotherhood of Carpenters and Joiners of America (UBC)—formed the Change to Win Coalition to push for new strategies that would focus on membership development and a return to large-scale worker organizing. Change to Win proposed to commit significantly more funding to union organizing efforts and encourage each union to focus its organizing efforts on a particular economic sector (Fine 2006).

Understanding the depth of the crisis within the labor movement, Jon Hiatt, then general counsel of the AFL-CIO; Ana Avendaño, then its director of immigration policy; and Stewart Acuff, then its organizing director, moved forward with an initiative in 2006 to forge new partnerships with worker centers. They used the day laborer national report and Janice Fine's book on worker centers to educate and persuade the AFL-CIO Executive Council and national union affiliates to garner sufficient support to launch the initiative.

In August 2006, the AFL-CIO's Executive Council unanimously passed a resolution, Creating a National Worker Center Partnership, that called on organized labor at all levels to build and strengthen ties with worker centers in their communities. The resolution acknowledged worker centers as "a vibrant and important part of today's labor movement" (AFL-CIO 2006). Soon after the Executive Council meeting, Hiatt and Avendaño reached out to Pablo Alvarado, executive director of NDLON, inviting NDLON to become the first major partnership initiative. They organized a leadership delegation from the AFL-CIO to come to Los Angeles to meet with NDLON and went together to the Agoura Hills day-labor site, where union officials watched the day laborers deliberating about whether to increase the minimum wage at the corner from $12 to $15. When 85 out of 100 day laborers raised their hands to increase the minimum, the AFL-CIO officials said, "That's how the unions began!"

AFL-CIO officials were moved by a desire to build support among immigrant workers. They were interested in connecting organized labor to the growing worker center movement. NDLON was motivated by a desire to create a strong political alliance that would strengthen their efforts to protect the rights of day laborers, who at that time were main targets of anti-immigrant groups. NDLON initiated a process of discussion and analysis among its affiliates about the proposed partnership. Many NDLON groups had negative experiences with construction unions in the past and needed to deliberate before moving forward with the partnership. For example, the Institute of Popular Education of Southern California (IDEPSCA), an NDLON member based in Los Angeles, attempted to open up a day laborer worker center in Pasadena during the early 1990s only to be blocked by a construction trades local through a court-ordered injunction (Fine 2006, 2007; Fine, Grabelsky, and Narro 2008).

Through a series of conference calls and face-to-face meetings, NDLON members selected a core group to begin the process of dialogue with the AFL-CIO. They knew that the AFL-CIO could become a formidable political ally in their efforts to influence the immigration reform debate so that day laborers would not be left out of reform policies or singled out for attacks. Furthermore, they believed that, over time, the relationship with the AFL-CIO could be deepened and that local unions might open their organizations to day laborers and accept them into construction apprenticeship programs and local membership. Moved by their observations of day laborer organizing, the AFL-CIO decided that a national partnership agreement with NDLON would be the best starting point to launch the new initiative that came to be known as the AFL-CIO National Worker Center Partnership (AFL-CIO 2018). Regarding this collaboration, John Sweeney, president of AFL-CIO stated:

> Day laborers in the United States often face the harshest forms of workplace problems and this exploitation hurts us all because when standards are dragged down for some workers, they are dragged down for all workers. The work being done by worker centers and NDLON in particular is some of the most important work in the labor movement today, and it's time to bring our organizations closer together. Through this watershed partnership, we will strengthen our ability to promote and enforce the workplace rights for all workers—union and non-union, immigrant and non-immigrant alike. (Narro, Poyaoan, and Waheed 2015)

Also in 2006, the AFL-CIO announced partnership agreements with other worker center networks, including Interfaith Worker Justice and ENLACE (a network of worker centers organizing low-wage workers in the United States and Mexico), and launched similar partnership agreements with the National Domestic Workers Alliance and the National Guestworkers Alliance in 2011.

IMPLEMENTATION OF THE AFL-CIO/WORKER CENTER PARTNERSHIP

For the most part, the partnership agreements have been aspirational and reflective of a commitment to work on issues of mutual benefit—specifically, immigration reform and legislation to combat wage theft, improve workplace health and safety, and other issues affecting low-wage workers. The partnership, however, has benefited AFL-CIO unions and local labor bodies by establishing channels to connect formally with local worker centers that expose abuses in various industries and help to project the moral authority of unions as vehicles for worker voice and protections.

Under the partnerships, worker centers are given the opportunity to apply to affiliate with state labor federations, local labor councils, and Working America—the community affiliate of the AFL-CIO. The partnerships authorize the AFL-CIO to issue certificates of affiliation to individual worker centers, or worker center networks, at the request of a state federation or central labor council (CLC), where the entities have decided on a voluntary basis to form a mutually beneficial partnership. When issued, the certificates authorize worker center affiliations with state federations and local central labor councils in order "to build ties between these organizations and enable them to work cooperatively on issues of mutual concerns," giving them a seat at the table where key labor strategies are discussed and developed (Narro, Poyaoan, and Waheed 2015).

The AFL-CIO developed procedures that require a CLC or state federation to submit an application for a worker center to the national AFL-CIO, certifying that the affiliation is in the mutual interest of the worker center and the CLC/state federation. CLCs and state federations are permitted to set the fees for such affiliations. The AFL-CIO president is required to consult with the national Executive Council before issuing a certificate of affiliation. The certificates can be revoked when the partnership is no longer mutually beneficial (Narro, Poyaoan, and Waheed 2015). Table 1, on the next page, shows the list of affiliations as of July 2014 (Narro, Poyaoan, and Waheed 2015)

In the years since the Executive Council authorized worker center affiliations, the AFL-CIO has issued over 30 certificates of affiliation, and there have been no requests for revocation. Affiliations have taken place in 24 cities and 12 states. Most recently, the Koreatown Immigrant Workers Alliance (KIWA) and the Carwash Worker Center of the CLEAN Carwash Campaign (discussed below) entered into an affiliation process with the

TABLE 1
Worker Center/AFL-CIO Affiliations (July 2014)

Worker Center	AFL-CIO Affiliation
Central Labor Council	Affiliated Worker Center
Austin Area AFL-CIO Council	Workers Defense Project
Greater Boston Labor Council	Chelsea Collaborative
Greater Boston Labor Council	Massachusetts Coalition for Occupational Safety and Health
Greater Lansing (Michigan) Labor Council	Lansing Worker Center
Harris County AFL-CIO Council	Fe y Justicia Worker Center
Mid-State (New York) Central Labor Council	Tompkins County Workers Center
North Bay (California) Labor Council	Graton Day Labor Center
NOVA (Northern Virginia)Area Labor Federation	Tenants and Workers United (merging with Virginia New Majority)
Northern New Mexico Central Labor Council	Somos Un Pueblo Unido
New York City Central Labor Council	New York Taxi Workers Alliance
Pioneer Valley (Springfield, Massachusetts) AFL-CIO	Alliance to Develop Power
San Diego Labor Council	United Taxi Workers of San Diego
San Francisco Labor Council, AFL-CIO	Mujeres Unidas y Activas
South Central (Madison, Wisconsin) Federation of Labor	Madison Interfaith Worker Justice
Washington State Labor Council and Martin Luther King County Labor Council	Casa Latina
Western North Carolina Central Labor Council	Western North Carolina Worker Center

Los Angeles County Federation of Labor, the largest central labor council in the country.

The affiliation processes of worker centers to central labor councils differ from one another, depending on a variety of factors relating to the working relationships that existed prior to affiliation as well as the local political landscape. For relationships where both parties shared common issues and where their interests converged, seeking a partnership was a logical next step. For example, the issue of wage theft is common to both worker centers and unions—especially those unions that are organizing low-wage workers. They both have a vested interested in combating wage theft, and a partnership to engage in policy and organizing campaigns toward that goal can be a strategic next step (Narro, Poyaoan, and Waheed 2015).

The Los Angeles Black Worker Center created the Black Labor Construction Council (BLCC), an organization of Black union members in the building trades, as a strategic way to build a relationship with the leadership of five local construction unions and establish joint efforts to improve conditions for Black construction workers. The collaboration stemmed from a powerful call initiated by Steven Pitts at the UC Berkeley Labor Center to address the national Black jobs crisis, and it has led to stronger partnerships with organized labor.

Worker centers and central labor councils have reported that, in many cases, significant coalition work and solidarity support for organizing and policy campaigns had already existed prior to affiliation. From these experiences, worker centers and unions concluded that affiliations were a natural progression from informal joint activities and alliances. They have found that formal affiliation has provided an opportunity to deepen and strengthen these efforts. The majority of worker centers and central labor councils currently work together on one to two campaigns a year. Moreover, the majority of these joint efforts have led to successful outcomes (Narro, Poyaoan, and Waheed 2015).

By working together, central labor councils and worker centers have been able to transcend conservative political climates to succeed in passing pro-worker legislation. In Austin, the Building Trades and the Workers Defense Project have successfully advocated for pro-worker legislation in a "real, red, Republican-dominated state." Campaigns have included fighting against wage theft and for a higher local minimum wage, as well as a getting a commitment from the local district attorney for more aggressive prosecution of wage theft. In Vermont, the state American Federation of Teachers (AFT) affiliate collaborated with the Vermont Worker Center to pass single-payer health care on the state level, putting forward the message that "health care is a human right"(Narro, Poyaoan, and Waheed 2015).

CLEAN Carwash Campaign

Another outcome of the AFL-CIO/worker center partnerships has been the CLEAN Carwash Campaign (CLEAN Carwash Campaign 2016). As a result of the increasing levels of collaboration and trust that the partnership had developed between a number of Los Angeles area worker centers and local unions, community groups approached the AFL-CIO and asked whether, together with a union affiliate, it would partner with the community to improve conditions in the carwash industry. The United Steelworkers stepped up, with USW President Leo Gerard committing to

reach out to immigrant workers in an industry that had never been organized into a union.

Today, there are over 30 carwashes with union contracts in Los Angeles,
and union organizing campaigns have spread to New York City and
Chicago. Worker centers are key partners in four carwash organizing
campaigns taking place in Chicago (Arise Chicago and USW), New York
(Make the Road New York and the Retail, Wholesale and Department
Store Union [RWDSU]), Los Angeles (various worker centers and USW),
and Santa Fe (Somos un Pueblo Unido). All four campaigns employ an
array of advocacy tools including litigation, heightened enforcement of
health and safety and wage and hour laws with state and local government
agencies, boycotts, and community pressure. The New York campaign has
won four National Labor Relations Board (NLRB) elections and three
collective bargaining agreements.

In addition to the strong labor–community partnership to unionize
carwashes, in 2016 the CLEAN Campaign incubated and launched a
Carwash Worker Center. This new worker center was the evolution of
leadership programs for carwash workers, a strong and active Carwash
Worker Organizing Committee, and the participation of carwash worker
leaders in citywide campaigns led by worker centers. The Carwash Worker
Center has become the central space for leadership development of carwash
workers who have yet to unionize. Additionally, the worker center is working
closely with United Steelworkers to provide services and programs to their
union carwash members.

AFL-CIO National Convention 2013

On September 8, 2013, the AFL-CIO kicked off its national convention
in Los Angeles. The last time it was held in Los Angeles was in 1999, when
the AFL-CIO announced its historic declaration in support of a legalization program for all undocumented immigrants, increased workplace protection for immigrant workers, and an end to support for employer sanction laws, which it had supported back in 1986 as part of the Immigration
Reform and Control Act (IRCA). The 2013 AFL-CIO national convention
in Los Angeles marked a historic opening by the AFL-CIO and signaled
a commitment to diversity, partnership, and new ideas to transform a labor
movement that had been in a steady decline for the past 30 years. However,
events leading up to the convention spotlighted a dramatic disjuncture in
the level of collaboration between the national federation and national
unions, and the national worker center federations and many of their local
counterparts. Despite close collaborations between some local worker centers and unions, major challenges remained in many parts of the country.
Unions and worker centers in many communities had profound cultural
differences, and they lacked a shared analysis about the situation of low-

wage workers and a common understanding of each other's history and strategic approaches.

At the same time, however, the necessity for collaboration on campaigns for immigrant rights and workplace justice was only growing. For example, a major challenge that worker centers raised is the issue of immigration. Most worker centers organize undocumented workers, which makes it necessary for central labor councils to recognize how their stance on immigration can affect relationships with worker centers. A few worker centers reported tensions or pushback because the issue of immigration came up. For example, if the affiliation process involved a day laborer worker center, then there might be vocal opposition from or tension with the local building and trades union leadership. Another example was the issue of inclusion. The majority of worker centers currently organize women and undocumented workers. Some of them noticed a lack of diversity right away when first going to the central labor council meetings. They realized that it would be important to take steps toward making a space that tends to be more White and predominantly male more inclusive (Narro, Poyaoan, and Waheed 2015).

Preceding the convention, working committees developed resolutions that would chart a new course for the AFL-CIO. The Committee on Growth, Innovation and Political Action created resolutions that called for central labor councils around the country to find ways to create opportunities for the affiliation process for worker centers; new organizing strategies, including a focus on the South and engaging young workers; labor law reform; and immigration reform with a pathway to citizenship. One of the resolutions specifically called on the AFL-CIO to expand its partnerships with worker centers, strengthen its Worker Center Advisory Council, and invest more in its work with foundations to seed union/worker center collaboration. It also called for the AFL-CIO in cooperation with worker centers and national associations of worker centers to expand and update existing research describing in detail the operation of worker centers and documenting examples of union/worker center collaboration (Narro, Poyaoan, and Waheed 2015).

Beginning with the first pre-convention diversity conference, where worker center, community, and labor activists came together to address the future of worker representation, the convention brought a number of nontraditional partners together to chart a new course for the AFL-CIO. For example, the election of Bhairavi Desai, executive director of the National Taxi Workers Alliance (NTWA), to the AFL-CIO Executive Council was the first time a representative from a worker center became a member of the federation's governing body. During his keynote address, AFL-CIO President Richard Trumka was joined on the stage by day laborers, domestic workers, taxi workers, carwash workers, and other groups of workers who had historically been excluded from the protections of labor laws. The AFL-CIO leadership moved further toward inclusion by honoring the International Domestic Workers Network (IDWN) in recognition of the rights of domestic workers everywhere. On June 16, 2011, government, employer, and labor delegates to the International Labour Conference (ILC) of the International Labour Organization (ILO) voted nearly unanimously to adopt Convention 189, Decent Work for Domestic Workers. This first international set of standards on paid household labor marks a tangible victory for both the labor movement and the global women's movement. The AFL-CIO worked on this initiative, and they invited the NDWA and its members to participate in the conference and provide testimonies (Fish 2017).

AFL-CIO Worker Center Advisory Council
In January 2012, the AFL-CIO established the Worker Center Advisory Council to help bridge these gaps and build on opportunities. The council consists of worker center leaders, state federation/CLC leaders, union leaders, and academic/research advisors. The advisory council met for the first time in January 2012. Four main themes emerged from the two-day meeting. First was the need for sustainable models for worker centers. Most worker centers relied on philanthropic dollars for the majority of their resources to function. Because of dwindling amounts from foundation grant awards, some worker centers had begun experimenting with alternative models to generate resources.

Second was the need for more research, documentation, and education. Participants felt that there was too little research on union/worker center collaboration, almost no documentation of existing collaborations, and a continuing need for education among worker centers and unions about each other's functions and strategies. Many worker centers and unions did not understand one another's role in the labor market. Third was a need for more avenues for collaborations between worker centers and unions. Although the number of unions that interacted in a nontransactional way with worker centers had increased over the past few years, many unions still had not yet explored what such collaborations could mean for them. At the same time, many worker centers did not have the opportunity to highlight their work or build relationships with unions outside of those they already knew. There remained a great need for additional experimentation with collaborative projects.

Finally, the organizations identified a need for deeper strategic thinking about synergies. They felt that there needed to be more discussion on the advantages for worker centers and unions for engaging in partnerships. In addition, they felt that dialogue was necessary to address the challenges posed by the partnerships. For example, worker centers are not labor organizations subject to the restrictions on secondary activity created by the Taft–Hartley Act or the reporting, disclosure, and elections requirements of the Landrum–Griffin Act. Some worker centers feared that a closer collaboration with unions would cause them to be subject to these constraints and requirements. The organizations realized that a deeper thought process was necessary in order to develop strategies for collaboration between particular affiliates and particular worker centers that could create synergies.

Since the first historic meeting, the advisory committee has met periodically and become an important vehicle for sharing best practices, developing strategies, and responding to urgent issues such as the attacks on worker centers by conservative groups.

LIFT Fund to Support Union/Worker Center Collaborations

In 2012, the AFL-CIO partnered with philanthropic institutions to establish the Labor Innovations for the 21st Century (LIFT) Fund to support "collaborative and innovative cross-sector learning between communities, the labor movement, and organizations working for a fair economy." The fund works to support collaborative work between unions and worker centers, document and disseminate new strategies, and promote advocacy within labor, philanthropy, and other sectors working to build worker power. The LIFT Fund has provided grant support to major organizing campaigns led by worker centers including the CLEAN Carwash Campaign, National Day Laborer Organizing Network and the National Domestic Workers Alliance. The union partners benefiting from these initiatives included the Laborers International Union of North America (LIUNA), the United Steelworkers, the American Federation of Teachers, and the United Food and Commercial Workers as well as central labor councils and state labor federations from various states and cities.

Examples of LIFT Fund–supported collaborations include the following:
- In Austin, Texas, the Workers Defense Project and its allies in the building trades are working together across the state to create a wage floor in the construction industry.
- In New Mexico, Somos un Pueblo Unido and the Santa Fe Central Labor Council are collaborating to build local workplace and sectoral committees of low-wage immigrant workers.
- LIUNA and NDLON worked with day laborer organizations in New York and New Jersey to build an associate membership program to bring workers into the union and conduct safety trainings for workers engaged in rebuilding after Hurricane Sandy devastated communities in both states.
- The National Taxi Workers Alliance has chartered its first new local in Austin and is building an ambitious membership drive to increase its density and dues payment in New York and Philadelphia.

- Centro de los Derechos Del Migrante and American Federation of Teachers together launched Authentic Voices, a cross-sector worker committee for international labor recruitment reform to bring worker voices to advocacy activities related to international labor recruitment.
- In Los Angeles, the Los Angeles Black Worker Center (LABWC) and the Los Angeles County Labor Federation are working to ensure an effective and timely implementation of the new anti-wage theft ordinance, with robust enforcement mechanisms in the city, including advocacy, worker outreach, trainings, and more in a multi-sector, multi-industry, and multi-ethnic collaboration.
- In Los Angeles, LABWC, the Sheet Metal Workers International Association (SMART) Local 105, and the International Brotherhood of Electrical Workers (IBEW) Local 11 worked together to increase access to quality jobs.
- Voces de la Frontera and the American Federation of Teachers are working together to build and share capacity to establish a strong neighborhood network of working-family committees in Milwaukee to demand the protection of public education and a strong pro-immigrant rights agenda in the schools.
- In New Orleans, the New Orleans Workers' Center for Racial Justice is working with the Southeast Laborers' District Council Laborers International Union, connecting to union training programs African Americans who are former union members and guestworkers on short-term contracts.

EVALUATING THE PARTNERSHIPS

In 2014, the LIFT Fund and AFL-CIO commissioned the UCLA Center for Labor Research and Education (UCLA Labor Center) to conduct a survey and assessment report of the 16 worker center affiliations into AFL-CIO state federations of labor and local central labor councils throughout the country. The report, entitled "Building a Movement Together: Worker Centers and Labor Union Affiliations," analyzed in-depth surveys of the worker centers and central labor council or state federation of labor involved with an affiliation process and created recommendations on how to strengthen this partnership model (Narro, Poyaoan, and Waheed 2015).

The study found that national worker center networks are playing a key role in local-level implementation of affiliations and recommended that the AFL-CIO explore ways to continue to strengthen its relationship with them through revising partnership agreements and developing tools to help members of the networks strengthen their local partnerships with central labor councils. However, the study also found that there were many important worker centers that were not connected to national organizations, and they called for specific strategies to develop affiliations with "stand-alone" worker centers and local networks of worker centers and connect them with central labor councils, especially in regions where the labor movement lacks political strength.

The study also found that the affiliation process itself had become a focal point of transformative action by creating spaces for dialogue, reflection, and the development of strategy as well a mechanism for the sharing of best practice models and creating solidarity support for organizing and policy campaigns. The report's authors noted that affiliation had already produced positive outcomes that have allowed partners to augment each other's work, collaborate on campaigns, and develop joint strategies. Throughout the survey and in-depth interviews, respondents repeatedly expressed a need for information about affiliations taking place in other parts of the country and showed a serious interest in the best practices and lessons learned elsewhere, and they recommended that the AFL-CIO create and distribute materials such as toolkits and guides on how to facilitate the affiliation process and best practices of successful affiliation models.

Another finding of the study was that many worker centers were struggling with financial, staffing, and capacity issues, and the lack of resources to address staffing and capacity had become a major crisis. While the affiliation process offered them opportunities for key alliance building and solidarity support for their campaigns, most worker centers were also looking to the partnerships with central labor councils as potential fund-raising opportunities. The report authors recommended that the AFL-CIO build on the success of the LIFT Fund to create more opportunities to generate funding for worker centers involved in the affiliation process.

Despite the partnerships, the surveys and interviews revealed that, for some unions, discussions about immigration and worker centers were still quite fraught and had been marked by misconceptions and misunderstandings. Strikingly, the study found that many worker centers lacked a clear understanding of unions, the AFL-CIO, and the history of the labor movement. Worker centers and their members often carried serious misconceptions about unions when they entered into an affiliation process. When one partner lacked a working knowledge of how the other's institution operated, miscommunication often followed. The authors argued that both parties needed to better understand how each other's structures work, and put a clear system of accountability in place.

The authors called on the AFL-CIO to create materials for central labor councils on issues relating to immigration and low-wage immigrant workers and to produce workshops dedicated to overcoming stereotypes and undoing misconceptions relating to undocumented workers as well as worker centers and their history. Likewise, the report called for unions to show greater sensitivity to issues relating to inclusivity and diversity and recommended partnering with groups that are experienced in these areas to produce workshops for worker centers and unions that are about to engage in a process of relationship building.

The authors also recommended that the AFL-CIO produce educational materials and a workshop curriculum that focused on the structure and culture of unions, as well as the history of the labor movement and the AFL-CIO (Narro, Poyaoan, and Waheed 2015).

LOOKING TO THE FUTURE

By linking with the AFL-CIO and its affiliates, worker centers have the potential to win substantial gains for low-wage workers. No other movement has been as successful as organized labor in driving systemic, long-term shifts in the redistribution of wealth. Even today, in its weakened state, labor is still the best-resourced and largest membership-based institution on the left in the United States.

There are important potential benefits to joining forces with worker centers. The most deeply ingrained theme of anti-union propaganda, despite voluminous evidence to the contrary (Lafer 2017), is that unions care only about their individual dues-paying members and do not represent the needs of *all* working people. Incorporating worker centers (at this point, nondues-paying members) into the AFL-CIO reinforces labor's moral authority. They are an enduring demonstration of the federation's commitment to representing the needs of all working people in the United States—especially those at the bottom—and enables it to reach immigrant and African American workers in the fastest-growing employment category in our economy: low-wage jobs.

Partnerships with worker centers position unions for low-wage worker organizing in several ways. They show that strong bases of solidarity can be constructed when occupational and industrial identities are united with those of ethnicity, race, immigration status, gender, and gender identity. As community-based institutions, they lend themselves to labor market–wide strategies necessary to organizing in overwhelmingly non-union environments. By going after end user companies at the top of industrial supply chains rather than individual employers who are often small, mobile, and whose brand names are unknown to the broader public, they shed light on how to raise standards across an entire industry in which subcontracting is rampant. For the increasing number of workers who are not in long-term relationships with a single employer, they offer access to education, training, legal representation, advocacy, and flexible agreements that allow for the raising of standards without collective bargaining.

Labor law in the United States is in need of dramatic reform in order to be utilized more effectively to organize workers. As a consequence of years of laws being weakened through Congress and the courts, employers are able to intimidate workers who wish to join unions, stall after union elections have been won, and refuse to bargain a first contract—in some cases, for years—until a new vote can be taken to decertify the union. As discussed above, as non-union entities, worker centers are not permitted to collectively bargain for workers, but they are not restrained by provisions of the Taft–Hartley Act that prohibit secondary boycotts. Recent attacks by the Chamber of Commerce and others are falsely claiming that worker centers are really unions by another name in order to narrow their strategic arsenal. Formal membership or partnerships with the AFL-CIO will certainly be cited as evidence of worker centers' union affiliations.

The labor movement needs organizing strategies outside of the National Labor Relations Act given the changes to how labor in the United States is structured, weakened protections under current labor law, and the trend toward right-to-work in many states around the country. Worker centers originated to meet the needs of low-wage workers in unorganized industries and are employing innovative strategies to win better protections for thousands of workers.

While labor unions remain the best-resourced progressive institutions in the United States, the rapid decline of dues-paying members threatens their longevity. Worker centers today are fledgling institutions highly dependent on government and foundation grants. Most worker centers currently lack the internal infrastructure needed to make them self-sufficient institutions. While better-resourced unions should commit financial resources to support worker centers, there is a broad concern among centers that they will be junior partners in the labor movement if they do not become more self-sufficient. Worker centers will have to develop self-sufficient organizational models, but this change will not occur overnight, and any partnership will have to recognize this fact. Moreover, the organizing experiments being conducted in worker centers, while promising for the labor movement as a whole, will need to focus more on income generation, first and foremost through membership dues, in order to be able to engage in the kind of experimentation and testing of new strategies necessary to the development of new models. Many worker centers argue that, given the income levels of their constituents, they could not generate enough revenue through dues, but unions have not had this experience. Members of SEIU's building services locals are overwhelmingly immigrants, people of color, and low income, yet they have repeatedly voted in favor of significant dues increases. Full-time workers pay an average of $65 and part-time workers $33 per month.

Many worker centers understand organized labor's long history of fighting for workers and have often sought guidance and resources from unions and central labor councils. After all, many worker centers believe unions are powerful with access to resources and strong political connections. Worker centers believe that organized labor brings a more established understanding of how workers can gain power in the workplace, what an organized shop looks like, and what steps are necessary to win a campaign. Some worker centers view themselves as a precursor for workers seeking union representation. Central labor councils admire worker centers for their creativity, their commitment to worker justice, and their ability to connect worker struggles with community issues to fight for victories beyond the workplace. They also recognize how worker centers are able to lead major policy campaigns for workers with few resources and accomplish major victories.

These combined efforts of unions and worker centers to organize immigrant and low-wage workers throughout the country have led to innovative partnerships, new models of organizing campaigns, and efforts to expand the base of the labor movement. These efforts laid the foundation for the innovations that took place during the 2013 AFL-CIO convention that focused on diversity, inclusion, and new organizing models and partnerships that will help to transform the labor movement.

CONCLUSION

Despite the gains from this partnership, which are felt mostly at the local or regional level, worker centers need the infrastructure and stability offered by the AFL-CIO to remain viable in the long term. Low-wage work is a growing sector of the economy, and coordination between established labor unions and worker centers is necessary to meet the growing need to organize new workforces and gain ground in industries that were once union dense but have suffered declining union membership. Both worker centers and unions have the opportunity to benefit significantly from working jointly to achieve important victories. For collaboration to be effective, however, worker centers need significant investments from unions to help them become self-sufficient institutions.

With the continuing attacks and looming threats against the labor movement, and the recent upsurge in workers mobilizing and taking to the streets, forging strong community–labor alliances is playing a major role in many of our victories. These alliances are not recent developments in the labor movement. Many are the outcomes of years of efforts and investment in relationship building and creating strategic partnerships. The AFL-CIO Worker Center Partnership is an example of labor–community alliance building that has led to major accomplishments and victories. The mutual benefit, respect, and synergy between worker centers and the labor movement are clear. Over time, many union and worker center activists have come to realize the labor movement's future depends not only on organizing prospective members but also on engaging all workers—union and non-union, immigrant and non-immigrant. Local partnerships have led to significant outcomes in local policy campaigns against wage theft and other forms of exploitation against workers, strong solidarity support for worker organizing efforts to win a union or address exploitation in the workplace, and ongoing local joint initiatives that combine collaboration and innovation. It is in local campaigns where the work leads to cross-sector relationships that the connection between these two types of organizations will reach greater numbers of union and worker center members and continue to mature.

REFERENCES

AFL-CIO. 2006. "A National Worker Center–AFL-CIO Partnership." http://bit.ly/2vxWsya
AFL-CIO. 2018. "Worker Centers." http://bit.ly/2vxWMNo
Bloom, Joshua, Ruth Milkman, and Victor Narro. 2010. *Working for Justice: The L.A. Model of Organizing and Advocacy.* Ithaca, NY: Cornell University Press.
Chishti, Muzaffar. 2004. "Employer Sanctions Against Immigrant Workers." *WorkingUSA* 3 (6): 71–76.
CLEAN Carwash Campaign. 2016. "Our Work." http://bit.ly/2vxLtEP
Erickson, Christopher L., Catherine L. Fisk, Ruth Milkman, Daniel J.B. Mitchell, and Kent Wong. 2002. "Justice for Janitors in Los Angeles: Lessons from Three Rounds of Negotiations." *British Journal of Industrial Relations* 20: 543–567. https://doi.org/10.1111/1467-8543.00246
Fine, Janice. 2006. *Worker Centers: Organizing Communities at the Edge of the Dream.* Ithaca, NY: Cornell University Press.
Fine, Janice. 2007. "A Marriage Made in Heaven? Mismatches and Misunderstandings Between Worker Centres and Unions." *British Journal of Industrial Relations* 45: 335–360. https://doi.org/10.1111/j.1467-8543.2007.00617.x
Fine, Janice, and Nik Theodore. 2013. "Worker Centers: Community Based and Worker Led Organizations." New Brunswick,NJ: Rutgers School of Management and Labor Relations. http://bit.ly/2vAoEAo
Fine, Janice, and Daniel J. Tichenor. 2009. "A Movement Wrestling: American Labor's Enduring Struggle with Immigration, 1866–2007." *Studies in American Political Development* 23 (1): 84–113. https://doi.org/10.1017/S0898588X09000042
Fine, Janice, Jeff Grabelsky, and Victor Narro. 2008. "Building a Future Together: Worker Centers and Construction Unions." *Labor Studies Journal* 33 (1): 27–47. https://doi.org/10.1177/0160449X07311858
Fish, Jennifer. 2017. *Domestic Worker Organizing in the Global Economy: The Convention 189 Campaign as a Mobilization Model.* New York, NY: Rosa Luxemburg Stiftung.
Gautié, Jérôme, and John Schmitt. 2010. *Low-Wage Work in the Wealthy World.* New York, NY: Russell Sage Foundation.
Interfaith Worker Justice. 2018. "Affiliates." http://www.iwj.org/affiliates

Lafer, Gordon. 2017. *The One Percent Solution.* Ithaca, NY: ILR Press.

Mason, Geoff, and Wiemer Salverda. 2010. "Low Pay, Working Conditions, and Living Standards." In *Low-Wage Work in the Wealthy World,* edited by Jérôme Gautié and John Schmitt. New York, NY: Russell Sage Foundation.

Milkman, Ruth. 2006. *L.A. Story: Immigrant Workers and the Future of the U.S. Labor Movement.* New York: Russell Sage Foundation.

Milkman, Ruth, and Ed Ott. 2014. *New Labor in New York: Precarious Workers and the Future of the Labor Movement.* Ithaca, NY: Cornell University Press.

National Employment Law Project (NELP). 2014. *The Low-Wage Recovery: Industry Employment and Wages Four Years into the Recovery.* New York, NY: National Employment Law Project.

Narro, Victor, Jassmin Poyaoan, and Saba Waheed. 2015. *Building a Movement Together: Worker Centers and Labor Union Affiliations.* Los Angeles, CA: Labor Innovations for the 21st Century (LIFT) Fund.

Narro, Victor, and Janna Shadduck-Hernández. 2014. "The Informality of Day Labor Work: Challenges and Approaches to Addressing Working Conditions of Day Laborers." In *Hidden Lives and Human Rights in the United States: Understanding the Controversies and Tragedies of Undocumented Immigration,* edited by Lois Ann Lorentzen. Santa Barbara, CA: ABC-CLIO.

Narro, Victor, Janna Shadduck-Hernández, and Kent Wong. 2007. "The 2006 Immigrant Uprising: Origins and Future." *New Labor Forum* 16 (1): 48–56.

Ness, Immanuel. 2005. *Immigrants, Unions, and the New U.S. Labor Market.* Philadelphia, PA: Temple University Press.

Passel, Jeffrey S. 2005. *Unauthorized Migrants: Numbers and Characteristics.* Washington, DC: Pew Research Center.

Schmitt, John, Margy Walker, Shawn Fremstad, and Ben Zipperer. 2008. "Unions and Upward Mobility for Low-Wage Workers." *WorkingUSA: The Journal of Labor and Society* 11: 337–348.

US Bureau of Labor Statistics. 2017. "Monthly Labor Review." http://bit.ly/2mocaEw

Valenzuela, Abel Jr., Nik Theodore, Edwin Meléndez, and Ana Luz Gonzalez. 2006. "On the Corner: Day Labor in the United States." Los Angeles, CA: UCLA Center for Study of Urban Poverty. http://bit.ly/2msKWwG

CHAPTER 4

Union Organizing, Advocacy, and Services at the Nexus of Immigrant and Labor Rights

Xóchitl Bada
University of Illinois at Chicago

Shannon Gleeson
School of Industrial and Labor Relations, Cornell University

Els de Graauw
Baruch College, City University of New York

INTRODUCTION

Much has been written about the ways immigrant workers are transforming the American labor movement and the role of unions in advocating for immigrant rights. The intersection of immigrant and labor rights is perhaps inevitable now that immigrants comprise nearly 17% of the US labor force, nearly half of them identifying as Latino and a quarter as Asian (US Bureau of Labor Statistics 2017). Also, worker issues have been central to recent political debates among policy makers and union leaders alike. Examples include the creation of employer sanctions in 1986 (which unions then supported but now oppose), recent proposals to expand guest worker programs (which unions are divided over), and legal challenges to undocumented immigrants' access to collective bargaining and other workplace rights (which implicate unions and other types of worker organizations).

While the growing immigrant workforce is bifurcated, labor issues are common to different types of immigrants. Many high-skilled immigrants work in the technology and health care fields where precarious conditions often leave them far from parity with their native-born counterparts (Ontiveros 2016). Low-skilled workers, especially those who are undocumented, are especially vulnerable owing to the much higher number of wage and hour violations and more hazardous work conditions in the jobs they tend to fill (Hall and Greenman 2014; Milkman, González, and Ikeler 2012). These latter workers often also confront language barriers, racial discrimination, and challenges resulting from their immigration status. Organized labor has taken a particular interest in the needs of low-wage immigrant workers, begrudgingly at first, but more proactively since the American Federation of Labor and Congress of Industrial Organizations (AFL-CIO) formally declared support for immigrant rights in 2000 (Burgoon, Fine, Jacoby, and Tichenor 2010).

Labor's increased support for immigrant rights has manifested itself through high-profile protests, more advocacy on behalf of immigrant rights, a growing number of immigrants in union leadership positions, and other ways discussed in this chapter.

Unions' increased engagement with immigrants has not been easy. Unions and other worker advocates are confronting a paradoxical legal context that affects how unions strategize and engage with immigrant communities. On the one hand, labor standards enforcement agencies—including the US Department of Labor, the Equal Employment Opportunity Commission, the National Labor Relations Board (NLRB), and state and local agencies—seek to uphold the rights of *all* immigrant workers. Yet immigration law often prevents undocumented immigrants from accessing full remedies, especially in the collective bargaining context. Furthermore, federal immigration enforcement agencies—most notably US Immigration and Customs Enforcement (ICE)—have increasingly singled out undocumented immigrants and focused on the workplace as a site for enforcement actions. In this paradoxical legal setting, with tensions between integrative and exclusionary policies and practices, the AFL-CIO has sought to influence national debates around visa allocations, enforcement processes and priorities, and legalization. Labor unions have also responded in other ways, by including innovative wording in collective bargaining contracts, influencing state and local policies that increase immigrant protections, and joining coalitions to provide immigrant members and their families with access to a range of critical social and legal services.

This chapter broadens the discussion of unions' engagement with immigrant workers by contextualizing unions within the broader field of immigrant rights advocacy. Unions rely on community partners to support their *worker* rights campaigns, but they have also played an important role in supporting *immigrant* rights campaigns. We draw on research in three traditional immigrant destinations with different state and local contexts for worker organizing—Chicago, San Francisco, and Houston—to highlight that unions have increased their activism on immigrants and their labor issues, though in locally distinct ways. We argue that key factors driving this variation include the amount of power unions enjoy locally, the political context in which unions operate, and the form and function of the local field of civil society organizations in which unions are embedded.

In what follows, we first provide a brief overview of the maze of US immigration laws and labor and employment laws, focusing on the challenges for both individual immigrant workers and the organizations that advocate on their behalf. Then, based on the typology first developed by Fine (2006), we discuss three ways in which organized labor—both unions and worker centers—have responded to these challenges, including through *collective organizing, public policy advocacy*, and the *provision of legal and other services*.

To do so, we draw on examples from union activism in three traditional immigrant-receiving cities, and we discuss (1) innovative labor organizing campaigns in Chicago, (2) successful campaigns to create living and minimum wages in San Francisco, and (3) key immigrant worker organizing efforts and evolving responses to the 2012 and 2014 DACA/DAPA federal executive initiatives in Houston. Our main findings illustrate the challenges of diversifying union leadership positions, the opportunities strong coalitions provide to advance pro-immigrant local legislation, and the effective ways to frame immigrant labor issues to build support across the aisle in anti-immigrant state environments. We conclude with a discussion of both best practices and challenges of union engagement with immigrant issues as illustrated by these three city case studies.

LEGAL CHALLENGES FOR IMMIGRANT WORKER RIGHTS

In the United States, laws on the books mostly offer foreign-born workers the same labor rights as native-born workers. However, undocumented workers in particular face workplace vulnerabilities as a result of their immigration status. They represent only 5% of the US workforce (Passel and Cohn 2016), but their precarious position in the labor market renders them the proverbial canary in the coal mine in the race to the bottom in workplace rights. This is because of closing opportunities for legal migration for low-wage workers, but also because of the increasing reliance of certain industries—most notably agriculture, residential construction, and the service sector—on undocumented laborers.

Immigration Law Challenges

The labor challenges of low-wage immigrant workers stem from the fact that many work in industries and workplaces with higher risks of workplace violations, including wage theft, occupational hazards, and workplace injuries (Bernhardt, Spiller, and Polson 2013; Hall and Greenman 2014). The rights afforded to low-wage immigrant workers without legal status are the most precarious in this regard. On the one hand, federal immigration authorities have routinely used the workplace to find, detain, and then deport undocumented immigrants. On the other, major federal labor standards enforcement agencies have been concerned with reaching out to these workers in order to promote compliance with labor laws among employers, who might otherwise exploit undocumented workers with impunity in efforts to lower labor costs. These tensions between federal immigration and labor laws were very notable under the Bush and Obama administrations, both of which used the workplace for enforcement through mechanisms such as Social Security No-Match Letters, E-Verify compliance, and Internal Revenue Service (IRS) audits of employer records (National Immigration Law Center 2012).

The situation has become more tenuous under the Trump administration, which has emphasized immigration enforcement priorities that affect many more undocumented immigrants and even legal immigrants. At the same time that the administration has pulled back on recently strengthened worker protections, it has also advocated a return to high-profile workplace raids and a willingness to conduct ICE arrests and removals at previously safe spaces such as courthouses, schools, churches, and hospitals. Earlier, various federal labor standards enforcement agencies had drawn up memoranda of understanding that preclude ICE from interfering in their investigations (Griffith 2011). However, the Trump administration has effectively ignored these goodwill and common-sense measures, even promoting immigration enforcement at worker dispute hearings. In this context, union leaders and other immigrant rights advocates remain concerned about both information sharing between employers and immigration officials and the willingness of federal authorities to respect sensitive locations as off-limits to ICE officials.

To be sure, immigration laws form the primary obstacle for undocumented workers to receiving fair, just, and equitable treatment in the workplace. One of the most important immigration policies shaping immigrant employment was codified in 1986 as the Immigration Reform and Control Act (IRCA). This federal law had both inclusive and punitive elements, creating a one-time large-scale legalization program benefiting more than 2.7 million undocumented immigrants and instituting employer sanctions that are still in effect. The latter policy, which unions championed at the time, mandated the use of the now-ubiquitous I-9 form that requires employers to verify the work eligibility of their employees. This, in theory, left employers vulnerable to hefty fines if they knowingly hired undocumented workers. Yet, in practice, worker advocates now point to the low levels of actual employer enforcement and the added power that status verification mechanisms give employers to retaliate against workers who speak out against or challenge workplace abuses, especially in an at-will employment environment.

Following IRCA, labor advocates litigated the right of undocumented immigrants to assert their workplace rights. Of biggest consequence here was the 2002 US Supreme Court decision in *Hoffman Plastic Compounds, Inc. v. National Labor Relations Board*. The decision in this case precluded undocumented workers from accessing key remedies, including receiving back pay, after being fired for participating in a union organizing campaign. The case, while limited in its application, has had ripple effects across other areas of case law. Since then, some states (e.g., California) have strengthened protections for undocumented workers, while other states (e.g., Arizona) have instead enacted more punitive measures, thereby widening the gulf in undocumented worker rights protections across states (Bohn, Lofstrom, and Raphael 2013; National Employment Law Project 2013).

Labor and Employment Law Challenges

Looking beyond immigration law, both undocumented and documented immigrants face a variety of workplace challenges in large part as a result of the precarious nature of the work they do in agriculture, construction, and the hotel and restaurant industries. Federal law provides a framework for upholding basic worker rights across the country for *all* workers, but labor policies and their enforcement can vary widely across levels of government in the US federal system. Distinguishing between different enforcement regimes can be difficult for immigrant workers experiencing problems, and there is little coordination between labor enforcement agencies at the federal, state, and local levels. Workers may also quickly find that they are ineligible for protections. Especially in the informal economy and the growing gig economy, so-called independent contractors abound, and the courts are struggling to settle what obligations companies such as Uber and Manpower have to their just-in-time employees. Such coverage, furthermore, can vary substantially by state and industry.

Worker advocates play an important role in educating workers of their rights in this confusing federated landscape of labor laws and practices. For example, many worker centers challenge the misclassification of day laborers as independent contractors to help them recover lost wages and access health and safety benefits (Nicholson, Bunn, and Costich 2008; Quinlan and Mayhew 1999). Many low-wage workers also struggle to navigate complicated management hierarchies, especially in industries such as agriculture and construction where subcontracting and sub-subcontracting are common. Here, worker advocates had recently been able to strengthen joint employer responsibility, but these efforts too have been rescinded by the Trump administration.

The ability of low-wage immigrant workers to access formal labor and employment protections often hinges on access to legal counsel or other advocates who can guide and assist them in the claims process. Having a lawyer at one's side can lead to more generous settlements and can bridge language gaps for immigrant workers who struggle with English. Yet even access to low-cost attorneys can be difficult, especially when lawyers rely on funding that restricts their ability to serve undocumented immigrants. With union membership levels at historic lows, new forms of worker advocacy have emerged to address the needs of these particularly disadvantaged immigrant workers. This in turn has prompted questions about the rights of non-union organizations to represent workers (Griffith 2015). Furthermore, these organizations must navigate IRS regulations that restrict the amount and type of political activities of not-for-profit, tax-exempt 501(c)(3) organizations. While these regulations do not stop advocates, they do shape the strategies and tactics they use to make rights real for their immigrant clients and members (de Graauw 2016).

ORGANIZATIONAL RESPONSES TO IMMIGRANT WORKER RIGHTS

The intersection of immigration and labor and employment laws has created many challenges for immigrant workers, but it has also produced a unique issue space in which different organizations are active. Most notably, these include labor unions, worker centers, and other nonprofit organizations; faith-based institutions; local government agencies; and foreign consulates. They all have an interest in advancing the rights of immigrant workers, though to varying degrees and with immigration-related issues differently articulated across organizations. These organizations also have different missions, core constituencies, access to resources, and abilities to engage in organizing and policy advocacy, making concerted action on immigrant worker rights challenging. At times, they have secured victories for immigrant workers when collaborating under the right circumstances. At other times, tensions and conflicts between organizations have resulted in missed opportunities for economic and policy change and setbacks for immigrant workers and their families.

Historically, relations between labor unions and immigrants, who were once seen as economic threats, were strained and at times openly hostile (Burgoon, Fine, Jacoby, and Tichenor 2010; Fine and Tichenor 2012). But in 2000, after years of grassroots organizing within the AFL-CIO and as the immigrant workforce continued to grow while unions suffered steep membership declines, organized labor formally embraced immigrants, including the undocumented, as legitimate members and an essential new source of organized labor's power (Greenhouse 2000; Hamlin 2008). Since then, the largest labor federation and its affiliates have stepped up to strengthen their commitment to immigrant workers by devoting more resources to mobilizing and organizing these workers and by exerting political and policy influence over immigration issues and worker legislation.

Labor's formal support for immigrants since 2000 has also meant that unions have built more partnerships with other organizations that promote immigrant rights and advocate for immigration reform. Notable collaborators include the National Partnership for New Americans (a coalition created in 2010 of 37 regional immigrant and refugee rights organizations spanning 31 states that work to influence immigrant rights policies at the local, state, and federal levels) and Working America (the community affiliate of the AFL-CIO that has championed a range of immigration issues). Unions continue to work with worker center coalitions, many of them immigrant led and immigrant focused, such as the National Day Laborer Organizing Network, and many central labor councils and regional federations have signed solidary charters with them. Local unions and central labor councils, especially following the announcements of Obama's executive immigration actions in 2012 and 2014, have worked more closely with immigration lawyers to make union-centered legal aid more readily available. In some cases, local labor councils have created new immigrant service centers, including the We Rise San Francisco Labor Center for Immigrant Justice that provides "one stop legal and wrap-around services to immigrant union members and their families" (San Francisco Labor Council 2017).

Besides unions, other member-based groups such as worker centers, immigrant advocacy organizations, and faith-based institutions have long been working with immigrants. These organizations, often located in the communities where immigrants live, help unions gain access to immigrant workers ripe for organizing. Many immigrants tend to work in industries that are difficult to unionize because of the small size of the workplace, the decentralized nature of the industry, or the isolated nature of work. In this context, worker centers, other nonprofits, and faith-based institutions provide safe havens for immigrant workers to address a variety of issues, and they can help unify disparate workers within a community and bolster support for grassroots union organizing campaigns (Cordero-Guzmán, Izvănariu, and Narro 2013; Martin 2012). Nonprofits also help rally support for unions among immigrants by expanding the union agenda to include broader concerns, such as poverty reduction, affordable housing, immigration reform, and a clean environment (Botein 2007; Wells 2000). Furthermore, nonprofits can help unions win recognition outside the traditional NLRB elections process, for example, by pressuring employers to recognize neutrality agreements (Sherman and Voss 2000). Finally, nonprofits legitimize union power in local policy making and community relations. While unions are still associated with strong-arm tactics to further their goals, nonprofits and faith-based institutions wield moral capital as a result of their association with charitable causes and social justice and faith initiatives (de Graauw 2016; Gleeson 2009).

Government entities, including local governments and foreign consulates, have also worked to advance immigrant worker rights. Between 1994 and 2006, with pressure from diverse coalitions of labor unions, community organizations, and churches, more than 140 municipalities around the country adopted living wage laws requiring employers with government contracts to pay their workers decent, living wages (Dean and Reynolds 2009). Some local governments have done more, enacting their own minimum wage laws (applying to *all* workers, including undocumented workers), wage theft prevention laws (to further protect immigrants and other vulnerable low-wage workers from unscrupulous employers who steal their wages), and other laws (such as paid sick leave, health care legislation, and municipal ID cards) that have benefited immigrants and other low-wage workers alike. Foreign consulates, most notably the Mexican consulate, have also increased efforts to protect immigrant workers (Bada and Gleeson 2014; Délano 2011). Since 2007, the Mexican consulate has organized the annual Labor Rights Week, a bilateral initiative that coordinates efforts among local consular offices, federal and state labor standards enforcement agencies, labor unions, and immigrant-serving nonprofits to enforce the labor rights of Mexican immigrant workers in the United States.

UNIONS AND IMMIGRANT LABOR RIGHTS ACTIVISM IN CHICAGO, SAN FRANCISCO, AND HOUSTON

Unions' engagement with immigrant workers varies from place to place, often depending on local union power, local political dynamics, and the characteristics of local civil society organizations. Here, we highlight notable developments in Chicago, San Francisco, and Houston to demonstrate the different ways in which unions in recent years have increased their activism on immigrants and their labor issues.

Building Coalitions for Collective Representation in Chicago

Chicago, the country's third largest city with about 2.7 million residents, has a long history of immigration and supporting immigrant and worker rights. Large numbers of European immigrants as well as Arab, Asian, Latin American, and Caribbean immigrants have called Chicago home for over two centuries. In 2015, 21% of city residents were born abroad, with the majority coming from Latin America (55%), followed by Asia (22%) and Europe (17%).[1] Fifty-eight percent of them had not acquired US citizenship in 2015, and the city has an estimated 183,000 undocumented immigrants who make up 23% of the foreign-born population (Paral and Associates 2011). Chicago is a Democratic stronghold, and more than three-quarters of the city's voters supported Democratic presidential candidates in recent elections. Chicago's first sanctuary city ordinance dates from 1985, and in recent decades, city officials have enacted various immigrant-friendly policies, including a Welcoming City Ordinance (2011), Minimum Wage Ordinance (2014), Anti-Wage Theft Ordinance (2015), Food Truck Ordinance (2015), Language Access Ordinance (2015), Paid Sick Leave Ordinance (2016), Municipal ID Ordinance (2017), and publicly funded legal services for immigrants facing deportation (2017). Most recently, the Chicago filed a federal lawsuit against recent efforts by the Trump administration to withhold federal funding from sanctuary cities. Finally, Chicago has an immigrant affairs office, called the Office of New Americans, which has promoted immigrant integration initiatives since 2011.

While the city's original packinghouse unions of the early 20th century included mainly Irish and German workers, today's meatpacking-related and service sector industries have many more Latino immigrants in the ranks of large and vocal locals such as United Food and Commercial Workers (UFCW) Local 881 and Service Employees International Union (SEIU) Local 1. Yet, over the past two decades, immigrant workers in Chicago have faced a steady decline in union density. Union-busting practices by private sector employers have contributed to this, also deterring long organizing campaigns and making long-term victories difficult to sustain. These challenges notwithstanding, traditional labor unions in Chicago still enjoy considerable power and visibility, and they remain major players in immigrant rights campaigns. Some of the leading immigrant unions include UNITE HERE! Local 1, UFCW Local 1546, SEIU Local 1, and Teamsters Local 743. As was the case across the country, the historic 2006 immigrant rights marches fell on the heels of previous mass mobilizations, including the 2003 Immigrant Freedom Ride, which drew support from the year-long UNITE HERE! campaign at the Congress Plaza Hotel on Michigan Avenue. This largely immigrant union workforce ultimately joined an even larger coalition of local hometown associations, faith-based groups, and other grassroots organizations in support of the ride. Several labor unions, including SEIU Local 1, also participated as part of a delegation from the Illinois Coalition for Immigrant and Refugee Rights, Illinois' largest immigrant rights coalition.

In Chicago and elsewhere, organizing low-wage immigrant workers remains very challenging, and the barriers to win an entire sector with large numbers of immigrant workers requires long-term union investments and unwavering support also from national union leadership. In the past decade, some Chicago metro-area unions serving immigrant workers have adopted innovative strategies to improve coalition building with local, national, and international actors with the goal of attracting wider public support for their organizing campaigns. These efforts, while showing Chicago unions' growing engagement with immigrant workers and their issues, have had only modest results and various degrees of sustainability, as our review of five paradigmatic cases of union coalition building shows.

The first case involves a sectorwide union campaign in 2012 by the United Steelworkers to organize car washers in Chicago, a largely male and immigrant workforce (Bruno, Quesada, and Manzo 2012). While local union organizers were fully committed to the campaign, their organizing drive ultimately failed in part because it lacked full support from the national leadership. Investing union resources in an industry with high worker turnover proved untenable. Learning from the experience of this failed car-wash campaign, other Chicago unions have since worked to strengthen their relationships with worker centers to build trust and buy-in before launching their organizing campaigns.

The second case involves workers in an egg processing plant in Lansing (Illinois) collaborating with the Chicago worker center ARISE in an effort to win an organizing campaign in 2016. It started out with a largely Latino immigrant workforce seeking to address labor disputes with the help of ARISE, which subsequently connected them with UFCW Local 881 (ARISE Chicago 2016; Trotter 2016). After a relatively short campaign, workers voted to have union representation in November 2016. The employer then retaliated and contacted the NLRB to challenge workers' eligibility to vote. After the union threatened to sue the employer for unlawful dismissal, the employer briefly desisted. During the organizing campaign, UFCW organizers elevated immigrant labor issues, and with worker center organizers, collectively decided that the best approach was to use the media to build public support. This collaborative approach aided the successful union vote and helped the majority of the dismissed workers to get certified for visas set aside for victims of crime. The early outreach to and empowerment of these otherwise isolated workers was a major win, and eventually the employer and union reached a favorable settlement with all dismissed workers.

The third case involves workers at Fox Valley, a metal factory in the Chicago suburb of Aurora. Here, workers collaborated closely with a local hometown association to build worker trust and ultimately win a unionization campaign via the International Brotherhood of Boilermakers Local 1600 in 2009. The workers were largely Mexican immigrants from Michoacán, many struggling with language barriers that prevented them from fully understanding their workplace rights. The social network of the hometown association became a key mechanism to support their organizing campaign, but the workers also enjoyed the backing of a local alderwoman, the AFL-CIO Solidarity Office in Mexico City, and Sisamex and Dana (two Mexican companies that boycotted Fox Valley exports during the long negotiation process). Immediately following the union election victory, union contracts were translated into Spanish. However, after two years of drawn-out negotiations, the employer ultimately decided to move most of the operations to the more business-friendly states of Ohio and Wisconsin. Despite the bad outcome for the workers involved in this campaign, this case illustrates the power of transnational civil society as well as the importance of unions to make basic language-access accommodations for their immigrant members.

The fourth case involves a union rallying support from unions in *other* countries to build international solidarity for an organizing campaign. In 2008, the Republic Windows and Doors factory abruptly closed its operations on Goose Island (an industrial hub in Chicago) and fired its entire workforce, 75% of whom were Mexican immigrants. Seeing an organizing opportunity, the United Electrical, Radio, and Machine Workers of America (UE) Local 1110 stepped in to lead a historic strike, even attracting the attention of President Obama. The strike garnered support from many local immigrant right organizations and a few European and Latin American labor groups (Lydersen

2009). A California-based company next acquired the factory, pledging to retain all the workers. Yet, by 2012, the factory closed again, prompting another worker strike and occupation. Shifting gears altogether, after the closure, the UE ultimately led the workers to form a successful, but smaller worker-run cooperative that continues today as the New Era Windows Cooperative. They did so with the key support of The Working World, a nonprofit organization that promotes a just and sustainable economy for low-income communities.

The final case involves a now institutionalized partnership between Chicago unions, foreign consulates, and other local organizations aimed at fighting wage theft. Traditionally, consulates provide legal services and basic documents such as birth certificates and passports. Collaboration with unions first started around 2006 when some union representatives began calling on consular officials in Chicago to help locate immigrant members in a detention center following workplace raids. Following the 2006 marches in Chicago, Teamsters Local 743, SEIU, UFCW, Jobs with Justice, and Workers United also started working with the Mexican consulate and the US Department of Labor (DOL) to organize the pilot Labor Rights Week (LRW) in 2007 to address wage theft and other labor complaints. The pilot would eventually be replicated in Los Angeles and across 15 other consulates in 2008. Today, the LRW is organized at all Mexican consulates in the United States and Canada, and 12 consulates from Latin America and the Philippines have also joined (Bada and Gleeson 2015). While the LRW is federally managed by DOL and the embassies in Washington, D.C., the implementation happens locally, and its success depends on the ongoing commitment from all governmental and nongovernmental partners, with a strong leading role for unions.

In sum, Chicago labor unions have enjoyed a rich history of organizing for worker power, which has allowed them to work creatively with non-union organizations, including worker centers, hometown associations, and even foreign consulates. Despite their coordination and framing challenges, these collaborations have strengthened various labor campaigns that have also benefited the rights of immigrant workers.

Exerting Policy Influence in San Francisco

San Francisco, the 14th largest city in the United States with about 840,000 residents, has a long and continuous history of immigration. In 2015, 35% of city residents were born abroad. The majority of immigrants come from Asia (65%), followed by Latin America (19%) and Europe (13%). Thirty-nine percent of them had not acquired US citizenship in 2015, and the city has an estimated 30,000 to 45,000 undocumented immigrants (Hill and Johnson 2011; Migration Policy Institute 2014). San Francisco is deep blue politically, and more than 80% of the city's voters have supported Democratic candidates in recent presidential elections. In recent decades, San Francisco officials have enacted various immigrant-friendly policies, including a Sanctuary Ordinance (1989), Equal Access to Services Ordinance (2001), Municipal ID Ordinance (2007), Due Process for All Ordinance (2013), and noncitizen voting in local school board elections (Proposition N, 2017). San Francisco has a strong union movement, and the greater Bay Area boasts higher than national average union membership rates in the private and public sectors (Hirsch and Macpherson 2017). Additionally, San Francisco is located in a state that offers labor protections that surpass federal standards and limits cooperation with federal immigration enforcement officials. In 2000, San Francisco created its own Office of Labor Standards Enforcement (OLSE) to enforce all wage and labor laws adopted by local legislators and San Francisco voters. Finally, San Francisco has two municipal agencies with specific immigrant-related mandates: the Immigrant Rights Commission, established by ordinance in 1997; and the Office of Civic Engagement and Immigrant Affairs, which in 2009 consolidated a handful of city administrative positions and offices responsible for immigrant integration programs.

Since 2000, San Francisco voters and policy makers have adopted several ordinances that have expanded the rights of immigrant and other low-wage workers. After a bruising and protracted campaign, the San Francisco Board of Supervisors enacted the Minimum Compensation Ordinance (popularly known as the Living Wage Ordinance) in 2000, raising the wages of an estimated 22,000 low-wage workers employed in businesses with city service contracts (Reynolds and Kern 2004). A broad Living Wage Coalition of more than 20 labor unions and worker centers, 28 religious leaders, 45 community organizations, and 10 immigrant rights organizations proposed and campaigned for a living wage of $14.50, at a time when the federal minimum wage was $5.15 and the California minimum wage was $5.75 (de Graauw 2016). The business community—especially the San Francisco Chamber of Commerce and the Golden Gate Restaurant Association—strongly opposed the $14.50 wage proposal and expended great resources in lobbying local policy makers to oppose it. In an attempt to find middle ground, Supervisor Tom Ammiano—at the time the board's foremost advocate for economic and social justice—introduced an $11 living wage proposal, for which there was no majority support on the board. The policy proposal nearly died in May 2000, but living wage advocates' threat to put the issue on the ballot forced all parties back to the negotiating table. As a result, in July 2000, a final compromise ordinance was enacted, calling for a $9 hourly wage (with provisions for paid and unpaid time off) for for-profit and nonprofit businesses with city service contracts.[2]

The Living Wage Coalition subsequently regrouped as the Minimum Wage Coalition and continued to campaign for a Minimum Wage Ordinance in 2003. This ordinance mandated that *all* low-wage workers in the city be paid

$8.50, an hourly wage higher than the federal and state minimums. This time, the advocates decided to put the issue on the ballot, allowing them to maintain control over the content of the ordinance at a time when the San Francisco economy was in a downturn and the business community opposed another wage increase. With an empowering electoral strategy targeting lower turnout neighborhoods of working-class people, immigrants, and people of color who would benefit most from the Minimum Wage Ordinance (including the Chinatown, Mission, and Bayview neighborhoods), 60% of San Francisco voters approved Proposition L, the Minimum Wage Ordinance. This made San Francisco one of the first of a growing number of cities with its own minimum wages. At the time that the ordinance was enacted, it was estimated that it would result in direct and indirect pay raises for more than 54,000 workers, or 12% of San Francisco's private and nonprofit sector labor force. It was also estimated that the city's minimum wage would disproportionately benefit immigrants, native-born minorities, and workers under the age of 25 (Reich and Laitinen 2003).

The city's minimum wage is adjusted annually based on the previous year's Consumer Price Index for urban wage earners in the San Francisco Bay Area. In early 2017, the San Francisco minimum wage was $13, compared with $10 at the state level and $7.25 at the federal level. The Minimum Wage Ordinance has an administrative enforcement mechanism through OLSE. The ordinance also provides for a private right of action for aggrieved workers and a representative cause of action, allowing unions and community organizations to file wage claims on behalf of duped workers. The ordinance also requires every workplace to post official bulletins announcing the current San Francisco minimum wage in English, Spanish, Chinese, and any additional language spoken by more than 5% of the workforce. Finally, the ordinance contains strong anti-retaliation language and prohibits employers from discriminating against workers who exercise their rights under the ordinance. Compared with the Minimum Compensation Ordinance, the Minimum Wage Ordinance contains more provisions aimed at protecting the rights of vulnerable immigrant workers who—owing to unfamiliarity with government agencies, undocumented status, or limited English proficiency—are less likely to contest labor law violations and speak up against unscrupulous employers (Gleeson 2012).

Labor and community organizations that campaigned for the Minimum Compensation and Minimum Wage Ordinances have since collaborated on several other policies that have further restructured the low-wage labor market in San Francisco. In 2001, the Board of Supervisors adopted the Health Care Accountability Ordinance, which requires city contractors and certain tenants on city property to offer health plan benefits to their employees or make payments to the city for use by the Department of Public Health.

In 2006, the Board of Supervisors adopted the Health Care Security Ordinance to provide comprehensive health care for the city's 73,000 uninsured adult residents, who include many immigrants (Katz 2008). The Paid Sick Leave Ordinance, legislated via initiative in 2006, requires all employers to provide paid sick leave to all employees, including temporary and part-time ones, who perform work in San Francisco. Also in 2006, the city's legislators adopted the Minimum Wage Implementation and Enforcement Ordinance to strengthen the enforcement of the Minimum Wage Ordinance against noncompliant private sector employers. The Board of Supervisors adopted the Wage Theft Prevention Ordinance in 2011, which further enhances the enforcement powers of OLSE and doubles the fines for employers who retaliate against workers exercising their rights under San Francisco labor laws. Finally, 77% of San Francisco voters adopted Proposition J in 2014, raising the city's minimum wage to $15 by 2018.

Although these ordinances did not directly benefit most union members, who already enjoyed relatively generous wage and benefit packages, San Francisco unions were very active in the coalitions behind the different campaigns. Unions, however, often were not the frontrunner advocates. Given the dense and well-developed infrastructure of immigrant worker advocacy groups in San Francisco, organizations such as the Chinese Progressive Association and La Raza Centro Legal (the Community's Legal Center) were able to play central leadership roles while working in partnership with unions sympathetic to immigrant labor rights.

High-Profile Organizing Campaigns and Legal Services in Houston

Houston, the fourth largest city in the country with about 2.2 million residents, is also very diverse. The sprawling city has experienced impressive growth in its immigrant population since World War II, and in 2015, 29% of Houstonians were foreign born, with the largest share hailing from Latin America (70%), followed by Asia (20%) and Africa (5%). Seventy-two percent of immigrants were not US citizens in 2015, and about 400,000 individuals in the larger metro area are estimated to be undocumented (Capps, Fix, and Nwosu 2015). Houston is located in a right-to-work state with weak labor and employment laws, and the city is marked by low union membership and unions that have relatively little sway over local politics. The countywide central labor council in Houston recently reinvented itself as the new Texas Gulf Coast Area Labor Federation, as part of a new "southern strategy" aimed at consolidating regional power (Miller 2016). While Houston is politically divided between Democrats and Republicans, it is flanked by staunchly conservative suburbs and rural areas. Houston has an Office of New Americans and Immigrant Communities that seeks to promote immigrants' civic, economic, and cultural integration, though it has been restructured twice since its creation in

2001 as a result of legislative opposition and mayoral leadership changes. Compared with the politically more progressive Chicago and San Francisco, Houston provides a more challenging context for worker and immigrant rights advocacy.

Some of the leading anti-immigrant voices in federal politics come from the Houston area, and Texas Governor Greg Abbott recently signed into law an anti-immigrant bill (SB 4) resembling Arizona's controversial "show me your papers" legislation from 2010. The American Civil Liberties Union issued a travel alert to Texas following the law's enactment (McLaughlin 2017), and while Harris County (which encompasses most of Houston) has not taken action against this state legislation, Houston recently joined the Mexican American Legal Defense and Educational Fund and four other Texas cities to challenge SB 4 in court (Associated Press 2017). Mayor Sylvester Turner has also declared Houston a "welcoming city" (short of calling it a sanctuary city, as advocates have been demanding), and the city's police chief has sharply criticized the racial profiling impacts that SB 4 will likely have. Houston is also home to some of the staunchest immigrant advocacy through a small but active group of organizations such as the Fe y Justicia (Faith and Justice) worker center, Familias Inmigrantes y Estudiantes en la Lucha (FIEL, Immigrant Families and Students in the Struggle), and the local United We Dream affiliate. Although the newly constituted regional labor council has chosen not to take up local immigration battles, including the campaign to rescind Harris County's 287(g) agreement with ICE, it passed a resolution in early 2017 calling on government agencies at all levels of government to protect immigrant families. The local business community, perhaps surprisingly, has played an active and vocal role in promoting immigrant integration and advocating for "sensible" federal immigration reform (de Graauw and Gleeson 2017).

While there have not been many labor organizing campaigns in Houston, some of the more high-profile ones have included organizing the Hilton Americas (Houston's largest convention center hotel) and SEIU's Justice for Janitors campaign. The latter resulted in first contracts for 5,000 janitors, in large part thanks to civil disobedience that resulted in $20 million in bail for those arrested during the campaign (Lerner and Shaffer 2015). In a massive 2012 janitor strike, even then moderate Mayor Annise Parker was persuaded to urge contractors to return to the bargaining table to consider the union's "good faith offers" on behalf of its mostly female workers of color (Casares 2012). Beyond winning that initial contract, advocates also succeeded in securing key immigrant protections and prohibiting employment reverification and translations of key union documents and communications. In each campaign, as in the other cities profiled here, unions relied on a wide range of community allies to support their organizing in immigrant-heavy workplaces.

Beyond these organizing campaigns, Houston has become an unlikely leader in local worker policy, and the advocacy efforts of local worker centers and immigrant rights groups have a lot to do with that. In 2001, for example, local advocates had formed the Justice and Equality in the Workplace Partnership with the Mexican consulate with the goal of better coordinating access to workplace protections for immigrants. At one time, the city also funded a series of day labor centers with federal community development block grants. These worker centers, however, were controversial, and they eventually closed under pressure from nativist anti-immigrant groups (Gleeson 2012). Yet, in 2013, the Houston city council unanimously passed an anti-wage theft ordinance, the result of a campaign spearheaded by a broad coalition of immigrant and worker advocates who sought to tie employers' outstanding wage violations and fines to their ability to renew their city business licenses (Morris 2013). This move that angered many employers, but others were supportive, arguing that such measures leveled the playing field for compliant employers who competed against noncompliant ones (de Graauw and Gleeson 2017).

In Houston, certain union and non-union advocates have also played important roles in connecting immigrants to legal services as federal immigration policies have changed in recent years. For example, key immigrant unions such as UFCW and SEIU have assisted immigrants through the naturalization process and introduced them to get-out-the-vote campaigns. Furthermore, in the wake of Obama's 2012 Deferred Action for Childhood Arrivals (DACA) program, and the proposed (and ultimately failed) 2014 Deferred Action for Parents of Americans and Lawful Permanent Residents (DAPA) and expanded DACA programs, union and non-union advocates have collaborated in connecting immigrants and their children to services that allow them to take advantage of these federal programs.

Local union leaders have viewed Obama's executive immigration actions of vital importance for workers, because they provide work authorization to undocumented immigrants and protection from deportation to many working-class families. Though the expanded DACA and DAPA programs were stalled in the courts, and the Trump administration has now formally blocked their implementation, in the aftermath of their original announcement there was a flutter of activity to educate and prepare the many eligible applicants for the programs. Houston nonprofits in particular have guided immigrants through the DACA process, through a series of public workshops and private consultations. In the wake of the attempted rescission of the 2012 DACA program, these advocates have also been vocal in demanding a federal legislative fix and helping eligible DACA beneficiaries renew their protected status. However, the city's relatively underdeveloped civil society sector has meant that private attorneys and sometimes unscrupulous *notarios* have had a large market share of would-be applicants (de Graauw and Gleeson 2016).

Houston's Office of New Americans and Immigrant Communities has provided some technical support to local community organizations, but neither the city nor Harris County have funded any of the DACA or citizenship outreach or services, unlike in other cities. This reflects the strength of conservative anti-immigrant constituencies in the city and larger metro area and an overall small-government and pro-market ethos. The financial support for recent immigrant-focused legal services has instead come from local foundations, most notably the Houston Endowment and the Simmons Foundation. These foundations have funded the staffing and operations of the Houston Immigration Legal Services Collaborative (HILSC), which emerged out of a 2013 meeting of the Greater Houston Grantmakers' Forum led by the United Way. Initially, HILSC focused on coordinating and streamlining local providers that offered legal services for undocumented immigrants who wanted to apply for the 2012 DACA program. With the shifting federal policy terrain, they now focus on serving a larger group of low-income immigrants who seek legal services while navigating the increasingly complex US immigration system. Unions have played only a minor role in HILSC, and legal service providers and other types of civil society organizations—including BakerRipley, the University of Houston Law Center Immigration Clinic, Catholic Charities, the YMCA International Services, and Boat People SOS—are at the heart of the collaborative.

In sum, the more hostile climate for immigrants and low-wage workers in Houston has led to a few, but powerful, high-profile union organizing campaigns and an eclectic collaborative of advocates who have worked together to influence local policy and provide social and legal services to immigrant workers and their families.

BEST PRACTICES

The city cases we discussed make clear that labor unions have come a long way, compared with several decades ago, in how they engage with immigrants and their issues. In cities with large immigrant populations, we see a range of creative and innovative responses that better position unions and their allies to represent the interests of immigrant workers. We see this in the new organizing strategies that unions have used in Chicago, the range of policy issues they have advocated for in San Francisco, and the greater number of services they have been providing to their immigrant members in Houston.

As we see in Chicago and San Francisco, two metropolises with large immigrant populations and historically strong labor movements, unions have attempted to increase their membership by using innovative organizing and advocacy campaigns. Collaborating with new allies—including worker centers, hometown associations, Mexican businesses, the Mexican consulate, and international social justice and labor solidarity groups—has been central to these efforts. Notwithstanding their modest results, Chicago's organizing campaigns in the past decade illustrate the diverse strategies unions are willing to explore to win the community's trust and increase their visibility among low-wage immigrant workers. In San Francisco, the labor movement has been actively involved in multiple advocacy campaigns to win cumulative policy victories for immigrant workers, including higher and stronger minimum wages and other immigrant-friendly policies. In these two cases, unions operate in labor-friendly states and enjoy the political advantage of heavily Democratic city constituents, who are more willing to support pro-immigrant and progressive labor laws.

Houston is perhaps more counterintuitive, as it is a city with a moderately progressive shine in a right-to-work state that is also among the most conservative and anti-immigrant states in the country. Unions in Houston, which has the largest undocumented population among the three cities we studied, have nonetheless been able to win a few significant organizing campaigns. Thanks to innovative partnerships with immigrant rights organizations, the Mexican consulate, business groups, and faith-based organizations, local unions have also provided essential outreach to immigrant members and drawn immigrants into get-out-the-vote campaigns to increase their political engagement. Despite Houston's more challenging political climate, its city council has become an unlikely leader in local worker and immigrant rights policies.

In sum, in order to evaluate how today's unions are engaging with immigrant communities, it is important to look at a wide range of their activities beyond traditional organizing campaigns. We need to consider also unions' public policy advocacy, service provision activities, and coalition building at the local level. And we also need to look at their losses and setbacks to understand how unions are adapting to a rapidly changing political landscape and a growing and diversifying immigrant workforce. Finally, it is essential, as we have demonstrated, to consider the work of non-union organizations, including worker centers and immigrant-serving nonprofits, in evaluating what strides are being made in immigrant worker rights.

CHALLENGES AHEAD

Unions cannot lead and have not led immigrant worker rights advocacy on their own, and how they go about their work and the effect they have depends also on the context in which they operate. Key considerations include how much power unions have in a particular place, what local political dynamics are like, and what kinds of partners in government and the nonprofit sector are available and willing to work with them. Also, while local unions need to count on support from national union leaders, national and local priorities do not always align, even within a particular industry. Besides long-standing immigrant unions such as SEIU, UNITE HERE!, and UFCW, it is important for other unions to proactively invest in immigrant workers as well. The former three unions have large numbers of immigrant members, and they are visible immigrant rights leaders in the three cities we studied. Yet it is clear that we need more unions that address the needs of immigrant workers. The recent bold actions of national leaders from the American Federation of State, County, and Municipal Employees (AFSCME) and the American Federation of Teachers (AFT) are instructive examples of unions whose members are not primarily immigrants but that nonetheless have institutionalized immigrant rights into their organizational platforms.

For unions to remain relevant, they have to engage with a range of issues that affect immigrant workers. In addition to traditional labor issues, they also have to heed issues such as language access, housing, policing, voter registration, legal services, and identification documents. This can be challenging for union leaders, who might not want to engage with immigrant worker issues unless they feel they can make a strong case to their membership that this investment is a priority and matters for *all* members.

The willingness of SEIU, UNITE HERE!, and UFCW to appoint first- and second-generation immigrants to key leadership positions has been critical in elevating a range of issues within their organizations. As such, local unions elsewhere may benefit from diversifying their leadership as well. Unions that lack diversity and that have been disengaged from immigrant worker issues can start addressing a broader range of issues by establishing partnerships with worker centers and unions that are doing this already.

Finally, for labor unions to be able to engage with immigrant worker issues more effectively, federal and state labor standards enforcement mechanisms need to work for immigrant workers, regardless of their citizenship and immigration status. In this regard, both the turn toward enforcement-only immigration policies and the recent federal retrenchment of worker rights are major concerns. The government officials of states such as California, which has vocally opposed the interference in worker rights enforcement by federal immigration officials, will remain critical for immigrant worker rights. Civil society actors—including unions, worker centers, and immigrant rights organizations—will need to work together to keep state and federal officials accountable to immigrant workers.

ENDNOTES

[1] Unless otherwise noted, all 2015 demographic data are from the American Community Survey, 2011–15 estimates, detailed table B05002 (US Census Bureau 2015).

[2] Exempted from the Minimum Compensation Ordinance in 2000 were contracts for goods, contractors with 20 or fewer employees, for-profit businesses with service

contracts of less than $25,000, nonprofit service providers with contracts less than $50,000, and nonprofit contractors that could prove that compliance with the ordinance would cause them economic hardship. These provisions continue to hold, but as of January 2017 the hourly wage is $13.64 for new and amended contracts with for-profits, and $13 in the case of nonprofits (Office of Labor Standards Enforcement 2017).

REFERENCES

ARISE Chicago. 2016 (Nov. 19). "Egg Workers Resist Challenge to Their Union Votes." Press Release. On file with the authors.

Associated Press. 2017 (Jun. 21). "Houston to Join Lawsuit against Texas 'Sanctuary City' Law." *Statesman*. https://atxne.ws/2o7Kpka

Bada, Xóchitl, and Shannon Gleeson. 2014. "A New Approach to Migrant Labor Rights Enforcement." *Labor Studies Journal* 40 (1): 32–53. doi:10.1177/0160449x14565112

Bernhardt, Annette, Michael W. Spiller, and Diana Polson. 2013. "All Work and No Pay: Violations of Employment and Labor Laws in Chicago, Los Angeles and New York City." *Social Forces* 91 (3): 725–746. doi:10.1093/sf/sos193

Botein, Hilary. 2007. "Labor Unions and Affordable Housing." *Urban Affairs Review* 42 (6): 799–822. doi:10.1177/1078087407299595

Bruno, Robert, Alison Dickson Quesada, and Frank Manzo. 2012. "Clean Cars, Dirty Work: Worker Rights Violations in Chicago Car Washes." Report. Urbana, IL: School of Labor and Employment Relations, University of Illinois at Urbana-Champaign. http://bit.ly/2ogcANX

Burgoon, Brian, Janice Fine, Wade Jacoby, and Daniel Tichenor. 2010. "Immigration and the Transformation of American Unionism." *International Migration Review* 44 (4): 933–973. doi:10.1111/j.1747-7379.2010.00831.x

Capps, Randy, Michael Fix, and Chiamaka Nwosu. 2015. "A Profile of Immigrants in Houston, the Nation's Most Diverse Metropolitan Area." Report. Washington, DC: Migration Policy Institute. http://bit.ly/2ogCill

Casares, Cindy. 2012 (Aug. 9). "Why the Houston Janitor Strike Was Historic." *Texas Observer*. http://bit.ly/2ocQ8oK

Cordero-Guzmán, Héctor R., Pamela A. Izvănariu, and Victor Narro. 2013. "The Development of Sectoral Worker Center Networks." *Annals of the American Academy of Political and Social Science* 647 (1): 102–123. doi:10.1177/0002716212474647

Dean, Amy B., and David B. Reynolds. 2009. *A New New Deal: How Regional Activism Will Reshape the American Labor Movement*. Ithaca, NY: Cornell University Press.

de Graauw, Els. 2016. *Making Immigrant Rights Real: Nonprofits and the Politics of Integration in San Francisco*. Ithaca, NY: Cornell University Press.

de Graauw, Els, and Shannon Gleeson. 2016. "An Institutional Examination of the Local Implementation of the DACA Program." New York, NY: Baruch College, CUNY. Center for Nonprofit Strategy and Management Working Papers Series. http://bit.ly/2oc2luC

de Graauw, Els, and Shannon Gleeson. 2017. "Context, Coalitions, and Organizing: Immigrant Labor Rights Advocacy in San Francisco and Houston." In *The City Is the Factory: New Solidarities and Spatial Strategies in an Urban Age*, edited by Miriam Greenberg and Penny Lewis, pp. 80–98. Ithaca, NY: Cornell University Press.

Délano, Alexandra. 2011. *Mexico and Its Diaspora in the United States: Policies of Emigration Since 1848*. New York, NY: Cambridge University Press.

Fine, Janice. 2006. *Worker Centers: Organizing Communities at the Edge of the Dream.* Ithaca, NY: ILR Press.

Fine, Janice, and Daniel J. Tichenor. 2012. "Solidarities and Restrictions: Labor and Immigration Policy in the United States." *The Forum* 10 (1): 1–21. doi:10.1515/1540-8884.1495

Gleeson, Shannon. 2009. "From Rights to Claims: The Role of Civil Society in Making Rights Real for Vulnerable Workers." *Law & Society Review* 43 (3): 669–700. doi:10.1111/j.1540-5893.2009.00385.x

Gleeson, Shannon. 2012. *Conflicting Commitments: The Politics of Enforcing Immigrant Worker Rights in San Jose and Houston.* Ithaca, NY: Cornell University Press.

Greenhouse, Steven. 2000 (Feb. 17). "Labor Urges Amnesty for Illegal Immigrants." *New York Times.* https://nyti.ms/2xXj4G5

Griffith, Kati L. 2011. "ICE Was Not Meant to Be Cold: The Case for Civil Rights Monitoring of Immigration Enforcement at the Workplace." *Arizona Law Review* 53 (4): 1137–1156. http://bit.ly/2og0aW6

Griffith, Kati L. 2015. "Worker Centers and Labor Law Protections: Why Aren't They Having Their Cake?" *Berkeley Journal of Employment & Labor Law* 36 (2): 331–349. http://bit.ly/2olSbHl

Hall, Matthew, and Emily Greenman. 2014. "The Occupational Cost of Being Illegal in the United States: Legal Status, Job Hazards, and Compensating Differentials." *International Migration Review* 49 (2): 406–442. doi:10.1111/imre.12090

Hamlin, Rebecca. 2008. "Immigrants at Work: Labor Unions and Non-Citizen Members." In *Civic Hopes and Political Realities: Immigrants, Community Organizations, and Political Engagement,* edited by S. Karthick Ramakrishnan and Irene Bloemraad, pp. 300–322. New York, NY: Russell Sage Foundation.

Hill, Laura E., and Hans P. Johnson. 2011. *Unauthorized Immigrants in California: Estimates for Counties.* San Francisco, CA: Public Policy Institute of California.

Hirsch, Barry T., and David A. Macpherson. 2017. "Union Membership and Coverage Database from the CPS." Atlanta, GA; and San Antonio, TX: Georgia State University and Trinity University. www.unionstats.com

Katz, Mitchell H. 2008. "Golden Gate to Health Care for All? San Francisco's New Universal-Access Program." *New England Journal of Medicine* 358 (4): 327–329. doi:10.1056/nejmp0706590

Lerner, Stephen, and Jono Shaffer. 2015 (Jun. 16). "25 Years Later: Lessons from the Organizers of Justice for Janitors." *The Nation.* http://bit.ly/2HtdOOA

Lydersen, Kari. 2009. *Revolt on Goose Island: The Chicago Factory Takeover, and What It Says About the Economic Crisis.* New York, NY: Melville House Publishing.

Martin, Nina. 2012. "'There Is Abuse Everywhere': Migrant Nonprofit Organizations and the Problem of Precarious Work." *Urban Affairs Review* 48 (3): 389–416. doi:10.1177/1078087411428799

McLaughlin, Eliott C. 2017 (May 9). "ACLU Issues 'Travel Alert' After Texas Sanctuary Cities Law Signed." *CNN.* http://cnn.it/2CvMNGu

Migration Policy Institute. 2014. "National and County Estimates of Populations Eligible for DAPA and DACA Programs, 2009–2013." Washington, DC: Migration Policy Institute/Data Hub. https://www.migrationpolicy.org/sites/default/files/datahub/County-DACA-DAPA-Estimates-Spreadsheet-FINAL.xlsx

The National Black Worker Center Project: Grappling with the Power-Building Imperative

Steven C. Pitts
UC Berkeley Labor Center

Power concedes nothing without a demand. It never did and it never will.

Frederick Douglass

INTRODUCTION

During the summer of 2015, the Bay Area Black Worker Center (BABWC) set up a table at the job fair hosted by the Allen Temple Baptist Church in Oakland, California. The staff prepared to distribute flyers and conduct brief surveys with the expectation that the vast majority of attendees would be jobless. However, the majority of attendees *had* jobs; they were there to find a *good* job. The tremendous need for jobs that paid well and provided benefits illustrates an overlooked dimension of the Black job crisis. While the dominant narrative about Black employment issues focuses on unemployment, *the reality of Black employment issues is that even though a large number of Black workers are employed, the quality of those jobs is poor.*

As BABWC continued its organizing and explored the employment challenges faced by its members, it found that the incarceration history of many individuals constrained their employment options. Some had been on jobs for a long time, but when the employer learned they were formerly incarcerated, they were terminated. Others were deterred by the employment application's question about any history of incarceration. Still others found that California's impressive legislation reducing some felony convictions to misdemeanor offenses did not benefit them because their felony convictions were not on the list of felonies to be reclassified. This led BABWC to form a coalition demanding that the Alameda County Board of Supervisors directly hire formerly incarcerated individuals into county government jobs. This successful campaign reflected another element of the Black job crisis: *solutions to the crisis must go beyond efforts at individual uplift and structurally transform employers' (public and private) hiring decisions.*

The root cause of the Black job crisis lies in the lack of collective power held by Black workers. This lack of power results in the durability of racial gaps in labor-market outcomes despite changing political–economic structures. For example, in 1973—before recessions wrecked the Rust Belt, the ratio of Black-to-White unemployment rates (using a three-month average to smooth out any monthly volatility) was 2.17. In 1986, after the back-to-back recessions of the late 1970s and early 1980s, the ratio was 2.43. In 2007, prior to the Great Recession, the ratio was 2.02. In 2017, the ratio was 1.96. This durability reflects the reality that Black workers don't have the collective power to engage a changing economy in ways that reduce racialized outcomes. Therefore, addressing the Black job crisis requires building the capacity to overcome the structural obstacles facing Black workers. This is the power-building imperative.[1]

Equally important, the need to build power must include recognition that structural racism is fundamentally intertwined with the existing political economy: race shapes the development of the political economy, and the political economy shapes the development of race. In his study of Blacks in Norfolk, Virginia, Earl Lewis said Black workers in the shipyard had a "racialized class consciousness": the occupational structure reflected class relationships needed by the elites to run the shipyard; at the same time, that structure was forged given the racial hierarchy of the times. Blacks had the worst jobs and Whites had the better-quality jobs.[2] This interweaving of race and political economy always exists. Unfortunately, dominant narratives about structural racism tend to sever its connection to political economy, resulting in sterile debates about "race" versus "class" and political organizing that fails to recognize class differences within the Black community. Equally important, the uncoupling of race and political economy results in the failure to understand the need to simultaneously fight for racial democracy *and* fight to transform the relationship between labor and capital.

The National Black Worker Center Project (NBWCP), a national network of which BABWC is an affiliate, is an effort to fulfill the power-building imperative. It aims to build power for Black workers and, implicitly, challenge the weaknesses of past approaches to achieve Black economic justice. This chapter highlights the efforts of NBWCP and its affiliates to address the Black job crisis. More than a chronicling of events, activities, and campaigns, this chapter uses the experiences of the network to elucidate the challenges of dealing with the imperative of power building. The crucial issues facing Black workers—unemployment, low-wage work, and discriminatory treatment on the job—result from the confluence of several structural forces. These labor-market outcomes will not change until Black workers amass sufficient power to transform these structures.

Next, the chapter presents an overview of the Black job crisis, which contains some data on the labor-market status of Black workers. It then provides a broader historical context of civil society and Black worker organizing that has taken place outside of NBWCP. After chronicling the efforts of NBWCP and its affiliates, I discuss key challenges and opportunities facing Black worker organizing in the immediate period going forward.

THE BLACK JOB CRISIS: AN OVERVIEW

The challenges facing Black communities in the United States are fundamentally challenges facing the Black working class. This statement is not to deny the very real issues of structural racism that affect Blacks regardless of class: Blacks who drive municipal buses experience racial discrimination as do Blacks who control financial portfolios. However, the vast majority of Blacks are workers who have very little control over their working conditions; this differs from the experience of members of the Black professional or managerial classes and certain Black businesspeople.

In addition, the specific challenges facing Black men and Black women are rooted in specific political economies. The challenges facing Black men in old industrial cities such as Gary, Indiana, are different compared with the challenges they might face in an economically thriving region such as the Bay Area. The challenges facing Black women in a city with rapidly changing racial demographics such as Los Angeles are different from the challenges they confront in a city severely impacted by climate change, such as Houston.

The notion that the Black job crisis is rooted in specific political economies means the current position and historical trajectory of the Black working class is qualitatively different from that of other working-class communities including (somewhat obviously) the White working class but also (not as obvious to many) other working-class communities of color. With respect to the latter, there are tendencies to assume that, because workers of color face racism, there should be an automatic sense of solidarity. In addition, there are tendencies to compare the political struggles of Black workers with those of immigrant workers as if the strategies used by immigrant workers are the yardstick against which all worker struggles should be measured. Both tendencies fail to be rooted in the concrete experiences of the communities in question and impede the development of the requisite power needed to transform the quality of life faced by workers.

Today's economic expansion is just the latest phase of the Age of Inequality—the period since the mid-1970s that has been marked by rising inequality and flat wages for most workers. These outcomes have been shaped by the changing nature of technology that has radically lowered transportation and informational costs of production, the changing relationship between finance and production, and the changing power dynamic between labor and capital. In this context, the Black job crisis can be characterized as a two-dimensional crisis of unemployment and low-quality work. This framework is important because the dominant framework is a near-exclusive focus on unemployment. Flowing from this narrow approach, strategies involving policy advocacy, organizing, and resource allocation target Black joblessness instead of addressing the real issue of low-wage work.

Some Data on Black Workers

This section first focuses on the unemployment picture by examining the basic unemployment rate and the employment–population ratio. Then, the focus shifts to the Black employment picture, presenting data on the industrial distribution of employment for Black workers, a portrait of Black low-wage work, and Blacks in unions. The section concludes by exploring issues of work, Black immigrants, and Black intra-racial inequality.

Before looking at the data, it is important to understand the limitations of data with respect to the power-building imperative. First, the data describing the various positions of Black workers in the labor market are the *outcome* of a variety of political and economy processes. Far too often, data are presented and analyzed as if the data exist outside of specific political economies. But just seeing racial disparities in unemployment or wages does not help the observer understand the precise ways race and political economy combine to produce those disparities. Similarly, just seeing the distribution of wages across industries or the wage premium earned by union workers relative to their non-union counterparts does not allow the observer to understand how power shapes the determination of wages. The pursuit of data cannot be undertaken outside of the social context that produces that data. Second, power building (and power wielding) is a function of relationships among groups and the strategic use of those relationships to impact a specific target. While data may paint a picture of a set of workers linked by common labor-market outcomes, the basic labor-market data usually presented provide limited clues as to how race, political economy, and on-the-ground relationships shape power asymmetries.

Figures 1, 2, and 3 present data on the joblessness dimension of the Black job crisis. Figure 1 reveals the widely understood racial disparity in unemployment.[3,4] The ratio of Black unemployment to White unemployment averaged 2.4 in the 1980s, 2.3 in the 1990s, 2.2 in the 2000s, and 2.2 between 2010 and 2016. What is not widely understood is that the highest annual unemployment rate for Whites was 7.2% in 2010; during only six years did the lowest annual unemployment rate for Blacks fall under 7.2%.

FIGURE 1
Unemployment Rate: Black and White, 1979–2016

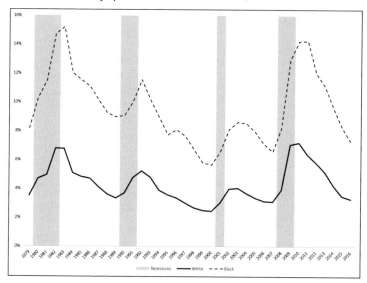

Note: Shaded vertical bars represent recessionary periods.
Source: Author's analysis of Bureau of Labor Statistics data.

FIGURE 2
Employment–Population Ratio: Black and White (ages 16–64), 1979–2016

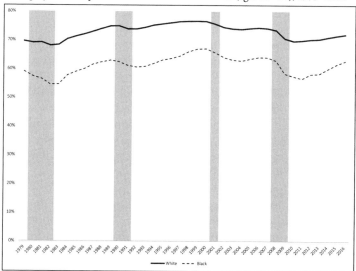

Note: Shaded vertical bars represent recessionary periods.
Source: Author's analysis of Bureau of Labor Statistics data.

FIGURE 3

Employment–Population Ratio: Black Women and Black Men (ages 16–64), 1979–2016

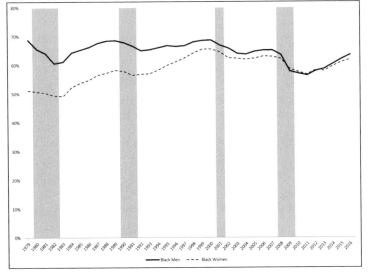

Note: Shaded vertical bars represent recessionary periods.
Source: Author's analysis of Bureau of Labor Statistics data.

(Note: the time trends of the two data series mirror one another. This is important because it captures the reality that Black and White workers experience similar and dissimilar fates in the labor market.) One shortcoming of the narrow racial disparity framework whereby everything is viewed through the lens of racial difference is that the framework glosses over those instances where changes in the political economy affect workers of all races.

Figure 2 presents a better measure of joblessness. As a measure of joblessness, the official unemployment rate has many weaknesses, chief among them the fact that the metric is a function of an individual's participation in the labor force. The employment–population ratio is a better measure of joblessness or, more precisely, employment probabilities. The ratio captures the proportion of the working-age population that is employed. As expected, Figure 2 shows that Whites have greater employment probabilities relative to Blacks. Once again, for the most part, the two data series move in tandem between 1979 and 2016. Recessions appear to cause a sharper decline in the employment–population ratio for Blacks than for Whites.

What is noticeable about the gender comparison within the Black population presented in Figure 3 is the convergence of the employment–

population ratios beginning in the mid-1990s, as the employed share of the Black female population rose at a faster rate than did the employed share of the Black male population. It is important to note that this ratio examines the civilian noninstitutionalized population, and so any interaction among gender, race, and incarceration would only come into play with post-incarceration employment prospects.

The six following tables present data on the other aspect of the Black job crisis: low-wage work. Table 1 presents data on where Black workers work: the industrial distribution of Black employment.[5] This is important because most policy interventions focus on industries. This chart and the four that follow it present a picture of the gender distinction with respect to employment within Black workers. While the public sector is an important employment niche for Black men and Black women, it is much more important for Black women compared with Black men. In addition, employment in the health care sector is key for Black women and not that important for Black men.

TABLE 1
Industrial Distribution of Black Employment
(pooled data: 2011–2016)

Industry	Men	Women	All
Public sector	15.6%	21.8%	18.9%
Health care and social services	7.5%	27.9%	18.4%
Professional and business services	11.5%	8.2%	9.7%
Retail trade	10.3%	9.2%	9.7%
Manufacturing	12.9%	5.4%	8.9%
Leisure and hospitality	7.6%	6.9%	7.2%
Transportation and utilities	10.6%	2.7%	6.4%
Financial activities	4.9%	6.9%	6.0%
Other services	4.3%	3.8%	4.1%
Construction	5.9%	0.5%	3.0%
Educational services	2.1%	3.6%	2.9%
Information	2.5%	1.9%	2.2%
Wholesale trade	3.1%	1.0%	2.0%
Agriculture and mining	1.2%	0.2%	0.6%
Total	**100.0%**	**100.0%**	**100.0%**

Source: Center for Economic and Policy Research, extract of Current Population Survey Outgoing Rotation Group (CPS ORG).

TABLE 2
Industrial Distribution of Black Employment, Rankings
(pooled data: 2011–2016)

Industry	Men	Women	All
Public sector	1	2	1
Health care and social services	7	1	2
Professional and business services	3	4	3
Retail trade	5	3	4
Manufacturing	2	7	5
Leisure and hospitality	6	5	6
Transportation and utilities	4	10	7
Financial activities	9	6	8
Other services	10	8	9
Construction	8	13	10
Educational services	13	9	11
Information	12	11	12
Wholesale trade	11	12	13
Agriculture and mining	14	14	14

Source: Center for Economic and Policy Research, extract of Current Population
Survey Outgoing Rotation Group (CPS ORG).

Table 2 paints a sharper portrait of these differences. Health care is the
seventh most important sector for Black male employment, while it is the
leading sector for Black women. Manufacturing is the second leading
employer of Black men but only the seventh leading employer for Black
women. Thus, public policies targeting specific industries are not gender
neutral with respect to impact: interventions to protect and strengthen jobs
in health care impact Black women more than Black men; conversely,
interventions designed to affect manufacturing impact Black men more
than Black women.

Tables 3 and 4 illustrate how concentrated Black female employment is
relative to the concentration of Black male employment. The three leading
sectors of employment for Black women capture 58.9% of all Black women
workers. For Black men, the three leading sectors capture 40.0% of Black
male workers. (Examining the three leading employers of Black women,
just 33.4% of Black male workers are in those sectors; examining the three
leading employers of Black men, 35.4% of Black women work in those
sectors; see Table 1.) The five leading sectors of employment for Black women
capture 74.0% of all Black women workers; the five leading sectors of Black
male employment capture 61.0% of all Black male workers.

TABLE 3
Top Five Industries, Black Women
(pooled data: 2011–2016)

Industry	Share
Health care and social services	27.9%
Public sector	21.8%
Retail trade	9.2%
Professional and business services	8.2%
Leisure and hospitality	6.9%

TABLE 4
Top Five Industries, Black Men
(pooled data: 2011–2016)

Industry	Share
Public sector	15.6%
Manufacturing	12.9%
Professional and business services	11.5%
Transportation and utilities	10.6%
Retail trade	10.3%

Source: Center for Economic and Policy Research, extract of Current Population Survey Outgoing Rotation Group (CPS ORG).

TABLE 5
Industrial Distribution of Employment by Nativity
(pooled data: 2011–2016)

Industry	Total	Foreign Born	Native Born
Public sector	18.9%	11.3%	20.2%
Health care and social services	18.4%	27.2%	16.9%
Professional and business services	9.7%	9.6%	9.8%
Retail trade	9.7%	9.4%	9.8%
Manufacturing	8.9%	7.2%	9.2%
Leisure and hospitality	7.2%	7.1%	7.3%
Transportation and utilities	6.4%	8.4%	6.1%
Financial activities	6.0%	5.5%	6.1%
Other services	4.1%	5.0%	3.9%
Construction	3.0%	3.3%	3.0%
Educational services	2.9%	2.7%	2.9%
Information	2.2%	1.5%	2.3%
Wholesale trade	2.0%	1.6%	2.0%
Agriculture and mining	0.6%	0.4%	0.7%

Source: Center for Economic and Policy Research, extract of Current Population Survey Outgoing Rotation Group (CPS ORG).

Because Black immigrants constitute a rising share of all Black workers, Table 5 presents a comparison of the industrial distribution of employment for native-born and foreign-born Black workers. With the exception of the public sector's and health care's share of total employment, the distribution of the two groups of Black workers looks remarkably similar.

Table 6 illustrates Black low-wage work by industry for Black women and Black men. The first panel of data presents the share of workers in each

TABLE 6
Industrial Distribution of Low-Wage Black Employment
(pooled data: 2011–2016)

Industry	Low-Wage Share of Industry			Industry Share of All Low-Wage Work		
	Men	Women	All	Men	Women	All
Public sector	18.5%	23.4%	21.5%	9.4%	13.7%	11.9%
Agriculture and mining	34.6%	24.2%	33.2%	1.3%	0.1%	0.6%
Construction	25.4%	21.7%	25.0%	4.8%	0.3%	2.2%
Manufacturing	27.0%	35.7%	29.8%	11.3%	5.2%	7.8%
Wholesale trade	25.9%	32.4%	27.7%	2.6%	0.9%	1.6%
Retail trade	44.8%	58.0%	51.5%	15.0%	14.4%	14.7%
Transportation and utilities	28.1%	33.3%	29.3%	9.7%	2.4%	5.5%
Information	18.7%	22.3%	20.4%	1.5%	1.1%	1.3%
Financial activities	17.3%	18.7%	18.2%	2.8%	3.5%	3.2%
Professional and business services	35.3%	33.0%	34.3%	13.2%	7.3%	9.8%
Educational services	20.8%	24.6%	23.3%	1.4%	2.4%	2.0%
Health care and social services	29.0%	40.0%	37.9%	7.0%	30.1%	20.4%
Leisure and hospitality	59.5%	69.7%	64.8%	14.6%	13.1%	13.7%
Other services	38.2%	51.1%	44.7%	5.4%	5.3%	5.3%
Total	**30.8%**	**36.96%**	**34.12%**	**100.0%**	**100.0%**	**100.0%**

Source: Center for Economic and Policy Research, extract of Current Population Survey Outgoing Rotation Group (CPS ORG).

industry that receives low wages.[6] In the public sector, 21.5% of all workers received $12.45 or less. We see that a greater share of Black women work for low wages (37.0%) compared with Black men (30.8%). The second panel presents each industry's share of total low-wage work. Low-wage workers in the public sector constitute 11.9% of all low-wage Black workers. Gender disparities in the second panel reflect the differential treatment within industries and the different industrial distributions of employment presented in Tables 1 through 4. For instance, the fact that 30.1% of low-wage Black women workers are in health care reflects that 40.0% of Black women in health care are low-wage workers (the first panel) and the fact that health care is the largest employer of Black women (1 3).

Figures 4 and 5 present data on special elements of Black work. Commentators are recognizing that the decline in unionization is a cause of the rising income inequality since the mid-1970s. Figure 4 shows how Black workers are impacted by this decline. The figure presents data on union density—the share of workers who are union members. In 1983, 36.4% of Black male workers were union members; the corresponding figure for Black women was 25.8%. These figures began to converge, so by 2016,

FIGURE 4
Black Union Membership Rate, 1983–2016

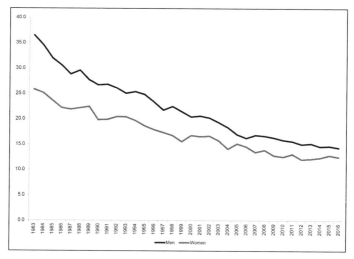

Source: Center for Economic and Policy Research, extract of Current Population
Survey Outgoing Rotation Group (CPS ORG).

FIGURE 5
Black Wages by Percentiles, 1979–2016

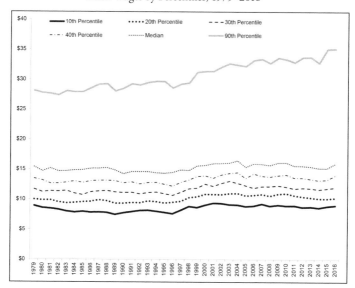

Source: Center for Economic and Policy Research, extract of Current Population
Survey Outgoing Rotation Group (CPS ORG).

the figures were 14.4% and 12.5%, respectively. (Overall, 31.0% of Black workers were union members in 1983 and 13.4% in 2016.)

Figure 5 presents data on Black intra-race wage inequality. Between 1979 and 2016, the median wage for Blacks in the lowest wage percentile rose by 0.7% ($8.94 to $9.00). For the 50th percentile (the overall median wage), the increase was 3.7% ($15.41 to $15.98), but for Black workers in the 90th percentile, the median wage grew by 24.8% ($28.12 to $35.08). Thus, the political and economic forces generating rising income inequality in the entire society have the same effect when examining just the Black community. These parallel trends raise a provocative question: if political advocates are increasingly clear on the damaging effects of rising income inequality on democracy in the United States, what are the effects of rising Black income inequality on Black politics?

BLACK WORKER ORGANIZING OUTSIDE OF THE NATIONAL BLACK WORKER CENTER PROJECT

A cursory glance at the history of Black activism reveals that whenever there has been a widely felt sense of Black activism, there has been a Black worker (or Black economic justice) manifestation of it. The first Great Black Migration (circa 1910–1930) triggered a radical change in Black civil society as Blacks left the rural South for urban destinations in the South, North, and West and caused what Joe William Trotter called "the proletarianization" of the Black community—the formation of an urban industrial Black working class.[7] As the new urban migrants interacted with established Black communities and forged a new world in the context of new racial hierarchies, a vigorous push for Black economic justice emerged. In many cities, residents began "Don't Buy Where You Can't Work" boycotts to force retail stores to end their discriminatory hiring practices. In 1935, Black organizers formed the National Negro Congress, and one of its main prongs of work was to build support in the Black community for the organizing conducted by the newly emerging industrial unions under the umbrella of the Congress of Industrial Organizations (CIO). Having successfully organized the Brotherhood of Sleeping Car Porters, A. Philip Randolph built the March on Washington Movement in 1940 to demand the federal government cease its discriminatory hiring practices. Under the threat of 100,000 marchers in Washington, D.C., President Roosevelt issued Executive Order 8802, which desegregated federal defense industries.

The second Great Black Migration (circa 1940–1970) envelops the Montgomery–Selma phase of the civil rights movement and the Black Power phase of that movement. While the traditional focus on the early years of the modern civil rights movement was on bus boycotts, Freedom Rides, and the struggle for voting rights, the period also saw significant campaigns for Black economic justice. Black unionists active in unions such as the Teamsters, the United Automobile Workers, the International Ladies' Garment Workers' Union, the United Steelworkers, and District 65 (a retail clerks' union) fought racial discrimination in their communities and in their unions. They formed the Negro American Labor Council and played a leading role in the March on Washington for Jobs and Freedom. Community activists fought against discrimination in hiring; in the construction arena, they developed the idea of "community control" of jobs (i.e., if development projects are taking place in the Black community, those jobs should go to community residents).

During the Black Power phase of the modern civil rights movement, Black workers in many unions formed caucuses to push for changes within their union. In addition, these years saw the increase in union organizing among Black workers as typified by the Memphis sanitation strike in 1968 and strikes among hospital workers in Charleston and Baltimore in 1969. On a broader scale, in response to the drift by A. Philip Randolph and Bayard Rustin to the political center—muting their criticism of the AFL-CIO and supporting US policy in Vietnam—and the overall conservatism of the AFL-CIO leadership, Black labor leaders formed the Coalition of Black Trade Unionists.

This relationship between Black civic activism and Black worker organizing continues today. In response to a spate of extra-judicial killings of Blacks, a vibrant Black Lives Matter movement arose. This activism sparked a variety of responses within the labor movement. The AFL-CIO established its Labor Commission on Racial and Economic Justice and held hearings on racism within unions around the country. The Service Employees International Union (SEIU) committed itself to becoming a racial justice organization. The United Food and Commercial Workers Union has supported efforts to restore a variety of rights for the formerly incarcerated. UNITE HERE has renewed efforts to address Black employment within the hotel industry. Several unions have endorsed an expanded use of collective bargaining under the umbrella of "Bargaining for the Racial Good." Outside the formal labor movement, the Fight for $15 has aggressively linked efforts to raise the wage in the fast food industry with efforts to fight police brutality. The Restaurant Opportunities Center has challenged racial segregation within the restaurant industry. The Organization United for Respect (OUR, formerly OUR Walmart) has deepened its racial justice work so that its members are more aware of racism felt by non-White Walmart workers. Groups in Chicago have fought anti-Black discrimination in temporary staffing agencies.

THE NATIONAL BLACK WORKER CENTER PROJECT

It is within this larger context that NBWCP has emerged as an effort to establish a network of local Black worker centers attempting to build power among Black workers in order to transform local conditions for Black workers and then leverage that power to have an impact nationally.

A Brief History of the National Black Worker Center Project

While NBWCP was constituted in 2014, the origins of its local affiliates have longer histories. One strand of activism emerging from the Black Power phase of the civil rights movement focused on organizing Blacks in the workplace as the central pathway toward Black liberation. Many young Black revolutionaries took it upon themselves to obtain jobs in factories or to use their professional skills in the direct service of the Black working class. From this milieu, the two oldest affiliates of NBWCP developed. The first, Black Workers for Justice (BWFJ) formed in 1981. Although based in Rocky Mount, North Carolina, its geographic focus was initially the entire state of North Carolina, and it eventually expanded its reach throughout parts of the South. Among its campaigns were efforts to form minority (nonmajority: where less than 50% of the workforce were members) unions in plants in North Carolina. It also supported the development of public sector unionism in the South in conjunction with United Electrical, Radio and Machine Workers of America. BWFJ recognized that Black working-class life did extend beyond the walls of the workplace, so it engaged in a variety of efforts to address the community interests of Black workers. Finally, BWFJ has worked with the Farm Labor Organizing Committee to promote solidarity between Black workers and the emerging Latino workforce in North Carolina. The second affiliate, the Mississippi Worker Center for Human Rights, was formed in Greenville, Mississippi, in 1995. Similar to BWFJ, the Mississippi Worker Center for Human Rights, while based in a small town, has a statewide focus. The worker center supported efforts to organize catfish workers in the state and has recently emphasized the enforcement of worker compensation laws as a way to improve the conditions facing workers throughout the state. In addition, the organization has been part of the progressive network in Mississippi.

The second period of Black worker center formation occurred between 2005 and today. The late 1990s through the early 2000s saw a rapid transformation of labor force demographics in the United States as immigration changed the composition of populations in most parts of the country. In response to these changes and the challenges facing these new workers, a vibrant worker center movement emerged. These new forms of worker organizations were largely focused on immigrant workers and their associated civil society and began to receive significant funds from philanthropy. At the same time, the Black job crisis continued to rage. Since the mid-1970s, the Black community was ravaged by deindustrialization, the crack epidemic, mass incarceration, and increasing attacks on a Black employment niche—the public sector. Yet a confluence of the particularities of anti-Black structural racism, transformations in Black civil society, and philanthropic indifference to Black organizing meant that there was not a growth in Black worker organizing similar to what occurred in immigrant communities.

However, a second wave of Black worker centers slowly emerged. In New Orleans, the devastation following Hurricane Katrina resulted in two shocks to the local labor market: large numbers of immigrants arrived to rebuild the city, and large numbers of Black workers found themselves initially displaced from the city and then, upon return, found themselves further marginalized in the labor market. The New Orleans Workers' Center for Racial Justice (NOWCRJ) formed initially to deal with the exploitation faced by immigrant workers, but quickly organizers found themselves needing to deal with the challenges facing returning Black workers. NOWCRJ initiated a special project called Stand with Dignity to deal with the special problems facing Black workers. Their first campaigns dealt with issues of public housing and the need to use federal housing monies to employ local residents.

In Los Angeles, Black organizers had been exposed to the vibrant immigrant worker center ecosystem and seen the possibilities of powerful Black workers organizing from their involvement in SEIU's security officers' organizing campaign, which intentionally projected the needs of Black security officers. Initially based out of the UCLA Labor Center, these organizers began to work with Black union leaders, staff, and members to analyze the possibilities of addressing the problems facing Black workers in Los Angeles, and the result was the Los Angeles Black Worker Center (LABWC), formed in 2009.

In Chicago, experienced labor and community organizers, responding to the twin impacts of a still-heavily racially segregated city and massive deindustrialization, began to explore forging new organizational forms that would be rooted in the city's Black working class. The result was the 2012 launch of the Workers Center for Racial Justice, with early campaigns examining employment practices associated with the expansion of the mass transit rail line on the city's South Side and a "Ban the Box" campaign that resulted with the state government removing from applications the check box that asks whether applicants have a criminal record.

In Washington, D.C., an organization emerging from the community development corporation movement transformed itself into a hub of organizing across a variety of issues. In the employment arena, ONE DC conducted campaigns around the right to income and racial equity in hiring on development projects. Around 2011, the organization began to explore the idea of forming a worker center as a component of the overall thrust of ONE DC, and its Black Workers Center was created. One unique feature of the work there was the combination of workforce development activity in conjunction with the Laborers' International Union of North America and the creation of a series of cooperatives.

With this Black worker center activism as a backdrop, NBWCP was created. During Phase One of this process, the UC Berkeley Center for Labor Research and Education (UCB Labor Center) incubated the organization. Specific outcomes were formalization of the organization with legal incorporation, including establishment of organizational bylaws and its inaugural board of directors; launch of two Black worker centers (the Bay Area in 2013 and Baltimore in 2016); organization of two major convenings of Black worker center staff, members, and supporters in Oakland (November 2014, November 2015). In 2015, Phase Two of the process began when the UCB Labor Center officially launched NBWCP, the organization became a fiscally sponsored project of the Movement Strategy Center (MSC), and MSC began to benefit from the funding relationships that had been cultivated by the UCB Labor Center. Most important, in July 2016, NBWCP hired its first executive director. This act led to an expansion of the funding base of the organization, an increase in staff for the organization, and the launch of its first major campaign—Working While Black—in Washington, D.C., in November 2016.

The Work of the National Black Worker Center Project

The work of NBWCP and its affiliates can be placed in three primary buckets:

- Building member-driven organizations
- Organizing and policy campaigns
- Changing the narrative

Building Member-Driven Organizations

Central to the functioning of the Black worker centers has been the development of member-driven organizations. Throughout NBWCP, several different activities have been used to identify potential members, including neighborhood canvassing, one-on-ones, information tables at various events, surveys, outreach at workforce development sites, and listening sessions. Often, these activities are not distinct but are seen as a progression of activities. For instance, having a table at particular events might lead to a one-on-one session with an organizer that might lead to an invitation to a listening session.

Once members have been identified and engaged in campaign work, member development activities include formation of street action teams so that members build community with each other during the campaign, member-engaged lobbying with key targets, involvement in other elements of the campaign work, political education sessions, and power-analysis training linked to the campaign in question.

Organizing and Policy Campaigns

Affiliates of NBWCP have been involved in a variety of organizing and policy campaigns that can be grouped into four areas: getting Black workers into good jobs, conducting broader policy fights, encouraging civic engagement, and exploring economic alternatives.

- *Getting Black workers into good jobs.* A major campaign undertaken by LABWC involved working in a broader coalition to impact the employment practices used by the Los Angeles County Metropolitan Transportation Authority as it expanded its rail system. Key policy planks included a project labor agreement to ensure good labor standards on the expansion, a local-hire provision so that Los Angeles residents could work on the expansion, and an innovative "diversity in hiring" provision so that Black workers would intentionally be included in the local hiring. As mentioned in the introduction to this chapter, BABWC was deeply involved in a coalition that successfully urged the Alameda County Board of Supervisors to pass and implement an ordinance that called for Alameda County to directly hire the formerly incarcerated into its county government jobs. This direct-hire approach is distinct from the "ban the box" approach inasmuch as the latter strives to lower the barriers to employment opportunities, while the former strives to result in direct employment opportunities. In Chicago, the Worker Center for Racial Justice has collaborated with UNITE HERE Local 1 to set up a hotel hiring hall. While this was not a classic hiring hall with a direct route into a hotel job, the partnership did open up a pathway into unionized hotel jobs for Blacks that heretofore had been closed.

- *Conducting broader policy fights.* As a second campaign, LABWC worked with other organizations in a coalition to increase labor standards enforcement. As they pushed the coalition to see that racial discrimination is a violation of basic labor standards ("employment discrimination is the ultimate form of wage theft"), they found out that state law did not sufficiently empower local entities to combat racial discrimination in employment. This sparked a campaign for a new state law correcting this oversight. The main partner with LABWC on this campaign was SEIU United Service Workers West. The resulting legislation—The California Anti-Employment Discrimination Action of 2017 (SB 491)—was passed by the California Assembly and Senate only to be vetoed by the governor. One of the earliest campaigns (2013) by the Worker Center for Racial Justice in Chicago was to join forces with other organizations in Illinois to get the governor to sign an executive order eliminating "the box" on applications for state jobs.

- *Encouraging civic engagement.* The civic engagement efforts of Black worker centers recognize that their vision to improve the lives of Black workers is not limited to workplace issues. Consistency requires attempts to improve the quality of life for the Black working class in and out of the workplace. Across the country, an important element of progressive activism has been the thrust to elect district attorneys with a reduced "law and order" mentality. In Chicago, the Worker Center for Racial Justice was active in the campaign to elect Kimberly Foxx as Cook County's district attorney in 2016. In New Orleans, the Stand with Dignity project approached the criminal justice issue from a different angle. In the midst of canvassing a local housing project, they ran across stories of many residents who could not obtain driver's licenses because of outstanding traffic fees. The worker center coordinated with local officials to host warrant clinics in the housing project that facilitated reduction of the fees. (In one case, $23,000 in fees and penalties was reduced to $9.)

- *Exploring economic alternatives.* Across NBWCP, some affiliates find that many of their initial members feel alienated from a political economy that devalues them as Black workers, and their response is a search for alternatives to the status quo. ONE DC is exploring the development of worker cooperatives. Two cooperatives already implemented are a child care cooperative and a cleaning cooperative. It's important to recognize co-op development within the organization's overall mission, which includes worker rights training, workforce development and job placement, and purchasing a building to house these activities.

Changing the Narrative

NBWCP and its affiliates recognize that a major component to building power is engaging in the battle to change the narratives around Black work and the Black job crisis. The dominant conservative narratives assume Blacks—as a group—lack the capacity to contribute to the US economy and that Blacks—once again as a group—assume some culpability for their subordinate position in the labor market. Dominant liberal narratives travel the spectrum along two themes: the role of individual behavior in racialized outcomes (relative to structural factors), and the role of state intervention and collective action in addressing the racialized outcomes. Neither set of narratives is sufficient to advance any qualitative solutions to the Black job crisis.

Given this, the primary national campaign of NBWCP has been Working While Black (WWB), a collaboration between the national office and local affiliates to gather stories from members, produce videos and other communication tools, and disseminate these stories. Any change in narrative surrounding the Black job crisis that challenges dominant narratives must be rooted in the experiences of Black workers. Therefore, WWB has been an effort to bolster the communications capacity of the affiliates, use this additional capacity to elicit member stories and campaign stories that provide a view of the Black job crisis "from below," and outline the efficacy of collective campaigns to address the crisis.

GOING FORWARD: KEY CHALLENGES FACING THE NATIONAL BLACK WORKER CENTER PROJECT

The challenges facing NBWCP can be grouped into two broad categories: developing vibrant local affiliates, and building the proper national "footprint."

Developing Vibrant Local Affiliates

In different degrees, each affiliate faces the interrelated problems of organizational development, sustainability and resources, scale and scope, and political education. It is important to recognize these challenges are faced by most emerging, small, and under-resourced worker centers regardless of the base of the organization. One can imagine an organizational life cycle trajectory where emerging organizations attempt to assume the functions of a maturing or mature organization with much less capacity. In this context, staff may be working without a job description or across multiple job descriptions; work plans might be, at best, loose parameters guiding the work; and norms and structures that support accountability within the organizations are weak. During the emerging phase, these challenges are amplified by limited financial resources and the reality that initial streams of revenue are either very small, tied to expectations that don't fully align with the actual needs of the organization, or both. Most NBWCP affiliates are in the early emergent phase of organizational growth.

In addition, these challenges are amplified by the reality that the affiliates are Black worker centers. This reality contains unrealistic expectations because emerging Black worker centers are improperly compared with immigrant worker centers across all phases of the organizational life cycle or they are quickly pigeon-holed into narrow workforce development efforts.

The dearth of philanthropic support of Black organizing over the past 20 years compared with the support of immigrant organizing means the networks and relationships that can support immigrant worker organizing as staff move along a variety of career paths that include organizer, lead organizer, different types of deputy directors, and executive director do not exist for Black worker organizing.

Linked to these issues are the issues of sustainability and financial resources. As noted previously, worker centers, and Black worker centers in particular, are under-resourced. While their work lies at the nexus of organizing and service delivery, the power-building imperative means that mainstream philanthropic resources and government support are difficult to acquire. The magnitude of the Black job crisis and some of the narrative surrounding worker centers ("filling the organizing gap where unions are not present") places immense pressures on Black worker centers to take on tasks that exceed the ability of available resources to successfully be tackled.

The gap between needs and capacity, the episodic nature of foundation support, and the push from many elements of philanthropy for "sustainable" revenue flows has led some Black worker centers to explore income-generating strategies. This is understandable—the bills must be paid—but it is important to remember that just as the failure of private markets to independently produce socially optimal amounts of certain goods like education and health care leads to the need for government intervention in the marketplace, a social system based on racial capitalism will never sustain efforts to support power building among Black workers. This is not a rationale for disengaging from the market system or maintaining funding streams dominated by philanthropy. It is a cautionary note that exhortations for sustainability without an explicit recognition of the challenges and limitations of doing so in this market economy fail the very constituencies who lie at the center of our concern.

An additional challenge involves the scale and scope of Black worker centers' programmatic thrusts. Within most geographically bounded networks, multiple organizations exist to satisfy the variety of needs of the fields: for example, multiple churches, mosques, and temples across several denominations address the faith needs of a region; several local unions address the diverse needs of workers in a region. However, the expectations—driven by a competition for scarce resources—are that one Black worker center can address the multiple dimensions of the Black job crisis in a particular region. The difficulty of this approach can be seen immediately when one considers, by way of an example, that New York City has a population of 8.6 million, with Blacks (native-born and immigrant) making up 24.4% of that total. Black worker centers (actually, all worker centers) must be allowed to grow within boundaries—geographic, sector, strata—

that make success more likely. This means developing organic connections with the Black working class based on deep organizing within designated targets and not developing into multiservice centers attempting to become a "Jack of all trades" with the associated implication of "master of none."

A final major challenge in this area lies in the arena of political education. While we "experience" race and capitalism in complicated, nuanced, and intertwined ways, we often "talk" about race and capitalism as if they are separate phenomena. These disconnects—between our experiences and our talk and between race and capitalism—manifest themselves in the activities of Black worker centers in a variety of ways. For example, often, the initial workers attracted to Black worker center activities have a strong racial consciousness and want to act against the racial discrimination they experience in a power hierarchy that is racially stratified. When key issues revolve around local hire, job access, and/or unemployment, some of these workers gravitate to the notion that the ultimate solution is "for us to hire our own people." A presentation of the problem that focuses on the racial disparity without linking the inequity to the dynamics of a market economy supports such solutions. The associated goals lead to strategies and tactics where key allies are no longer Black workers but rather the Black elite who have the requisite entrepreneurial resources and inclinations, along with government and corporate actors who have access to financial capital. To avoid this trajectory (and similar ones that are rooted in a disconnect between racism and capitalism), Black worker centers need political education efforts that are founded on members' experiences and that facilitate a learning process where members can see their experiences through a racialized political economic framework.

Building the Proper National "Footprint"

The ultimate strength of the modern civil rights movement and the expansion of the labor movement has been dynamic local activism. At the same time, the victories of those movements also were a function of a nationwide presence in a national narrative about social justice and in the national arenas where federal policies were determined. Consequently, a challenge facing NBWCP is how to address this dialectic in today's context. The historical trajectory of the network has correctly placed a great deal of weight on the importance of developing local Black worker centers. Still, if done properly, the synergy between local affiliates and a national center can be very powerful and enhance the implementation of the power-building imperative at both levels.

One question is what is the "value added" of the national to local work? If the value added is nonexistent, then the national federation will crumble as affiliates cease thinking of themselves (and more importantly, acting) as members of a national network. The notion of "value added" cannot be imposed from above. Local Black worker centers must see concrete ways that a well-resourced national center enhances their work. Some possibilities include a series of "communities of learning" where local experiences can be shared across affiliates or a set of capacity-building working groups (including a potential training institute) where members or staff from affiliates participate to advance their skills in specific areas (e.g., communications).

A second question is what are the appropriate national campaigns led by the national center? Related to that question, when should the national center initiate and lead a campaign with a federal target? In these campaigns, what is the appropriate expectation of the role of affiliates? When should the national campaign consist of coordinated local campaigns (e.g., several local Black worker centers advancing a similar policy campaign to target state legislatures)?

A third question: What is the effective relationship between the national center and other segments of the larger progressive movement? There is a very strong networking tendency among progressives. While this aggregation can be very powerful, it can also reallocate scarce resources away from essential power-building tasks. As the progressive movement grapples with the realization of the persistence of anti-Black racism and the need to fight it on several fronts, there is a tremendous demand on NBWCP (and other Black organizations) to enter into non-Black spaces. This activity is important. However, to approach these spaces with integrity and power, the activities must not overwhelm the need to deepen connections with the Black working class, forge dynamic Black worker centers locally, and build coalitions and networks that stitch together elements of Black civil society.

CONCLUSION

Probably the most critical problem in the Other America is the economic problem. By the millions, people in the Other America find themselves perishing on a lonely island of poverty in the midst of a vast ocean of prosperity. But the problem is not only unemployment, but it's UNDER employment or SUB employment. People who work full-time jobs for part-time wages.

Martin Luther King, Jr.

Just three weeks before he was assassinated, Dr. Martin Luther King, Jr., spoke before the Drug, Hospital, and Health Care Employees Union, District 1199 (commonly known as Local 1199—the predecessor union to today's 1199SEIU United Healthcare Workers East and the National Union of Hospital and Health Care Employees). The epigraph to this section, above, captures his characterization of "the economic problem": poor people facing unemployment and underemployment. His prescription accurately captures the Black job crisis today. King's final efforts—supporting the striking sanitation workers in Memphis and organizing the Poor People's Campaign—indicates he understood the need for the power-building imperative.

At the time of this writing (2018), residents of the United States face an extraordinary situation whereby the levers of federal power are controlled by political forces whose actions and words are hostile to core values of justice and equality. Simultaneously, around the country, bright rays of hope are emerging as people from all walks of life seek to re-assert those values. However, the success of these efforts depends on successfully merging an assertion of values with efforts to build power.

This chapter discussed efforts of the National Black Worker Center Project to build this power among Black workers. It described the Black job crisis in detail, sketched the linkages between broader Black community activism and Black worker activism, and discussed the efforts of NBWCP and its affiliates to address the Black job crisis through organizing Black workers. It closed by detailing the challenges facing these organizing efforts. Hopefully, the lessons here can be absorbed and applied as we attempt to forge what Dr. King and others called "the Beloved Community"

ACKNOWLEDGMENTS

I would like to thank Cherrie Bucknor, doctoral student in sociology at Harvard University, for providing the initial data analysis presented in this chapter.

ENDNOTES

[1] Earl Lewis, *In Their Own Interests: Race, Class and Power in Twentieth-Century Norfolk, Virginia* (Berkeley, CA: University of California Press, 1993).

[2] A full discussion of the power-building imperative is beyond the scope of this chapter, but a brief sketch of it entails the following: political organizing where the principal goal is building collective power not advancing individual advancement; political work that understands the dialectical relationship between service provision and member-driven organizing; and the understanding that movement-building requires building locally based membership organizations, developing a progressive narrative about social change, and forging a broad coalition around that progressive narrative.

[3] These (and subsequent racial) data are non-Hispanic Black and non-Hispanic White.

[4] The shaded vertical bars represent recessionary periods.

[5] This is in contrast to a focus on what Black workers do—the occupational distribution of Black employment—which is not presented in this chapter.

[6] Our analysis used two thirds of the overall median wage as the threshold for low wages; using these data, the median wage was $18.68 and the low-wage threshold was $12.45.

[7] Joe William Trotter, Jr., *Black Milwaukee: The Making of an Industrial Proletariat, 1915–45* (Urbana, IL: University of Illinois Press, 1985).

"Greedy" Institutions or Beloved Communities? Assessing the Job Satisfaction of Organizers

JANICE FINE

*School of Management and Labor Relations, Rutgers University,
and the Center for Innovation in Worker Organization*

HAHRIE HAN

University of California Santa Barbara

AARON C. SPARKS

Elon University

KYOUNG-HEE YU

University of Technology, Sydney[1]

INTRODUCTION

In June 2018, the Supreme Court issued a decision on *Janus v. AFSCME*, which eliminated the ability of labor unions to collect an agency fee from non-union members to cover the cost of collective bargaining. The decision has significant implications for the way many unions recruit and build their membership bases. This is thus an opportune moment to take stock of core union assets, in particular the professional organizers, who will be essential to preserving and expanding the membership base. Unlike most modern-day progressive organizations that depend on foundations and donors to support their efforts and recruit like-minded individuals to participate in campaigns, unions must rely on their own members (and thus the organizers who build that membership) for the vast majority of their funding. Unions are not able to pick and choose their members—they must persuade workers who have been selected by the employer to make the decision to join up, most often in the face of sophisticated and well-funded efforts to discourage them from doing so. Employers resist unionization because they do not want workers to have their own independent bases of power in the workplace. For unions, the source of that power comes from their ability to build an active membership base, and a set of committed leaders who are willing and able to act collectively.

At the core of every anti-union campaign is the attempt to *other* the union, portraying it as an alien third party. Fundamentally, professional organizers have to seed a consciousness and build a community in the workplace through intensive one-on-one relational organizing conversations and concerted leadership identification and development. They must drive the campaign through systematically building worker support for the union by identifying and recruiting key workplace leaders and providing the training and support necessary for them to recruit their colleagues and stand up to the anti-union deluge that is certain to come. The work does not end when a union campaign is won. It is the organizer's role to work with leaders to embed a union culture at the workplace where workers are in relationship with each other and comfortable with exercising their collective power to defend conditions of work and improve them over time. The work entails establishing a dynamic organization that is compelling to members to want to take part in, working with a leadership group that is always thinking about how to deepen and broaden worker identification and engagement. Union organizing is incredibly creative and rewarding work, but it is also extremely challenging.

Despite the importance of organizers to building, preserving, and expanding union membership and helping unions achieve their core purpose, we have only limited research on the factors that affect organizers' ongoing satisfaction with and commitment to their jobs (notable exceptions are Bunnage 2014 and Rooks 2004). Existing research focuses on job satisfaction among people who do "careers as calling," including those who do "justice jobs," or jobs focusing on service provision to underserved communities (Rooks 2004). While there are undoubtedly parallels, that research does not examine job satisfaction in relation to the power-building purpose of careers such as organizing. Understanding the factors that shape job satisfaction among organizers helps us understand some of the broader struggles unions and other organizations have had related to building power to achieve their goals.

This chapter draws on survey data to examine the job satisfaction and occupational challenges of career organizers, particularly as related to the power-building purposes of unions. We present original data from a 2015 survey of 570 participants in events surrounding the AFL-CIO Organizing Institute's 25th anniversary. Founded in 1990, the Organizing Institute is a center within the AFL-CIO whose mission is to help recruit and train organizers for affiliated unions. In March 2015, the Organizing Institute hosted a National Organizers Workshop in Washington, D.C., bringing together union and non-union organizers from across the country as part of a series of events celebrating its 25th anniversary. We worked in partnership with the Organizing Institute to design and conduct a survey of the organizers invited to the conference. We examine this data in light of a systematic review of existing literature to predict job satisfaction in organizing as a function of the lived experience of organizers in the context of their jobs and organizations.

Overall, we find that a significant percentage of organizers are not spending the bulk of their time on the core tasks associated with power building (such as recruiting and developing leaders) and, relatedly, that those key power-building tasks are the ones they find most challenging. In addition, we find that organizers report challenges related to management, supervision, and other job characteristics, and that these challenges are felt disproportionately by women. These findings thus point to clear, actionable ways in which organizing jobs can be changed to improve the trajectory and experience of organizers in a way that could also orient them more toward the core work of building power. We discuss these implications in the conclusion.

ORGANIZERS AT THE CENTER OF THE LABOR MOVEMENT

From at least the 1930s to the present day, full-time organizers have played crucial roles in unions, leading unionization efforts and contract fights. Years of militant action and membership gains led by organizers and rank-and-file leaders characterized the 1930s and 1940s. Long-running ideological warfare within the New Deal coalition and the labor movement itself, however, culminated with the 1947 Taft–Hartley law. Requiring all trade unionists to sign affidavits declaring that they were not Communists, this law led to a wholesale purge of many talented and committed organizers and rank-and-file activists (Goldfield 1989; Lichtenstein 2002). The depoliticization of the movement during this period presaged an acute loss of power from the late 1970s onward. In the 1980s, the Reagan administration's famous busting of PATCO, the air-traffic controllers' union, chilled unions and exacerbated this ongoing loss of power for the movement (McCartin 2006).

Nevertheless, even throughout these difficult years, unions have continued to mount organizing drives and contract fights and to employ large numbers of full-time organizers (McCartin, this volume; Windham 2017). In the 1990s and 2000s, labor experienced a revival of interest from activists in the progressive movement. An influx of post-1960s organizers with strong social justice ideals went to work for labor unions, some of which had grown bureaucratic and distanced from their militant roots (Fantasia and Voss 2004; Ganz et al. 2004; Voss and Milkman 2004; Voss and Sherman 2000; Zald and Ash 1966). They also brought significant skills to movement work (Compa 2004).

Data shows that approximately 6.7% of private sector workers and 12% of public sector workers are unionized in the present day, although union density varies dramatically between states (Hirsch and Macpherson 2017). Although unionization rates have declined dramatically since the 1980s, approximately 14 million American workers still belong to unions. Further, alt-labor organizations, such as worker centers and labor/community coalitions, have expanded their reach in recent years. In alt-labor, a 2018 census of worker centers (for this volume) identified 226 organizations, in addition to the 41 and 17 affiliates, respectively, that the community/labor coalitions Jobs With Justice and Partnership for Working Families have (Fine and Theodore 2012;

Jobs With Justice 2016; Partnership for Working Families 2015). Unions, along with social movement organizations, are thus still formidable institutions with substantial budgets and staff that continually recruit and employ professional organizers in significant numbers at the national, state, and local levels.

Organizing has been at the center of recent debates about the direction of the labor movement. During the 1990s, the AFL-CIO experienced its first contested election in the history of the federation, in which the "organizing" candidate, John Sweeney, president of the Service Employees International Union (SEIU), was victorious. A decade later, its affiliates engaged in a pitched battle over the strategic direction and leadership of the movement. The need for unions to focus more effort and resources on organizing figured prominently at both junctures.

In 1995, as part of its program for revitalization, the AFL-CIO established the Organizing Institute to recruit and train organizers for its affiliated unions. The Organizing Institute established a pipeline for students and other activists to enter the labor movement. Despite the strenuous efforts of the Sweeney administration, only six unions made a substantial commitment to organizing. The rest—whether as a consequence of the high cost; internal politics; gender, racial, and ethnic disparities between existing leaders and members and the unorganized; and other internal structural and cultural factors, or some combination—did not move organizing the unorganized to the center of their work (Milkman and Voss 2004). In 2005, a set of unions led by SEIU split from the AFL-CIO. Calling themselves Change to Win, five AFL-CIO member unions (SEIU, UNITE HERE, the Laborers, the Teamsters, and the United Food and Commercial Workers) that were disappointed in the lack of progress made by the federation in reversing labor's decline, pushed for a near-total redefinition of the AFL-CIO's role, which, they argued, was necessary to stimulate a return to large-scale worker organizing. Established through the merger of the American Federation of Labor and the Congress of Industrial Organizations in 1955, the AFL-CIO was set up as a voluntary coalition with little formal power over its affiliated unions. Change to Win proposed to streamline the federation while also giving it substantial power over member unions, with particular emphasis on the need for each union to focus its organizing efforts on a strategic economic sector—its "core industry." While unable to fulfill its vision, over the years, Change to Win has focused the great majority of its staff and resources on strengthening the strategic organizing and research capacities of affiliates.

DESCRIBING THE EXPERIENCES AND CHALLENGES OF ORGANIZERS

Despite the importance of organizers and organizing to the labor movement, there has been only a limited set of studies about the experience of organizers.

Although a handful of qualitative studies have emerged (Rooks 2004; Schurman 2005), there are, to our knowledge, no large-scale studies of organizers' job experiences and satisfaction. Not only do we lack an empirical picture, we also lack a theoretical one; industrial relations theory provides little guidance in theorizing the relationship between organizers' individual aspirations and organizational roles and structures. We can draw some ideas from the literature on "careers as calling" because organizers are also motivated by a commitment to helping others, feel morally compelled to do what they do, and make significant sacrifices as a result. Organizing is also, however, a distinct occupation. Unlike in other professions, organizers work toward systemic solutions to social problems by working with people who are directly affected by them to build organizations and take action.

To fill this gap and provide a picture of the unique experience of organizers in the United States, we worked in partnership with the Organizing Institute to field an original survey in March 2015 of approximately 700 union and non-union organizers from around the country. The goal of the survey was to examine the day-to-day experiences and perspectives of organizers, to deepen our understanding of what the experience of organizing is like, and to enable organizations to make better strategic choices about how to recruit, train, and retain professional organizers. The survey asked a range of questions, including questions about pathways into organizing, job satisfaction, the day-to-day experience of organizing, respondents' perspectives on what elements of the job were most challenging, and demographics. The survey was conducted online. All registrants were invited to complete the survey in the month prior to the conference, and extensive outreach was carried out at the conference itself so that those who had not done it ahead of time could do it at the conference. As a result of diligent efforts by digital organizers prior to the conference and conference staff working with the Organizing Institute, just under four hundred organizers completed the survey online prior to the conference; an additional two hundred organizers completed it at the conference. In the end, we had 570 respondents, representing more than 80% of the total number of people who attended the conference.

Table 1 shows some basic descriptive data on our respondents: 65% of our respondents were full-time, paid organizers, and 67% worked for labor unions. Approximately equal proportions of men and women completed the survey, with about 1.7% of respondents reporting that they were gender nonconforming. Our sample also had relatively high rates of racial diversity. Fifty-two percent self-identified as White, 15% as African American, 18% as Latino, 9.8% as other or mixed race, and 5% as Asian. The majority of our respondents were either college graduates or had some college education. Our respondents ranged in age from 20 to 72, with the median age being 37. Among our respondents,

TABLE 1
Descriptive Statistics for Key Independent Variables

Variable	Percentage
Type of Organization	
Labor union	67%
Community organization	8%
Multi-stakeholder organization	3%
Multi-issue campaign organization	5%
Worker center	8%
Issue organization	1%
Electoral campaign	1%
Other	8%
Gender Distribution	
Female	48%
Race Distribution	
White	52%
Black	15%
Hispanic	18%
Asian	5%
Other/mixed race	10%
Education Level	
Less than high school	2%
High school graduate/GED	8%
Some college	23%
College graduate/BA	43%
Some graduate work	8%
Graduate degree	16%
Number of Years Organizing	
Less than 1 year	10%
1–3 years	19%
4–6 years	20%
7–9 years	13%
10 or more years	37%
Median Age	37 years

9.8% had been in organizing for less than one year, 19% for one to three years, 20% for four to six years, 13% for seven to nine years, and 37% for more than ten years.

We do not have a good way of knowing how representative our sample is of organizers working across the country because there is not any such census of organizers. There is potential bias in our sample based on who self-selected to attend the Organizing Institute's conference. Nonetheless, despite bias that may exist, our data provides an important glimpse into the experience of a diverse group of union and non-union organizers across the country.

The best way to understand the day-to-day experience of organizing is to examine the way organizers spend their time. Overall, as shown in Figure 1, we find that organizers largely have to split their time between doing the core

FIGURE 1
Number of Hours per Week Spent on Each Organizing Task

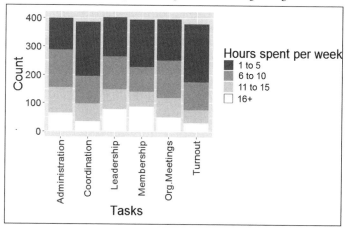

work of organizing—membership recruitment, relational engagement, leadership development, community building and the like—and administrative work. Over 40% of organizers spent five hours a week or less on membership recruitment while 35% spent 11 hours or more. Thirty-five percent spent five hours or less on leadership recruitment and development, and 34% spent 11 hours or more. Thirty-five percent spent five hours or less on internal organizational and staff meetings while close to the same number spent six to ten hours per week. Close to 60% spent six to fifteen hours per week on other and administrative work.

To understand what organizers found most challenging about their jobs, we examined six categories of potentially challenging work in the survey:

- *Organizing,* including membership recruitment and asking people to take on a task, a responsibility or leadership role, or responsibility for recruiting others
- *Mobilizing,* including public speaking, running meetings, doing turn-out for events and organizing actions
- *Strategic capacity,* including development of strategy, campaign planning, and research
- *Self-management,* including time management and developing and sticking to a work plan
- *Managing others,* including supervising and managing other organizers and staff
- *Administration and fund-raising,* including database maintenance and writing

Not surprisingly, close to 20% of organizers ranked the core practices of building power in the workplace—namely, getting people to take on leadership roles and getting people to take responsibility for recruiting others—their top challenges. Further, 17% also ranked developing leaders and recruiting members as one of their top challenges. Seventeen percent identified time management and 13.5% identified supervision of staff as one of their top challenges.

These perceptions of what was most challenging were not evenly distributed across our respondents, however. All ages ranked organizing-related tasks to be their greatest challenges, but organizers 30 years and younger and those with less than one year of organizing experience ranked self-management as a significant challenge. Organizers between ages 31 and 50 and those with ten or more years of experience identified managing others as a significant challenge, but organizers with one to six years of experience identified organizing-related tasks as the most challenging aspect of their work.

EXPLAINING JOB SATISFACTION AMONG ORGANIZERS

With this picture of the day-to-day experience of organizers and the challenges they face, we can now turn toward examining the sources of satisfaction (or dissatisfaction) among organizers. Research on job satisfaction within "careers as calling" can provide a useful starting point. This research concludes that those who feel morally compelled to do these jobs accept significant sacrifices in income, family life, and well-being to do work they love (Bunderson and Thompson 2009; Thompson and Bunderson 2003). Those who seek these jobs show a greater commitment to their work and express satisfaction regardless of the material benefits associated with it (Bunderson and Thompson 2009). Nonetheless, despite the commitments that bring people to this work, research shows that many organizations employing these kinds of workers experience high turnover. Research shows that structural job characteristics can crucially affect people's willingness to stay in these jobs. Scholars find that workers are most likely to leave justice jobs as a response to restrictive organizational policies, voice, a lack of training and mentoring opportunities, and the nature of the job (Bunnage 2014; Rooks 2004). This suggests that structural factors such as job characteristics, organizational structure, the availability of adequate training, and working environment are equally, if not more, important than status and salary in determining turnover in these organizations.

Based on our own experiences and scholarship, we submit that similar patterns should emerge in examining job satisfaction among organizers. Organizers care deeply about the extent to which they can participate and be heard in organizational decision making, and about the distribution of authority in their organizations and the quality of leadership. Studies have shown that the distribution of authority in local unions, for example, affects the allocation of resources for organizing and strategies for organizing, as well as organizing outcomes (Martin 2007). As one female organizer stated in a previous study of organizers, "I would do anything for an organization if I am heard" (Foley 2010).

To assess satisfaction, we develop a conceptualization of satisfaction that draws on the literature on justice careers (Thompson and Bunderson 2003), as well as the high-performance work practices literature in the industrial and human relations fields (Becker and Huselid 1998; Cappelli and Neumark 2001; Combs, Liu, Hall, and Ketchen 2006; Kochan and Osterman 1994; Kochan and Rubinstein 2000; Kochan, Eaton, McKersie, and Adler 2013; Macduffie 1995). The literature on justice careers has stressed the importance of alignment of moral values at work, while the literature on high-performance work practices has emphasized the importance of voice, participation, and job design (Freeney and Fellenz 2013; Grant 2007).

We also look particularly at satisfaction levels affected by participation and assessment of leadership. Unions, in particular, are large organizations in which careers are impacted by effective leadership at the local level as well as meaningful mentoring and development between people at different levels of experience and positions in the hierarchy (Dutton, Roberts, and Bednar 2010). Therefore, satisfaction with the relational and interactional dynamics with the immediate supervisor can be an important dimension of job satisfaction. In the past, union jobs often provided little formal training and mentoring, leaving organizers to acquire skills through "lay apprenticeship" (Feekin and Widenor 2000, 2001). Eaton (1995) found that many labor leaders reported learning their trade through a "sink or swim" approach.

Finally, we also examine organizers' satisfaction with work–life balance and the emotional aspects of the job. Rooks (2004) argues that dissatisfaction with the lack of work–life balance in organizing, and the physically and emotionally demanding nature of the work were two of the main reasons behind graduates of the Organizing Institute leaving the union movement. Organizing can exact a significant emotional toll. Organizers often have to manage their own emotions, such as despair after a failed campaign, as well as others' emotions—such as fear and anger among workers—in situations that can often be highly conflictual (Kurtz 2002; Lopez 2004; Rooks 2004; Rooks and Penney 2016). Indeed, in our own survey, we found that job stress was the thing people would most like to change about their job.[2] To capture all these dimensions of job satisfaction, the survey listed 27 different aspects of people's jobs and asked them to list their satisfaction with each item on a five-point scale of "very unsatisfied," "somewhat unsatisfied," "neither unsatisfied nor satisfied," "somewhat satisfied," or "very satisfied." As shown in Table 2, if we just look descriptively at the data, we find that, overall, the highest levels of dissatisfaction had to do with job-related stress as well as the organization's willingness to challenge unproductive members of the staff. The next highest levels of dissatisfaction related to size of workload, performance evaluation, opportunities for upward mobility, and the ability to influence organizational decisions and practices. There was a significant gender gap, with males reporting statistically significant higher levels of overall job satisfaction, satisfaction with how well their voice was heard in their organization, and satisfaction with the quality of their supervisors. There was no difference between males and females in terms of their satisfaction with the type of tasks they perform in their jobs or with organizational leadership.

In addition to looking at *what* organizers found satisfying (or not) about their jobs, we also wanted to examine the individual, organizational, and experiential correlates of job satisfaction. To identify possible correlates of job satisfaction, we drew on previous research examining job experience, gender, race, education, income, and job characteristics. We discuss each of these factors in turn.

Experience

Several studies have pointed to the high concentration of youth in justice jobs (Bunnage 2014; Rooks 2004). These jobs allow youth to fulfill their idealistic goals and have the kind of flexibility they want (Beadle and Knight 2012). Because they tend to be relatively unattached and geographically mobile, younger people are able to take on the grueling hours required in organizing (Rooks 2004). As workers age, however, they accumulate family and community responsibilities that often conflict with the extensive demands of organizing. Rooks (2004) found that older organizers cope with the tension by leaving these occupations altogether in search of less demanding work. Others move off the front lines into supervisory roles, which allows them to minimize occupational stress and reduce work hours without abandoning their global commitment to social change. The same study found that organizers who stayed had learned to compromise their idealism to conform to the demands of bureaucratic unions (Rooks 2004).

Gender

Most unions have had a male-oriented culture built around the assumption that men could work long hours and be away from home for long periods of time than women could (Schurman 2005). Rooks (2004) memorably described this occupational culture—a willingness to work all the time, extensive travel, social isolation, and giving up on having multidimensional interests and activities—as the "cowboy mentality." Even as more women have entered the field, these basic parameters of union organizing jobs have not changed. Because many women are still the primary caregivers for younger children and aging parents, the demands of organizing present a significant challenge for women, and many of them choose to leave the field as a result (Rooks 2004).

TABLE 2
Descriptive Statistics for Dependent Variables

Question Wording	Mean	Standard Deviation	Cronbach's Alpha
Have Voice in Organization	3.69	1.06	0.90
Ability to air questions or concerns without fear of retaliation	3.83	1.27	
Decision-making authority or independent freedom to take action	3.84	1.19	
Ability to influence organizational practices	3.51	1.24	
Ability to influence strategic direction as a whole	3.47	1.30	
Organization's willingness to share information with you	3.75	1.27	
Satisfied with Job/Task	3.66	0.81	0.89
Hours required	3.43	1.23	
Employment security	3.65	1.30	
Flexible work arrangements/scheduling	3.95	1.15	
Travel required	3.69	1.14	
Basic job duties	4.02	1.05	
Size of workload	3.54	1.17	
Promotion	3.37	1.25	
Physical work environment	3.80	1.17	
People with whom you work closely	4.14	1.03	
Level of job-related stress	2.93	1.22	
Amount of fund-raising you are expected to do	3.52	1.10	
Quality of Supervisor	3.66	1.04	0.91
Supervisor's appreciation of your knowledge, skills, and abilities	3.85	1.27	
Quality of feedback from your supervisor	3.55	1.34	
How your work performance is evaluated or appraised by your supervisor	3.49	1.32	
How you are acknowledged or rewarded for good work by your supervisor	3.65	1.26	
Productivity of others on your team	3.78	1.11	
Clarity of what you are supposed to be doing and what the priorities are	3.62	1.28	
Learning and training opportunities offered to you	3.77	1.26	
Organizational Leadership	3.63	1.08	0.82
Organization's overall vision	3.99	1.17	
Leadership's ability to carry out vision	3.82	1.25	
Organization's willingness to challenge unproductive members of staff	3.10	1.28	
Job Satisfaction (Composite)	3.66	0.85	0.95

Note: 1- to 5-point scale, from very unsatisfied to very satisfied. Matrix format.

A 2005 study of female organizers found that "by far the greatest challenge for these women revolves around balancing the demanding schedule and extensive travel typically required of organizers with their roles as family and community members" (Schurman 2005: 14). Emotional conflict and additional pressures built up when the job precluded women from fulfilling their roles as wives, partners, mothers, and community activists. One organizer's quotation summed up the dilemma: "Women are raised as social creatures. … [We] have families. … [H]ow do you have a life and organize?" (Schurman 2005: 16). Rooks (2004) has argued that this dominant culture of organizing, in concert with the demands of the work itself, has undermined the labor movement's ability to diversify its organizing ranks, particularly along gender lines.

Race

Previous scholarship on the experience of organizers of color offers a mixed view. On the one hand, evidence suggests that organizers of color have much to be dissatisfied about in the union movement. While membership of people of color has increased in unions, the hierarchical ranks remained predominantly White (Bronfenbrenner and Warren 2007; Hunt and Rayside 2000). Not only have the upper ranks of union jobs remained typically White and male, seniority systems in many unions historically discriminated against people of color and women (Riccucci 1990). In a study of Union Summer participants (a paid internship program for young people to become involved in organizing), Bunnage (2014) found that although the program expended considerable effort to recruit people of color, the retention rate was a little more than half that of whites. Women of color, in particular, were least likely to be retained in the labor movement after completing the program.

The union movement has also been heavily critiqued for placing economic and class-based issues above issues of gender and race, and failing to find intersections among these platforms (Kurtz 2002). On the other hand, unions have consciously expanded diversity in their ranks, especially since John Sweeney was elected president of the AFL-CIO (Fairbrother and Yates 2003; Hunt and Rayside 2000; Kelley 1998). The change in organizing philosophy of the AFL-CIO led by unions such as SEIU and UNITE HERE (Bronfenbrenner and Juravich 1998) galvanized first- and, especially, second-generation immigrants to work as organizers in unions (Milkman 2006; Yu 2008). Second-generation immigrant union organizers report a great appreciation for their jobs as opportunities to serve their communities and right the injustices they witnessed (Yu 2008). Many describe their jobs as a calling (Yu 2008). Among union occupations, the percentage of people of color in organizing leadership has increased. The percentage of lead organizers of color increased from 15% to 21% from the late 1980s to the late 1990s (Bronfenbrenner and Warren 2007).

Organizers of color also were found to have achieved better outcomes than their White counterparts. As Bronfenbrenner and Warren (2007: 145) found:

> While the overall win rate in [National Labor Relations Board] campaigns for female lead organizers averages 53 percent (compared to 42 percent for men), the average win rate for lead organizers of color is 58 percent (compared to 41 percent

for White leads), and for lead women of color organizers is 69 percent (compared to 43 percent). And when the lead organizer is a woman of color in units with over 75 percent women of color, the NLRB election win rate is an astounding 89 percent.

Similarly, Ganz (2009) argued that diversity within the leadership group of the United Farm Workers stimulated tactical and organizational innovation.

Education

In the past few decades since the 1980s, a "new breed" of organizers has entered labor organizing. These organizers are younger and relatively highly educated, especially in service sector unions (Reed 1990). Higher education levels of union staff have been associated with innovation and greater effectiveness, although the relationship to organizing win rates is mixed. For example, Voss and Sherman (2000) found that the presence of staff with higher education along with technical skills and organizing experience outside of the labor movement are necessary preconditions for unions to fully innovate. While Reed (1989, 1990) found that higher levels of education of organizers are linked to campaign success, Bronfenbrenner and Juravich (1998) found education level to be statistically insignificant in its relationship to rate of success.

High levels of education present other challenges for organizations: college-educated organizers expect more from their organizations. Rooks (2004) documented the initial expectations of college graduates who enrolled in the Organizing Institute. They believed "new labor" was more ideologically progressive compared with traditional unions, that unions would be diverse workplaces and also fight for greater diversity in society, and that the strategies espoused—such as militant organizing—would lead to "true worker empowerment" (Rooks 2004: 214–215). Disillusionment upon having these expectations violated was the most common reason that graduates left the labor movement within 18 months of graduation (Rooks 2004: 211).

Income

In Rooks' (2004) study of recent graduates from the Organizing Institute, no one reported income as being a source of grievance in their organizing jobs. While this would suggest that income should have no effect on organizer satisfaction early in their careers, our own work over the years has indicated that union staff appreciate being able to do justice work in an environment that provides a minimum level of income and job security. This was often cited to us as a reason for transition to labor from community and other social movement organizations. Moreover, studies on commitment to and satisfaction from work have shown in general that higher levels of income are correlated with increased commitment and satisfaction (Gao-Urhahn, Biemann, and

Jaros 2016; Richter, Naswall, Bernhard-Oettel, and Sverke 2014; Zheng, Diaz, Tang, and Tang 2014).

Working mothers, in particular, report greater ability to focus on their work and greater satisfaction at higher levels of income because extra income enables outsourcing childcare and other tasks that facilitate work–family balance (McManus, Korabik, Rosin, and Kelloway 2002). Often, those who dedicate themselves to justice jobs who are themselves socioeconomically disadvantaged are forced to choose between low-paying justice jobs and the need to make a living. Perhaps relatedly, in Bunnage's (2014) study of Union Summer program participants, no people of color from working-class backgrounds stayed in the union movement after completing the program.

Job Characteristics

Characteristics of the job and task, such as workload and hours worked, stress, and the nature of work tasks, are important factors influencing job satisfaction. The literature on justice careers stipulates that those who undertake work in this field tolerate long hours and high workload out of commitments to the larger mission (Bunderson and Thompson 2009; Thompson and Bunderson 2003). However, evidence suggests that those in justice jobs care deeply about the nature of the task, and particularly whether the tasks they are given serve to advance their personally held cause (Berg, Grant, and Johnson 2010). Tasks that do not directly lead to serving the mission, or that are seen to jeopardize the cause, can be a source of dissatisfaction for those in justice jobs. When tasks challenge core values that workers view as central to the mission, they can constitute a "violation of expectation" severe enough to trigger exit (Thompson and Bunderson 2003).

Based on earlier studies that found organizers believe new labor's emphasis on militant organizing tactics should translate into true worker empowerment (Rooks 2004), it is our view that organizer satisfaction will correlate with tasks that are associated with worker empowerment. These tasks include recruiting and providing support to worker leaders, recruiting workers through house calls and worksite visits, and motivating and inoculating workers to withstand anti-union tactics. Beyond organizing drives and contract campaigns, organizers engage leaders and members in public policy and electoral campaigns, and organize workers to sign up for recurring monthly donations to the union political action committee. In recent years, however, overall administrative tasks carried out in unions have been on the rise as a result of an increase in mergers across unions, a rising staff-to-member ratio, and changes in the nature of organizing that place more emphasis on researching employers' vulnerabilities and mounting corporate campaigns (Bronfenbrenner and Hickey 2004; McAlevey 2016). Also, negotiated settlements have increased the amount of administrative tasks performed by organizers (Behrens, Hurd, and Waddington 2004).

Local Versus National Levels of Organization

One of the recommendations made by Schurman and the Berger–Marks Foundation (2005) was that organizing should be based locally. For organizers, working on national campaigns often translates into constant traveling and the social and emotional isolation that accompanies it (Rooks 2004). Furthermore, mentoring and development is likely to be both more available and personalized when an organizer is rooted in relationships with colleagues and worker leaders in a local organization (Feekin and Widenor 2000; Fletcher and Hurd 1998).

To examine the relationship between these individual, organizational, and experiential characteristics and job satisfaction, we ran a series of multivariate ordinary least-squares regressions for most of our analyses. Our goal in these analyses was to identify what the correlational patterns were among people's individual characteristics, their experience of organizing, and their levels of satisfaction with their job. At the individual level, we included variables for gender, the number of dependents under the age of 17, marital status, age, education, whether the respondent was a person of color, whether the person worked full time, personal income, and whether the respondent had a partner who was employed part time or full time. In addition, we included variables related to the person's organization and their experience of organizing. These variables included the number of previous organizing jobs a person had had; whether they worked for a union; whether the organization was a local, state, or national organization; and the amount of time they spent on administrative work in their job. Finally, we included some interaction terms.

The results of our regression analyses are shown in Table 3. If we look at each of our measures of satisfaction, we find some interesting patterns. First, having had more organizing jobs is related to lower levels of overall satisfaction, satisfaction with voice in the organization, satisfaction with job characteristics and tasks, and satisfaction with supervisor. Note that bivariate analyses show that there appears to be a drop-off in terms of job satisfaction between the four- and six-year and seven- and nine-year marks and that satisfaction increases after ten years or more.

We also found an interesting set of patterns related to demography. Women who work for unions have less overall satisfaction than their union counterparts who are male, and they have less satisfaction with job characteristics and tasks, supervisors, and organizational leadership. Women of color in particular were less satisfied with organizational leadership. Respondents with more children under the age of 18, however, were more likely to be satisfied with job characteristics and tasks. Overall, however, organizers of color were more satisfied in general, and, in particular, more satisfied with the quality of supervision they received. Consistent with previous research from Bunnage

TABLE 3

Impact of Individual Characteristics on Job Satisfaction

(OLS regression coefficients; standard errors in parentheses)

	Job Satisfaction (Composite) (1)	Have Voice in Organization (2)	Satisfied with Job/Task (3)	Quality of Supervisor (4)	Organizational Leadership (5)
Number of organizing jobs in career	0.074 (0.125)	0.057 (0.159)	0.016 (0.116)	0.134 (0.153)	0.164 (0.164)
Female (dummy)	0.359 (0.285)	−0.095 (0.362)	0.283 (0.264)	0.563 (0.349)	0.602 (0.374)
Number of children under 18	0.057* (0.031)	0.038 (0.039)	0.067** (0.029)	0.041 (0.038)	0.058 (0.041)
Married (dummy)	0.130 (0.150)	0.181 (0.189)	0.080 (0.139)	0.163 (0.183)	0.170 (0.197)
Age (years)	−0.0004 (0.007)	−0.006 (0.009)	0.003 (0.007)	0.005 (0.009)	−0.004 (0.009)
Education	−0.048 (0.051)	−0.085 (0.065)	−0.004 (0.048)	−0.040 (0.063)	−0.127* (0.068)
Person of color (dummy)	0.260 (0.283)	−0.107 (0.358)	0.213 (0.262)	0.680* (0.346)	0.253 (0.372)
Household income	0.121* (0.072)	0.102 (0.092)	0.109 (0.067)	0.099 (0.088)	0.147 (0.094)
Partner employed (dummy, full or part)	−0.075 (0.151)	−0.033 (0.191)	−0.151 (0.139)	0.105 (0.184)	−0.013 (0.198)
Employed by union	0.095 (0.273)	−0.232 (0.345)	0.093 (0.253)	0.281 (0.333)	−0.168 (0.359)
Organizational level (local to national)	0.005 (0.075)	−0.032 (0.095)	0.002 (0.069)	0.012 (0.091)	0.054 (0.099)
Time spent on administrative tasks	−0.026 (0.056)	0.013 (0.071)	−0.024 (0.052)	−0.023 (0.068)	−0.043 (0.074)
Employed full time (dummy)	−0.27 (0.156)	−0.087 (0.197)	0.001 (0.144)	−0.049 (0.190)	−0.064 (0.205)
Female * number of children under 18	−0.008 (0.049)	0.025 (0.062)	−0.009 (0.045)	−0.005 (0.060)	−0.010 (0.064)
Female * work for union	−0.576** (0.276)	−0.394 (0.350)	−0.449* (0.255)	−0.804** (0.338)	−0.627** (0.362)
Person of color * work for union	−0.029 (0.272)	0.198 (0.350)	−0.075 (0.251)	−0.185 (0.331)	0.197 (0.357)
Person of color * female	−0.227 (0.256)	0.035 (0.323)	−0.134 (0.237)	−0.457 (0.312)	−0.567* (0.336)
Number of organizing jobs * income	−0.038 (0.023)	−0.041 (0.029)	−0.027 (0.022)	−0.051* (0.028)	−0.056* (0.031)
Constant	3.488*** (0.602)	4.479*** (0.760)	3.317*** (0.577)	2.920*** (0.733)	3.756*** (0.790)
Observations	206	205	206	205	206
Adj. R²	0.043	0.045	0.035	0.057	0.051

(2014), our findings indicate that unions are particularly challenged in working with organizers who are women of color. More highly educated people, however, were less satisfied with organizational leadership.

DISCUSSION AND CONCLUSION

When we put all of the analyses together, our data raises questions that get to the heart of how the field thinks about power building. In particular, we wonder whether organizers are developing the skills and spending the time on the tasks that are most essential to building collective power. Strikingly, organizers ranked core organizing tasks such as membership recruitment and getting people to take on leadership roles and responsibility for recruiting others as the most challenging aspects of organizing. Many of them also reported spending relatively little time on these tasks. Yet, from the perspective of building power and growing the union, they are arguably the most important, especially if unions will no longer be able to rely on the collection of agency fees.

Organizers are labor's most precious resource in terms of the essential work of growing the movement. To do this work, organizers need to want to spend the lion's share of their time recruiting members, developing leaders, and building organizations. Yet they must feel confident that they know how to do these things effectively. Recruitment, leadership development, and getting people to take responsibility for recruiting others are difficult tasks. If solid practices are not implanted and nurtured, many organizers will gravitate to less challenging ones.

Taken together, our results also suggest that there appear to be some general questions about managerial and cultural styles confronting the field of union organizing as a whole. Stress and workload have consistently emerged as the number one issue for organizers, raising the question of whether there have been attempts to implement alternate models, what became of these experiments, and whether there are interventions that could be made in the future to lower the level of stress. Is stress a fact of life that is endemic to organizing, or is it endemic to a particular managerial and cultural style of organizing that could be changed? Are there counterbalancing measures that organizations might take to reduce the level of stress among organizers?

In 2005, based on focus groups with women organizers, the Berger–Marks Foundation made a series of recommendations including basing organizers locally rather than requiring them to travel long distances, creating organizing teams and opportunities for organizers to share lead organizer jobs, providing more time off between assignments, and offering more assistance with child and dependent care. They also recommend upgrading the status of the organizer job within unions and providing better ongoing training and mentoring (Schurman 2005). We are not aware of many unions that have implemented these recommendations.

Quality of supervision and organizers' ability to manage others also emerged from our data as critical issues for organizers. Young organizers, female organizers, and newer organizers identified time management and self-management as a key challenge. The social justice field in general has long been notorious for a lack of training regarding management and supervision. This is likely due to some combination of ambivalence toward hierarchy and/or bureaucracy, a lack of exposure to managerial techniques, and a lack of resources. In recent years, some programs have emerged to fill this void, especially with respect to providing training and coaching for organizational leaders. The question is how to ensure that more unions and other economic justice organizations implement them and make them more broadly and deeply available within their organizations.

To understand more about how unions build a diverse base of organizers, it would seem important to pay attention to trends among particular subpopulations. In order to grapple with challenges facing the field not only with regard to entry-level positions, but also at the most senior levels, attention should also be paid to the leadership pipeline. In this regard, there seems to be some gender bifurcation, where women report feeling more challenged by strategic capacity issues such as strategy development and campaign planning and men report greater challenges with managing others. These findings suggest that the Organizing Institute, individual unions, and allied organizations might be advised to develop a strategy for working with women organizers in particular around strategic capacity issues and for supervisory trainings to be sensitive to gender dynamics.

In thinking about long-term retention, there was a palpable drop-off in job satisfaction at the six-year mark, which anecdotally also seems to be around the time when many organizers leave the field. This raises the question of what steps might be taken to raise levels of job satisfaction for organizers at this stage in their career so that they are more likely to remain. Some of these steps would likely be similar to those discussed previously in this chapter. In addition, sociologists have pointed to the value of communities of learning and practice that offer practitioners at similar points in their careers a space to come together to identify issues they are interested in exploring, to learn from what others are trying, to share their own experiences, and to bring in outside experts to present on specific subject areas (Van Maanen and Barley 1984; Wenger 2000).

In this study, we have found that the issues union organizers identify today are remarkably consistent with earlier qualitative studies of the field. Thus, we are left with a fundamental question: why has the occupational structure of organizing changed so little? Even as enormous shifts have taken place in the nature of work, technological advances have revolutionized communication, and the occupational ranks of organizing have diversified, the structure of the job itself seems to be frozen in time. It does not have to remain so. At this moment when American democracy is under terrible assault and social inequality has reached unprecedented levels, making union organizing a viable career for a broad range of people is more important than ever.

ENDNOTES

[1] Authors are listed in alphabetical order and contributed equally to the article. We would also like to acknowledge our superb collaborators at the AFL-CIO led by Lynn Rodenhuis and Allison Porter of the Alvarez/Porter Consulting Group.

[2] When asked what they would like to change most about their jobs, after the level of stress, organizers ranked the size of the workload, employment security, hours and compensation, and quality of supervision (especially with respect to clarity of their role and priorities and opportunities for learning and training).

REFERENCES

Beadle, Ron, and Kelvin Knight. 2012. "Virtue and Meaningful Work." *Business Ethics Quarterly* 22 (2): 433–450.

Becker, Brian E., and Mark A. Huselid. 1998. "High-Performance Work Systems and Firm Performance: A Synthesis of Research and Managerial Implications." *Research in Personnel and Human Resources Management* 16: 53–101.

Behrens, Martin, Richard W. Hurd, and Jeremy Waddington. 2004. "How Does Restructuring Contribute to Union Revitalization?" In *Varieties of Unionism: Strategies for Union Revitalization in a Globalizing Economy*, edited by Carola M. Frege and John Kelly, pp. 117–136. New York, NY: Oxford University Press.

Berg, Justin M., Adam M. Grant, and Victoria Johnson. 2010. "When Callings Are Calling: Crafting Work and Leisure in Pursuit of Unanswered Occupational Callings." *Organization Science* 21 (5): 973–994.

Bronfenbrenner, Kate, and Robert Hickey. 2004. "Changing to Organize: A National Assessment of Union Strategies." In *Rebuilding Labor: Organizing and Organizers in the New Union Movement*, edited by Ruth Milkman and Kim Voss, pp. 17–61. Ithaca, NY: Cornell University Press.

Bronfenbrenner, Kate, and Tom Juravich. 1998. "It Takes More Than House Calls: Organizing to Win with a Comprehensive Union-Building Strategy." In *Organizing to Win: New Research on Union Strategies*, edited by Kate Bronfenbrenner, Sheldon Friedman, Richard W. Hurd, Rudolph A. Oswald, and Ronald L. Seeber, pp. 19–36. Ithaca, NY: ILR Press.

Bronfenbrenner, Kate, and Dorian T. Warren. 2007. "Race, Gender, and the Rebirth of Trade Unionism." *New Labor Forum* 16 (3/4): 142–148.

Bunderson, J.S., and Jeffery A. Thompson. 2009. "The Call of the Wild: Zookeepers, Callings, and the Double-Edged Sword of Deeply Meaningful Work." *Administrative Science Quarterly* 54 (1): 32–57.

Bunnage, Leslie A. 2014. "Interrogating the Interaction of Race, Gender, and Class Within US Labor Movement Revitalization Efforts." *Women's Studies International Forum* 47 (A): 63–76.

Cappelli, Peter, and David Neumark. 2001. "Do 'High-Performance' Work Practices Improve Establishment-Level Outcomes?" *Industrial and Labor Relations Review* 54(4): 737–775.

Combs, J., Y. Liu, A. Hall, and D. Ketchen. 2006. "How Much Do High-Performance Work Practices Matter? A Meta-Analysis of Their Effects on Organizational Performance." *Personnel Psychology* 59 (3): 501–528.

Compa, Lance A. 2004. "More Thoughts on the Worker–Student Alliance: A Response to Steve Early." *Labor: Studies in Working Class History of the Americas* 1 (2): 15–22.

Dutton, Jane E., Laura M. Roberts, and Jeffrey Bednar. 2010. "Pathways for Positive Identity Construction at Work: Four Types of Positive Identity and the Building of Social Resources." *Academy of Management Review* 35 (2): 265–293.

Eaton, Susan C. 1995. "Union Leadership Development in the 1990s and Beyond." *Workplace Topics* 4 (2): 5–17.

Fairbrother, Peter, and Charlotte A.B. Yates. 2003. "Unions in Crisis, Unions in Renewal?" In *Trade Unions in Renewal: A Comparative Study*, edited by Peter Fairbrother and Charlotte A.B. Yates, pp. 1–32. London, UK: Routledge.

Fantasia, Rick, and Kim Voss. 2004. *Hard Work: Remaking the American Labor Movement.* Berkeley, CA: University of California Press.

Feekin, Lynn, and Marcus Widenor. 2000. "Organizer Training in Two Hemispheres: The AFL-CIO Organizing Institute and the Australian Council of Trade Union's Organizing Works." Unpublished Paper.

Feekin, Lynn, and Marcus Widenor. 2001. "Helping New Organizers Survive and Thrive in the Field: The Essential Role of Training and Mentoring." Unpublished Paper.

Fine, Janice, and Nik Theodore. 2012. "Worker Centers 2012: Community Based and Worker Led Organizations." Map prepared for the Center for Faith-Based and Community Partnerships. Washington, DC: US Department of Labor. http://bit.ly/2JLVQXS

Fletcher, Bill, and Richard W. Hurd. 1998. "Beyond the Organizing Model: The Transformation Process in Local Unions." In *Organizing to Win: New Research on Union Strategies*, edited by Kate Bronfenbrenner, Sheldon Friedman, Richard W. Hurd, Rudolph A. Oswald, and Ronald L. Seeber, pp. 37–53. Ithaca, NY: ILR Press.

Foley, Linda. 2010. "Stepping Up, Stepping Back: Women Activists 'Talk Union' Across Generations." Prepared for the Berger–Marks Foundation, Washington, DC. http://bit.ly/2H652Ez

Freeney, Yseult, and Martin R. Fellenz. 2013. "Work Engagement, Job Design and the Role of the Social Context at Work: Exploring Antecedents from a Relational Perspective." *Human Relations* 66 (11): 1427–1445.

Ganz, Marshall. 2009. *Why David Sometimes Wins: Strategy, Leadership, and the California Farm Worker Movement.* Oxford, UK: Oxford University Press.

Ganz, Marshall, Kim Voss, Teresa Sharpe, Carl Somers, and George Strauss 2004. "Against the Tide: Projects and Pathways of the New Generation of Union Leaders, 1984–2001." In *Rebuilding Labor: Organizing and Organizers in the New Union Movement*, edited by Ruth Milkman and Kim Voss, pp. 150–194. Ithaca, NY: Cornell University Press.

Gao-Urhahn, Xiaohan, Torsten Biemann, and Stephen J. Jaros. 2016. "How Affective Commitment to the Organization Changes Over Time: A Longitudinal Analysis of the Reciprocal Relationships Between Affective Organizational Commitment and Income." *Journal of Organizational Behavior* 37 (4): 515–536.

Goldfield, Michael. 1989. *The Decline of Organized Labor in the United States.* Chicago, IL: University of Chicago Press.

Grant, Adam M. 2007. "Relational Job Design and the Motivation to Make a Prosocial Difference." *Academy of Management Review* 32 (2): 393–417.

Hirsch, Barry, and David Macpherson. 2017. Unionstats. http://www.unionstats.com

Hunt, Gerald, and David Rayside. 2000. "Labor Union Responses to Diversity in Canada and the United States." *Industrial Relations* 39 (3): 401–444.

Jobs With Justice. 2016. "Partnerships and Projects." http://bit.ly/2J116uP

Kelley, John E. 1998. *Rethinking Industrial Relations: Mobilization, Collectivism, and Long Waves*. London, UK, and New York, NY: Routledge.

Kochan, Thomas A., Adrienne E. Eaton, Robert B. McKersie, and Paul S. Adler. 2013. *Healing Together: The Labor–Management Partnership at Kaiser Permanente*. Ithaca, NY: ILR Press.

Kochan, Thomas A., and Paul Osterman. 1994. *The Mutual Gains Enterprise: Forging a Winning Partnership Among Labor, Management, and Government*. Boston, MA: Harvard Business School Press.

Kochan, Thomas A., and Saul A. Rubinstein. 2000. "Toward a Stakeholder Theory of the Firm: The Saturn Partnership." *Organization Science* 11 (4): 367–386.

Kurtz, Sharon. 2002. *Workplace Justice: Organizing Multi-Identity Movements*. Minneapolis, MN: University of Minnesota Press.

Lichtenstein, N. 2013. *State of the Union: A Century of American Labor*. Princeton, NJ: Princeton University Press.

Lopez, Steven H. 2004. *Reorganizing the Rust Belt: An Inside Study of the American Labor Movement*. Berkeley, CA: University of California Press.

Macduffie, John P. 1995. "Human Resource Bundles and Manufacturing Performance: Organizational Logic and Flexible Production Systems in the World Auto Industry." *Industrial and Labor Relations Review* 48 (2): 197–221.

Martin, Andrew W. 2007. "Organizational Structure, Authority and Protest: The Case of Union Organizing in the United States, 1990–2001." *Social Forces* 85 (3): 1413–1435.

McAlevey, Jane. 2016. *No Shortcuts: Organizing for Power in the New Gilded Age*. Oxford, UK: Oxford University Press.

McCartin, J.A. 2006. "PATCO, Permanent Replacement, and the Loss of Labor's Strike Weapon." *Perspectives on Work* 10 (1): 17–19.

McManus, Kelly, Karen Korabik, Hazel M. Rosin, and E.K. Kelloway. 2002. "Employed Mothers and the Work–Family Interface: Does Family Structure Matter? *Human Relations* 55 (11): 1295–1324.

Milkman, Ruth. 2006. *LA Story: Immigrant Workers and the Future of the U.S. Labor Movement*. New York, NY: Russell Sage Foundation.

Milkman, Ruth, and Kim Voss. 2004. *Rebuilding Labor: Organizing and Organizers in the New Union Movement*. Ithaca, NY: Cornell University Press.

Partnership for Working Families. 2015. "National Network of Affiliates." http://bit.ly/2J0 C92J

Reed, Thomas F. 1989. "Do Union Organizers Matter? Individual Differences, Campaign Practices, and Representation Election Outcomes." *Industrial and Labor Relations Review* 43 (1): 103–119.

Reed, Thomas F. 1990. "Profiles of Union Organizers from Manufacturing and Service Unions." *Journal of Labor Research* 11 (1): 73–80.

Riccucci, Norma. 1990. *Women, Minorities, and Unions in the Public Sector*. Westport, CT: Greenwood Press.

Richter, Anne, Katharina Naswall, Claudia Bernhard-Oettel, and Magnus Sverke. 2014. "Job Insecurity and Well-Being: The Moderating Role of Job Dependence." *European Journal of Work and Organizational Psychology* 23 (6): 816–829.

Rooks, Daisy. 2004. "Sticking It Out or Packing It In? Organizer Retention in the New Labor Movement." In *Rebuilding Labor: Organizing and Organizers in the New Union Movement,* edited by Ruth Milkman and Kim Voss, pp. 195–224. Ithaca, NY: Cornell University Press.

Rooks, Daisy, and Robert A. Penney. 2016. "Outsiders in the Union: Organizing, Consent, and Union Recognition Campaigns." *Social Movement Studies* 15 (5): 498–514.

Schurman, Sue. 2005. "Women Organizing Women: How Do We Rock the Boat Without Getting Thrown Overboard?" Berger–Marks Foundation. http://www.bergermarks. org/download/WOWreport.pdf

Thompson, Jeffery A., and J. S. Bunderson. 2003. "Violations of Principle: Ideological Currency in the Psychological Contract." *Academy of Management Review* 28 (4): 571–586.

Van Maanen, John, and Stephen R. Barley. 1984. "Occupational Communities: Culture and Control in Organizations." *Research in Organizational Behavior* 6: 287–365.

Voss, Kim, and Rachel Sherman. 2000. "Breaking the Iron Law of Oligarchy: Union Revitalization in the American Labor Movement." *American Journal of Sociology* 106 (2): 303–349.

Wenger, Etienne. 2000. "Communities of Practice and Social Learning Systems." *Organization* 7 (2): 225–246.

Windham, Lane. 2017. *Knocking on Labor's Door: Union Organizing in the 1970s and the Roots of a New Economic Divide*. Chapel Hill, NC: University of North Carolina Press.

Yu, Kyoung-Hee. 2008. "Between Bureaucracy and Social Movements: Careers in the Justice for Janitors." Unpublished Doctoral Dissertation, Massachusetts Institute of Technology.

Zald, Mayer N., and Roberta Ash. 1966. "Social Movement Organizations: Growth, Decay and Change." *Social Forces* 44 (3): 327–341.

Zheng, Xingshan, Ismael Diaz, Ningyu Tang, and Kongshun Tang. 2014. "Job Insecurity and Job Satisfaction: The Interactively Moderating Effects of Optimism and Person–Supervisor Deep-Level Similarity." *Career Development International* 19 (4): 426–446.

Chapter 7

Innovative Union Strategies and the Struggle to Reinvent Collective Bargaining

Joseph A. McCartin

*Kalmanovitz Initiative for Labor and the
Working Poor, Georgetown University*

The story of US labor history over the past few decades is usually presented as a narrative of steady decline in union membership and the inability of unions to successfully organize against growing employer opposition and eroding legal protections. The ascendancy of Donald J. Trump to the presidency in 2016 only reinforced that declension narrative. Trump's election, facilitated by the erosion of union density and corresponding suffering of working-class families in key Midwestern states such as Michigan, Pennsylvania, and Wisconsin, called attention to the failure of unions to thrive during the administration of President Barack Obama. Obama's 2008 election had raised hopes that a union revival was in the offing. But not only did unions not revive during the Obama years, union density dropped to 10.7% from 12.4% during his presidency. Although Obama signed an executive order that raised wages for federal contractors, his appointees to the National Labor Relations Board (NLRB) streamlined its procedures, and the Affordable Care Act helped many working families gain health insurance, a string of policy defeats outweighed these achievements for the union movement: the Employee Free Choice Act (EFCA), a long-anticipated reform of aging US labor law, was derailed by a Senate filibuster; Congress refused to take up comprehensive immigration reform; five states enacted "right-to-work" laws (raising the number of right-to-work states to 27); 15 states enacted curbs on public sector collective bargaining or the ability of public employee unions to collect "fair-share fees" (or agency fees) from the workers they represented; and the US Supreme Court edged toward overturning state laws that allowed public sector unions to collect agency fees from the workers they represent.[1]

While the major outlines of this declension narrative are undeniable, the way it is often presented has tended to distort our understanding of the forces that have led to union decline and to obscure the rich variety of promising innovations that have emerged from the labor movement and its allies over the past generation that, taken together, might point the way forward for 21st-century worker organization. Building on research I conducted with my colleagues Jennifer Luff and Katie Corrigan, this chapter offers a corrective on both counts.[2] First, it argues that the roots of labor's crisis stem less from the failure of unions to prioritize organizing than from the sharp erosion of worker bargaining power produced by economic reorganization and by the related collapse of workers' ability to engage in successful collective actions to counteract their diminishing bargaining power. Second, it argues that the loss of bargaining power and reliable traditional vehicles for collective action prompted a range of experiments as unions and their allies attempted innovations in collective bargaining and collective action in light of new developments in the economy. Although these innovations have not yielded a "magic bullet," and labor's policy agenda has lagged in response to them, in their broad outlines we might be able to glimpse labor's future. As this chapter suggests, these innovations might harbor the seeds of a 21st-century revival of worker organization and bargaining power.

MORE THAN A FAILURE TO ORGANIZE

To grasp the significance of the innovations that have emerged from the labor movement and its allies in recent years, we must first free ourselves from the relentlessly single-minded attention on unions' failure to organize, which has tended to dominate both academic literature and discussion around the labor movement.[3] From the 1970s to the early 21st century, labor reformers and academics focused overwhelmingly on organizing as the tool that would revive labor's fortunes. This led them to propose changes in labor law that would better protect workers' rights to form unions and, beginning in the 1990s, to push unions to commit more resources to organizing. Both efforts—the push to reform policy and the bid to increase unions' commitment to organizing—yielded frustration.

The inability of labor's allies to amend the law to protect workers' right to organize against the increasing opposition of employers was the clearest failure. By the mid-1970s, unions were well aware of the degree to which the National Labor Relations Act (NLRA) no longer protected workers' rights to organize. With the election of Jimmy Carter in 1976 and Democrats in firm control of the House and Senate, labor's allies attempted to pass a comprehensive reform of the NLRA only to see their effort die in a Senate filibuster in 1978. The same fate would meet the effort to pass the Employee Free Choice Act (EFCA) during the Obama administration in 2010.[4]

Having failed to pass laws that would ease union organization, unions nonetheless saw no choice but to increase their efforts to organize new members if they were to survive. "There must be a renewed emphasis on organizing," as argued in "The Changing Situation of Workers and Their Unions," the 1985 special report of the AFL-CIO's Committee on the Future of Work. The report's recommendations that unions spend more on organizing, reach beyond their traditional ranks to organize professionals and white-collar workers, and create associate membership programs produced little change. While most AFL-CIO unions changed little in response to the AFL-CIO's prodding, a number of organizations made a concerted effort to prioritize organizing.[5]

One of these was the Service Employees International Union (SEIU). In many ways, SEIU had been a rather traditional organization before the Reagan era. Its roots stretched back to an effort by Chicago's building janitors to organize in 1902. It was chartered as an affiliate of the American Federation of Labor in 1921. By the 1960s, it had amassed a quarter of a million members. Under the leadership of George Hardy, the union took an aggressive and expansive approach to organizing. "If they're breathing, organize them," Hardy famously urged his colleagues. John Sweeney, the leader of the union's large New York City local, 32BJ, was fully committed to this vision. He rose to the local's presidency in 1976 and succeeded Hardy as general president of SEIU in 1980.[6]

Under Sweeney's leadership, SEIU revamped its internal culture to make organizing its top priority. In 1984, Sweeney tapped Andy Stern, then president of Local 668, the Pennsylvania Social Services Union, to come to Washington as the union's new organizing director. He also brought in a young organizer named Stephen Lerner to run the union's property services division. With support from Sweeney and Stern, Lerner launched the Justice for Janitors campaign in 1986, which led to breakthroughs organizing low-wage janitors— many of whom were immigrants—in major cities such as Denver, Los Angeles, and Washington, D.C.[7] Justice for Janitors helped change SEIU. Before the mid-1980s, like most unions, SEIU prioritized membership service above new organizing. "Promotion, power, and glory came from being a tough bargainer and fighting for existing members that voted in union elections," Stern explained. Consequently, "organizing workers into unions was underfunded and undervalued."[8] SEIU helped make organizing the center of attention in the labor movement.

By 1989, the AFL-CIO was devoting increased attention to organizing, creating the Organizing Institute (OI) in 1989. With initial funding from SEIU, the Amalgamated Clothing and Textile Workers Union (ACTWU) (forerunner of the Union of Needletrades, Industrial and Textile Employees [UNITE]), the American Federation of State County and Municipal Employees (AFSCME), and the United Food & Commercial Workers International Union (UFCW), the OI developed a training program available to any AFL-CIO–affiliated union. The OI recruited from university campuses as well as among rank-and-file members, and thousands of organizers got their start as OI trainees. Many unions created their own organizing training programs as well.[9]

Yet while a number of unions began prioritizing organizing by the early 1990s, union membership continued to slip. In response to that erosion and to Republican takeover of the Congress in 1994, Sweeney sought election as president of the AFL-CIO in 1995, pledging to commit massive resources to organizing. He won on a ticket that included Richard Trumka of the United Mine Workers and Linda Chavez Thompson of AFSCME.

Sweeney's election marked the ascendancy of the organizing model of unionism. A number of unions dramatically stepped up their commitment to organizing. In 1998, the Steelworkers boosted its organizing budget from $13 to $40 million, funded by a special dues assessment. At the same time, AFSCME increased dues to generate an additional $8 million for organizing. In 2002, the Teamsters pledged to spend $60 million per year on organizing. The AFL-CIO issued a Federation-branded credit card and used a portion of the profits to create a special organizing fund. Although the AFL-CIO never reached the goal Sweeney promised in 1995 of spending 30% of its budget on organizing, it doubled organizing expenditures during his tenure.[10]

Unions achieved their most significant organizing successes in property services, the public sector, and in health care organizing. The biggest gains arose from unions' creative collaboration with friendly state and local governments to classify homecare and childcare providers who received public subsidies as state workers who could bargain collectively with state and local governments, as happened when 74,000 homecare workers in Los Angeles County joined SEIU in 1999. But most organizing campaigns failed to achieve such large breakthroughs. Outside of health care and the public sector, few new organizing campaigns succeeded, regardless of the union responsible.[11]

Sweeney's effort to jump-start organizing across the labor movement soon ran into stiff headwinds, suffering three staggering blows in quick succession. In 1998, his ally, Teamster president Ron Carey, was deposed by James Hoffa after a bitter election battle. Then–vice president Al Gore, a union ally, lost the controversial 2000 presidential election to union opponent George W. Bush. Finally, the terrorist attacks of September 11, 2001, pushed the nation in the direction of conservatism and xenophobia. This sapped the union movement of much of the energy that it had gained from alliances it had struck with environmentalists and other anti-globalization activists during the protests against the World Trade Organization in Seattle in 1999 and with immigrants and their advocates after the AFL-CIO reversed its long-standing opposition to immigration reform in 2000.[12]

By the time George W. Bush won re-election and Republicans consolidated control of Congress in 2004, the organizing spirit that had suffused the AFL-CIO in the early days of Sweeney's rise to power had given way to dissatisfaction and internal division. Andy Stern, by then president of the SEIU, emerged as Sweeney's most pointed critic. Together with several of the AFL-CIO largest unions, Stern argued that Sweeney had not done enough to energize organizing across the movement. When Sweeney refused to step aside in 2005, Stern and his allies—including the Teamsters and UFCW—withdrew their unions from the AFL-CIO in 2005 to create a rival federation, Change to Win. As Sweeney had done a decade earlier, they too pledged to make organizing the top priority of their federation. "Organizing is our core principle," explained Change to Win's chair, Anna Burger. "It is our North Star."[13] But Change to Win's effort to jump-start mass organizing proved no more successful in the long run. Within a decade of its founding, its membership had dwindled.[14]

For four decades, the union movement had endeavored to revive organizing through labor law reform and increased investments by unions themselves, yet union membership continued to decline. Some have argued that a commitment to organizing was never embraced by enough unions to produce a turnaround for the movement. There is some truth in this critique. Sweeney, Stern, and other proponents of the organizing model never made converts of many of their colleagues. But labor's commitment to organizing was stronger than many critics allow, and its failures cannot be attributed primarily to the timidity of some union leaders, their inability to enact labor law reform, or even to the increased opposition they faced from employers.[15] Rather, the primary cause for union decline lies in the convergence of a set of developments larger than the unions or their employers—a wholesale transformation of the nation's economy and the relationship of that economy to the government.

This transformation included changes in structure of the national and global economy, the rise of neoliberal policies, the changed structure and function of corporations, the increasing influence of financial markets over corporate governance, the decreased leverage that the workplace holds as an arena for coalescing and deploying collective power, the privatization of public services and underfunding of the public sector, and the degree to which the political system has become both polarized along party lines and paralyzed by that polarization. Together, these developments sharply eroded worker bargaining power and undercut collective action. By doing so, they made it harder to organize workers no matter how much energy and commitment unions devoted to organizing. Grappling with these structural changes would increasingly force labor activists to look beyond organizing efforts alone to experiment with new ways to bargain and act collectively.

STRUCTURAL EROSION OF BARGAINING POWER AND COLLECTIVE ACTION

Many commentators cite globalization and automation as key developments undermining workers' ability to exercise collective power. To be sure, trade liberalization, the offshoring of jobs, and the introduction of computer-based technologies did help undermine bargaining power in manufacturing and other pockets of the economy. But other developments proved more broadly damaging. These included deregulation, the financialization of the economy, and the "fissuring" of the labor market.

Three forms of deregulation eroded worker bargaining power in the late 20th century. First, a bipartisan embrace of deregulation led to the adoption of policies that devastated worker bargaining power in parts of the economy that had once been labor strongholds, such as transportation. The Airline Deregulation Act of 1978 introduced increased competition in the airline industry, triggering mergers, layoffs, and restructurings that forced airline workers to compete with each other as never before. The Motor Carrier Act of 1980 led to a proliferation of low-cost, hypercompetitive trucking companies that undercut the Teamsters' ability to protect wages and benefits through its master freight agreement.

Second, key elements of federal regulation affecting workers, including the minimum-wage and immigration law, became subject to policy drift. The creation of a national minimum wage through the passage of the Fair Labor Standards Act (FLSA) in 1938 had once helped buttress the industrial union movement. "No more important labor legislation has ever been introduced into Congress," said Sidney Hillman of the Amalgamated Clothing Workers (ACW). But by the late 20th century, efforts to update the FLSA ran into increased opposition. The minimum wage was never raised during the two-term presidency of Ronald Reagan. It lagged behind cost of living increases and has never caught up. Between its passage in 1938 and 1981, the minimum was raised every 2.87 years on average. Since 1981, the average length between increases has nearly doubled to 5 years. Even more problematic was the policy drift that affected immigration law in the years after the passage of the Hart–Cellar Act in 1965. As US immigration law remained inert—except for the temporary fix that came from the 1986 Immigration Reform and Control Act—tens of millions of immigrant workers entered the US workforce without legal status and were vulnerable to exploitation.[16]

Finally, the agencies responsible for enforcing regulations that protected workers were starved for resources. As David Weil has documented, inflation-adjusted spending devoted to the enforcement of the FLSA remained almost unchanged between the Reagan and Obama administrations, even as the size of the nation's workforce ballooned.[17]

The rise of neoliberalism and its deregulatory tendencies facilitated another process that disempowered workers: financialization. In some ways, financialization fed on the achievements of organized labor. The first modern pension fund was not created until General Motors and the United Automobile Workers signed the Treaty of Detroit in 1950, but by 1990, pension funds controlled $2.5 trillion in assets, half of which were invested in common stocks. The deregulatory spirit that rose to the fore by the late 1970s created new opportunities for the large pools of capital that were now seeking improved return on investment. Wall Street gave rise to new entities, including hedge fund and private equity investors; new methodologies, including leveraged buyouts; and a new ideology—"maximizing shareholder value." Together these developments transformed the economy, and the FIRE sector (finance, insurance, and real estate) doubled its share of the GDP.[18]

Financialization changed the behavior of corporate employers. Between the 1920s and the 1970s, corporate consolidation and efforts to vertically and horizontally integrate led to the rise of *managerial capitalism*. It produced corporate giants whose place in the economy was secure enough that their decisions could take into account not only the interests of their stockholders but also of some of their stakeholders, including in some cases their workers. Unions were well suited to deal with these corporate entities. In the last quarter of the 20th century, however, as the principle of maximizing shareholder value became dominant, driven by growing pools of capital seeking short-term returns, managerial capitalism gave way to *shareholder capitalism*. As this happened, investors came to see large-scale, diversified conglomerates as worth less than the sum of their parts and to pursue strategies of selling off their pieces and making them leaner profit-driven machines with a single corporate mission: raising their stock value. This gave rise to what Gerald Davis calls management by markets, in which corporate managers were increasingly hostage to strategies that promote stock values. While managerial capitalism grudgingly tolerated unions, shareholder capitalism was increasingly anti-union when corporate managers found that weakening, shedding, or avoiding unions and downsizing, outsourcing, and automating jobs positively influenced stock values.[19]

Deregulation and financialization in turn paved the way for a dramatic reorganization of the employer–employee relationship, driving a process that David Weil calls the fissuring of the American workplace. This was a process whereby employers sought to contract-out work, construct global supply chains, rely increasingly on temporary employees or independent contractors, and expand their businesses through strategies such as franchising that dispersed ownership responsibilities and accountability for workers' welfare. By the end of the 20th century, it was becoming less common for workers to be directly employed by the entities in whose workplaces they labored, unlikely that they would remain with the same employer for most of their working lives, and more likely that they be temporary employees or independent contractors who lacked regulatory protection or the right to organize and bargain collectively.[20]

Deregulation, financialization, and fissuring has sharply eroded worker bargaining power since the 1980s. The decline in union membership figures only hints at the extent to which bargaining power plummeted. A better measure is the precipitous decline in workers' abilities to engage in collective action that would enhance their bargaining leverage. While strikes had been the most reliable form of worker collective action in the 20th century, they suddenly lost their punch. The number of major work stoppages (involving at least 1,000 workers) dropped from 289 per year in the 1970s to 35 per year in the 1990s and never recovered (the average has been 15 per year in the 2010s). The extent to which unionized workers, fearful of replacement, came to view strikes as dangerous or futile suggests how far bargaining power had tipped toward employers.[21]

By the late 20th century, it was becoming clear to a growing number of labor activists that unless unions could find ways to reconstitute bargaining power in light of the late 20th-century transformation of the economy, no amount of money and effort poured into organizing was likely to produce a turnaround in organized labor's fortunes. Out of necessity, activists were forced to develop new approaches to organization, bargaining, and collective action.

MOTHER OF INVENTION: THE EMERGENCE OF INNOVATIVE STRATEGIES

Two things characterized the labor innovations that began emerging in the late 20th century. First, successful organizing campaigns tended to pair organizing strategy with creative ways of marshaling bargaining power. Organizing success increasingly depended on the existence of a sound bargaining strategy and mechanisms that could either prod government into supporting or encouraging bargaining relationships or create extra-governmental forms of pressure or encouragement that might function in lieu of effective government regulation. Developing bargaining strategies that might win the support of actors other than the union and the employer was often crucially important to an organizing success. Second, innovative strategies tended to emerge in an ad hoc fashion to address deep-seated dysfunctions in a labor relations system that was devised for a form of economy that was receding into the past. To navigate that disjuncture, successful campaigns frequently had to devise ad hoc workarounds, tactics that might be characterized as "hacks" of a broken system of labor relations.

Cataloging and characterizing the full range of experiments and innovations is challenging. Any taxonomy is bound to create some arbitrary distinctions between related innovations. But, after surveying a wide range of strategic innovations, my colleagues and I found that grouping them into six basic categories helped illuminate key contributions of the innovators. We called these categories Reconstructing the Bargain, Public Goods Unionism, Capital Strategies/Public Investment, Alternative Union Recognition Strategies, Creative Militancy, and Alternative Worker Organizations.

Reconstructing the Bargain was an innovation that involved devising strategies to organize and bargain beyond the individual employer, such as organizing entire markets rather than individual companies, bargaining with purchasers or financiers up and down supply chains, establishing public authorities as employers of record for collective bargaining, securing retention agreements with public authorities, and creating public and private mechanisms to enforce such agreements. Examples of this innovation included SEIU's Justice for Janitors campaign, the fair food campaign of the Coalition of Immokalee Workers (CIW), and the successful organization of homecare workers by SEIU and AFSCME. Justice for Janitors targeted building owners in an effort to pressure them to agree to labor standards that would allow SEIU to get their building service contractors. The CIW used a boycott of large-scale tomato purchasers to force growers to agree to labor standards and the creation of the penny-a-pound fund for tomato workers. SEIU and AFSCME pushed states such as California and Illinois to have the government act as the employer of record for homecare workers for the purposes of collective bargaining. In each of these cases, bargaining with the direct employers of workers was infeasible. However, reconstructing the bargaining table to bring other entities into the bargain—building owners, tomato purchasers, or state and local governments— was necessary before successful organization could be accomplished.[22]

Public Goods Unionism sought to align organizing and bargaining with broader community interests such as the achievement of living wages, affordable housing, environmental justice, public health, or food justice. This approach is embodied by Jobs to Move America, which is attempting to link urban mass transit solutions to the creation of union jobs, the Don't Waste LA campaign of the Los Angeles Alliance for a New Economy (LAANE), which seeks to build a modern sustainable system of waste removal that will address the issues of poor communities and create decent-paying unionized jobs, or the Supermarket Task Force organized in Detroit by MOSES (Metropolitan Organizing Strategy Enabling Strength) and the UFCW, which is advocating for the alleviation of "food deserts" through the construction of unionized supermarkets and improved transit. The widespread use of community benefit agreements or project labor agreements that ensure the hiring of local, demographically representative, and either unionized or union-eligible workers is perhaps the most common form of this approach.[23]

Capital Strategies/Public Investment entailed using investment strategies, such as shareholder mechanisms, labor-friendly private equity, and public financing to advance organizing and bargaining objectives. With this strategy, unions try to use capital as leverage; invest in quality, union-friendly jobs with public and private resources; and secure contract language on profit sharing, executive compensation, and other issues not traditionally part of bargaining. Examples of this approach range from the AFL-CIO's Housing Investment Trust, which has used its capital to promote projects employing union labor, to Vital Healthcare Capital, a spinoff of SEIU Capital Strategies, created with the help of a Ford Foundation grant, which provides flexible financing and development services to support quality health care and good, unionized health care jobs in low-income underserved communities. Other examples include the Green Justice Campaign of Community Labor United in Boston, which won public subsidies and outreach programs that made home weatherization affordable and accessible to low-income communities, while increasing wages and improving labor standards for weatherization workers, or the Emerald Cities Collaborative, a national nonprofit network of organizations working to make cities more environmentally and socially sustainable through infrastructure projects that promote union jobs with high wages and career paths for their residents, especially women and minorities.[24]

Alternative Union Recognition Strategies saw unions pursue a variety of strategies to avoid bitterly contested elections under an NLRB regime in which the employer has an inherent advantage. These strategies have included pushing employers to agree to neutrality and card-check union recognition, a strategy widely used by UNITE HERE in its organizing of hotels and food service providers. A related strategy is the securing of neutrality agreements from employers, in which the employer agrees not to contest a union's bid for recognition in an unorganized workplace (an approach often paired with card-check recognition). This was the approach the United Automobile Workers (UAW) took in organizing the Dana Corporation in 2003. Yet another example is the negotiation of election procedure agreements in which employers and unions agree to rules of engagement that govern a union election campaign. Typically, both sides agree not to use certain weapons, and elections are expedited. SEIU's organization of Catholic Healthcare West employed this approach.[25]

Through *Creative Militancy*, unions attempt to revive and redefine strikes and related work actions. In some cases, unions infused traditional strikes with the spirit of human rights struggles. This happened in 1989 when 37,000 mineworkers in Kentucky, Virginia, West Virginia, and participated in a wildcat, or unsanctioned, strike, joining 1,900 already striking Pittston Coal mineworkers, who had walked out in protest of Pittston's termination of healthcare and retirement benefits. That wildcat strike helped Pittston workers prevail and helped pave the way for the 1992 Coal Act mandate that forced companies to provide certain health and retirement benefits. In other cases, workers unprotected by law engaged in work stoppages. This happened in 1998 and 2007, when the New York Taxi Workers Alliance (NYTWA), an organization of independent contractors, organized strikes that improved wages and won an AFL-CIO charter for its organization in 2011. But the most creative repurposing of the strike occurred in the one-day walkouts by small numbers of Walmart associates affiliated with the OUR Walmart campaign or fast-food workers affiliated with the Fight for $15 intended to dramatize their plight. These walkouts sought to use strikes primarily as political or public relations actions rather than efforts to shut down businesses. In some cases, it gave workers the power to change the terms and conditions of employment or muster the political will for legislative or regulatory change; in many ways, the successful use of militant tactics depended on other structural factors.[26]

The development of *Alternative Worker Organizations* represented perhaps the most significant of all of the innovations to emerge in the late 20th century. In an economy where unionization proved increasingly difficult, activists created a range of alternative organizations to advance worker power. Worker centers and minority workplace organizations (or minority unions) were the two most significant iterations of this tendency.

The worker center idea can be traced back at least to the 1970s and the organization of the national working women's membership organization 9to5. Building a membership base through creative campaigns such as the Heartless Employer and Scrooge of the Year awards and brandishing the threat of anti-discrimination lawsuits effectively, 9to5 advocated for "pink collar" workers. By the early 1980s, other non-union low-wage workers began turning to local advocacy centers. African Americans in the Carolinas, and immigrants in New York City's Chinatown and in El Paso, Texas, organized the first modern worker centers. A wave of organizing in the late 1980s and early 1990 among Latinx and Southeast Asian immigrants spread the worker center idea and led to the founding of model efforts such as the Centro de Derechos Laborales (the Workplace Project) in suburban Long Island and the Korean Immigrant Workers Alliance, both launched in 1992. These early worker centers offered social services and legal advice and orchestrated local campaigns against wage theft and discrimination. By the early 2000s, worker centers, such as the Restaurant Opportunities Center, began focusing on workers in specific industries. By 2015, there were more than 200 worker centers around the United States.[27]

Worker centers helped give birth to several national networks. Among these were the National Day Laborer Organizing Network (NDLON), founded in 2001, which organized immigrant day laborers; the National Guestworker Alliance (NGA), established in 2006, which advocated on behalf of H2 visa workers in the United States; and the National Domestic Workers Alliance (NDWA), founded in 2007. These organizations adapted to conditions unfavorable to unionization. Traditional collective bargaining was difficult to envision for day laborers who might have a different employer each day, or for domestic workers whose employers were as numerous as the workers themselves, but collective action could win improvements in these workers' lives. NDLON affiliates set up day-laborer cooperatives in some cities, the NGA exposed US employers who exploited guest workers, and the NDWA helped secure passage of a bill of rights for domestic workers in New York State.[28]

Worker center-like organizations also served those outside of the low-wage labor market. The Freelancers Union (founded in 2001), like NDLON, NDWA, and NGA, advocated for workers who could not readily unionize. It signed up dues-paying members who worked in a variety of jobs, especially in the entertainment and media industries, offering them access to a group health insurance plan, legal advice, and more.[29]

A second model of alternative worker organization workplace-based organizations lacked official certification as collective bargaining representatives but functioned as minority unions. Such organizations emerged in settings where unions were either not strong enough to win certification or were not allowed to win it under law. Several minority unions are affiliated with the Communications Workers of America (CWA). Alliance at IBM, Washington Alliance of Technical Workers (WashTech), and Working at GE (WAGE) formed in response to imminent company takeaways or a failed organizing campaign (in the case of WAGE). Another CWA affiliate, the Texas State Employees Union, exists as a minority union owing to the restrictions on collective bargaining for public employee in Texas.[30] Other examples include the Graduate Employees and Students Organization (GESO) at Yale University, affiliated with UNITE HERE; and the Dick's (Sporting Goods) Employee Council, affiliated with the Steelworkers. In 2006, the Steelworkers unsuccessfully attempted to use Dick's Employee Council as a test case for a legal theory that the NLRA grants minority unions collective bargaining rights, yet that strategy continues to draw adherents among legal theorists.[31]

Although minority organizations have not won the right to bargain collectively with their employers, some of them have found ways to take collective action and win improvements in wages, benefits, and working conditions. OUR Walmart, launched in 2011 by the UFCW, is a case in point. At its peak, OUR Walmart membership was made up of past and present Walmart employees from more than 600 stores in over 43 states. It fought to get its members more respect at work, better pay, improved health care, and predictable scheduling by engaging in public actions such as one-day strikes and pickets outside Walmart stores on Black Friday, the stores' busiest day. Rather than seeking recognition as a bargaining agent, OUR Walmart sought to take advantage of workers' rights to engage in collective action under Section 7 of the NLRA. By some measures, OUR Walmart made significant headway. In 2015, Walmart announced wage increases that many observers attributed to OUR Walmart's success in drawing negative attention to the company's labor practices. The UFCW ultimately found it difficult to sustain OUR Walmart, which produced negligible income from its own membership. In 2015, the union withdrew its support, and OUR Walmart became an independent and scaled-down entity. Even so, it continued its agitation by developing a smartphone application called WorkIt, which acts as a digital shop steward informing employees of their rights and helping them navigate the company's internal regulations and grievance procedures.[32]

Alternative worker organizations have struggled to become financially self-sufficient. But recently they have made headway in addressing this problem. OUR Walmart hopes to realize revenues from its WorkIt app. Fast-food workers involved with the SEIU's Fight for $15 in New York City have developed another creative alternative. After years of organizing and intense lobbying, they pressured the New York City Council to adopt a law in 2017 that gives fast-food employees the ability to make voluntary contributions to not-for-profit organizations of their choice through payroll deductions. The creation of Fast Food Justice, a 501(c)(4) group funded by fast-food workers' payroll deductions and capable of advocating on their behalf, stops well short of giving the workers a collective bargaining vehicle. But it does not take much imagination to see how such an organization might lay the experiential basis for a future self-funded union of fast-food employees.[33]

The examples above suggest that as unions and worker activists struggled to deal with an economy reshaped by deregulation, financialization, and fissured employment, they developed a wide range of innovations from "reconstructing the bargain" to building new forms of organization. Taken together, these innovations suggest some of the features that might define a 21st-century revival of worker organization and bargaining power.

MOVING INNOVATION TO THE NEXT LEVEL: COMMON-GOOD BARGAINING

Perhaps the most thoroughgoing effort to reinvent collective bargaining in response to the erosion of worker bargaining power and collective action has emerged from a group of public sector unions and their allies who have embraced an initiative called *Bargaining for the Common Good*.[34] As was the case with other innovations, this initiative arose in response to urgent necessities. The Great Recession propelled a generation of militantly anti-union Republicans into office, including governors Scott Walker of Wisconsin, Rick Snyder of Michigan, and Chris Christie of New Jersey. They promptly implemented austerity budgets and launched attacks on public sector unions, characterizing their members as a new elite who enjoyed expensive benefits—such as defined benefit pensions—that were unavailable to most of the private sector workers whose taxes paid for those benefits. Capitalizing on such sentiments, Walker, the most successful of the bunch, pushed Act 10 through his state legislature, effectively ending collective bargaining for most state and local government workers. These anti-unionists also found allies on the US Supreme Court: in 2012, Justice Samuel Alito signaled that it was time to review and overturn state laws that allowed public sector unions to collect agency fees from the workers they represented.

Realizing their vulnerability in this new context, some trade unionists advocated an approach that would soon be called Bargaining for the Common Good. They argued that the continued pursuit of traditional collective bargaining would isolate unions, allowing their opponents to pit union members against taxpayers. An entirely new approach was called for.

The outlines of that approach first became visible in Chicago under the leadership of the Chicago Teachers Union (CTU). Just as several Midwestern states elected anti-union governors in 2010, union reformer Karen Lewis and her Caucus of Rank-and-File Educators (CORE) were elected to office within the CTU. Lewis's team were determined to take a different approach to the union's contract negotiation in 2012. They resolved to go into bargaining arm in arm with community allies and parents, merging the union's traditional demands with a range of new proposals that went far beyond the parameters of traditional bargaining. The CTU joined with a range of groups including the Grassroots Collaborative, a network of 11 membership organizations; Parents for Teachers; and Stand Up Chicago, a union-sponsored group that specialized in direct action protests. They issued a report called *The Schools Chicago's Students Deserve*, which laid out demands for smaller class sizes, improved facilities, wrap-around programs, and other items that went beyond the confines of the wages, hours, and narrowly defined work issues about which the union was legally permitted to bargain. Significantly, the CTU challenged the financing of the school system, exposing the fact that the school district lost hundreds of millions to toxic interest rate swap deals struck with Wall Street firms. By making the financial industry's exploitation of the school district an issue and demanding that this issue be taken up in negotiation, the CTU placed itself in the position of defending the interests of Chicago taxpayers. The union's demands attracted broad-based support and placed Chicago Mayor Rahm Emanuel, a Democrat who had embraced an austerity agenda, on the defensive. When the union went on strike in September 2012, Emanuel was forced to accede to many of its key demands.[35]

Similar creativity was displayed by state workers in Oregon and teachers in St. Paul the following year. Oregon's SEIU Local 503, which represents homecare, childcare, university, and state workers pursued a campaign called In It Together in preparation for their 2013 contract negotiations. Local 503's demands extended well beyond pay and benefits for its members, calling for a broad investigation into the ways in which banks were ripping off Oregonians, demanding tuition freezes for the state university, and a state lawsuit that would recoup millions lost by state retirement funds resulting from banks' secret manipulation of the London Interbank Offered Rate (LIBOR). Meanwhile, the St. Paul Federation of Teachers (SPFT) took a page from the CTU's playbook, convening community allies and jointly drawing up a list of 29 items to advance at the bargaining table. Included among them were demands for an expanded preschool program; additional nurses, counselors, librarians, and social workers; a reduction of standardized testing; and a commitment that the school district would cease doing business with any banks that foreclosed on the families of school-aged children during the academic year. Although neither Local 503 nor the SPFT won all of their demands, their approach to collective bargaining shattered the taxpayer-versus-union dynamic that had come to characterize so much public sector bargaining.[36]

In May 2014, activists involved in these efforts convened at Georgetown University in Washington, D.C., in a conference that helped to popularize the term Bargaining for the Common Good to describe their approach. Participants included a delegation from Los Angeles that was in the process of launching a campaign called Fix LA. It allied the city's leading public sector unions— SEIU Local 721 and District Council 36—with a broad cross-section of 20 community groups and faith-based organizations in a common cause to restore cuts made in city services in response to the recession and to improve the lot of LA's struggling public sector workers. In March 2014, the campaign released a report titled *No Small Fees*, which noted that Los Angeles was spending more taxpayer money paying fees to the private firms that marketed its municipal bonds and other financial services ($290 million) than it was spending on caring for the city's streets ($160 million). The report blamed the financial industry for forcing austerity on the city and demanded that LA use its $106 billion worth of assets, payments, and debt issuance as leverage to "demand better deals with Wall Street, so that it can invest more in our communities." After a year-long contract campaign, the union won most of its demands, including the city's commitment to hire 5,000 workers and a commitment by the city to study and seek to reform its relationship with Wall Street.[37]

Bargaining for the Common Good (BCG) campaigns drew inspiration from many of the innovations or "hacks" that had emerged from the labor movement over the previous few decades. But these campaigns took the most significant step yet in the effort to redefine collective bargaining to meet the needs of 21st-century workers. BCG campaigns sought to revise three fundamental elements of traditional collective bargaining: its participants, its processes, and its goals.

BCG campaigns sought to expand the stakeholders represented at the bargaining table. Whereas traditional collective bargaining was premised on a simple bilateral bargain between management and labor, BCG campaigns sought to give the community a voice in bargaining by jointly crafting bargaining demands and in some cases—such as St. Paul—to have community representatives physically present during bargaining. Even as they pulled community allies into bargaining on their side of the table, BCG campaigns also attempted to bring the powerful economic actors that so often dominate public policy to the table on the other side. Realizing that public sector employers often functioned on austerity budgets, the campaigns attempted to "bargain with Wall Street" by making the relationship between the financial industry and government a subject of bargaining.

BCG campaigns also transformed the processes of bargaining. Rather than constructing coalitions in which unions recruited community allies at the last minute to support pre-formulated union demands in a quid pro quo transactional relationship that was not intended to survive beyond the contract campaign, these efforts sought to build enduring alignments of interest groups that shared a common vision and narrative and worked to accumulate lasting power over time through campaign victories. BCG campaigns were also prepared to use Creative Militancy when necessary. The campaigns operated from the assumption that traditional political action and bargaining strategies would no longer give public sector workers sufficient leverage. Chicago teachers struck, St. Paul teachers threatened to strike, and Fix LA protesters blocked streets to dramatize their demands. In each case, unions found that militancy or the threat of militancy was most effective if the union was advocating goals that served the common good, not the narrow interests of their members.

Finally, the BCG campaigns broadened the goals of collective bargaining. Since the inception of public sector bargaining in the 1960s, unions have been forced to bargain over a narrow range of economic issues that allowed union opponents to argue that public employees' gains came at the taxpayers' expense. At the same time, unions were forbidden from bargaining over a whole range of issues that might allow them to make common cause with the community. BCG campaigns made a conscious effort to break out of this box, even advancing demands that were outside the scope of what the law permitted. Even if they failed to resolve these issues, the simple act of raising them changed the bargaining dynamic.

Despite their promise, BCG campaigns have spread slowly. Public sector bargaining is highly decentralized, and any effort to change it must be embraced at the local level. At the same time, unions are tradition-bound organizations—and arguably, nothing in the union movement is more impervious to radical reinvention than the bread-and-butter act of bargaining. In perilous times, some unions fear the risks of reinvention. But they might soon have little choice. As this chapter goes to press, indications are that the US Supreme Court will soon overturn the long-standing precedent that permits unions to negotiate contracts that require the workers they represent to pay for the costs of their representation through agency (or fair share) fees. If the court does as expected in the case of *Janus v. AFSCME*, it will force on the entire nation elements of the anti-union regime that Scott Walker enacted in Wisconsin—and the results could be devastating for union finances and strength. If they are to resist the anti-union forces that are now gathering, public sector unions will need all of the allies they can find, and BCG campaigns provide a good model for how to build such alliances.[38]

Finally, the BCG approach need not remain confined to the public sector. Private sector bargaining continues to deteriorate. Not only do employers resist unionization, the very structure of employment continues to change in ways that disempower workers. The application of BCG principles to the private sector might provide new leverage for workers who are experiencing this disempowerment. An intriguing implementation of the BCG approach can be found in the campaign to organize bank workers that is currently being bankrolled by CWA, which has made an effort to link the organization of these workers to efforts to reform the nation's corrupt finance industry. "The importance of this campaign extends beyond improving, or maintaining, conditions for individual workers," the union insists. CWA asserts that "many of the abuses of the financial industry which caused the 2008 crash, including unethical actions and predatory lending, could in fact have been prevented if workers had the protection to speak with an independent voice and whistleblower protections."[39] If they ever hope to unionize the powerful banking industry, workers will require such a broadly conceived mission in which their union fights not only to protect its members through collective bargaining but uses their collective power to protect the public from predatory financial practices.

TRAVELING AN UNCHARTED PATH

Organized labor has been in crisis for a generation. Over time, that crisis has generated a growing list of creative innovations, as the brief survey offered here makes clear. While none of these innovations by themselves have provided a resolution to the crisis, a consensus is beginning to emerge around one fundamental proposition: labor cannot simply organize its way out of this crisis; it must also *reorganize* itself, *reframe* its approach to bargaining, and *revive* its capacity for creative militancy in the service of the common good. Doing so means traveling down an uncharted path, for 20th-century methods will not suffice in meeting the needs of workers in the 21st century. But as this survey suggests, a growing number of labor activists are ready to meet the challenge.

ENDNOTES

[1] Martin H. Malin, Brenda D. Taylor, and Timothy T. Gardner, "Bargaining and Post-Recession Years," Paper Presented to the Tenth Annual ABA Section of Labor and Employment Law Conference, Nov. 11, 2016.

[2] This chapter draws on a 2012 study I co-authored with Jennifer Luff and Katie Corrigan called "Bargaining for the Future: Rethinking Labor's Recent Past and Planning Strategically for Its Future" (http://bit.ly/2EoIthe). For background, see Joseph A. McCartin, "Launching the Kalmanovitz Initiative: A Labor Historian's Labor History," in *Civic Labors: Scholar Activism and Working-Class Studies*, eds. Dennis Deslippe, Eric Fure-Slocum, and John W. McKerley (Champaign, IL: University of Illinois Press, 2016), 197–216.

[3] See, for example: *Organizing to Win: New Research on Union Strategies*, eds. Kate Bronfenbrenner, Sheldon Friedman, Richard W. Hurd, Rudolph A. Oswald, and Ronald L. Seeber (Ithaca, NY: Cornell University Press, 1998); *Rebuilding Labor: Organizing and Organizers in*

the New Union Movement, eds. Ruth Milkman and Kim Moody (Ithaca, NY: Cornell University Press, 2004); Jane F. McAlevey, *No Shortcuts: Organizing for Power in the New Gilded Age* (New York, NY: Oxford University Press, 2016).

[4] Dorian T. Warren, "The Politics of Labor Law Reform," in *The Politics of Major Policy Reform in Postwar America*, eds. Jeffery A. Jenkins and Sidney M. Milkis (New York, NY: Cambridge University Press, 2014), 103-128.

[5] AFL-CIO Committee on the Evolution of Work, *The Changing Situation of Workers and Their Unions* (Washington, DC: AFL-CIO, 1985), 27.

[6] Hardy quoted in Don Stillman, *Stronger Together: The Story of SEIU* (White River Junction, VT: Chelsea Green Publishing, 2010), 17–18.

[7] John B. Jentz, "Janitorial/Custodial," in *Encyclopedia of U.S. Labor and Working Class History*, Vol. 2, ed. Eric Arnesen (New York, NY: Taylor & Francis, 2007), 711.

[8] Stern quoted in Stillman, *Stronger Together*, 20.

[9] Amy Foerster, "Confronting the Dilemmas of Organizing: Obstacles and Innovations at the AFL-CIO Organizing Institute," in *Rekindling the Movement: Labor's Quest for Relevance in the Twenty-First Century*, eds. Lowell Turner, Harry C. Katz, and Richard W. Hurd (Ithaca, NY: ILR Press, 2001).

[10] Financial Reports, AFL-CIO Executive Council Reports, 1980–2009, cited in McCartin, Luff, and Corrigan, "Bargaining for the Future."

[11] Lydia Savage, "Justice for Janitors: Scales of Organizing and Representing Workers," *Antipode* 38:3 (2006): 645–666; Eileen Boris and Jennifer Klein, *Caring for America: Home Health Workers in the Shadow of the Welfare State* (New York, NY: Oxford University Press, 2012), 183–210.

[12] Timothy Minchin, *Labor Under Fire: A History of the AFL-CIO since 1979* (Chapel Hill, NC: University of North Carolina Press, 2017).

[13] Burger quoted in Steven Greenhouse, "Breakaway Unions Start New Federation," *The New York Times*, September 28, 2005, A17.

[14] Rachel Aleks, "Estimating the Effect of 'Change to Win' on Union Organizing," *Industrial & Labor Relations Review* 68, No. 3 (2015): 584–605.

[15] For background on labor organizing in the 1970s, see Lane Windham, *Knocking on Labor's Door: Union Organizing in the 1970s and the Roots of a New Economic Divide* (Chapel Hill, NC: University of North Carolina Press, 2017).

[16] Hillman quoted in Steven Fraser, *Labor Will Rule: Sidney Hillman and the Rise of American Labor* (New York, NY: Free Press, 1991), 394; Jerold Waltman, *The Politics of the Minimum Wage* (Champaign, IL: University of Illinois Press, 2000), 28–47; Carol M. Swain and Virginia M. Yetter, "Federalism and the Politics of Immigration Reform," in *The Politics of Major Policy Reform in Postwar America*, eds. Jeffrey A. Jenkins and Sidney M. Milkis (New York, NY: Cambridge University Press, 2014), 179-202.

[17] David Weil, *The Fissured Workplace: How Work Became So Bad for So Many and What Can Be Done To Improve It* (Cambridge, MA: Harvard University Press, 2014).

[18] Peter F. Drucker, "Reckoning with the Pension Fund Revolution," *Harvard Business Review* 69, No. 2 (March–April 1991): 106–114; John D. Martin and J. William Petty, *Value-Based Management: The Corporate Response to the Shareholder Revolution* (Cambridge, MA: Harvard University Press, 2000); Thomas I. Palley, *Financialization: The Economics of Finance Capital Domination* (New York, NY: Palgrave Macmillan, 2013).

[19] Rana Foroohar, *Makers and Takers: How Wall Street Destroyed Main Street* (New York, NY: Crown Business, 2016); Eileen Appelbaum and Rosemary Batt, *Private Equity at Work:*

When Wall Street Manages Main Street (New York, NY: Russell Sage Foundation, 2014); Gerald Davis, *Managed by the Markets: How Finance Reshaped America* (New York, NY: Oxford University Press, 2009).

[20] Weil, *The Fissured Workplace*; David Van Arsdale, "The Recasualization of Blue-Collar Workers: Industrial Temporary Help Work's Impact on the Working Class," *Labor: Studies in Working-Class History of the Americas* 5, No. 1 (Spring 2008): 75–99.

[21] Josiah Bartlett Lambert, *If the Workers Took a Notion: The Right to Strike and American Political Development* (Ithaca, NY: Cornell University Press, 2005), 129–208; Joseph A. McCartin, "Approaching Extinction? The Declining Use of the Strike Weapon in the United States, 1945–2000," in *Strikes Around the World, 1968–2005: Case Studies of Fifteen Countries*, eds. Sjaak van der Velden, Heiner Dribbusch, Dave Lyddon, and Kurt Vandaele (Amsterdam, Netherlands: Aksant Academic Publishers, 2007), 133–154.

[22] Boris and Klein, *Caring for America*, 189–200; Susan Marquis, *I Am Not a Tractor! How Florida Farmworkers Took on the Fast Food Giants and Won!* (Ithaca, NY: Cornell University Press, 2017).

[23] Jobs to Move America (http://jobstomoveamerica.org); Don't Waste LA (http://www.dontwastela.com); Metropolitan Organizing Strategy Enabling Strength (http://www.mosesmi.org); Herbert R. Northrup and Linda E. Alerio, "'Boston Harbor–Type' Project Labor Agreements in Construction: Nature, Rationales, and Legal Challenges," *Journal of Labor Research* 19 (Winter 1998): 1–63; Bradford W. Coupe, "Legal Considerations Affecting the Use of Public Sector Project Labor Agreements: A Proponent's View," *Journal of Labor Research* 19 (Winter 1998): 99–113.

[24] *AFL-CIO Housing Investment Trust Annual Report* (Washington, DC: AFL-CIO, 1998); Vitalcap (http://vitalcap.org); Green Justice Campaign (http://bit.ly/2EqjES3); Emerald Cities Collaborative (http://emeraldcities.org).

[25] Forrest Stuart, "From the Shop to the Streets: UNITE HERE Organizing in Los Angeles Hotels," in *Working for Justice: The LA Model of Organizing and Advocacy*, eds. Ruth Milkman, Joshua Bloom, and Victor Narro (Ithaca, NY: Cornell University Press, 2010), 191–210; Gary T. Pakulski, "Dana, UAW Cut Deal on Union Effort to Organize," *Toledo Blade*, August 14, 2003 (http://bit.ly/2EpMxOo); Adam D. Reich, *With God on Our Side: The Struggle for Workers' Rights in a Catholic Hospital* (Ithaca, NY: ILR Press, 2012).

[26] Richard A. Brisbin Jr., *A Strike Like No Other Strike: Law and Resistance During the Pittston Coal Strike of 1989–1990* (Baltimore, MD: Johns Hopkins University Press, 2010); Mischa Gaus, "Not Waiting for Permission: The New York Taxi Workers Alliance and 21st Century Bargaining," in *New Labor in New York: Precarious Workers and the Future of the Labor Movement*, eds. Ruth Milkman and Ed Ott (Ithaca, NY: Cornell University Press, 2014), 246–265; Erica Smiley, "Collective Bargaining 3.0," *Dissent* 62, No. 4 (Fall 2015): 69–72.

[27] Lane Windham, *Knocking on Labor's Door: Union Organizing in the 1970s and the Roots of a New Economic Divide* (Chapel Hill, NC: University of North Carolina Press, 2017), Chap. 7; Janice Fine, *Worker Centers: Organizing Communities at the Edge of the Dream* (Ithaca, NY: ILR Press, 2006); Saru Jayaraman, *Behind the Kitchen Door* (Ithaca, NY: ILR Press, 2014).

[28] Walter Nichols, "Politicizing Undocumented Immigrants One Corner at a Time: How Day Laborers Became a Politically Contentious Group," *International Journal of Urban & Regional Research* 40, No. 2 (March 2016): 299–320; Josh Eidelson, "Guestworkers as Bellwether," *Dissent* 60, No. 2 (Spring 2013): 53–59; Ai-jen Poo and Carol Whitlatch, "Caregiving in America: Supporting Families, Strengthening the Workforce," *Generations* 40, No. 4 (Winter 2016/2017): 87–93.

[29] Atossa Araxia Abrahamian, "The 'I' in Union," *Dissent* 59, No. 1 (Winter 2012): 40–44.

[30] WashTech (https://washtech.org); Rand Wilson, "Hooksett GE Workers Want a New Voice for Workers," March 26, 2007 (http://geworkersunited.blogspot.com); David Nack and Jimmy Tarlau, "The Communications Workers of America Experience with 'Open-Source Unionism,'" *WorkingUSA* (2005): 721–732.

[31] US National Labor Relations Board, Office of the General Counsel, Advice Memorandum, June 22, 2006, to Gerald Kobell, Regional Director Region 6, Regarding Dick's Sporting Goods, Case 6-CA-34821 530-3067 (http://bit.ly/2EqksX0); Catherine Fisk and Xenia Tashlitsky, "Imagine a World Where Employers Are Required to Bargain with Minority Unions," *ABA Journal of Labor & Employment Law*, 27, No. 1 (Fall 2011): 1–22.

[32] David Moberg, "The Union Behind the Biggest Campaign Against Walmart in History May Be Throwing in the Towel. Why?" *In These Times*, August 11, 2015 (http://bit.ly/2EoJs0U); Yael Gauer, "A Third Party App Helps Walmart Workers Understand Company Policies," *Motherboard*, November 25, 2016 (http://bit.ly/2EqkONk).

[33] Fast Food Justice, see https://www.fastfoodjustice.org.

[34] For a fuller account of the emergence of Bargaining for the Common Good, see Joseph A. McCartin, "Bargaining for the Common Good," *Dissent* 63, No. 2 (Spring 2016): 128–135.

[35] Micah Uetricht, *Strike for America: Chicago Teachers Against Austerity* (New York, NY: Verso, 2014); Steven K. Ashby and Robert Bruno, *A Fight for the Soul of Public Education: The Story of the Chicago Teachers Strike* (Ithaca, NY: ILR Press, 2016).

[36] Joseph A. McCartin, "Public Sector Labor Under Assault: How to Combat the Scapegoating of Organized Labor," *New Labor Forum* 22, No. 3 (September 2013): 60; Mary Cathryn Ricker, "Teacher–Community Unionism: A Lesson From St. Paul," *Dissent* 62, No. 3 (Summer 2015): 72–77.

[37] Patrick M. Dixon, "Fixing LA and Remaking Public Sector Bargaining: A Case Study of Bargaining for the Common Good," Kalmanovitz Initiative for Labor and the Working Poor, 2016 (http://bit.ly/2Em9kui).

[38] Joseph A. McCartin, "Labor's Janus-Faced Juncture," *Democracy: A Journal of Ideas*, October 24, 2017 (http://bit.ly/2EmrFaG).

[39] On the bank workers' project, see Communications Workers of America (http://bit.ly/2EkKHOP).

CHAPTER 8

The Strike as the Ultimate Structure Test: Rebuilding Working-Class Power Through Mass Participation Strikes

JANE MCALEVEY

2016'S MOST SUCCESSFUL U.S. UNION ORGANIZING DRAWS ON THE POWER OF MASS STRIKES

> *To abandon the strike is to abandon the concept of wage labor;*
> *for the essence of wage labor as opposed to slave labor, is*
> *refusal to work when conditions of work become unbearable.*

John Steuben[1]

In September 2015, at 4:30 in the morning of his night shift, nurse Michael Winn cold-called nearby Temple University Hospital in Philadelphia, which is unionized, to ask about its conditions and its union. Winn didn't know the nurses he was calling. He and his co-workers in the emergency department at the nearby non-union Hahnemann University Hospital had just experienced a heartbreaking and deeply frustrating patient-care crisis caused by systemic short staffing. When he reached the switchboard, he asked to speak with the charge nurse in the emergency department.

"Hi. Temple ER. May I help you?" the charge nurse asked.

"Hi. My name is Michael. I'm a nurse over at Hahnemann's, and we are having an incredible staffing crisis. I want to pick your brain for a minute: I know you have a union at Temple. Do you like your union? Does your hospital get away with substandard care and nurse abuse the way our hospital management's does?"[2]

"We'd never tolerate those conditions, and I love my union!" Temple's charge nurse answered.

When Winn heard the response, he and his co-workers decided they needed a union. Within days, union nurses from Temple University Hospital, who were members of the Pennsylvania Association of Staff Nurses and Allied Professionals (PASNAP), began meeting with their non-union counterparts at Hahnemann Hospital. By January 20, 2016, Winn and his 850 co-workers overwhelmingly voted yes (516 to 117) to forming a union through a National Labor Board Relations (NLRB) election. Yes, an NLRB election.

Had Winn reached a nurse who didn't know or care about the hospital's union, it's fair to say he wouldn't have considered that the solution to his problem could be forming a union.

In Philadelphia, the union at Temple University Hospital seems as strong as any union in the heyday of the American labor movement described in the 1940s and 1950s—and for some of the same core reasons. As in those earlier decades, the Temple workers forged intense solidarity through one of the largest strikes in the United States. In 2010, 1,600 nurses and technical workers at Temple walked off the job in an open-ended strike. It garnered strong support actions from the city's unions, as well as from politicians, editorial boards, and the general public. The central issue in the strike was a gag order on nurses proposed by hospital management during the successor contract negotiations for the Temple workers' fourth contract with PASNAP as their union. The gag order was intended to silence mounting complaints about dangerous short-staffing levels lodged by empowered union nurses through a special State of Pennsylvania reporting hotline, Project DISCLOSE.[3] The management-proposed gag order read: "The Association [PASNAP], its officers, agents, representatives and members shall not publicly criticize, ridicule or make any statement which disparages Temple, or any of its affiliates or any of their respective management officers or medical staff members."[4]

Adding to the fury of the nurses and technical staff, Robert Birnbrauer, a Temple human resources department director, was quoted by the news media as saying to the nurses and techs, "If you want your constitutional rights, you need to go somewhere else."[5] Taking Birnbrauer at his word, the nurses and techs decided that "somewhere else" would be the streets of Philadelphia. They were there for 28 days until they defeated management in a public relations romp. The strike received so much press that it would be difficult even today to find a nurse in Philadelphia who wasn't aware of the month-long Temple strike. Area nurses like Winn also knew that as a result of the strike, Temple had the best-paid nurses and staffing safeguards in Philadelphia, won through their union strike and struggle.

Days before the lopsidedly pro-union vote at Hahnemann Hospital on January 19 to January 20, 2016, however, the 330 nurses at Delaware County Memorial Hospital (DCMH) had voted 164 to 130 to unionize on January 15 to January 16 (164 to 130). Two weeks later, on February 8, just off Broad Street—the same street as Temple—470 nurses at St. Christopher's Hospital voted 311 to 49 to unionize. Over the next two weeks in February, two more units of both outpatient and technical workers at St. Christopher's and DCMH would vote yes to joining the nurses in their hospitals. And on April 8, the nurses at Einstein Medical Center—also on Broad Street, to the north of Temple, the biggest hospital of the 2016 campaign and most strategically important because of its ranking and prestige in the Philadelphia labor market—voted to unionize (463 to 343).

But seeing the handwriting on the wall from the successive elections, Einstein management had hired one of the top union-busting firms in the United States: IRI, Inc. There were a dozen union busters in the hospital in the weeks leading up to the election.[6] In fact, the first sighting of IRI consultants inside the hospital was in late March 2015, when the union had leafleted about unionization outside the hospital. The consultants, therefore, had been trying to work the Einstein nurses into an anti-union crusade for almost one full year by the time of the election, resulting in a narrower win than in most of the other recent contests. There were 926 nurses eligible to vote, of whom 806 cast ballots (86% of all nurses cast a ballot). The 463 yes votes were equal to the number of no votes combined with the 120 who hadn't voted (343 no votes, with 120 who didn't participate in the vote).

Within the byzantine NLRB-defined legal period of seven days from the date of the election—the number of days either side in an election has to file objections to a union election—an urgent fax stated what a courier simultaneously hand-delivered to the union offices: an official objection by management's lawyers to the union election at Einstein, seeking immediate relief and stating that the hospital refused to recognize the union because of its allegations of malfeasance on the part of the union.

METHODOLOGY

I used mixed qualitative and quantitative methods in writing this chapter. I was a participant observer in the 2016 organizing campaign in Philadelphia. Prior to that year, starting in 2013, I was an occasional consultant to PASNAP, conducting training on power and strategy. I was in regular discussion with union leadership starting in January 2016 but was unable to move because of my post-doc requirements at Harvard, which involved teaching full-time in January and February. In April 2016, eight days after the Einstein hospital management filed election objections with the NLRB, I delivered the keynote speech to the annual convention of PASNAP. There I met with top nurse leaders who urged me to move to Philadelphia to help the campaign. On May 1, PASNAP hired me to do two jobs: to coordinate the citywide first contract campaign across the hospitals and to try to win recognition of the union at Einstein, which would include negotiating the contract if we overcame hospital management in the fight to win union recognition.

The legal charges filed by the hospital had the potential to lock the workers into what is typically five years of legal appeals and judicial rulings, a process that we understood from experience was developed by A-level union busters to destroy the workers' hopes of forming the union, despite their voting yes in a sanctioned NLRB election.[7] I moved to Philadelphia in May, just in time for the first of a series of legal hearings that were to be conducted about the employer's objections—hearings where we were preparing dozens of nurse witnesses to testify. I remained there until late October. I continued to fly in and out in November and phone in regularly for December's end-game strategy.

During the course of the campaign, we held weekly shift-change meetings (at seven in the morning and seven in the evening, to make them accessible to all workers) where we had discussions with hundreds of nurses, city and state elected officials, journalists, lawyers for our side and the opposing counsel, and hospital management. As part of the organizing work, the staff team held roughly 1,000 face-to-face, semistructured conversations with nurse and technical staff rank-and-file organizers (those workers elected or actively and regularly participating in organizing committee meetings and eventually as members of the negotiations committees). The 1,000 nurse and technical rank-and-file organizers conducted roughly another 5,000 conversations with an additional 1,500 semistructured one-on-one conversations with their co-workers between May and October. All of these semistructured conversations were based on what organizers call "written raps": raps typically being a one-page model conversation practiced first among paid union organizers, then between union organizers and rank-and-file organizers. These conversations are structured to ensure that consistent information is distributed to the mass of the workers and to ensure that consistent information will be returned from the same mass of workers (an example of one of the dozens of raps intended to have a mass number of semistructured conversations is shown in the appendix to this chapter). As part of the staff development effort, weekly raps had to be written for all hospital teams and sent to me by 5 P.M. each Sunday. I refined, changed, adjusted, or corrected key aspects of the rap if needed; the organizing teams met every Monday morning to practice the final weekly raps. I conducted full staff team meetings every Monday at 9 A.M. across the hospital teams and attended hospital-specific meetings that were held later and staggered throughout each Monday.

In preparing this chapter, I conducted ten semistructured interviews in March and April 2016 with nurses and union organizers. I did archival research, primarily retrieving key statements and exchanges posted to both the pro-union and anti-union websites put up for each hospital. I also led a second team, a four-person research team, during the same period. The job of the research team was to do a comprehensive geographical power structure analysis (PSA) on the Philadelphia labor market. The PSA team did extensive research on the health care labor market in Philadelphia, including top-performing hospitals, and obtained hospital rankings by public patient satisfaction reports, strategic planning documents made by each hospital, and deep background searches on the CEOs and members of the board of trustees or directors for each hospital in which we were engaged in active campaigns.

Additionally, our PSA research team conducted 40 structured interviews with journalists, academics, political appointees in various agencies, and management staff. The team sat in on and observed agency meetings, city council meetings, and meetings of other public bodies that had relationships to either hospital management board members or hospital financial plans. The PSA team exhaustively researched election contributions, especially all contributions by the hospitals engaged in the campaign, as well as contributions of the Hospitals & Healthsystem Association of Pennsylvania and its subgroups. The team also geo-mapped the newly organized members of the union by political districts and precincts. In total, the PSA research team logged roughly 1,000 hours of research time into the Philadelphia power structure, mostly over the months of July and August. I conducted several PSA interviews personally as a method of initially teaching and training the researchers how to conduct a structured PSA interview conversation.

As coordinator of the citywide campaign, I had full access to the PASNAP database. The system for data collection and management that PASNAP uses, called Broad Stripes, is designed for social movement organizing. It is capable of holding many strands of segmented and mergeable data per worker. For the Philadelphia 2016 contract campaign, we had just under N = 3,200 for the newly organized workers, plus an additional 2,000 workers at the already unionized Temple University Hospital. The Temple union's existing contract, by coincidence and great luck, expired on September 30, 2016. These 2,000 workers, the ones who conducted one of the largest strikes of the new millennium, were added to the contract coordination. As such, the data pool I was working with was N = 5,200.

This chapter focuses primarily on one hospital, Einstein, where the top union busters had decided there would be no union. Specifically, it focuses on the effort to move the most virulently anti-union department—what organizers call the "biggest worst"—from anti-union to pro-union. This chapter examines a small section of union actions. It is a story of significant success in a period of massive union decline. My aim is to understand in depth the dynamics and strategies in which particular hard-fought victories are achieved and how workers build resilient organizations. I argue that understanding the success at Einstein offers important insights into attempts to rethink and revitalize the future labor movement.

HIGH-PARTICIPATION STRIKES AS STRUCTURE TESTS, STRUCTURE TESTS AS UNION DEMOCRACY TESTS, PASNAP'S ORIGINS, AND ROUTINIZATION OF STRIKES

Strike leadership should be much broader than the regular union leadership; for the greater the participation of the rank and file, the stronger the strike.

John Steuben[8]

The US working class is at its weakest power in a hundred years. Working-class unity in the workplace, as measured by successful strikes, is at an all-time low.[9] Working-class solidarity in the electoral arena has given way to working-class disunity; workers vote for anyone who promises any form of radical change, whether progressive or reactionary. This chapter makes four interrelated arguments, and all four points are interdependent:

1. There have always been strategic sectors where workers position structurally in the labor market enables them to conduct and win strikes, versus more general masses of workers less structurally capable of using the strike weapon and therefore less capable of challenging the ruling class.
2. Within the strategic sectors, examples from the 1930s include auto, steel, and coal workers and today include health care, education, and transport and logistics, to name a few.
3. Once union leadership *within the strategic sectors* stopped using strikes as their most powerful weapon, they no longer needed to build strong worksite organization.
4. Thus, weak worksite organization lies at the root of the power crisis of the US working class today. The result is that the vast majority of what's left of today's unions, including many in strategic sectors, are unprepared for the kind of attacks that began in earnest with the 2010 elections, and continue with the Supreme Court case *AFSCME v. Janus.*

Writing in the 1920s, John Steuben remarked in his book *Strike Strategy,*[10] the first of its kind, "The strike organization must have a wide, democratic base; that is a large section of strikers must be involved in the various phases of activity. A strike needs active participants, not observers."[11] Although Steuben gives many reasons rank-and-file workers must be fully engaged in the planning for and execution of what he calls the "strike machinery," no single reason is more important than his simple statement that "a strike needs active participants, not observers." Steuben, a machinist who eventually became a full-time organizer for the CIO, was on the team that helped organize steel workers in the 1930s. I use his definition of a strike: "A strike is an organized cessation from work. It is the collective halting of production or services in a plant, industry, or area for the purpose of obtaining concessions from employers. A strike is labor's weapon to enforce labor's demands."[12] This definition of a strike stands in contrast to today's symbolic strikes, which have the character of a protest but lack the power of the collective withdrawal of labor.[13]

In the post-Reagan era in the United States, to overcome or defeat the efforts by employers to replace workers during a strike, strike strategists generally won't consider a strike unless and until no fewer than 90% of the workers are ready to unite and walk off the job. In addition, the workers have to possess some strategic capacity to even contemplate using the strike weapon. With the exception of rare highly specialized or individually significant workers—say, 19 engineers at a jumbo aircraft maker such as Boeing, who are the only people who can certify that a new plane is ready to fly without its crashing—most worker power comes from their large numbers and their unity, not their irreplaceability. But this has always been true; there have always been workers with more capacity to strike and workers with less capacity to strike. In the 1930s and 1940s, the radical leaders inside the CIO weren't equally focused on all sectors of workers. They weren't even somewhat focused on all types of workers; rather, they were very focused on industries that they believed presented the best opportunity for workers to exercise the strike. This chapter focuses on one such key strategic sector today, health care. In thinking through the factors that enable workers to strike, strategists of any era have to consider a long list of criteria, including the following:

- Are the workers hard to replace or easy to replace?
- Are the concessions costs high or low?
- Is it possible to stop production, or seriously constrain production, by the withdrawal of labor?
- Is the broader community likely to support the workers or the employers if a strike is held? Can the workers' actions change the likelihood of whom the public sides with by their actions?
- Is the time of year good or bad for a strike, encompassing factors such as weather and climate, major holidays, or specific events such as elections or major conventions?
- Reflecting some criteria that originate with modern globalization, can the physical workplace itself be moved to another region, state, or part of the world, or are there structural factors that limit the mobility of the facility? Is the employer an identifiable target?

The answers to these questions are essential to strike outcomes.

In the United States, as a result of 40 years of globalization, the dominant industries of the new millennium are characterized by service provision and service workers, who are easily or fairly easily replaced.[14] In addition to the active engagement of the rank-and-file workers, Steuben spent considerable energy in his nearly 100-year-old *Strike Strategy* discussing the importance of paying close attention to the most vulnerable workers, and indeed, the unemployed: "Should the thousands upon thousands of unemployed in any given industry develop a feeling that their union is not concerned with their welfare and does not put up a fight for their immediate needs, they will look upon the union as a 'fair weather friend' and may turn against organized labor."[15] Steuben even provides a chapter focused on persuading spouses, families, and communities to embrace the cause of a strike. For example, according to Steuben, beyond being sure that key facilities or departments are ready to strike, "similar committees should meet with the Mayor, City Councilmen, church leaders, civic organization leaders, heads of political parties and other influential persons in the community. All of this must be done as part of strike preparations. The problem of molding public opinion in support of the strike must not be left until after the strike begins."[16]

PASNAP was birthed by nurses who were dissatisfied by the union they were a part of in the 1990s and who decided to break away and form a new, independent union in 2000. According to Patty Eakin, a recently retired nurse who worked at Temple University Hospital for 29 years and is the founding president of PASNAP, she and her co-workers at Temple originally formed a union with the Pennsylvania Nurse Association (PNA). But by the early 1990s, PNA had come to be dominated by management-side nurses, not bedside or staff nurses. (Management nurses are not eligible to be part of collective bargaining or unions in the United States.) Tired of PNA, the Temple nurses decided to leave the organization, along with nurses at 17 other hospitals.[17]

> In 1995 at Temple we de-certified PNA and joined PSEA HC (Pennsylvania State Education Association, Health Care, a new division created by the teachers' union in Pennsylvania to capture the many groups of nurses who were unhappy being in an association with management nurses). We were actually the 17th local [hospital] to de-cert PNA. By 1999 everyone in PSEA HC was pissed off and disgusted with our terrible contracts and wanted out, or wanted to do something. In early 2000, we made our plans to exit PSEA. Our agreement with PSEA was re-negotiated every two years and happened to be up in April of 2000. One of the best days of my life was going into the meeting with the PSEA officials with my other two comrades and giving them a letter stating we were out. They were blown away![18]

On May 29, 2000, there was a founding convention where the Temple nurses voted officially to leave the PSEA and founded PASNAP. By the time of the convention, another group of nurses from Butler Memorial Hospital, who had already left the PSEA, decided to join the Temple nurses in PASNAP. By late June 2000, the nurses had decided to hire a small staff team with experience in organizing and negotiations. Both of PASNAP's early staff hires came from what was then an independent national union called simply 1199, a union widely considered an effective and politically left and militant union. Its origins and methods today are steeped in the socialist-dominated era of the US labor movement.[19]

The preamble of an unpublished training manual written by Bernie Minter— the only of its kind used by 1199 when it was still an independent national union,[20] states that a union is defined as the following:

Progressive Trade Unionist
- To raise the class-conscious level of working people.
- To clarify the fact that there are sides and define them.
- To work for rank and file control and collective decision making on all levels.
- To maximize participation in union life, understanding that people participate based on their understanding.

Later in the same manual, in a section describing the two directions unions can go (democratic or top-down control), Minter wrote:

> A union cannot choose who shall be members. We have no choice but to organize whoever the boss hires. Therefore, we will constantly have thousands of new members who have never gone through struggles and who reflect the thinking of society at large. The overwhelming majority see three sides. The boss is one authority the union is another (good) authority. The workers have to maneuver to get the most they can from both sides. The basic strength of the union depends on how well we can change three sides to two.

Since their founding as a union, nurses and technical workers in PASNAP have walked off the job eight times. Seven of those strikes happened since 2010.

As Table 1 demonstrates, workers who are presumed to self-identify as professional have no trouble deciding to strike when the leadership of the union places a premium on teaching workers that they win the most by exercising class power. In fact, in the 1199 tradition, gleaning from experience, interviews, and manuals, it is clear that what workers can win has everything to do with how much power they themselves can build. On the heels of a union election, no matter the percentage of workers voting for or against the union, PASNAP's organizers continue the same aggressive organizing approach that they used during the initial organizing drive. If the union didn't prioritize raising workers' expectations that they can win a life-changing contract by being ready to "strike to win," they'd have no incentive to build mass participation and a resilient workplace structure once they had secured a yes vote in a union election. This goes to the heart of the issues that Bernie Minter addressed in his 1199 manual, written in the early 1960s, where he discussed the two directions in which a union can go.

If the purpose of the union is to teach workers to win, which is PASNAP's understanding of its purpose, strike preparation is key to every aspect of the organization's core work—including its approach to the ongoing life of the

TABLE 1
PASNAP Strikes Since Its Founding in 2000

Hospital (and Unit, If Applicable)	Date of Strike	Duration of Strike	Unit Size and % Not Crossing	Date of Contract
Wilkes-Barre General Hospital	Jan. 30–Feb. 18, 2003	21 days	500; 92%	Feb. 14, 2003
Temple University Hospital	Apr. 1–28, 2010	28 days	1,000 RNs, 600 techs; 97%	Apr. 29, 2010
Wilkes-Barre General Hospital	Dec. 23, 2010	1-day strike, 4-day lockout	510; 89%	May 3, 2010
Wilkes-Barre General Hospital	Dec. 3–5, 2013	1-day strike, 2-day lockout	485; 92%	Sep. 5, 2014
Wilkes-Barre General Hospital	Jul. 4–9, 2014	5-day strike	485; 90%	Sep. 5, 2014
Crozer Chester Medical Center	Sep. 21–25, 2014	2-day strike, 3-day lockout	570; 100%	Jun. 15, 2015
Armstrong County Memorial Hospital techs	Mar. 31–Apr. 2, 2015	1-day strike, 2-day lockout	125; 90%	Jun. 8, 2016
Delaware County Memorial Hospital, RNs and techs	Mar. 6–10, 2017	2-day strike, 3-day lockout	460; 98% (100% of RNs out; 7 lab techs crossed)	Apr. 20, 2016

With regard to the "not crossing" column, the number was never less than 90%, though accurate numbers for the 10% who might have crossed was not available for all strikes. Also, lockouts are considered strike days in this table because the workers are aware during voting for a strike authorization that the employer is likely to lock them out for more days, with more loss of pay, less time to return to their normal life routines, etc.

union, the governance phase. PASNAP represents a growing trend of independent unions—unions filled with workers who have been disappointed with the approach to the work that lowers workers' expectations, an approach that is commonly understood as business unionism. In the new millennium, most unions considered to be progressive in the larger social-change movement are the same unions that deliberately lower workers' expectations about what they can expect or hope to win in the collective bargaining process.

One of the sister unions to PASNAP is the Massachusetts Nurses Association (MNA). Like PASNAP, MNA is independent of any national union or national federations, but both pay dues to their local central labor councils (CLCs, bodies of the AFL-CIO) and collaborate with other unions on local politics and other key labor solidarity efforts. PASNAP and MNA have codified their solidarity by forming an overt and contractual partnership, the Northeast Nurses Association (NENA), whose sole purpose is to pool union dues money and union-organizing staff to assist workers in the hardest organizing fights. The organizing wins that workers achieved in Pennsylvania were due in part to the strategic partnership the two unions have forged, facilitated by their geographic proximity and their shared sense of the purpose of the union. A third, far smaller, union is part of the strategic organizing collaborative, the New York Association of Nurses. (In the case of New York, there is a much larger nurses' union that is not a party to the NENA collaboration.)

NENA reflects the focus on teaching workers to win as a core value of the union in its approach to the very definition of what new organizing or external organizing means. In the unions considered to be the dominant national unions in the service sector, and in fact for two decades at the AFL-CIO, "new organizing" or "external organizing" refers only to the moment the workers win the union but not to the struggle to achieve the first collective agreement. In NENA, the first contract fights are understood to be a legitimate component of new organizing. In the early 1990s in one of the largest unions in the United States, and certainly in the largest hospital workers unions, SEIU made its position on this issue official and carried its own philosophy that workers' contracts don't matter to the national AFL-CIO. That set the tone of the new organizing department at the national labor federation as one focused exclusively on dues growth—not the expansion of worker power.

SEIU led the breakup of the national labor movement and created a breakaway alternative federation, Change to Win (CTW), founded by seven unions, all of which projected in a substantial public relations effort that they were the organizing unions, the unions that were going to grow the US labor movement. And their definition of growth was completely divorced from the quality of contracts that workers would win when they formed a union. Collective bargaining was downgraded entirely, with dues growth metrics replacing teaching workers how to win strong contracts. From the view of workers themselves, the irony that seven unions broke away, declared themselves the organizing unions, and explicitly decided to jettison collective bargaining was hard to miss. Yet because the vast majority of so-called progressive allies—including community groups, philanthropists, journalists, and faith-based groups—have such a limited understanding of how unions function and what workers want when they survive a tough union election, the same irony was lost on them.

EINSTEIN MEDICAL CENTER: EXHIBIT A IN HOW UNIONS THAT STRIKE TEND TOWARD INTERNAL DEMOCRACY AND HIGH WORKER AGENCY

> *Buying munitions is one thing, tactical preparation is another. Employers do not stock up on gas and revolvers and then just sit back and wait for things to develop; often they hire men with military training and background to survey their plants and outline plans for a "tactical situation."*
>
> John Steuben[21]

In mid-April 2016, when Einstein management filed a bevy of legal charges challenging the workers' election, the workers and PASNAP leadership understood the strategy was intended to destroy the union by legalizing the fight for half a decade. The vote to form the union was 463 to 343. If the purpose of the union is to teach workers to win—and winning includes actually achieving a contract that addresses the core issues negatively affecting the workers every day—the approach of the union is to immediately make a plan to win over the 343 no votes to the cause of the union. To build a 90% active unity, the percentage required to make a credible strike threat, there's no possible way to achieve those numbers without directly engaging the 343 no's to shift their position radically from anti-union to pro-union. In a view that came to predominate the so-called organizing unions, those 343 no votes don't matter because there would never be a plan to focus on the contract negotiations at all, thus mitigating the need to teach the workers to build a strong worksite organization.

Part of the reason I was hired by PASNAP was to figure out how to beat the employer and develop a strong union despite Einstein management's decision to kill the union with a long, protracted legal fight that would demobilize the workers who voted yes, refuse to start any contract negotiations, and snuff out the entire union victory with a series of proven tactics designed to defeat unions in the post–Ronald Reagan era. There were two things I understood from prior experience. First, we had to force the employer to actually *drop* its legal charges. It simply would not work to allow the legal fight to run its course, even if the workers won the fight at every stage. The strategic employer approach is to automatically and endlessly appeal at each ruling in the legal fight, which drags on for years. Second, the workers themselves would have to overcome the internal divisions and build the worksite organization strong enough to demonstrate supermajorities for the union if we were to have a credible campaign to convince the broader general public that the employer's actions were immoral and anti-democratic. The challenge was that to achieve supermajorities meant moving a substantial number of workers from equating union with bad to equating union as a force for good. And doing so at the same time that the employer was publicly steadfast, the workers would never have a union.

Because Einstein management had hired an A-level union-avoidance firm, the full-time consultants brought in to devise and direct the management's anti-union campaign hadn't left when the election was over. The consultants remained and built their anti-union beachhead in several departments. The biggest was in the telemetry unit (Tele), where 66 nurses had all but shut out the union and voted no in the election. Even though NLRB union elections are conducted by secret ballot, good organizers and strong worker committees that practice a discipline called worksite charting can predict how each worker will vote. The method relies on endless structure tests, essentially a mechanism to assess each worker's opinion of forming a union throughout the campaign. From the view of winning a strong contract, 7% of the anti-union animus resided in this single unit. Although there were smaller pockets of scattered no votes throughout the hospital, the largest block of anti-union nurses resided in a unit that is literally walled off from other units. Tele nurses are the nurses who sit, astutely staring at computer screens that are hooked to patients in almost every room, monitoring their oxygen level, heart rate, status of liquid medications, and so forth. Without the support of this unit, the Einstein workers couldn't achieve a credible strike threat.

Because the workers there had actually led the anti-union campaign, just how to approach Tele was particularly challenging. They regularly contributed to an anti-union Facebook page and an official website. In the posts, there was not only hostility but also a virulent strain of anti-unionism. In conversations with pro-union worker leaders about what had happened during the campaign, they would throw up their hands and exclaim there was no way to change the nurses' view in Tele. They believed they had tried everything. But with an approach to unionism centered on teaching workers to win, the conversation from the union staff with the pro-union workers was consistent: you (not the paid union staff) have to win over the no votes to be able to seriously win anything substantial in this hospital.

The initial strategy was to step back and do a serious assessment of the leadership in Tele, who were the most respected workers among all the workers in that department. Had we correctly assessed who the real, informal, or organic leaders were among their peers? What had been the effort to move the department previously? One conclusion was that the assessments to identify Tele's most respected workers might easily have been wrong because the union-avoidance firm had instructed the workers not to talk to anyone about their unit or the union. While conducting the review of the anti-union effort in Tele, several names surfaced as people identified as holding some leadership. Out of 66 workers, Liz Miller on the night shift was the only functioning contact the union had. And the night shift of any hospital is always significantly smaller than the day shift because management's incorrect assumption is that patients sleep at night and are not in need of nearly the same attention as they are during the day. Of course, anyone who has ever been hospitalized overnight knows that at night, patients are either awake in pain or fear, or are woken up for various tests, IV bag changes, administration of medications needed in short-time intervals, lab tests, and so forth.

So one person would talk to us: Miller, who had voted yes for the union. She is close to retirement, a seasoned nurse working in a unit with many new and young nurses, many of who were people of color. Miller is a classic case of someone who is a pro-union activist but not a leader. She is a songwriter and musician when she isn't working the night shift. Miller was recently elected the Pennsylvania representative for the American Songwriters Association (a membership group for songwriters, but not a union). She identifies as a feminist, as someone who experienced second-wave feminism in the 1970s and the changes that women, including registered nurses, had to fight for to secure basic decent treatment and respect. I like Miller: she is funny, exuberant, and incredibly strong with her opinions. She makes me want to hear her sing in a smoke-filled Nashville bar. She was interesting and easy to spend time with.

But as the lead on a campaign where my job was to teach the workers to win and, specifically, to overcome the significant crisis of the Tele department, there wasn't much Miller could do. In my discussions with her, and in a formal interview conducted after the campaign, she discussed at length that, to her, the union idea was an obvious one: Why wouldn't the workers want a union? She was extremely frustrated by her inability to move the younger nurses. She loved her unit and felt very good about her co-workers, except for on the vexing issue of how to get them to see what she saw: a union as a good choice for nurses.

Miller began attending pro-union meetings in December 2015, when the effort to build a union at Einstein was picking up energy after it had faltered seven months earlier. There was an uptick in energy again because management had done what corporate management does at some point: cheated the workers, all of them. In late August 2015, management made hospital-wide internal changes to sick-leave and attendance policies. Interestingly, the policies were changed, according to the management memo, by the city of Philadelphia's becoming one of the first cities in the United States to affirm a citywide sick-leave ordinance, run by progressive activists on the heels of New York City's passing an extremely limited policy of three paid days of sick leave per year. Philadelphia's new ordinance was similar to New York City's, and those high up in management at one of the biggest hospitals in Philadelphia decided that if they must amend the sick-leave policy for what they considered low-level employees and contractors, they'd make higher-paid workers foot the bill by taking away and seriously restricting *their* sick-leave policy. Here, we are discussing the prospect of registered nurses losing sick time and having a more stringent attendance policy as a response to progressive social policy.

According to Miller, the imposition of the policy was an affront to all the nurses. Teams of managers explained to all workers in the hospital that if they were late a few times, it would be considered a day missed. If they were sick, they must bring a doctor's note to prove it. The nurses who had been trying to form the union early in 2015—but who had hit the wall not only with no one in Tele being interested but also in the critical cardiac and other units—were suddenly having other nurses approach them asking about unionization. Miller, who had always been the one person in her unit who wanted the union, was able to convince one day-shift worker, whom she identified as someone that other nurses listened to, to attend her first union meeting on the heels of the sick- and attendance-leave policy debacle. That day-shift nurse was Marne Payne.

Payne was an energetic, 29-year-old nurse, who, like Miller, loved working in her unit. She had been there for nine years prior to the start of the discussion of a union. Payne was still finishing nursing school during her first two years of working at Einstein, and she was doing an externship at the hospital. She started as a nurse in the Tele unit in August 2009. For Payne, Tele was a smart choice because there was upward mobility from it: if you were a Tele nurse, you worked next to the cardiac critical care unit (CCU), and you could grow into becoming a cardiac nurse, considered a highly skilled position. And upward advancement was important to Payne. As she tells it, although her parents didn't go to college, they pushed hard for her and her two siblings to succeed. All three work in health care in Philadelphia, which is not surprising given that health care and education are the backbone of modern Philadelphia's economy. Growing up Black in the Philadelphia suburbs, Payne lived in a house that was very academic. She describes how her father, who had not attended college, pressured her in school: "I could get a 92 on a test, and my father would say, 'Why didn't you get a 96?' He was never pleased."[22] For Payne, hitting key life milestones, like graduating from high school with good grades, buying a house, and securing a job with decent pay and room for growth, mattered a lot. "Remaining independent and a free thinker mattered, and that's how I approach Einstein, my patients, and the union," she says.

Not long after the hospital imposed the new sick-leave and attendance policies, Payne says she literally yelled that they needed a union. "I remember the first time I said anything about a union, I went running down the hallway at work saying we needed a union," she says. "I started screaming that we needed a union."[23] Payne liked and respected the manager in Tele. She considered her to be straightforward and an advocate for the nurses in her unit. But the new sick-leave and attendance policies, in Payne's and many other nurses' minds, were completely disrespectful. She says that her own manager knew it but couldn't protect the nurses from the hospital-wide policy.

This dynamic—when workers realize that even if they like their manager, their manager doesn't control key decisions—is often crucial to worker self-awareness that they themselves might have to do something to restore their dignity.

Not long after Payne expressed the need for a union, she was called into the office by her nurse manager and told she wasn't allowed to talk about a union in the hallway. After having been a loyal nurse for years, and one who by her own description prizes her free-thinking ways, being told that she was forbidden to talk about something probably compelled Payne to attend her first union meeting just weeks after the incident.

At Miller's urging, Payne attended what they experienced as their first union meeting. It was December 2015. The meeting was at Chickie's and Pete's sports bar. Payne remembers that she thought it was a good enough conversation, but it was way too loud: "I couldn't hear anything." During the next meeting, she listened to a union staffer describe the types of things they could win if they formed a union. Payne began to do research to fact-check the discussion about what a union could and couldn't do. Not long after, hospital management began holding daily anti-union meetings. By Payne's description, her manager was very good at telling nurses why they shouldn't have a union. "My boss was right out there from the starting gate, pushing hard against the union," she says. "Anyone who hadn't made up their minds yet, my manager got them. She did a really good job keeping the atmosphere on our floor very anti-union."

A combination of factors informed Payne's initial decision to be against the union, including her manager and most of her co-workers' acquiescing that they had it okay and that a union might disturb that. This is exactly what A-level union-avoidance consultants do: as with the highly paid public relations consultants that are front groups for the fossil-fuel industry, their goal is to drive serious doubt about any union claims of workers winning a better life.

And if that fails, they resort to fear: fear of job loss and fear of change, of something bad happening. The professional fossil-fuel-doubter industry is somehow better understood by progressives and liberals in the United States, but it created its playbook from the union-busting industry. Doubt, then fear.

In Payne, IRI, Inc., the professional union busters who were by then throughout the hospital, found their leader. Despite going to a second union meeting, Payne decided that "everyone at the union was a liar." She decided to run against the union. True to her spirit, when she made up her mind that the union was making promises it could not keep, her drive made her all-out against the union. It's worth noting that no successful union organizer *promises* workers anything. In fact, a cardinal rule of such unions as PASNAP and 1199 is that organizers never make promises. That Payne came to believe she had heard union organizers making promises was likely a result of intense penetration of IRI, conducting what Miller described as "nonstop mandatory meetings."

The kind of meetings and the intensity and pace of them are a trademark A-level union-busting strategy. In the lingo of union battles, the consultants from the union-avoidance industry were conducting what are called captive audience meetings. *Captive* because the meetings are on work time and mandatory. If a worker, even a free thinker, thinks she can say no when they call her in—even if she is caring for a patient—she is wrong. Refusing to attend mandatory captive audience meetings is considered gross insubordination and an offense that can be grounds for firing. IRI was in full swing in the Tele unit.

According to Miller,

> We were getting letters in our mailboxes at work every day from our manager, saying, "As a personal favor to me, I want to ask you to vote no to the union." And I was thinking, this was really not fair, this isn't personal, we are doing this because you can't get it done, you can't make things change—we have to.

But the manager was working the day-shift nurses hard. Miller says,

> They are afraid of Maryanne [the manager]. I was arguing with the day-shift nurses, but they were being told if they supported the union, they were going to be traitors. And management was pulling everyone away from the patients for these meetings for one hour or more at a time to move the traitor message.

To Miller, the meetings were infuriating. But to most nurses in her unit, they were effective. From Miller's view, the young, new nurses never had to advocate for themselves. They didn't go through the experience years earlier of being told they had to wear dresses every day at work. Miller remembers in the 1970s, when everyone in her unit decided to come to work the next day wearing pants not dresses. Overnight, they won the right to wear pants to work. Such experiences are what separated Miller from the young nurses who dominated the day shift.

Payne became one of the most vocal and visible anti-union nurses. She says that she would monitor the pro-union Facebook page, and "if PASNAP was on social media pushing something, I went on social media and pushed for the opposite. The people I trusted were against the union, so I went all out and campaigned against PASNAP."

The day before the vote, Payne took to social media, imploring nurses to vote no. She used an analogy about a highly recruited and highly touted star player coming to Philadelphia's storied football team and failing spectacularly. The team was locked into a long contract with a player who just couldn't deliver what everyone promised he would. The nurses were the fans, and they would be humiliated forever by a union, like the fans of the football team. Similar to climate-change-denier messaging, she wrote, "Not all unions are bad, but I believe PASNAP is the devil." She closed the piece by writing, "Service above self!! VOTE NO!! VOTE HELL NO!!!"

BUILDING THE WORKERS' CONFIDENCE

> *Strike preparations must necessarily vary. What they are depends on the character of the expected struggle. If the strike is to take place in a factory or industry where hitherto collective bargaining was not in effect, the major task is to bring the workers into the union. This means to develop the organizing to a peak. In such an intensified recruiting and union building drive, care must be taken that the key plants and departments receive special attention.*
>
> John Steuben[24]

In every weekly meeting with the Einstein nurses who had voted yes to the union and who were attending regular Wednesday meetings, the problem of what to do about the Tele unit was a key topic. They simply couldn't get to supermajority numbers without moving the Tele department and a few other clusters of anti-union nurses in other units.

The union strategy was to act like a union and move forward, despite the vexing and frankly terrifying legal charges that at that point no one saw a way out of. In late May 2016, the first ruling of the local NLRB came down in the nurses' favor. The local tribunal dismissed all of the employer's allegations of wrongdoing and recommended that the hospital recognize the union. And immediately, as if the union-avoidance law firm had already long prepared its appeal, the employer started what we knew it would: the appeals game of endless delays. The nurses issued a flier to their co-workers declaring victory, and management put out a long memo to all nurses explaining that they were immediately appealing the ruling and would not recognize the union, ever.

This was the work of the union-avoidance consultants from IRI: this phase of the operation is called futility. It's standard in their playbook. Futility is a special type of doubt. The message, delivered constantly, is that even though you vote to form a union, you will never have one. You will never win. And true to the moment, just after the hospital filed the appeal to the next-level court in the appeals process, nurse attendance plummeted at the regular 7 A.M. and 7 P.M. Wednesday meetings. The nurses who limped in to what had been robust evening meetings reported that others throughout the hospital had read the long e-mail from management stating that they'd never have a union and that the hospital would appeal it all the way, as long as it took.

The goal of the union at this stage is to raise expectations again that workers can win. How to do this successfully in the face of the formidable management memos would be key. The fact that we had one favorable legal ruling wasn't a real comfort because it read just like a legal ruling: the only people who could understand nearly any sentence in the 30-odd pages of legalese were lawyers. Nurses aren't lawyers, and although they can easily decipher endless complexities in medical terms, a 30-page legal ruling wasn't going to lift the spirts of 1,000 nurses.

We knew who could understand the legal language, however: politicians, probably half of whom are lawyers. We knew someone other than nurses or the nurses' union had to send the message to the nurses that the hospital was going to eventually lose. One of the PASNAP organizers had formerly been a very successful fund-raiser to key politicians in the area—likely the most highly valued position to almost any politician. She was tasked with getting a letter written, on official letterhead, to the hospital CEO from powerful Pennsylvania politicians. It would state that they were aware of the hospital's tactic of stalling unionization, that the legal ruling in favor of the nurses would prevail, and that they stood with the nurses.

This letter had two objectives: to lift workers' spirits and give them hope, and to have them see people perceived as more important than the hospital CEO challenging his authority. The CEO, Barry Freedman, considered himself a liberal Democrat. He was known to attend fund-raisers for Democrats running for office. We had researched him not only by talking with the nurses but also with key players in unions in New York City, where Freedman had previously been a hospital CEO. On June 7, ten senators, including ones who hailed from the important Appropriations Committee, signed the letter siding with the nurses and against management. It stated their awareness of the nurses' election and that the NLRB had ruled in favor of the nurses. The final paragraph of the letter stated:

> We support the nurses' efforts to improve the quality of care of
> their patients by creating an organized, collective voice in their
> workplace. We believe it is in the best interest of our constitu-
> ents and the community for [Einstein Medical Center] to respect
> that decision. Instead of spending healthcare dollars on expensive
> "union avoidance" consultants, put those funds toward building a
> partnership with your nurses, who interact with the patients you
> serve every day.[25]

Within minutes of knowing the letter had been sent to the CEO, we made
hundreds of black-and-white copies, as well as more expensive color copies,
showing the official, gold-leaf stamp of the Senate of Pennsylvania. We quickly gave copies to the nurses, and they went floor to floor, handing out the letter
as if it were Halloween candy.

It worked. More nurses attended the subsequent Wednesday meetings, and
those who came once again believed they could win the fight. It's hard to un-
derestimate the value of outsiders, important ones, validating workers' dreams
while union busters are simultaneously presenting nightmarish futility. The
discussion at the meeting centered on what must happen next. From experience, the staff of the union understood that management, and particularly the
CEO, would immediately sow doubt in the minds of the senators that there
was actually real nurse support for the union. In fact, we predicted that because
of an inflated hiring binge just as the union vote occurred—a strategy to make
management look as if it was listening to the nurses and would hire more staff
to lessen the crushing patient load—the CEO was likely to tell the senators
there wasn't even majority support for the union: out of 1,000 staff nurses,
only 463 had voted yes, and he would claim the numbers of support were
falling.

To combat the CEO's message, the nurses needed to quickly get a hand-
signed, real majority petition to show, rather than tell, that the CEO was lying.
The nurses in the room were worried about getting a supermajority of no less
than 65%. They'd never gotten a majority to do anything up to that point.
The discussion was simple: the nurses had to achieve a supermajority or
management would get the upper hand.

For the union staff, the hand-signatures-only petition was a structure test,
a mechanism to help assess where worker organization was strong, weak, or
middling. A structure test is a key tool to help understand which nurses had
serious support among their colleagues and which were enthusiastic but couldn't
persuade colleagues to sign the open-letter petition to the CEO. Structure tests
are crucial at every phase of a tough union campaign. Without them, everyone
walks blindly, having no idea whether, or where, there's real majority support.
Because time was of the essence, we decided not to focus on the Tele department and instead use the petition mostly to reassess how nurses were feeling,

given the legal ruling's rambling. Would nurses who had previously taken any kind of pro-union action quickly sign the petition demanding the employer drop its legal appeal, recognize the union, and get to the negotiations table?

There was pushback from some nurses who thought we should take the letter from the senators and hold a press conference. But we explained that nothing other than a supermajority of nurses signatures would counter the boss's likely challenge that a majority in fact wanted a union. These moments, where union staff who have experience in many rounds of employer warfare teach the worker leaders—all of whom are new to a union fight—are key to winning in high-risk, high-tension, high-stakes union wars. We understood this petition was a test, but that it was also urgent for the fight. If the nurses could demonstrate a real majority, it would also help in the effort to move Tele and other anti-union departments because management's message to the senators was the same as it was to the anti-union clusters: no nurses really want the union, even if a few accidentally voted for it in April. It was late June at that point, and there was still no legal recognition of the union. Every other hospital that had voted yes was already many sessions into their negotiations. That was the employer's futility message.

Weeks later—certainly longer than was ideal—the nurses reached a majority, then a bare supermajority, on their petition. Good enough to go, and "go" was the order of the day. The plan was for the nurse leaders to march the petition to the CEO, an act of challenging authority. Enabling workers to constantly make acts of defiance is key to the long buildup to having a credible strike threat—because a strike is the highest act of defiance. But marching the petition into the CEO's office would be only the first act. The second act would be groups of nurses meeting and hand delivering the petition (enlarged to 3 by 6 feet) to each member of the hospital's board of trustees. We needed to do this to expand the universe of nurses acting defiantly. There were a couple dozen community VIPs on the board of trustees, and hand delivering the giant, signed petition and a packet that contained the legal ruling and the senators' letter would provide an opportunity for many nurses to experience acting defiantly.

Experienced organizers also know how union busters hide their destructive tactics from everyone other than the nurses and line managers. In the United States, private hospital boards are typically made up of prominent members of the community—including philanthropists who donate to the children's cancer wing and get their names on hospital buildings. Board members most certainly do not want negative publicity nor do they want well-loved nurses appearing unannounced at their offices, pronouncing that their hospital is anti-democratic and attacking its employees.

The union began to get reports that the CEO was increasingly agitated. He had called the senators to tell them what we had predicted he would—that nurses didn't want the union and that the union was just a money-grubbing special interest group. But when the hospital trustees began calling the CEO to demand that nurses stop coming to their offices—and in the case of a few liberals on the board, questioning the CEO's leadership—the dynamic was shifting. In all the right ways.

With pressure mounting and nurses themselves getting stronger and stronger, the next opportunity for action was clear: the national Democratic Party Convention in late July, where Hillary Clinton would be anointed as the presidential nominee. We knew this was a key moment, with national and international media focused on the city with its proud liberal political structure about to spread its wings like a peacock to show off its success to the world. The idea that thousands of nurses, beloved in all opinion polls as the most trusted workers in America—and women to boot—would be potentially walking picket lines, protesting union busting and unsafe staffing conditions was a specter we were certain that local politicians would not tolerate.

The timeline, however, was moving faster than the nurses' organization was growing. Futility and fear were still being driven by the union busters daily. Despite the real pressure hospital management felt from the nurse's actions, they weren't backing down. More leverage was needed: the leverage of nurses walking picket lines during the Democrats' convention. Union president Eakin, herself a nurse who had been part of the 2010 Temple University Hospital strike, was a sitting member of the local Labor Council, where all unions coordinated in endeavors such as political campaigns. We decided that Eakin needed to get a resolution from the Labor Council that called on all unions to support the nurses who would be picketing the Democratic National Convention.

We didn't know until Eakin arrived at the Labor Council meeting that months earlier, the Labor Council had signed an actual no-protest agreement with the official Host Committee of the Democratic Party! Furious texting went back and forth between Eakin—sitting in the meeting and being told the other unions could not support the nurses—and our team. Despite the foolish "labor peace" accord holding the council back, we knew that the discussion at the Labor Council was about to ripple straight into the halls of Democratic Party power. From the view of the unions who were complicit with the idea of labor peace during the convention, Eakin's description of nurses—most of whom are female—walking picket lines while the first serious female candidate for president was accepting an already troubled nomination was about to explode in front of elite Democratic Party circles.

I was looking at my watch, counting the minutes until a strong-arm from the Dems called Eakin to tell her what she could *not* do. I was inoculating with her, getting her ready to stand her ground, and at that moment, had we not already had a supermajority petition hand-signed by the nurses demanding the CEO drop his legal appeal, the entire effort would have unraveled against us. This is a superb example of why majority petitions matter. Behind the scenes, calls began between myriad players: What would it take to back the nurses down? Democratic leaders and the male leaders of the Labor Council were consternated. Meanwhile, we were frantically trying to move the nurses who had just barely pulled off their first supermajority petition to take a strike vote, an act way too serious for such an early stage of worker development. So discombobulated were the politicians and labor leaders that we realized if we could only get a credible picketing threat, we would likely have the leverage needed to get the Democratic Party elite to tell—forcibly tell—the CEO that he must withdraw his legal charges.

Nurse organizers in the hospital had put up thousands of fliers throughout the hospital calling for an emergency all-nurses' vote about picketing in ten days. One of many quirks of labor law (which should more aptly be called boss or management law) is that to even picket, a legalized, formal ten-day notice of intent to picket must be sent in order for workers not to be punished. The clock was ticking: the Democratic Convention was ten days away, and the moment of leverage would disappear fast.

We decided to have Eakin ask the Labor Council to send a letter to the hospital CEO, cc'd to the Democratic Committee, simply stating his concern about the nurses' plight and how unfortunate it would be if there were labor action during the convention. Key to everything happening at this frenetic moment was the fact that PASNAP had conducted a strike at Temple University Hospital six years earlier, which was considered highly successful. Had that not been true, the threat of action would likely have fallen on deaf, or at least highly suspicious, ears.

The affable elected head of the Labor Council liked Eakin, and he and the other unions had supported her and her 1,600 colleagues during the Temple strike. We knew that we needed to get the plan moving quickly by suggesting a way for him to go on record supporting the nurses. In his mind, writing the letter wasn't violating the no-protest agreement. Even though we had a supermajority petition demanding that the hospital drop its legal appeal, recognize the union, and start collective bargaining negotiations, we knew that in order to make our request of others legitimate, we had to have an affirmative vote from the nurses to authorize the sending of a legal, formal, ten-day picket notice.

We held a hastily called meeting and had do what real organizers do best: be honest, be straightforward, be clear, explain exactly what the strategy is, make it compelling, and lay the decision squarely on the nurses. Everyone was nervous about the 7 A.M. and 7 P.M. meetings: it was unfortunate that we had to have a night-shift vote first because our top nurse supporters worked the day shift in most units.

We were either winning this vote or missing the biggest act of leverage possible. I laid it out exactly as Bernie Minter—of 1199 fame and the author of the manual that taught it was a sin to lie by omission or commission—had instructed. Our 7 A.M. meeting was in a church basement two blocks from the hospital. A statue of Jesus stood behind me as I described the options: take a really strong action—an action people didn't feel ready for—and defeat their boss and win the union, or be consumed with fear of direct action and lose our moment of maximum power.

After many questions and much discussion of concerns, the affirmative vote from the night-shift nurses was unanimous. We took a picture of all hands raised, and we put it on slides for the 7 P.M. meeting of the day-shift nurses. By then, news was spreading through the day shift that the night-shift nurses had voted to authorize the ten-day picket notice. By the evening meeting, held in the basement of Nick's Roast Beef, a restaurant near the hospital where we could get maximum turnout, an overflowing crowd of nurses voted to send the CEO a picketing notice.

Every politician in town knew the nurses were voting. The Labor Council knew the nurses were voting. By 8 the next morning, Eakin, the public face of a massive and successful strike at Temple University Hospital, faxed the letter from the nurses authorizing the ten-day notice to picket to the entire power structure. Exactly three hours later, I received a phone call from the hospital legal counsel—the law firm Fox & Rothschild, long entrenched in the Democratic and Republican power structures—offering to meet to see whether we could work out the differences between nurses and the hospital.

The first thing I told the hospital's lawyer was that any actions we would take would have to be ratified by the nurses themselves. I explained that neither I nor PASNAP leadership were the kind of unionists who would make decisions for the nurses—only they could decide their future. I explained, therefore, that if we were to meet, these meetings would not be secret, and the union would cut no deal. The lawyer hung up after telling me that there was "no way, no way in hell" the CEO would agree to meet if it wasn't secret. My nerves were fraying. I called the head of union and quickly explained that I had said no to a secret meeting with the CEO. We were tense about the moment, about my decision, about everything.

Before we could decide whether to give in, just enough time had passed—one hour—before the lawyer called back, saying, "Okay. Give us dates for a meeting."

Days later, after three rounds and many hours of high-stakes meetings between CEO Barry Freedman and me, along with the hospital's law firm and the executive director of the union, and done in consultation with key nurse leaders, we had a deal. Interestingly, despite the fact that the three meetings were premised on my telling the management team that any deal we hammered out would have to be ratified in a formal vote by the nurses themselves, the CEO and his lawyer were furious that PASNAP stuck to our guns that there was no deal until the nurses voted to withdraw the notice to picket. We were three days from the planned picket, which meant we were two days from the day Clinton would make her acceptance speech.

We called an emergency meeting, which was packed with even more nurses than the recent meetings. I explained the deal: if they voted to rescind their picketing action, the employer would withdraw its legal appeal, recognize the union, and start contract negotiations immediately. There was very little discussion, and the nurses voted immediately to accept the deal. Why not? They had a massive victory, surrendering basically nothing and learning the most important lesson of all: by standing strong and taking high-risk action, they had won big. Although negotiations hadn't started, the nurses had won their union after management emphatically said they would never have one.

FROM "PASNAP IS THE DEVIL" TO "THANK YOU, JESUS"

As a rule, unorganized or newly organized workers have no appreciation of the value of organization and solidarity. Their chief concern is whether or not they will derive immediate material benefits from joining the union, or by going out on strike.

John Steuben[26]

After teaching the workers how to build their worksite organization from the narrow vote back in April to moving some April no voters to pro-union—enough to produce the crucial supermajority petition demanding that their employer drop its legal appeal—it was finally time to focus entirely on the intransigent Tele nurses. In most departments of the hospital, the nurses' exhilaration was palpable. But Tele was dug in. Throughout the summer, with the exception of Miller, Tele nurses refused to talk to any other nurses or union staff. Candace Chewing, the staff organizer assigned to Tele, was fearless and fearsome. She hatched a new idea: to have PASNAP president Eakin phone every Tele nurse with a personal message that the union was heading to negotiations and everyone else would be making decisions for Tele if they didn't participate. We took Payne off her call list, deciding that based on a bad interaction between them months earlier, Eakin would not be effective with her.

Our theory was several fold, based on decades of experience. First, we already knew that this group had not decided, as had some others who had also voted no, to simply change their minds post-election and join the winning side. Second, we were using the authority of the union president to call them all and either get them live or leave a voice mail message. We assumed this would at least be interesting to some nurses. Third, we crafted a very particular message: the heart of it was that other nurses in the hospital would be making decisions about the Tele unit if it didn't participate in making its own decisions. We role-played and practiced the message with Eakin: "Every unit has elected negotiations committee members but yours. All nurses are presently reading drafts of the contract and on crucial issues, no one has any idea what nurses in your unit want, so they will just make it up for you if you continue to not be involved."

We added something else: "Management told you over and over and over you wouldn't ever have a union and now you do. Do you still believe them when they tell you nurses can't win raises and improvements through the upcoming negotiations?" We borrowed the tactic of climate-change deniers and union busters of sowing doubt. We were turning doubt against management, however, which was already putting out a message that just because it recognized the union, it would not give in to any demands in negotiations.

We also had Eakin make the calls from her cell phone, not the office, so the nurses in Tele would not know who was calling, or at least they would not know it was PASNAP calling. And we knew all the calls had to happen in a flurry so that the union busters wouldn't hear about it and tell nurses not to talk to the union president. Not surprisingly to us, Eakin did not get through to most nurses. One day-shift Tele nurse, Evan, picked up the phone. Eakin is charming and sincere, like most nurses. She was reading from her written rap because she wanted to say it all just right. When Evan asked, "Okay, what should I do next?" Eakin answered, "Agree to take a follow-up call from your union organizer, Candace Chewing, and talk the steps through with her." Evan agreed. Within an hour, Chewing was on the phone, having her first phone conversation in three months with a unit of nurses who had hung up on her previously.

Chewing asked Evan to gather some Tele nurses and meet her in the cafeteria the next day (the staff organizers had decided to start sneaking into the hospital cafeteria, blending in with patients' families, and holding meetings). He agreed. While Chewing and I were making plans for exactly how to handle the meeting, we had been debating whether I should go, as the chief negotiator, or whether a key worker leader should attend with her. We decided she needed to take one of our most effective nurse leaders with her, one who was strong and had a great way of talking union all on his own.

The nurse we decided to send was Pat Kelly, who had spearheaded the entire drive back in 2014 and stuck with it all along. Kelly was a single father of three kids who had to work the night shift: he could be home to take his kids to school and be there when they got off the bus to feed them, start their homework, and head off to the hospital. Kelly was definitely the leader of the leaders at this point, and he'd proven persuasive in several earlier tough meetings with nurses who once believed the union to be a bad idea.

I was waiting anxiously by the phone the next day. Who would show? Would they show? What would happen? When my cell phone lit up with the message on the screen saying, "Candace calling," I stared for a minute, hoping for good news.

First, Chewing explained she wanted to give me the good news. Payne and Evan showed up, along with another nurse we had a hunch was also a leader among nurses in the unit, Patricia Graves. Three of them. The bad news was that Payne still hated the union, and she was angry that Kelly was at the meeting. She yelled at him, really yelled at him. "Okay, keep going," I said to Chewing. "Tell me everything you said, everything Pat said, and everything they said." That level of detail is exactly what lead organizers use when we are doing what's called a debrief with a more junior organizer, when we are teaching them the craft of good organizing. Chewing continued but wanted to cut to the chase first and informed me that the next step—the only next step she could think of in a very tough meeting—was to ask them to return the next day and meet with me, the chief contract negotiator, to hear exactly how negotiations would work.

I blurted out the first thing that came to my nervous mind, "Candace, am I wearing a suit or a dress? Which one?" That level of detail is also just as important when trying to move the most important leader in a big unit from anti-union to pro-union.

Without missing a beat, Chewing told me that a dress would work better; otherwise, someone in management might notice me in the cafeteria. I called Kelly next because I wanted to hear what he thought about the meeting, as well as to reassure him. When he answered, he told me, "I am not sure how that meeting went. I didn't play a big role because the first thing that happened was Marne looking at me and said, 'What are *you* doing here?'" He was still shaken: he wasn't used to be yelled at by anyone, let alone the leader of the anti-union effort.

Later, when I interviewed Kelly about the meeting and his entire history with the Tele unit, he said that from the very beginning, Tele had been a problem for him. He said that back in January, before the vote, before management's legal appeals and everything else,

> Tele was the first place I came across two nurses who said, "Absolutely not. No, we aren't interested. The union won't do anything for us. We don't want to pay dues." It was the first negative response when we were trying to form the union. In other units they were disengaged, but in Tele, they said a very loud *no* to me and to all our attempts.[27]

I asked Kelly what he thought I should do the next day when I met with Payne and Graves. We agreed the entire focus would be my discussing the contract, walking through the draft line by line with them.

Chewing and Kelly, at my instruction, had left a draft marked "confidential" with the Tele nurses, a bit of a risk because we didn't want management to have our proposals before negotiations. But it was a risk worth taking if we would earn their trust. The draft was in good shape already. If anything would to get them to move, it was the realization that negotiations really were about to start and they actually had had no say up to that point.

By the next day when I walked into the cafeteria, there were a couple other top nurse leaders lingering in the cafeteria. They wanted to listen nonchalantly, as if paying no attention, to the conversation! Everyone, every nurse leader, was nervous with me. We had spent so much time talking about Tele, and the importance of Tele with the entire committee, that we couldn't ever get to a credible strike threat or therefore a great contract without moving Tele. This moment reminded me of many other moments just like it (especially when two other top nurse leaders pretended to eat their food at the next table, just so they could listen).

Chewing and I waited at the table, fidgety. When Payne and Graves entered, on their lunch break, they had the contract draft in hand and marked up from the night before. Good sign, I thought: not just that they showed, but they had been reading the draft contract. They were clearly uncomfortable. I made myself more relaxed at that point, friendly but not too friendly, more serious than friendly, and I had my Harvard Law School business card for them as the first order of business.

Thirty minutes later, after I had walked them through how negotiations worked in a good union such as PASNAP—since I was considered an outsider from Harvard at that meeting—and how in a democratic union, all workers were invited and encouraged to attend their own negotiations and that it would be crucial to have Tele nurses participating, the meeting had to end because their lunch break was over. We asked Payne and Graves to take union membership cards and sign up more than half their unit—the number they would need to hold elections in their unit for seats on the formal negotiations committee. They took the cards, said they'd think about it, and left. Everyone ran over as soon as Marne and Pat left to ask what happened.

At nine the next morning, less than 24 hours later, Payne called Chewing to say she had some signed union membership cards, and her unit had decided whom they wanted to represent them in negotiations. Chewing called me excitedly, but she literally couldn't talk coherently. She kept blurting something out about cards in her hands. I asked her to text me so I could understand. I couldn't tell whether she was crying or sick. The text read: "*34 signed union membership cards from Tele.*" The nurses had done it. They had cracked the "biggest worst."

To keep teaching her, I told Chewing she had to call back Payne and explain that they had to have an election—this was a democratic union; they could not simply appoint their representatives. Neither Payne nor Graves, clearly the two real leaders, were nominating themselves. They had decided that the representatives would be Miller and a male nurse whom we had not met nor knew of. So I told Chewing to add, "Jane said she and Patricia actually have to be nominated for their unit to be taken seriously."

Within days, a compromise was reached, and Graves and Miller were elected to represent Tele. And at the opening of negotiations on August 17, Payne and Graves attended the first negotiations. Management was astounded, and they seemed to understand the fight was over. We had moved every single unit in the hospital.

During the course of the negotiations, Kelly built a solid relationship with Payne and with all the leaders from Tele. I had to leave in November, just after the US election because I had way overstayed the date by which my director at Harvard had said I needed to return to teaching. I handed the negotiations over to the PASNAP organizing director, Mark Warshaw. When I first told the nurses I had to leave and that we had a transition plan, they were nervous. Terrified, actually, but I knew that by that point they knew, really deeply knew, that they were winning and almost done. They were confident in themselves, and I stressed repeatedly that I was only a tactician in a serious power fight between them and management.

In early December 2016, by the time a real strike vote was needed—not a vote for picketing, but a vote to strike—to get management to move off their insistence that only small raises would be given, Payne didn't just participate in the strike vote, she helped lead it. It was even more important than the vote she had ignored back in July—the vote to send the ten-day legal notice to picket. Trump had been elected US president, and management was smelling blood. At that crucial moment, Tele stepped in to become central actors in winning a terrific first collective agreement. The workers had forged an unbreakable solidarity bond through their unpaid, all-volunteer, high-participation, open, democratic negotiations.

Payne told me that in the final days, actually the final 18 hours—there was an 18-hour round-the-clock last day of negotiations, "I wouldn't leave. I couldn't leave. I am for fair pay, and I was not letting management *not* give us a fair pay raise." Miller, who was inseparable at that point from Payne, told me:

> I kept saying to people the process is fascinating, a slow chisel away, all the way to the end, with 18-hour days, with people saying, "I am not going to leave. I am going to sit right here to the end." I remember when it was finally over, that last day, we got the wages, we got some remaining little stuff, too, but it was big, and the raises were big. And it's all big—especially when they [management] don't want to give you anything. We were so burnt out. And then I went home thinking, "Oh, my God. I can't believe this shit happened." I even cried when I drove home, I was crying.

On the blackboard, on that final, 18-hour day, as she walked out, Payne wrote, "Thank you, Jesus." On December 23, the day the workers voted to ratify their first contract, she sent a text message to Kelly. He gave it to me, and Payne agreed I could include it here in its entirety:

Hey Patrick. I wanted to personally thank you for all the work and time you sacrificed on this contract. Up until the very end, I still did not believe our contract could be this good the first time around. I know myself that I was not easy to deal with. I have very strong convictions. And so does my floor, telemetry. It was hard for myself and the floor to swallow that the union got in. I did not believe in the process. After last night and waking up this morning I have now realized that we are in fact stronger together. And we can accomplish so much in this profession together. Thank you for being one of the lead organizers and helping to push this through. We now have a true voice and damn good contract!!! Enjoy your holidays with your family. I am sure they miss you!

CONCLUSION: BECAUSE WORKERS, NOT PROFESSIONAL STAFF, HAVE TO DECIDE TO STRIKE, REAL WORKER AGENCY AND UNION DEMOCRACY PRODUCE AND RESULT FROM REAL STRIKES

> *Trade union and strike leaders who have experienced genuine union democracy know that the rank and file have a great deal to teach them.*
>
> John Steuben[28]

I asked Payne recently what she would say if it were five years from now and someone in a non-union hospital was asking her opinion about forming a union. She thought for a couple of seconds and said:

> I would tell somebody if they need a union, to be patient and be prepared to fight for what you believe in, and, you have to fight for every nurse in the hospital, you can't have a union and be self-ish. You can't be I, I, I. It's not about you, it's about the people, the entire population.

In the end, as Payne herself said to Kelly in the pre-Christmas text, she wasn't convinced about the union in the beginning and even after she had first changed her mind about participating (and convinced her entire unit to back the union). Had Tele not completely flipped its position about building a strong union, they would not have won a life-altering contract. That Payne became the strike vote leader—in a department with a 100% strike vote and after running the anti-union campaign—is a powerful lesson in how best to build worker agency.

This real-life struggle, set against the backdrop of a horrible year for the working class in the United States, one characterized by disunity and division, reaffirms the argument laid out by Judith Stepan-Norris and Maurice Zeitlin in *Left Out: Reds and America's Industrial Unions*.[29] Their book details with exacting evidence that the unions of the CIO heyday that were least oligarchic and the most democratic were also the most radical. Today, PASNAP—but not just PASNAP—proves the same point. Unions prove it in today's strategic sectors, mainly but not exclusively the service sector, where schools, universities, hospitals, and health care systems are growth industries where workers still have strategic labor market power.

The mostly female workers who dominate in these two sectors of the economy—sectors increasingly under attack from accounting firms, hedge funds, and Wall Street that attempt to suck the life out of education and health care, to turn students and patients into profit centers—have the capacity to hold the line on austerity. They are building or rebuilding unions like those built in 2016 at Einstein Medical Center and by nurses and techs in a half dozen other hospitals in Philadelphia in the same year. Building strong, democratic unions in strategic sectors, sectors made up of enough workers who are hard to replace, and workers who have a kind of moral authority in mission-driven work, is a strategic choice of leadership, not something dictated by the constraints of global trade deals, though priorities on sectors should be informed by the effects of neoliberalism. Of course, there are many sectors of workers where using the strike weapon is not feasible, but that was also true a hundred years ago. The key to rebuilding working-class power is a more intense focus on questions of strategy—the strategy of which workers to focus on, why, when, where, and how.

TABLE 2
PASNAP 2016 New Organizing Snapshot

Hospital (and Unit, If Applicable)	Date of Election	Vote Count (Yes–No)	Total Unit and % Turnout	First Contract Vote
Eagleville Hospital RNs	Aug. 20, 2015	78–8	94 of 100 voted (94%)	Sep. 13, 2016
Eagleville Hospital techs	Sep. 11, 2015	62–9	71 of 90 voted (79%)	Sep. 13, 2016
Delaware County Memorial Hospital RNs	Jan. 15–16, 2016	164–130	294 of 330 voted (90%)	Apr. 20, 2017
Howard University Hospital RNs	Jan. 19–20, 2016	516–117	633 of 838 voted (76%)	Dec. 5, 2016
St. Christopher's RNs	Feb. 8–9, 2016	311–9	360 of 470 voted (77%)	Dec. 7, 2016
St. Christopher's outpatient	Feb. 10, 2016	18–2	20 of 29 voted (69%)	Dec. 7, 2016
Delaware County Memorial Hospital techs	Feb. 19, 2016	61–17	78 of 102 voted (76%)	Apr. 20, 2016
Einstein Medical Center RNs	Apr. 8, 2016	463–343	806 of 926 voted (87%)	Dec. 23, 2016
Mercy Hospital of Philadelphia	*Sep. 7, 2016*	*117–125 (lost)*	*242 of 296 voted (90%)*	——
Pottstown Hospital	Sep. 7, 2016	189–129	318 of 360 voted (88%)	2017
Total newly organized in 2016 (excluding 2015 numbers)	3,005 newly organized; 3,300 with growth in new units since election			

APPENDIX: EINSTEIN WEEK OF 7-25 CONDENSED RAP

I'm sure you've heard the good news—Einstein has officially caved, and agreed to not appeal again and to come to the negotiations table! Why do you think they finally agreed to respect your decision?

Einstein finally caved because of all the hard work you and your co-workers have been doing, and the power you've built in the hospital. Getting to a majority on the petition, talking to the Board of Trustees, getting the support of Philly state senators, and sending a 10-day notice to Einstein informing them that you'd be picketing in front of the hospital—this is why Einstein is coming to the table, you've built real power.

Our official first negotiations date is August 17th. The most important thing to know about negotiations is that you don't win a contract at the nego-tiating table, you win it in the hospital and in and with the community. If you have a lot of power in the hospital with 80% of nurses involved and signing petitions and wearing buttons, you win a strong contract—if not, you win a weak contract.

The plan to build that power is to get a majority of nurses to sign full mem-bership cards by the time we get to the negotiating table. Einstein management fights in two major arenas day in and day out; inside the workplace to make a profit, and in Harrisburg and Washington DC to reap more money and keep the rules stacked in favor of management and against the nurses. We have to be able to go toe to toe with management, which is why it's important for everyone to sign a political dues and a union dues card. Paying political dues keeps you strong in Harrisburg and DC so you can win crucial legislative fights such as the law that banned mandatory overtime. Remember when Senator Leach and 9 other senators sent a letter to Barry Freedman asking him to stop the appeals (show the letter)? The only reason the senators sent that letter is because nurses from other hospitals pay political dues, and PASNAP has built relationships with these senators. If you want to continue to have their support and to have political power, it's important to sign both cards.

The other card is a membership card, which makes you a full member with voting power to vote on your contract and to elect your future union leader-ship. Temple and Crozer both have about 98% membership, which a key reason why they have been able to win such strong union contracts. You don't start paying workplace or political dues until you and your co-workers have won a union contract that you yourselves have approved.

What kind of message does it send to management if only 20% of nurses are signed up as full members? Do you think we can win if we don't get a ma-jority of nurses to sign up as full members? Great, so let's make a plan for your unit of how you're going to get to majority over the next few weeks!

ENDNOTES

[1] John Steuben, *Strike Strategy* (New York, NY: Gaer Associates, 1950), p. 14 (note, however, that introductory pages to this version of the volume state the first printing of Steuben's book was in 1923, and it was subsequently added to and eventually published later with various claims for the copyright. This version states that the copyright is held by no one and is in the public domain).

[2] Michael Wynn, interview with author, April 29, 2016.

[3] Linda Briskin, "Resistance, Mobilization and Militancy: Nurses on Strike," *Nursing Inquiry* 19, No. 4 (2012): 285–296.

[4] Id., 292.

[5] Id., 292.

[6] In President Obama's second term, he began to make some progressive changes administratively, via rule and regulation changes in various agencies. One bone he threw to national unions frustrated by lack of progress on anything to do with union elections was to mandate that firms or companies that hire union avoidance consultants had to file monthly paperwork with the National Labor Relations Board naming the basics, the firm or union avoidance consultants, and the amount of money being spent on union busters. I am in possession of the monthly reports that demonstrate that Einstein had hired IRI, Inc.

[7] Kate Bronfenbrenner, *Organizing to Win, New Strategies for Unions* (Ithaca, NY: Cornell University Press, 1998).

[8] Steuben, op. cit., p. 100.

[9] Bureau of Labor Statistics, Major Work Stoppages in 2016. Press release, February 9, 2017.

[10] Steuben, op. cit.

[11] Id., p. 98.

[12] Id., pp. 13–14.

[13] Jörg Nowak and Alexander Gallas, "Mass Strikes Against Austerity in Western Europe—A Strategic Assessment," *Global Labour Journal*, 5, No. 3 (2014): 306–321 (https://doi.org/10.15173/glj.v5i3.2278; http://bit.ly/2r0g5Ju).

[14] Joseph A. McCartin, "Unexpected Convergence: Values, Assumptions, and the Right to Strike in Public and Private Sectors, 1945–2005," *Buffalo Law Review*, 57 (2009): 727–760.

[15] Steuben, op. cit., p. 111.

[16] Steuben, op. cit., p. 96.

[17] Patty Eakin, interview with author, April 3, 2017.

[18] Id.

[19] Leon Fink and Brian Greenburg, *Upheaval in the Quiet Zone: A History of Hospital Workers' Union, Local 1199* (Champaign, IL: University of Illinois Press, 1989); Jane McAlevey, *No Shortcuts: Organizing for Power in the New Gilded Age* (New York, NY: Oxford University Press, 2016).

[20] In author's possession. Also, in 1990, what was a national union, 1199, voted district by district to merge into either SEIU or AFSCME, with the vast majority of the members voting to join SEIU. The biggest 1199 local, NYC 1199, voted to stay independent, but by 1998, voted to merge into SEIU.

[21] Steuben, op. cit., p. 74.

[22] Marne Payne, interview with author, April 2, 2017.

[23] Id.

[24] Steuben, op. cit., p. 91.

[25] Letter in author's possession.

[26] Steuben, op. cit., p. 91.

[27] Pat Kelly, interview with author, April 2, 2017.

[28] Steuben, op. cit., p. 100.

[29] Judith Stepan-Norris and Maurice Zeitlin, *Left Out: Reds and America's Industrial Unions* (Cambridge, UK: Cambridge University Press, 2002).

Section Two:
Bargaining

CHAPTER 9

Bargaining for the Common Good: An Emerging Tool for Rebuilding Worker Power

MARILYN SNEIDERMAN
Center for Innovation in Worker Organization, School of Management and Labor Relations, Rutgers University

JOSEPH A. MCCARTIN
Kalmanovitz Initiative for Labor and the Working Poor, Georgetown University

One of the most significant innovations to appear during the last decade of struggle for the labor movement and its allies is an initiative called "Bargaining for the Common Good" (BCG).[1] Emerging from public sector unions—especially teachers' unions—in the wake of the Great Recession and the austerity regimes it imposed on state and local governments, BCG is an ambitious effort to redefine collective bargaining. Its practitioners have sought to bring community allies into the bargaining process by forging strategic alignments around a shared commitment to the preservation of public services and use of the public sector as a tool for building a fairer economy for all; they have sought to challenge the narrow parameters of bargaining in order to highlight the structural inequalities and exploitative power relations that are undermining the public sector and broad-based prosperity; and they have sought to hold financial elites accountable for policies that are starving the public sector. As this initiative matures, it promises to point the way toward the revitalization of collective bargaining as a tool for building a more democratic and egalitarian economy. We believe that it will become particularly relevant in a landscape reshaped by restrictions on union security that are likely to follow the Supreme Court's decision in the case of *Janus v. American Federation of State, County and Municipal Employees, Council 31*. In what follows, we will describe the emergence of this initiative and suggest a course for its evolution in the decade ahead.

ORIGINS, EVOLUTION, AND CHARACTERISTICS

BCG builds on a long tradition of community–labor alliances and community unionism. That tradition dates back at least to the "mixed

assemblies" of the Knights of Labor (founded in 1869), organizations that
worked in conjunction with the Knights' trade assemblies and functioned
as community unions that mobilized worker political power.[2] It is a tradition that has been repeatedly revised and updated in response to changing
conditions over the years. In 1930s Chicago, the Congress of Industrial
Organizations supported the efforts of former CIO organizer Saul Alinsky
as he built the Back of the Yards organization, the prototype for postwar
community organizing.[3] In 1950s St. Louis, Teamster Local 688 developed
an innovative "community stewards" program under the leadership of
Harold Gibbons and Ernest Calloway, through which the union sought to
advance a vision of "total person unionism."[4] Flashpoint struggles by workers of color in the 1960s and 1970s, including the Memphis sanitation strike
and the struggles of the United Farm Workers, helped forge strong alliances between unions and community allies.[5] Jobs With Justice, was founded in 1987 with the vision of lifting up workers' rights struggles as part of
a larger campaign for economic and social justice and institutionalized
community–labor alliances, eventually spreading to 45 affiliates in 25 states.[6]
And in 1996, the AFL-CIO's Department of Field Mobilization launched
Union Cities, an effort to work with key central labor councils to rethink
labor's relationship with community groups, an effort that included mapping corporate power structures, building a shared infrastructure for
political work, increasing diversity in leadership and activists, and supporting organizing of unrepresented workers in local communities.[7]

The Great Recession put the long tradition of labor–community alliances to a new test and revealed the need for rethinking old models. Over
the years, as union resources were stretched thin, all too often labor–
community alliances had devolved into strictly transactional relationships.
Unions did little to build community support for organizing or bargaining
campaigns. It was common for a union to pay little attention to community allies until the eve of a campaign and then to approach allies with an
offer of financial support or some other quid pro quo in return for their
solidarity. Community groups, meanwhile, remained disconnected in particular from union bargaining. Unions rarely sought the input of their allies
when crafting bargaining demands. If a form of labor–community alliance
that some have disparaged as "the mutual backscratch" had worked in an
era when unions were strong enough to win what they needed at the bargaining table with minimal community support, such an approach was
clearly inadequate in an era when private sector union density was dipping
toward 6% and when governors such as Scott Walker (Wisconsin), Tim
Pawlenty (Minnesota), Mitch Daniels (Indiana), and Chris Christie (New
Jersey) were leveling attacks on public sector workers as a "new privileged

class," whose wages and benefits were paid by taxpayers whose own wages and benefits were fast eroding.[8]

It was not only the need for allies in troubled times that drove some unions to begin to rethink their approach to labor–community alliances, it was a growing realization that the same forces that were undermining the bargaining power of public sector workers were also wreaking havoc on the communities served by those workers and their governmental agencies. Unless union and community joined together, it would be impossible to confront these forces. Public sector bargaining had first developed in the 1960s and early 1970s in an economy that had not yet been reshaped by privatization, subcontracting, outsourcing, and financialization. These trends began deconstructing the private sector economy in the mid-1970s, and by the 1990s they were also increasingly affecting the public sector. Even before the Great Recession hit, "austerity bargaining" had become well entrenched in the public sector—even when conditions could not justify it, as when New York City's Metropolitan Transportation Authority (MTA) sought to institute a two-tier system of health and retirement benefits at a time when the system was boasting a billion-dollar surplus.[9] Financial elites, who were exercising increasing influence over governmental institutions ranging from New York City's MTA to local school boards before the Great Recession, used that calamity to push aggressive austerity agendas aimed at increasing their influence and at opening the public sector further to the incursions of a rapacious neoliberal order bent on privatizing public goods.[10]

Confronting these developments demanded going beyond transactional community–labor relationships and temporary alliances of convenience to build lasting *alignments* between unions and community groups, both of which were being threatened by the forces that were transforming American capitalism in the 21st century. BCG did not emerge as a full-blown strategy fostered in a top-down fashion. Instead, it took shape from the bottom up, developing incrementally from the experiences of unions and their community allies, who began to push back against the austerity agenda in discrete local settings.

As suggested in Joseph McCartin's contribution to this volume, "Innovative Union Strategies and the Struggle to Reinvent Collective Bargaining," the general outlines of BCG began to emerge in the Chicago Teachers Union bargaining campaign and strike of 2012. But it was only in the aftermath of the Chicago fight as St. Paul teachers, Oregon state workers, Los Angeles municipal workers, and others began adopting similar strategies that the phrase "Bargaining for the Common Good" emerged to describe their approach. That phrase was further popularized in a conference by that name that attracted many of practitioners of these early efforts to Georgetown University in May 2014. Nonetheless, not every union that has adopted the BCG approach has done so under that explicit banner. There is no exclusive franchise or centralized control of this initiative, which to date has involved the locals of unions both inside and outside the AFL-CIO, including the American Federation of State, County and Municipal Employees (AFSCME), the American Federation of Teachers (AFT), the Communications Workers of America (CWA), the National Education Association (NEA), and the Service Employees International Union (SEIU).[11]

While BCG is an evolving approach, emerging organically from the activities of a broad range of unions and community allies, a menu of nine key features, present in varying combinations and to varying degrees, tend to define BCG-style campaigns. They are the following:

- *Expanding the scope of bargaining.* BCG campaigns seek to attack head-on the endlessly repeated claim by anti-union forces that public sector unions are greedy, self-interested, and willing to protect the wages, benefits, and pensions of their members even at the expense of community needs. Mindful of the increased traction such arguments have achieved in a climate of economic insecurity, wage stagnation, and union erosion in the private sector, unions adopting the BCG approach have attempted to break free of the "paradox" of public sector unionism, the fact that unions are generally permitted to bargain only over those issues—wages and benefits—that are most likely to divide them from community allies.[12] BCG campaigns have advanced nontraditional bargaining demands—such as that tuition costs at state universities be frozen, that governments cease doing business with banks that foreclose on home loans of distressed borrowers, and that commissions be formed to investigate government financing—and in so doing have assumed the role of defenders of the public's interest. Such demands seek to publicly redefine who the union represents when it goes to the bargaining table.

- *Bringing the community to the table.* BCG campaigns realize that expanding the scope of bargaining means also expanding the bargaining table so that community interests—and in some cases even key community groups themselves—are represented. This means incorporating the community into the formulation of bargaining demands early in the process and developing an alignment of union and community interests that will persist through the bargaining process and beyond.

- *Unifying identities.* Even as they seek to bring together unions and their community allies, BCG campaigns also seek to address the multiple identities of union members. Union members (or potential members) are also parents, homeowners, renters, taxpayers, neighbors, and human beings with their own gender, racial, and class identities. By seeking to expand the range of bargainable issues beyond simply wages, benefits, and working conditions, BCG campaigns attempt to use the bargaining process to serve the needs of their members not only as workers but also as individuals who wear multiple hats and are embedded in larger communities with particular needs. BCG campaigns attempt to center both community and labor struggles in the heart of union work—the bargaining table—and use bargaining to connect traditional worker issues and broader community issues.

- *Confronting systemic/racial injustice.* BCG campaigns tend to realize that traditional collective bargaining has proven to be an inadequate instrument with which to confront systemic injustices like institutionalized racism, the roots of which invariably extend beyond the confines of the workplace and are deeply imbedded in the structure of communities and reinforced by a broad range of policies. By breaking out of the box of traditional bargaining, BCG campaigns seek to identify, expose, and attack systemic injustices. For example, teachers' unions embracing BCG have attempted to break the school-to-prison pipeline by calling for an end to disciplinary policies that tend to criminalize students and by demanding wraparound services that can better serve vulnerable populations.

- *Strengthening internal organizing and member engagement.* BCG campaigns seek to capitalize on the fact that union members are rarely more engaged with their organizations than during collective bargaining, using increased member interest to further deepen and expand member engagement. Union members involved in BCG campaigns often report feeling energized and prouder than ever to be union participants because they know that they are fighting not only for themselves and their coworkers but also for their neighbors and the broader community they serve.

- *Identifying, exposing, and calling to account the economic elite.* In the public sector, BCG campaigns work on researching and naming those who are profiting from the austerity agenda that has been imposed on the public sector. Long before bargaining begins, BCG campaigns do deep research to map the corporate power structure that dominates the setting of government priorities. They identify the corporate actors who claim there are insufficient funds to pay for public services even as they profit from tax cuts and generous public subsidies. Exposing the forces behind lucrative privatization schemes and showing who benefits from cuts to public services and taxes, BCG campaigns reframe the dominant narrative and expose calls for austerity as unjustified.

- *Challenging wealth inequality.* BCG campaigns call attention to one of the greatest injustices of our time: the fact that the public sector is being starved for funds as a small sliver of Americans wallow in unprecedented wealth, paying taxes at a rate that is but a fraction of what the wealthy paid in the post–World War II era. BCG campaigns call for progressive revenue solutions that address the obscene growth of inequality. By demonstrating how wealth has been increasingly concentrated in the hands of a small elite, these campaigns help create a public debate that will help us build support for efforts to eliminate tax loopholes and raise the revenue needed to fund good schools and public services.

- *Putting capital to work for the common good.* By seeking to hold financial powers accountable, BCG campaigns open up opportunities to ensure that labor's capital is put to work on behalf of the common good. Many union pension funds have been hurt not just by underfunding and skipped contributions but also by investing in high-fee hedge and private equity funds that all too often provide mediocre returns even as they engage in socially damaging activities that range from profiting from private prisons to promoting subcontracting, downsizing, and offshoring of jobs. (In many cases, hedge and private equity fund managers use their mega-earnings to fund candidates and groups that are leading the fight against public sector labor.) BCG campaigns increasingly seek to ensure that labor's pension funds invest in projects that provide good returns and benefits to the community, putting billions of dollars of workers' capital to use benefiting underserved communities.
- *Building a positive perception of organized labor.* For years, labor struggled with a negative press that bred defensiveness among unions, defensiveness that in turn led to more losses. In recent years, unions have experienced increasing popularity as the general public focuses on the dangers of growing inequality. BCG campaigns seek to build on this recent turn by positioning unions as defenders of the common good.

RECENT DIRECTIONS IN BARGAINING FOR
THE COMMON GOOD

The promise that BCG holds as a game-changing approach for rebuilding worker power has become clearer in the last few years in work taking place around issues of education, racial justice, and financialization. An overview of some of this work indicates how BCG is evolving as unions and their allies struggle with problems in specific contexts.

No area has been a more fertile ground for the development of common-good approaches to date than education. Indeed, in many ways this sector has provided an ideal setting for BCG campaigns. As an indispensable public institution, public schools constitute an essential part of the social fabric of every community. Public schools have been hard hit by severe funding inequities and privatization efforts even as public demands for excellent schools have been rising in response to the needs of the job market for better-educated workers. Teachers' unions have been repeatedly scapegoated for their alleged subversion of educational reform efforts and blamed for every problem besetting public education. Common-good campaigns have helped teachers reframe bargaining in that sector in ways that align the union's interest with that of the community, pushing demands meant to correct fundamental inequities. Both the NEA and AFT have encouraged their locals to embrace common-good principles in their collective bargaining campaigns.

The recent work of the St. Paul Federation of Teachers (SPFT), an affiliate of both the AFT and the NEA, is a particularly representative case in point. In its 2013 and 2015 contract campaigns, the SPFT framed and won a set of demands that went significantly beyond the normal scope of bargaining. SPFT bargained for reduced class sizes and increases in the number of school nurses, counselors, social workers, and librarians employed by their school district. They also challenged their district's standardized testing regime and called for the expansion of parent-led family engagement programs. They even demanded and won funding for restorative practices and mechanisms meant to address institutional racism. These restorative practices, framed as an alternative to punitive discipline policies that were pushing students of color out of the classroom and into the school-to-prison pipeline, were intended to radically shift the way members of a school community relate to one another and focused on intentional relationship building and shared problem solving. In their second year of implementation, these restorative practices have transformed the way pilot schools function, helping students, educators, and parents build deep, lasting relationships within their communities.[13]

The SPFT contract negotiations in 2015 also resulted in an agreement to form a task force to examine the school district's relationship with the financial institutions with which it does business. This task force included SPFT members, district officials, and parents. It was created in response to the predatory lending practices of banks like Wells Fargo and US Bank, which have a major presence in Minneapolis–St. Paul. In its bargaining demands, the SPFT also asked the school district to stop doing business with any financial institution that forecloses on the mortgages of students' families while the school year is in progress.

The SPFT has continued to follow this path of expanding the issues taken up in bargaining. As part of their 2017 negotiations, SPFT targeted large corporations and nonprofits—especially private colleges and medical institutions—that pay no taxes or receive public subsidies. The union is demanding that these often generously endowed institutions, whose administrators earn millions, shoulder some of the financial burden of maintaining decent schools. In order to press its demands, the SPFT launched a popular education campaign called Teaching and Inquiring about Greed, Equity and Racism (TIGER), which has been documenting the tax avoidance by large corporations and wealthy nonprofits that is contributing to school underfunding.

Several factors help account for the SPFT's success. First, the union was blessed with strong progressive leadership. Presidents Mary Cathryn Ricker (who moved on to be elected executive vice president of the AFT in 2014), Denise Rodriguez, and Nick Faber were visionary leaders and effective communicators of the union's vision. Equally important, however, was the activation of rank-and-file union members who have gotten involved in the bargaining process and in programs like TIGER. Active and involved community partners were also crucial to the success of the union's bargaining campaigns. By including those partners in the shaping of bargaining demands, and even seeking to bring them to the table during bargaining, the union built durable and broad-based community support. Parent engagement and involvement was especially important in that process. Finally, the political climate of St. Paul proved to be a propitious one for articulation of a BCG agenda.

While local conditions and the forward-thinking orientation of the SPFT made St. Paul an especially favorable location for developing BCG strategies, the SPFT has demonstrated the exportability of its approach. In 2016 it established the Saint Paul Leadership Institute to train teachers from other jurisdictions how to bargain for the common good. In 2016–2017, 26 teams, including a total of 130 educators and union staff from teachers' locals in 17 different states, participated in trainings at the institute.[14]

Racial justice is another area in which BCG approaches are gaining ground. "As with most strategies in this moment, the need for Bargaining for the Common Good to focus on racial justice cannot be understated," argues Maurice BP-Weeks, co-executive director of the Action Center on Race and the Economy. "As our opposition's tactics focus more and more on wealth extraction from communities of color, we need strategies that fight back with specificity and collective strength."[15] BCG strategies in education have served as important incubators of such work. Seattle teachers have helped show the way on this front. When members of the Seattle Education Association went on strike in September 2015, they elevated issues of racial equity to a central place in their demands. The union denounced racism within schools, citing the disproportionate disciplining of African American children in the schools, where blacks were suspended at four times the rate of whites. One of the achievements of their strike was the creation of racial-equity teams at schools throughout the district, which would work to reform practices that placed students of color at risk.[16] AFSCME Local 3299 has also made racial justice central to its approach. Inspired by the Black Lives Matter movement, the union formed a Racial Justice Working Group in 2014 at the same time reactivating an Immigration Committee. After extensive internal organizing, the local developed an ambitious bargaining agenda that featured racial justice demands when it went to the table to negotiate for a contract covering 21 hospitals and the University of California's (UC) campuses. Among their demands were the creation of local-hire and training programs for disadvantaged workers of color and a demand that UC commit to not collaborate with draconian immigration enforcement.[17]

The inflammatory approach of the Trump administration to issues of racial and immigrant justice has sparked growing interest among unions and their allies in using collective bargaining to advance racial justice. In March 2017, the Center for Innovation in Worker Organization (CIWO) at Rutgers School of Management and Labor Relations and Georgetown's Kalmanovitz Initiative for Labor and the Working Poor partnered with the Action Center for Race and the Economy (ACRE) to host a conference in Silver Spring, Maryland, that drew 150 key activists and leaders from racial justice groups from across the nation to explore how BCG approaches can open new avenues to confront racism and White supremacy. The conference drew support from the AFT, NEA, and SEIU, as well as racial justice community organizing groups such as Black Youth Project 100 (BYP 100) in Chicago and community organizations such as Neighborhoods Organizing for Change (NOC) of Minnesota and Alliance of Californians for Community Empowerment (ACCE). Conference participants worked on developing bargaining demands and campaigns that address structural racism in the workplace and how structural racism impacts the quality and types of services provided by schools and the public sector. By directly challenging racism and highlighting this as part of the analysis of how the public sector is being defunded, participants created openings that will allow unions and racial justice groups to connect more strategically.[18]

In addition to providing a tool to address racial inequalities, BCG is also beginning to expand beyond K–12 education to address issues such as funding, access, and immigrant rights in higher education. Unions in Oregon and California have helped lead the way. In 2015, SEIU Local 503, which represents 55,000 workers in Oregon, including 4,500 classified support workers at state university campuses, demanded a restoration of state funding for higher education to pre–Great Recession levels and a tuition freeze, arguing that protection of access to higher education is of "utmost importance for Oregon families and our economy."[19] AFSCME Local 3299, which represents workers in the UC system, joined with students and other

}coalition partners to document and expose how the university's endowments were invested in hedge funds that had poor returns, high fees, and socially irresponsible investments. They have now built into their bargaining demands a proposal to create local-hire and training programs for disadvantaged workers and to ensure that UC follows "fair-chance" hiring procedures. They are also proposing expanding their existing immigrant rights language. In a past contract campaign, they won nondiscrimination provisions that restrict UC's ability to use government-initiated reverification of immigrant documents against members. Now, in 2017, they are demanding that UC make stronger commitments not to collaborate with immigration enforcement.[20]

Higher education provides a particularly propitious arena for the expansion of BCG. Institutions of higher education often act as "anchor institutions" in their communities, helping to set standards that influence local labor markets for better or worse. Their social function as economic incubators and training centers for workers gives them influence over the direction of the economy. They depend on public subsidies—even private institutions rely heavily on taxpayer funding of research and federal and state student loan programs. Their students borrow heavily from a rigged student loan market. Their boards of directors are influenced to an inordinate degree by financial interests. And both the endowments of private institutions and the pension funds of public university employees are often tied up with hedge funds and private equity concerns whose profits stem from the pursuit of job-destroying strategies.[21]

In higher education, BCG offers a way of bringing diverse constituencies together and using the bargaining process to transform educational institutions into nodes for the construction of a fairer and more sustainable economy. In February 2018, the CIWO at Rutgers University hosted a convening cosponsored by the Kalmanovitz Initiative and ACRE, which brought together more than 200 activists, including members of United Students Against Sweatshops (USAS), faculty unionists, and allies from around the country to strategize about transformative bargaining campaigns. If the enthusiastic response to the Rutgers convening is any measure, higher education might well become an increasingly central arena for the development of BCG in the years ahead.[22]

Finally, while BCG to date has focused on public sector bargaining, there are indications that it could hold promise for the private sector in the years ahead. One promising sector for this work happens to be a key target identified in public sector BCG campaigns: the banking and finance industry. In recent years, public sector unions have repeatedly targeted banks and Wall Street firms for the role they have played in fleecing public coffers through toxic interest rate swaps and high fees—for example, the Chicago Teachers

Union occupation of the Bank of America in February 2016.[23] But banks themselves could soon become the incubators of worker organizations that pursue common-good strategies within those institutions.

CWA has worked in recent years with the Committee for Better Banks to organize bank workers with the twin goals of winning better wages and benefits for the workers and challenging and reforming a business model that ties employee compensation to the promotion of predatory financial products. Bank workers involved with this effort were the whistleblowers who helped expose Wells Fargo's cheating scandal, in which workers were encouraged and even coerced into opening fake accounts on behalf of bank clients in order to create the illusion of a rapidly expanding depositor base. Bank workers are unionized in other nations, such as Brazil. There is no reason a bank workers' union could not emerge in this country. BCG strategies could help build support for such a movement, encouraging everyday depositors to see organized bank workers as consumer watchdogs.[24]

THE FUTURE OF BARGAINING FOR THE COMMON GOOD

As the relentless legal, political, and economic attacks on unions, the public sector, and the broader movement for social justice continue into the immediate future, there is good reason to believe that the BCG initiative will continue to develop and spread. In many ways, the initiative is responsive to both the central underlying dynamics of these times and the needs and capacities of unions and their allies. BCG is an ambitious attempt to come to terms with the way capitalism has changed since the rise and subsequent unraveling of collective bargaining in the last two thirds of the 20th century. By attempting to rethink bargaining's participants, methods, and purposes, BCG is opening up a conversation about the sort of bargaining that will be necessary if working people are to help shape a 21st-century economy that serves their aspirations. Moreover, as a decentralized phenomenon that has taken shape from local experiments, BCG is well suited to a time when union resources are harder to come by and big top-down campaigns are difficult to facilitate. It builds on an essential function that unions must continue to perform— bargaining—and leverages that function into a broader, movement-building strategy.

The suitability of the BCG strategy to the conditions labor confronts today was exemplified by the teacher strikes and mass mobilizations of the spring of 2018. As teachers in Arizona, Colorado, Oklahoma, West Virginia, and elsewhere staged strikes and marches on state capitals, they did not explicitly adopt the mantle of BCG, and yet they pressed BCG-style demands by connecting their cause with that of community allies and attacking the austerity regimes that were starving their schools. West Virginia teachers refused to end their walkout until all state employees received the same raise they had won for themselves; Oklahoma teachers demanded levies on the state's enormously wealthy and notoriously tax-dodging oil and gas industry; and Arizona teachers insisted that no new tax cuts be enacted until per-pupil funding reaches the national average. Whether they adopt the BCG label or not, the extent to which teachers in Seattle and St. Paul, and from Logan County, West Virginia, to Logan County, Oklahoma, have begun converging around the same logic should alert us that something important is afoot: public sector workers are beginning to redefine how they bargain and for whom.[25]

How might this phenomenon spread in the years ahead? We can imagine growth occurring along geographic and sector-based lines and spreading increasingly from the public to the private sector. National convenings, such as the May 2014 meeting at Georgetown, helped plant the seed for common-good campaigns in some settings. But as activists gain experience with common-good campaigns in different regions, regionally based trainings are likely to serve as the key platforms for the expansion of the initiative. As BCG gains ground in specific sectors, institutions are likely to emerge that can help spread it further in those sectors, as the Saint Paul Leadership Institute has been doing for K–12 education. One could imagine similar institutions helping spread BCG in higher education, municipal employment, or other sectors. As common-good strategies gain ground in public sector bargaining, they should draw increased interest from private sector unions.

The Supreme Court's attack on public sector union security is likely to facilitate the spread of BCG over the next few years. The spread of common-good strategies in the public sector, where they began, was initially hampered by fears of judicial intervention. Just as the Chicago Teachers Union was outlining its common-good demands in 2012, laying the groundwork for its strike, the Supreme Court was signaling the beginning of its attack on public sector agency fees. In *Knox et al. v. Service Employees International Union, Local 1000* (2012), Justice Samuel Alito authored a majority opinion in which he called for a reconsideration of the constitutionality of state laws that allowed unions to collect agency or "fair share" fees from the workers they represented. Alito made clear his intention to overturn the 1977 Supreme Court decision in *Abood v. Detroit Board of Education,* which upheld the constitutionality of agency fee laws. Contending that public sector unions were inherently political vehicles and that public sector bargaining was an inherently political process, Alito believed that the collection of agency fees amounted to an infringement on the First Amendment rights of workers who might not share their unions' politics. As such, he judged laws allowing for the collection of those fees to be unconstitutional. An Alito-led majority accepted a like argument in *Harris v. Quinn* (2014) and indicated that it was prepared to examine the question in full if given the right case. If not for the sudden death of Justice Antonin Scalia in February 2016, *Friedrichs v. California Teachers Association* (2016) would have been that case. Without Scalia, the court deadlocked, and it would take two more years and Donald Trump's election before *Janus v. AFSCME* allowed the court to continue the work Alito had first envisioned in 2012.[26]

During the years between 2012 and 2018, as this legal drama played out, unions worried about the legal sword of Damocles that hung over their heads, and some hesitated to embrace common-good principles in part because they feared that this approach would be used by anti-union justices as evidence of the political nature of bargaining, thereby endangering agency fees. Over time, the near certainty that the Supreme Court battle was already lost had begun to diminish such reticence. If the court overturns agency fees in the *Janus* case, one of the unintended consequences of that decision will be to inspire unions to continue to innovate in their approaches to collective bargaining. They will have nothing to lose and much to gain by doing so. Should that happen, it will not be the first time in US labor history that necessity has become the mother of groundbreaking invention.

ENDNOTES

[1] This chapter draws on Marilyn Sneiderman and Secky Fascione, "Going on the Offensive During Troubled Times," *New Labor Forum* 27: 1 (December 2017) (http://bit.ly/2HzI9dW); Joseph A. McCartin, "Bargaining for the Common Good," *Dissent* 63:2 (Spring 2016): 128–131.

[2] On the Knights of Labor's use of mixed assemblies to build local political power, see Leon Fink, *Workingmen's Democracy: The Knights of Labor and American Politics* (Champaign, IL: University of Illinois Press 1983).

[3] On labor and community in industrial Chicago, see Lisabeth Cohen, *Making a New Deal: Industrial Workers in Chicago, 1919–1939* (New York, NY: Cambridge University Press 1990); Sanford D. Horwit, *Let them Call Me Rebel: Saul Alinsky, His Life and Legacy* (New York: Knopf 1989); Robert A. Slayton, *Back of the Yards: The Making of a Local Democracy* (Chicago: University of Chicago Press 1988).

[4] Robert Bussel, *Fighting for Total Person Unionism: Harold Gibbons, Ernest Calloway, and Working-Class Citizenship* (Urbana, IL : University of Illinois Press 2015).

[5] Laurie B. Green, *Battling the Plantation Mentality: Memphis and the Black Freedom Struggle* (Chapel Hill: University of North Carolina Press 2007); Miriam Pawel, *The Union of Their Dreams: Power, Hope, and Struggle in Cesar Chavez's United Farm Workers* (New York, NY: Bloomsbury 2009).

[6] *Jobs with Justice: Twenty-Five Years, Twenty-Five Voices*, ed. Eric Larson (Oakland, CA: PM Press 2013).

[7] David Moberg, "Union Cities," *American Prospect*, December 19, 2001 (http://bit.ly/2HF9GKMO).

[8] Amy B. Dean and Wade Rathke, "Beyond the Mutual Backscratch," *New Labor Forum* 17:3 (Fall 2008): 46–56; Joseph A. McCartin, "Convenient Scapegoats: Public Workers Under Assault," *Dissent* (Spring 2011): 45–56.

[9] Joshua B. Freeman, "Anatomy of a Strike: New York City Transit Workers Confront the Power Elite," *New Labor Forum* 15:3 (Fall 2006): 8–19.

[10] This aggressive effort was anticipated by Naomi Klein's *The Shock Doctrine: The Rise of Disaster Capitalism* (New York, NY: Metropolitan Books 2007); Elliott Sclar, "Looting the Urban Commonwealth: Privatization and the Politics of Austerity," *New Labor Forum* 22:3 (Fall 2013): 46–53.

[11] See AFSCME, *Strong Unions, Stronger Communities* (2017) (http://bit.ly/2HCcCrC).

[12] On this paradox, see Martin H. Malin, "The Paradox of Public Sector Labor Law," *Indiana Law Journal* 84 (2009): 1369–1399.

[13] For an account of the evolution of the SPFT's thinking about collective bargaining, see Mary Cathryn Ricker, "Teacher–Community Unionism: A Lesson from St. Paul," *Dissent* 62:3 (Summer 2015): 72–77.

[14] St. Paul Leadership Institute, "Organizing to Bargain for the Common Good Contract Campaigns" (http://bit.ly/2HCSfeb).

[15] Maurice BP-Weeks, Action Center on Race and the Economy, "What Is ACRE?" (http://bit.ly/2HCSiqn).

[16] Tatiana Cozzarelli, Seattle Teachers Strike for Better Pay, Conditions, Racial Justice," *Left Voice,* September 15, 2017 (http://bit.ly/2Hz28cF); Keith Ervin and Maureen O'Hagan, "Feds Probing Seattle Schools Treatment of Black Students," *Seattle Times,* March 5, 2013 (http://bit.ly/2HEmRvx); Claudia Rowe, "Race Dramatically Skews Discipline Even in Elementary Schools," *Seattle Times,* June 23, 2015 (http://bit.ly/2HClAFx).

[17] Luster Howard, Maricruz Manzanarez, and Seth Newton Patel, "How We're Setting Our Contract Bargaining Tables to Advance Racial Justice," *Labor Notes,* March 15, 2017 (http://bit.ly/2HBCq7s).

[18] Kalmanovitz Initiative for Labor and the Working Poor, "Community and Labor Organizers Plot to Bargain for Racial Justice," April 24, 2017 (http://bit.ly/2HzK16s).

[19] "Len Norwitz to Ways and Means Sub Education Committee," Local 503 SEIU, April 14, 2015 (http://bit.ly/2HAng2b).

[20] "Missing the Mark: How Hedge Fund Investments at the University of California Shortchange Students, Staff, and California Taxpayers," AFSCME Local 3299, January 2016 (http://bit.ly/2HFaOhu).

[21] On universities as anchor institutions, see Walter Wright, Katherine W. Hexter, and Nick Downer, *Cleveland's Greater University Circle Initiative: An Anchor-Based Strategy for Change* (Washington, DC: The Democracy Collaborative 2016) (http://bit.ly/2HBdWeB); on financial interests' influence on university boards, see Gary W. Jenkins, "The Wall Street Takeover of Nonprofit Boards," *Stanford Social Innovation Review* 3:13 (Summer 2015): 46–52.

[22] For a report on the Rutgers conference, see "Activists Strategize to Bring Common Good to Higher Ed," Bargaining for the Common Good, March 1, 2018 (https://bit.ly/2HZ77Xt).

[23] Bill Chambers, "Chicago Teachers, Union Supporters March and Occupy Bank of America for Fair Contract," *Chicago Monitor,* February 6, 2016 (http://bit.ly/2HCMsFs).

[24] Stephen Lerner, Rita Berlofa, and Molly McGrath, "Making Banks Better: Frontline Workers Can Assist in 'Regulation from Below,'" Freidrich Ebert Stiftung, 2018 (https://bit.ly/2rfrO7p).

[25] Maurice BP-Weeks, Stephen Lerner, Joseph A. McCartin, and Marilyn Sneiderman, "Before the Chalk Dust Settles: Building on the 2018 Teachers Mobilization," *The American Prospect*, April 24, 2018 (https://bit.ly/2Hxm3IQ).

[26] Garrett Epps, "The Court's Scott Walker Moment," *The American Progress*, June 21, 2012; *Knox et al. v. Service Employees International Union, Local 1000* 10–1121 (2012); *Harris et al. v. Quinn, Governor of Illinois et al.* 11-681 (2014).

CHAPTER 10

A Primer on 21st-Century Bargaining

ERICA SMILEY
Jobs With Justice

For the overwhelming majority of the past century, a union contract has been the best weapon to ensure that working people in the United States have access to staples of a social safety net such as health care, retirement income, and other benefits often provided in other democracies directly by the government. Unlike in other parts of the world, the modern progressive movement in the United States has not been consistent in forcing the government to provide a social safety net that includes many of the things unions bargain over.

This approach is attributable to the decisions movement leaders made during and after World War II when tackling the question of who is responsible for providing for the common good and welfare of working people—employers or the state? At that moment in history, many European countries used their leverage to force the government to provide a strong social safety net that included many of the things American unions bargain over—health care, retirement, sick time, and leave. This freed up European unions to negotiate for all workers in a sector and not simply over wages but also over worksite conditions, production practices, and in some instances overall business model.

Meanwhile, US leaders used their leverage in the New Deal to increase the union's role in negotiating these same social welfare items from each company on an enterprise-by-enterprise basis—in many ways letting the government off the hook. And that's the system still present today, a system that puts undue pressure on unions to win piecemeal social welfare benefits for small universes of people while leaving the rest of the population to fend for themselves at the policy level.

In another New Deal compromise that continues to haunt us today, movement leaders compromised with southern Democrats to exclude protection for sectors that employed predominantly Black and Brown workers and shortly afterward allowed states to undermine and even ban various protections for workers attempting to form unions.[1] Continuing this legacy, corporations and union-busting consultants have actively and intentionally used White supremacy to keep working people from organizing in any way.[2] They led with White supremacy while training managers how to avoid unions—playing on the fears executives had of an active, diverse workforce that was clear on the rights they'd won. They led with it to keep workers divided—painting unions not only as

235

outsiders but also as a Black worker thing … something that would benefit
only workers of color.[3] This is not just the history of worker struggles at Cannon
Mills or Teneco,[4] but also the recent story of southern workers at Boeing[5] and
Nissan.[6]

This legacy of the New Deal is that only a small section of the US workforce
is currently able to consistently negotiate a collective bargaining agreement in
the face of employers' successful efforts to undercut unions through legal restrictions, retaliation, and intimidation.[7] Because of this, some have already
sounded the death knell of collective bargaining and the US labor movement.[8]

And yet, many non-union workers are building a vibrant movement that
is shaping the future of bargaining in ways that could engage the 90% of working families without access to a union contract.[9] Like their forebears, working
people today are not waiting until the perfect legal framework is in place before
creating a new democratic platform for having a say, as equals, over their working conditions. In fact, the harder some employers have worked to restrict
workers' ability to collectively bargain, the more nimble and creative the modern
labor movement is actually becoming. They are building a 21st-century labor
movement.

Birthing the new framework for collective bargaining will not happen simply
by rallying only those who already have access to 20th-century rules and protections. Certainly, unions and other institutions must protect what they've
won. And those who still have the power to win a traditional union contract—
particularly a first contract—under the current circumstances should continue to go forth and prosper. But for the remaining 90% plus of working
people, most of the traditional channels are completely blocked. So building
the organizing and collective bargaining power required for this phase of global
capitalism requires the kind of creativity and militancy that could ultimately
set up the foundation for establishing a bargaining framework that goes beyond
what was won in the New Deal—expanding the ways in which working people
collectively negotiate together, the types of binding agreements they can win,
what they can bargain over, and whom they can bargain with.

This chapter highlights a snapshot of pioneering bargaining models and
experiments that help working people call more of the shots and achieve lasting gains. Some of the efforts have been proven successful, some are actively
being tested today, and others are still in incubation. The models, by and large,
all require that working people are directly at the table with employers and
decision makers, that an enforceable agreement or other means of collective
accountability exists, and that the outcome builds enduring, longer-term power
for working people.

These models fall into three distinct approaches, discussed in more detail
in the pages that follow:

COLLECTIVE BARGAINING DEFINITION

When working people take collective action in negotiating with any entity that has power over their wages, conditions, and overall well-being in a way that produces an enforceable or contractual agreement that can be renegotiated as conditions change.

Disclaimer: The definition of bargaining used here is expansive and should not falsely implicate any of the organizations noted as seeking sole representation of a group of workers for the purpose of negotiating with a direct employer unless they otherwise state that themselves.

- *Broadening the scope of traditional bargaining.* This approach involves worker-driven bargaining that expands the scope of a traditional bargaining unit and broadens the topics subject to negotiation with a set employer.
- *Bargaining with the ultimate profiteer.* These strategies attempt to establish shared bargaining units of formal and informal workers in any given sector to increase their collective power.
- *Community-driven bargaining.* In this approach, working people organized as community members and/or some other non-union entity is the key negotiating party, and they negotiate not necessarily with an employer but with other entities with economic power over their lives—such as building owners/landlords, bankers/financiers, and developers, to name a few.

As a central strategy to expanding the bargaining power of working people, all of these approaches offer opportunities to confront White supremacy. When worker organizations centralize the struggle against White supremacy, accounting for the impacts of structural racism in their efforts to expand the scale and scope through which ordinary people are able to organize and collectively negotiate against shared targets, they win. And they do not simply win short-term compromises for a small number of members. They win in ways that alter our shared understanding of what is possible—providing the political space for the majority to essentially govern in ways that match our values of putting people and our environment over the profits of a tiny few.

Here is the problem. Far too often when confronted with this situation, movement organizations clam up. They don't want to deal with it head on for fear of alienating some White members whom they believe might quietly disagree. And yet the 2016 elections were a sobering reminder of what happens when institutions avoid the issue of race—the silent "hard hat" voters transforming the legislature, judiciary, and executive branch into a five-finger giveaway for corporate interests. This was a far cry from what unions did to address race directly while canvassing for Barack Obama in 2008.[10]

Combating racism and White supremacy is not an insurmountable challenge. Despite buying into the easy racist rhetoric of the Right that makes them fearful of extinction and scapegoats everyone who is not a White Christian man, these White men and women are actually suffering. Lane Windham's *Knocking on Labor's Door* demonstrates the power of trusting in working people's innate ability to struggle and grow over issues of race when organized around our shared values. In the book, Cannon Mills worker, Tim Honeycutt, acknowledged that he was actively racist in high school, having participated in a "race riot." But when the union organized around his shared values and economic goals with Black workers in his plant, he supported it.[11]

The labor movement needs all workers to make this whole thing work. It's not fair to workers of color to let their White colleagues stand on the sidelines while they get their butts kicked. And it's not fair to White workers to deny them the opportunity to be heroes in their own narratives.

What follows are a few examples of how some unions and organizations have led in expanding the ways in which working people come together to collectively negotiate for themselves, in ways that unite individuals across race to build a stronger foundation for a 21st-century labor movement.

BROADENING THE SCOPE OF TRADITIONAL BARGAINING

Social justice unionism has experienced a recent resurgence.[12] One of the more popular approaches to using the collective bargaining process to negotiate over issues beyond the worksite is Bargaining for the Common Good. Coined by fellows at the Kalmanovitz Institute of Georgetown University,[13] this phrase describes an approach rooted in the reality that unions and community-based organizations are actually in the same struggle.

Over several generations, community organizations and unions have fought for quality public schools, hospitals, mass transit, affordable housing, and the regulation of health and the environment to create a civil society that serves everyone. These institutions are in jeopardy after years of attack from the financial sector and global capital, which lust hungrily after the opportunity to profit off of these sectors. The same forces that seek to defund government and privatize services are dismantling the social safety net, destroying good public sector jobs, and driving ever-increasing wealth inequality. Communities of color are directly impacted because they are often more vulnerable to cuts in public services and where public sector jobs are often among the last opportunities for decent wages and benefits. Harms to the public sector also hurt working-class White communities, who are similarly dependent on Medicaid, Social Security, public schools, or public hospitals. In fact, White workers make up the majority of families who benefit from many of these services.[14]

Whether directly or indirectly, public sector unions address some of the same issues at the bargaining table that community organizations fight for in corporate and legislative campaigns. Community organizations organize where workers live. The same can also be true in the private sector. In both cases, these unions can advance the common good by working together with community partners. Negotiating in a united front can help both organizations move beyond reactive, defensive battles toward aligned and proactive approaches.

Luster Howard, Maricruz Manzanarez, and Seth Newton Patel offer a prime example of how to align the needs of working people and community members through their multiracial coalition negotiating for the common good. The trio introduced racial justice demands into their union's contract negotiations with the University of California (UC) state system.[15] Inspired by the Black Lives Matter movement, they formed a racial justice working group in 2014. They created space for members the American Federation of State, County and Municipal Employees (AFSCME) Local 3299, who are overwhelmingly people of color, to tell their personal stories about racism and police violence. After identifying individual cases of discrimination and systemic inequities that their members face on the basis of race and nationality, the union local pressed for several reforms to the UC system. They demanded the creation of local-hire and training programs that would open up jobs for low-income people of color who live in communities near the worksites and commitments from the school system not to collaborate with immigration enforcement. The union went beyond the traditional jurisdiction of bargaining—which directs unions to focus almost exclusively on self-interested workplace conditions—and expanded it to include the conditions of their entire community, their broader workplace.

Working people and their advocates can also look to legislative and regulatory policies as a tool to improve and expand bargaining. By working in partnership with government enforcement agencies, worker organizations can broaden the base of people able to engage in collective bargaining by using the leverage of labor law enforcement to contact more and more working people in particularly exploitative industries or jobs. In 2014, Jobs With Justice San Francisco led a successful campaign to have the city enact the first set of laws in the nation ensuring more predictable and fair workplace schedules for nearly 40,000 people who work in retail and restaurants in San Francisco. Armed with the leverage of the scheduling ordinances, women and men who work at Macy's in the Bay Area were able to renegotiate a better contract. Beyond these individuals, the coalition had to navigate how to maximize the policy's implementation to create new channels for organizing.

Any organizer can validate the common experience of laws getting easily overturned, repealed, watered down, or ignored. And while labor and employment laws on the books may technically grant working people more protection—those who have a union worksite are in the best position to maintain standards. Therefore, organization is key to enforcement, to holding employers accountable and keeping working people's concerns and voices heard long after the initial legislative lobbying and victory phase.

Co-enforcement policies can solve for lax enforcement and provide another path for expanding the scope of traditional worker-driven bargaining. As Janice Fine has noted, these processes prioritize the participation of working people, worker organizations and high-road firms in enforcement and greater cooperation among government, workers, and worker organizations.[16] Jobs With Justice and other groups collaborated with the agency charged with enforcing the scheduling statutes to adopt co-production/co-enforcement mechanisms. The Office of Labor Standards and Enforcement then reserved funds to community-based organizations to increase compliance with the law and make sure workers' rights are respected. The coalition is working with the Central Labor Council, the Organization United for Respect (OUR), and other partners to organize the people affected by the San Francisco ordinance to monitor implementation store-by-store. Legitimized by the local government, the coalition is set up to talk to retail employees specifically about scheduling and hours in a way that opens up organizing discussions. The co-enforcement model may catalyze a more collective engagement of individuals working in the retail industry in San Francisco who share common interests and goals.

BARGAINING WITH THE ULTIMATE PROFITEER

In the era of Uber and TaskRabbit, what defines a person's "boss"? Is it the person who signs the paycheck? Perhaps it is the person who invests in the company or organization. Or is it the person(s) who sets prices, wages, or standards industry wide? Jobs structured with the traditional employer/employee relationship have shrunk dramatically in proportion to nonstandard employment, or jobs that muddy the employment relationship with the ultimate benefactor(s).[17] This phenomenon is what scholars like David Weil have often referred to as the fissured workplace.[18] With whom do workers negotiate in such a climate?

To understand what today's working people are up against, workers must target the individuals who own these various enterprises and thus hold significant positions of power in our economy. Those in power are not simply vague systems to analyze or generic companies to be angry at. They are people making decisions that ultimately benefit a small select few at the top to the detriment of everyone else. There simply is no winning plan to build a shared prosperity without confronting these individual owners and their corporate power directly.

Luckily, working people have modeled various approaches to doing just this over the past few years.

Workers at many gig companies are experimenting with different ways to negotiate over their conditions.[19] In some instances, this takes the form of outlining a new set of labor protections for independent contractors or other workers not considered direct employees who are clearly tied to an ultimate benefactor. Uber and Lyft drivers in Seattle successfully got the local council to approve a law pushing those companies to negotiate with them.[20] Meanwhile, groups such as the New York Taxi Workers Alliance[21] and several unions have attempted to win protections for similar drivers under traditional labor law, claiming that they are in fact employees.[22] Both examples are proving that the only thing inevitable about the gig economy is that, as with business innovations of the past, working people will eventually figure out how to organize.

In another example, a group of guestworkers took on the largest employer in the world by targeting the ultimate benefactors of their seasonal migration cycle—the Walton family.

Walmart is worth more than $100 billion, greater than the combined wealth of the bottom half of the US population. They directly employ 2.2 million workers but also have their tentacles stretched throughout our economy. Consider one Walton in particular, Greg Penner, Walmart's chair and son-in-law to Rob Walton. He has his own investment firm, sits on the boards of Walmart and Hyatt Hotels, and funds anti–public school initiatives through a set of nonprofit organizations. All the workers he touches, whether or not they are directly employed by one of these companies, is a massive list. It would include Walmart sales associates as well as the Louisiana and Maryland seafood workers whose employers supply exclusively to Walmart. The list would also include subcontracted workers at the Hyatt in Los Angeles, the guestworkers on visas at the Hyatt in Colorado, and the temporary construction workers building the new Hyatt in New Orleans. It would include the janitors in the Silicon Valley building of Penner's investment firm and, yes, the teachers and staff at the charter schools he funds. It would include these workers and many, many others. Together, all of these are "Greg Penner's workers."

In Breaux Bridge, Louisiana, a group of guestworkers at C.J.'s Seafood, a Walmart supplier, faced abuses not visibly seen in the United States since sharecropping. They were forced to work 24-hour shifts. They and their families were threatened with violence. They grew ill from standing so long in the heat, and at times they were locked inside the facility to work.[23]

What are 11 guestworkers going to do to change Walmart?

Actually, they can do quite a lot. Instead of targeting a small supplier, their technical "boss"—C.J.'s Seafood—they targeted the end of the supply chain: Walmart. They organized, at great risk to their safety, engaging other guest-workers and direct employees alike to pressure the company to shift the conditions of their and other suppliers. And when the *New York Times* published "Forced Labor on American Shores," an editorial about Walmart,[24] it changed the scale and scope of the fight demanding justice for Walmart workers.

They essentially created a small bargaining unit to negotiate directly with the 0.01% at the top of their food chain, seeing the ultimate benefactor of their labor not as C.J.'s Seafood, but as Walmart and its top executives. Because they took this approach, these loosely documented workers in Breaux Bridge, Louisiana got Walmart to the table. The company ended its contract with C.J.'s and ultimately revisited its relationship with suppliers and their practices. More still is necessary to push Walmart and other companies to take full responsibility for the workforce throughout their supply and labor migration chains, and with other employees directly impacted by their policies and practices. But the guestworkers demonstrated what is possible when modeling this strategic framework.

The Asia Floor Wage Alliance (AFWA)[25] provides another great illustration of bargaining with the ultimate profiteers, this time targeting multinational brands throughout their supply chains. This transnational collaborative effort among unions and worker-based organizations in Asia allows working people to negotiate with their direct employer in the garment factories and undermines the ability of multinational corporations to pit one country's workers off of another's in search of the lowest price.

Across Asia, the minimum wage varies as governments try to compete for business, and suppliers are loath to pay more than the minimum, given the pressures from the large multinational brands such as H&M, Walmart, and the Gap to keep costs low.[26] So in 2005, the alliance assessed what a living wage would be across Asia. This calculation[27] established a shared floor wage, allowing working people in the garment sector to make consistent wage demands and negotiate with large garment suppliers. The unions within the alliance want the garment suppliers to pay the minimum wage and have the multinational brands pay the difference between the minimum wage and the calculated floor wage. This approach gets to the heart of 21st-century bargaining in supply chains. It is a tripartite approach allowing garment workers to negotiate with their governments, who set the floor and living wages; their direct employers in the factories; and the profiteers, the multinational corporations controlling industry wages—all in a transnational collaboration among unions.

COMMUNITY-DRIVEN BARGAINING

Consider the Justice for School Workers campaign in Atlanta, Georgia. In the spring of 2012, the Georgia commissioner of labor, Mark Butler, cut off access to unemployment benefits for contracted school workers in the state—the majority of whom were Black women. These jobs—held by cafeteria workers, bus drivers, school support staff, and even some charter school teachers—had once been considered good jobs based in the public sector. In fact, it was public sector jobs like these that created many pathways out of poverty for African American workers. But by 2012, these same jobs had been contracted out to companies like Sodexho, Aramark, and others—limiting the state's responsibility for these workers and introducing a level of flexibility that helped a set of corporations but ultimately devastated workers. Butler's action sent thousands of school workers, again primarily African American women, into crisis.

Atlanta Jobs With Justice took it on with both organized union workers and unorganized workers. They fought a battle with the Georgia Department of Labor and the Georgia state legislature to prevent the cuts from being permanent and to restore the benefits that had been previously denied. Instead of developing a short-term "give us our unemployment back" transactional victory, the coalition took a very different, worker-centered approach. The coalition framed the issue not simply as an attack on the social safety net, but as an issue of wages and income contingent school workers in Georgia depended on. In addition, they uncovered the real systemic problems regarding the nature of work in Atlanta, asking "Whose city is it? Ours or Sodexho's?" By doing so, the coalition was able to win $8 million in previously denied unemployment benefits, paid directly back to the workers. They were also able to establish an organizing hub, "Justice for School Workers," that functioned across several existing unions, included non-union workers, and that positioned workers to counter future attacks while setting an agenda to redefine the value and standards of school worker jobs in Atlanta and throughout Georgia. Some of these workers were able to go on to collectively bargain agreements the traditional way with the companies they now worked for. Others are still organizing, trying to identify opportunities to collectively confront the powers that be in Georgia's public/private education sector.[28]

Collective bargaining, at its best, is a system by which workers are able to exercise power in a way that directly confronts the owners of capital, and that reclaims portions of that capital for working people and our communities. It has served as a direct mechanism to fight for a fair return on the labor workers put into building, operating, servicing, or moving something. And the Atlanta case study demonstrates how and why collective bargaining must be expanded in ways that allow modern workers to confront their bosses and the owners of capital in new and creative ways.

Another model of community-driven bargaining centers on the creation and administration of a trust board that governs a public fund to advance community interests. In this model, representatives from the community, a particular workforce, government officials, and the private sector sit on the board. The approach derives from the Center for Community Change's Housing Trust Funds, which involve housing advocates and low-income residents in decisions about affordable housing. Workers, in their role as tenants, drive negotiations with housing advocates and elected officials. These funds aggregate streams of public and private revenue for affordable housing, which a board oversees and negotiates over the funds. A board holds regular meetings, often open to the public. Through their representatives on the board, community members thus have a voice in determining fund spending.[29]

The Maine People's Alliance and Caring Across Generations—a joint national campaign of Jobs With Justice and the National Domestic Workers Alliance—seek to employ this strategy in the care sector. The groups are campaigning for the passage of universal family care legislation to improve wages and working conditions for family and professional caregivers and allow families to have affordable access to care.[30] Universal family care could address both childcare and eldercare needs, although in Maine the campaign may focus on care for the elderly and people with disabilities. Their proposal would create a dedicated funding stream, likely through a tax on income from wealthy individuals that is not subject to Medicare and Social Security taxes.

Instead of directing government agencies to oversee enrollment targets, set standards that employers of care workers must meet, and otherwise oversee implementation, the campaign purposely rests power and decision making with a governing board comprised of stakeholders elected by the constituencies they represent. The tripartite board would include care workers, families using the care benefit, and industry representatives. Thus, working people can more directly bargain for both improvements in the workplace and better access to care rather than trying to pressure government officials to represent their needs.

These are just a few of many examples that counter the perverse misconception that the labor movement is dead. The struggles of working people, not legal parameters of union density, have always defined the labor movement. Black Americans did not wait for the Voting Rights Act to pass before showing up at the polls in North Carolina. Undocumented youth did not wait for the DREAM Act to pass before enrolling in colleges around the country. And the American labor movement did not wait for the National Labor Relations Act to organize and vie for collective power.

Efforts to organize new bases of individuals in order to position them to bargain, to vote, and to disrupt blaze the path toward building an economy that works for everyone. This requires directly confronting corporate power,

White supremacy, and all of the systems of exploitation that allow a small number of individuals to benefit from everyone else. There is no magic pill to solve the problems of working people in the current economy without doing this.

Corporations and their friends in government have long aligned to weaken the 20th-century weapons that workers have used to claw wealth and security back from the 1%.[31] Leaders of a budding 21st-century labor movement cannot arm the new troops with Iron-Age swords when the leaders of global capital fight with drones. Progress requires innovation and creativity beyond the frameworks of the past century. But it also requires some old basics as well—organizing like there's nothing to lose. And in all of this, movement leaders must reach far beyond their existing memberships to the overwhelming majority of workers who are yet protected by a collective bargaining agreement—way beyond the narrow reaches of a traditional bargaining unit and a bargaining agreement—to meet the modern-day worker and in the economy she or he functions in.

While labor law reform is needed, waiting for the balance of power to change in Washington to fix the current rigged system is foolish. Early industrial unions were bargaining long before the Wagner Act codified the practice, leveraging their ability to halt production when necessary. Only through exercising their power, and even breaking some rules, were these unions able to win the legal protections to back up the ability of working people to negotiate equally with employers. Incremental change alone won't overcome the incredible inequity and obstacles getting in the way of working people's leading a good life.

Around the country, working people are organizing to change the rules so they are able to live with dignity. They have turned many crises into opportunities to make powerful strategic interventions to expand models of organizing, bargaining, and policy remedies that build out a framework for collective bargaining in the 21st century.

ACKNOWLEDGMENTS

This was written with the research support of Adam Shah, Senior Policy Analyst at Jobs With Justice. Acknowledgment is given to Saket Soni and Stephen Lerner, who wrote the original concept paper (not published) outlining some of these ideas, including the original version of this example about the Walton family.

ENDNOTES

[1] Ira Katznelson, *Fear Itself: The New Deal and the Origins of Our Time* (New York, NY: Liveright 2013), p. 163.

[2] Lane Windham, *Knocking on Labor's Door: Union Organizing in the 1970s and the Roots of a New Economic Divide* (Chapel Hill, NC: University of North Carolina NC Press 2017), Chapter 3.

[3] Windham, *Knocking on Labor's Door*, Chapter 3.

[4] Windham, *Knocking on Labor's Door*, Chapters 4 and 5.

[5] Noam Scheiber, "Boeing Workers Reject a Union in South Carolina," *New York Times* (Feb. 19, 2017), https://nyti.ms/2HSvJSw

[6] Dominique Briggins, "Under the Hood of Nissan's Campaign to Stop Thousands in Mississippi from Earning a Fair Return on Their Work," Jobs With Justice (Aug. 7, 2017), http://bit.ly/2IbZ35Q

[7] US Department of Labor Bureau of Labor Statistics, "Union Members Summary," Economic News Release (Jan. 19, 2018), http://bit.ly/2HUAjLU

[8] Teresa Ghilarducci, "Farewell to America's Middle Class: Unions Are Basically Dead," *The Atlantic* (Oct. 28, 2015), https://theatln.tc/2wiXQ8c; Rick Wartzman, "The Most Successful Union Organizer in America Thinks Traditional Organizing Is a Lost Cause," *Fast Company* (Jan. 13, 2018), http://bit.ly/2wiXZZi

[9] Harold Meyerson, "Unions Confront Race at the Doorstep," *The American Prospect* (Oct. 23, 2008), http://bit.ly/2whHKLY; US Department of Labor Bureau of Labor Statistics, "Union Members Summary," Economic News Release (Jan. 19, 2018), http://bit.ly/2HUAjLU

[10] Philip Bump, "Donald Trump got Reagan-Like Support from Union Households," *Washington Post* (Nov. 10, 2016), https://wapo.st/2weSqLh

[11] Windham, *Knocking on Labor's Door*, p. 47.

[12] For a definition of social justice unionism and a description of its modern resurgence, see Bill Fletcher, Jr., and Fernando Gapasin, *Solidarity Divided: The Crisis in Organized Labor and a New Path Toward Social Justice* (Berkeley CA: University of California Press 2009).

[13] "Bargaining for the Common Good" was first characterized in this way by fellows at the Kalmanovitz Initiative for Labor and the Working Poor at Georgetown University, http://bit.ly/2IeqyeZ

[14] Arthur Delaney and Alissa Scheller, " Who Gets Food Stamps? White People, Mostly," *Huffington Post* (Feb. 28, 2015), http://bit.ly/2IiPpyg

[15] Luster Howard, Maricruz Manzanarez, and Seth Newton, "Setting Our Bargaining Tables to Advance Racial Justice," Labor Notes (Mar. 15, 2017), http://bit.ly/2IiPtOw

[16] See Janice Fine, "Co-Production: Bringing Together the Unique Capabilities of Government and Society for Stronger Labor Standards Enforcement," The LIFT Fund (2015), http://bit.ly/2JOtOeu

[17] Harold Meyerson, "Low Unemployment Doesn't Increase Wages Like It Used To," *The American Prospect* (Oct. 4, 2017), http://bit.ly/2IhiaeN

[18] David Weil, *The Fissured Workplace: Why Work Became So Bad for So Many* (Cambridge, MA: Harvard University Press 2014).

[19] "Uber Deal Shows Divide in Labor's Drive for Role in 'Gig Economy'," *Fortune* (May 23, 2016), https://for.tn/2IirYp0

[20] "Law Allowing Uber and Lyft Drivers to Unionize Temporarily Halted in Seattle," *Guardian* (Apr. 4, 2017), http://bit.ly/2HV0nGR

[21] New York Taxi Workers Alliance, http://www.nytwa.org

[22] Matthew Hamilton, "Judge Finds NYC Uber Drivers to Be Employees; Upstate Impact Debated," *Albany Times Union* (Jun. 14, 2017), http://bit.ly/2HVoGVd

[23] Cecilia Garza, "Meet the Crawfish-Peeling Guestworkers Who Inspired Walmart Walkouts," *Yes Magazine* (Oct. 11, 2012), http://bit.ly/2HVfLDh

[24] "Forced Labor on American Shores," Editorial, *New York Times* (Jul. 8, 2012), https://nyti.ms/2wf8LPZ

[25] Asia Floor Wage, https://asia.floorwage.org

[26] Mark Bain, "A Web of Terror, Insecurity, and a High Level of Vulnerability": H&M, Gap, and Walmart Are Accused of Widespread Worker Abuse," Quartz (May 31, 2016), http://bit.ly/2HTQtVZ

[27] "Calculating a Living Wage," Clean Clothes Campaign (Oct. 18, 2013), http://bit.ly/2weVwin

[28] For more information on this effort, see "Georgia School Workers Stand Up Across State!" Atlanta Jobs With Justice (Jul. 4, 2012), http://bit.ly/2HUeD2N; "Victory! Justice for Georgia Public School Workers," Jobs With Justice (Apr. 11, 2013), http://bit.ly/2weWxqH

[29] For more information, see "What Are Housing Trust Funds?" Center for Community Change, http://bit.ly/2HSr6I2

[30] For more details on this campaign, see Ben Chin, "Universal Family Care: A Plan for Maine," Caring Across Generations (Feb. 2017), http://bit.ly/2weGedn

[31] Windham, *Knocking on Labor's Door.*

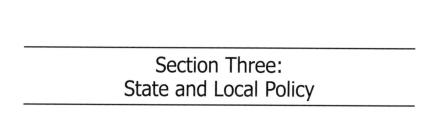

Section Three:
State and Local Policy

Chapter 11

"$15 and a Union": Searching for Workers' Power in the Fight for $15 Movement

Chris Rhomberg
Fordham University

In the summer of 2012, the federal minimum wage in the United States stood at $7.25 per hour, a rate at which it remained in 2017. Yet, even in 2012, a full-time, year-round job at $7.25 per hour produced an annual income below the federal poverty guidelines for a family of two (US Department of Health and Human Services 2012). In 2012, 18 states and the District of Columbia had higher minimum wages, with Washington State the highest by far at $9.04 (Burnett 2011). In July of that year, US Representative Jesse Jackson, Jr., introduced a bill in Congress to immediately raise the federal minimum to $10 per hour. With a Republican majority in the House, however, a spokesperson for Jackson's office admitted that the bill almost certainly would not come up for a vote (Berg 2012).

Less than five years later, 29 states mandated higher-than-federal minimum wages and 16 of them required at least $9. Cities such as the District of Columbia, Los Angeles, Minneapolis, San Francisco, and Seattle had enacted laws to phase in a local minimum of $15, or more than twice the federal standard (Franco 2017; Tung, Lathrop, and Sonn 2015). In April 2016, both California and New York approved measures to do the same statewide, and in August, the Democratic National Convention made a $15 minimum wage part of the party's election platform (Bacon 2016). A demand that only recently had seemed "outlandish" and politically impossible was being swiftly adopted in major states and metropolitan areas (Finnegan 2014). The momentum for such reform was widely attributed to the Fight for $15 campaign, which was initiated by the Service Employees International Union (SEIU) and sparked by numerous and highly publicized strike actions by workers in the fast food industry.

What explains the rapid spread and impact of this movement for economic change? In many ways, it both follows and departs from both traditional and contemporary models of labor mobilization. While the campaign organizers insist on workers' rights to organize along with wage increases, the strikes do not emerge from established relations of collective bargaining, and the workers are as yet far from gaining union recognition from the employers. Although the movement is backed by SEIU, its organizational form resembles the independent worker center model of advocacy (Avedaño and Hiatt 2012; Fine

251

2015). Yet it also stands out in its focus on workplace militancy and its engagement with the National Labor Relations Board (NLRB) to try to open up space for union organizing.[1]

In this chapter, I examine the Fight for $15 campaign as an example of innovative practice in the American labor movement. I begin by briefly sketching an analytic framework for understanding the features of the campaign and its strengths and limits. I then review conditions for low-wage workers, including in the fast food industry, and the emergence in recent decades of labor movement strategies to address those conditions. This sets the stage for a narrative account of the Fight for $15 mobilization, from its first walkout in New York City in November 2012 through some of its notable landmarks and victories. Finally, I try to assess some of the outcomes to date and the ongoing challenges facing the movement.

ANALYZING WORKERS' POWER IN THE EMPLOYMENT RELATIONSHIP

We can situate our analysis here by identifying the types of power workers can use to regulate the employment relationship, starting with Wright's (2000) distinction between structural and associational power (see also Lambert, Webster, and Bezuidenhout 2012; Silver 2003). Structural power, rooted in the economy, includes (1) labor market bargaining power arising from low unemployment or high demand for scarce skills, and (2) workplace power from strategic location within an integrated production process or supply chain. In turn, associational power describes "the various forms of power that result from the formation of collective organizations of workers [including] such things as unions and parties but [also] a variety of other forms, such as works councils or forms of institutional representation of workers on boards of directors in schemes of co-determination, or even, in certain circumstances, community organizations" (Wright 2000: 962).

Associational power draws on (1) the institutional authority and legal rights exercised through the state and (2) the organizational forms and strategies for collective action developed in the labor movement. In this way, associational power spans the arenas of the state and civil society as both a dependent and an independent variable. That is, labor's associational power is channeled by the legal and political institutions of the state, but it also may have recursive effects on public policy, including the laws governing workers' collective organization, and on the opportunities for further mobilization. In civil society, movement organizations build on existing repertoires of action and relationships among workers, but also generate tactical and strategic innovations to address problems that emerge in the course of ongoing conflict.

Civil society is especially important for a third form of power that Chun (2009) calls "symbolic." In the United States, marginalized immigrant, racial minority, and women workers in low-wage sectors were historically often excluded from legal protections and face a prior struggle for acknowledgment of the legitimate status of their labor and rights as workers. Chun argues that such workers can mobilize by using symbolic power not within formal institutional channels but through the moral order of the public sphere. Workers can exert symbolic leverage by organizing "public dramas" that transform workplace disputes into "moral crises" for the larger community, pressuring employers to respond to public opinion (2009: 17–18).

Structural, associational, and symbolic power are not historically separate or opposing types but rather coexist in varying combinations, grounded in relations in the economy, the state, and civil society. Thus, the organization of the workplace and the labor market, the nature of state-sanctioned rights and regulatory processes, and the development of workers' capacities for collective action all affect the kinds of power that workers can bring to bear on the employment relationship. The intersection of patterns across these arenas can create opportunities, threats, or leverage for different actors, and the key question for the movement is not just the material concessions it may win but whether it can institutionalize forms of workers' associational power. In what follows, I review these issues in the fast food industry and the low-wage economy, and I highlight the evolution of strategic responses from within the labor movement as a prelude to the emergence of the Fight for $15 campaign.

THE RESTRUCTURING OF EMPLOYMENT AND THE RISE OF PRECARIOUS WORK

For several decades, the American economy has seen a growing polarization of employment and the expansion of low-wage jobs (Autor 2010; Kalleberg 2011). The shifts have been attributed to the offshoring and automation of many previously middle-range jobs and the decline of unions and other forms of labor market regulation. In addition, Weil (2014) argues the changes have coincided with a "seismic shift" in the structure of jobs, as employers outsource even core functions through subcontracting, third-party management, and other forms of "fissured" employment. As large firms transfer work to smaller providers operating in highly competitive markets, the result is often "downward pressure on wages and benefits, murkiness about who bears responsibility for work conditions, and increased likelihood that basic labor standards will be violated" (2014: 8).

These trends have contributed to the growth of precarious conditions for many low-wage workers, including unstable employment; involuntary part-time or temporary work and irregular, unpredictable hours; few—if any—health, retirement, or leave benefits; weak enforcement of safety standards and protections for workers' rights; and a general shift of the burden of risk from employers to employees (Kalleberg 2014). Many of these characteristics are illustrated in the fast food industry, with its franchise system of ownership linking large "brand" corporations with retail outlets operated by franchisees. Franchising represents another type of fissured work, through which the brand corporations dictate exact standards and procedures for products, services, management, training, and marketing while denying responsibility for wages or compliance with the National Labor Relations Act (NLRA) and other labor laws. The franchisees, on the other hand, pay royalties to the corporations based on revenues rather than profits and so face pressures to reduce costs, thus contributing to higher rates of violation of wage and hour laws and other employment regulations (Bernhardt et al. 2009; Weil 2014).

On the Front Lines: Fast Food Workers

The fast food industry employed an estimated 3.6 million people in 2012, the year the Fight for $15 movement began in earnest. Median hourly wages for front-line employees ranged from $8.69 to $8.94 and median hours from 24 to 30 per week (Allegretto et al. 2013; National Employment Law Project 2013; Ruetschlin 2014). According to Schmitt and Jones (2013), half of all fast food workers were age 23 or older, 31% had some college experience or college degree, and 12% were born outside the United States. Among core front-line workers in fast food, Allegretto et al. (2013) found that 73% were women, 23% were African American, and 20% Latino. Sixty-eight percent were single or married adults who were not in school, and 26% were raising children. Moreover, around 20% of core front-line workers lived in families with incomes below the federal poverty level, compared with just 5% of workers as a whole.

A survey of New York City fast food workers in 2013 found that 57% experienced some form of wage theft, including off-the-clock work, not receiving time-and-a-half pay for overtime, working while on a break, or waiting to clock in after arriving for a scheduled shift (Fast Food Forward 2013). A 2015 study of fast food workers in Chicago found respondents worked an average of 27 hours a week, and weekly hours fluctuated by as much as 10 to 14 hours for nearly 25% of employees and by 15 to 19 hours for another 18%. Over 70% of respondents said they were not guaranteed a minimum number of hours per week, and almost one third received notice of their work schedules less than one day in advance (Dickson, Bruno, and Twarog 2015).

In many ways, the fast food industry defines the popular image of precarious, low-wage work, and a "McJob" is a common term for a range of low-quality, dead-end service jobs. The conditions in the industry also make it difficult for workers to organize, and the unionization rate is less than 2% (Tung, Lathrop, and Sonn 2015). Workers lack both forms of structural power: labor market bargaining power is limited by low skill requirements and easy replaceability, while workplace power is minimized by the vertically fissured production process scattered among thousands of franchisee employers. The average number of employees per establishment is 17, and even a complete shutdown of any one site would not necessarily affect the labor process at other sites (Weil 2014: 129). Yet this structural dispersal is in part an artifact of the legal construction of the fissured workplace and the regulatory institutions that allow lead corporations to avoid liability for labor practices.

THE RESPONSE FROM THE LABOR MOVEMENT: REMAKING ASSOCIATIONAL POWER

The rise of low-wage, nonstandard, and precarious work is not new, and neither is the impact on workers' power. Apart from those in skilled trades, integrated production systems, or supply chains, most workers in most sectors would seem to lack structural power most of the time (Silver 2003). With the decline of union density and the weakening of traditional protections for collective bargaining, however, workers have been forced to search for new ways to exercise associational power. The last few decades have seen a proliferation of new forms and strategies of worker organization, both apart from and in alliance with unions and collective bargaining (Avendaño and Hiatt 2012; Fine 2015). There is no need here for a full review of this movement repertoire, but three types stand out as important precedents for this case.

First, the SEIU's Justice for Janitors (JfJ) campaigns that emerged in the late 1980s directly confronted the outsourcing of work in building services. Rather than organizing for NLRB elections at each subcontractor, the JfJ strategy targeted the building owners or corporations who were the prime contractors for the cleaning firms (Lerner, Hurst, and Adler 2008). Organizers focused as much on the urban community as on the workplace, building solidarity among members and mobilizing symbolic power through "guerilla-style, 'in your face,' media-oriented events" designed to create public dramas and bring pressure on building owners (Milkman 2006: 157). The goal remained a collective bargaining agreement covering all contractors, but organizers typically sought voluntary recognition or filed for NLRB elections only at end of the process when the parties were already prepared to come to table (Rosenblum 2017: 95).

A second form includes nonprofit worker centers that organize groups such as independent contractors, domestic workers, undocumented immigrants, and others who lack access to collective bargaining rights under the NLRA (Fine 2006). Such worker centers enjoy greater tactical flexibility by operating outside the laws governing unions and often mobilize symbolic power to sway public opinion against unfair employers. They may also find leverage from other areas of law and state power—for example, using local authorities such as city taxi commissions to govern working conditions, the judicial system to win back pay and consent orders for legal violations, or local and state legislation to establish new regulations such as a domestic workers' bill of rights (Milkman, Bloom, and Narro 2010; Milkman and Ott 2014).

Finally, labor and community groups have joined to support local government ordinances or ballot initiatives requiring higher-than-minimum "living" wages for designated groups of workers (Luce 2014). Such laws typically cover employees of firms contracting with local government or benefiting from tax incentives or public subsidies. Starting in 1994 in Baltimore, by 2014 more than 125 living-wage laws and policies were in effect nationwide, and, while they help only a small fraction of all low-wage workers, they are credited with fostering labor–community political alliances and reinforcing popular opinion on the need for a higher minimum wage.

By 2012, these types of actions had become an established part of the repertoire of American labor, and SEIU and other labor and community groups had achieved some two decades of experience with them. As the traditional institutions of postwar industrial relations in the United States have declined, workplace struggles have expanded into other arenas of the state and urban civil society (Rhomberg 2012). With that, organizers have encountered a variety of institutional rules and resources that affect workers' ability to exercise associational and symbolic power. When the Fight for $15 emerged in 2012, it drew on this body of experience and extended it, beginning with a new group of previously unorganized workers in the fast food industry.

The Fast Food Workers' Strikes

In May 2010, Mary Kay Henry was elected president of SEIU, and the following spring the union introduced its Fight for a Fair Economy (FFE) program focused on income inequality and outreach to unorganized low-wage workers, including those in fast food (Eidelson 2012). Working through SEIU's long-standing partnerships with community groups such as New York Communities for Change in New York City and Action Now in Chicago (both local successors to the Association of Community Organizations for Reform Now), the FFE program initially avoided direct identification with the union. "We made a decision not to make it an SEIU thing," said Neal Bisno, head of the SEIU health care workers division in Pennsylvania. "We literally took off our purple T-shirts" (Eidelson 2016b). Starting in early 2012, SEIU paid for the campaign to hire dozens of organizers, spending an estimated $2.5 million in New York and $3 million in Chicago by the year's end. Campaign staff began canvassing fast food workers and holding meetings away from the workplace, and, despite risks of reprisal from their employers, workers began to get involved (Finnegan 2014; Gupta 2013.)

On November 29, 2012, around 200 workers from some 40 fast food outlets in New York City, including Burger King, Domino's Pizza, KFC, McDonald's, and Taco Bell, engaged in a one-day walkout, the largest work stoppage in the industry to that time. Mobilizing under the name Fast Food Forward, strikers and supporters gathered in front of a McDonald's in midtown Manhattan and raised core demands of a $15 per hour wage and the right to form a union without intimidation (Eidelson 2012; Finnegan 2014). Underlining the latter point, in the days afterward, religious and community allies accompanied workers back to the job to ensure they would not be fired for their actions (Brown 2013). Coming one week after the first Black Friday walkout on November 23 by workers at Walmart, the New York City strike attracted wide attention and quickly sparked a larger movement throughout the country.

Within six months, the campaign had spread to cities across the United States, with each local coalition organizing under its own banner, including Fight for 15 in Chicago, Detroit-15 in Detroit, Raise Up MKE in Milwaukee, and Stand Up KC in Kansas City (Gupta 2013). At the end of July 2013, the first set of coordinated strikes occurred in seven cities over four days, followed by a nationwide action involving 60 cities on August 29 (Eidelson 2013a; McVeigh 2013). The actions continued to escalate, featuring walkouts in 100 cities in December 2013 and rising to 150 cities in May 2014, along with solidarity actions in some 30 other countries. In July 2014, 1,300 fast food workers from 50 cities gathered in suburban Chicago for a first national convention (Finnegan 2014; Speri 2014). That September, the movement for the first time engaged in mass nonviolent civil disobedience, with hundreds of protesters arrested nationally—including in Southern cities such as Atlanta, Charleston, Durham, and Little Rock (Resnikoff and Richinick 2014). By the end of 2016, the campaign had mobilized a dozen nationally coordinated one-day strikes with participation from tens of thousands of workers and supporters (Greenhouse 2016).

At a time when legal protections for the right to strike have eroded and strike rates among American workers have reached historic lows, the fast food walkouts have stood out as an extraordinary example of labor militancy and courage. The strikes have been crucial to the larger Fight for $15 mobilization, although not for their exercise of structural power: even with tens of thousands of participants, the strikers as yet have comprised only a tiny fraction of the total number of fast food employees nationally, and only a small share of the total number of outlets has been affected. Despite the rallies and sit-ins, the one-day demonstration actions have rarely shut down the restaurants, causing little disruption for most consumers and imposing almost no direct economic costs on the brand corporations. Rather, the walkouts have been important to the movement for their use of symbolic power, both internally and externally.

Symbolic Power: The Meanings of Action

Internally, the strikes reinforced solidarity among the workers, allowing them to overcome their fears and experience the power of collective action. Douglesha

Nicholson, a 23-year-old Pizza Hut worker from Kansas City, recalled, "When I first heard about it, I'm not gonna lie, I was kind of skeptical. I was thinking, 'I'm gonna lose my job, I'm gonna get in trouble.'" But after the first strike, "It was a big rush of adrenaline, going out and being able to yell without the risk of being fired. Just to let you know 'Hey, I'm here, this is what I'm demanding, this is what I want'" (Speri 2014). The act of striking itself was, for many, personally transformative and important for their emergence as leaders. Naquasia LeGrand, a 21-year-old KFC worker from New York making $200 a week, became a prominent spokesperson for the movement. "What do we have to lose? We're already working for pennies," she said. "This could be a breakthrough to something different in our life, to actually be worth something" (Johnston 2016). The initial strikers emboldened others to follow them: New York strikers traveled to Chicago to help persuade workers there to go out, and a group from St. Louis was motivated after returning from a bus trip to support strikers in Chicago (Brown 2013; Gupta 2013).

With a heavily minority and female workforce, organizers also explicitly invoked the cultural legacy of the African American civil rights, women's rights, and immigrant rights movements. The April 4, 2013, action in New York was scheduled on the 45th anniversary of the assassination of Dr. Martin Luther King, who at the time of his death was supporting striking African American sanitation workers in Memphis, Tennessee. Organizers brought two surviving strikers from that 1968 campaign to New York to speak to workers in a series of pep talks before the action (Harris 2013). In Detroit a few weeks later, the Reverend Charles Williams II, head of the Michigan chapter of the National Action Network, told protesters, "You have decided to sit down in the spirit of Rosa Parks and Fannie Lou Hamer. We will continue to fight until we get $15" (Bukowski 2014). Such themes resonated with workers whose grandparents fought for and won access to unionized manufacturing jobs that now scarcely exist in many urban areas. "This kind of organizing is new to us, people my age, but we know where we come from," said one young striker from St. Louis (Freed Wessler 2013).

Externally, the walkouts captured public attention in a way traditional media campaigns and even boycotts and demonstrations alone could not achieve. When workers risked their jobs for dignity in a sector that was both the epitome of the low-wage economy and as ubiquitous as the restaurant around the corner, the image told a powerful story. The narrative was amplified with the help of the elite public relations firm BerlinRosen (2017) and reinforced by commissioned research reports on wage theft in New York City fast food restaurants (Fast Food Forward 2013) and on poverty and reliance on public assistance among fast food workers nationally (Allegretto et al. 2013).

Along with the 2011 Occupy protests and the similar walkouts at Walmart, the fast food strikes dramatized the problems of income inequality and low-wage work and transformed mainstream political discourse. As SEIU president Henry remarked, "The individual courage of these few hundred workers making a bodacious demand galvanized the next stage of the national conversation about inequality" (Johnston 2016). By 2015, the broader movement had clearly captured the moral debate. In February, Walmart announced it would raise its base wage to at least $9 per hour, followed shortly thereafter by similar raises at Target and the retailers T.J. Maxx and Marshall's, and opinion polls showed strong majorities across the country in favor of raising the minimum wage to $15 (Dreier 2015; Tung, Lathrop, and Sonn 2015).

Beyond Symbolic Power: Changing the Industry

The problem remained, however, how to convert symbolic power into concrete gains in associational power and institutional change. By the summer of 2013, discussions within SEIU centered on two strategies: first, escalating pressure on the top brand corporations to push for improved standards and a path toward union negotiations, and second, legislative action for local living-wage laws to raise incomes for workers (Eidelson 2013b). Following the JfJ model, the campaign avoided seeking NLRB elections at the franchisee outlets, instead targeting the brands as the actors with enough resources to undo the low-wage, non-union pattern in the industry. In particular, the campaign focused on industry leader McDonald's, applying pressure from any available angle. In May 2014, one week after the walkouts in 150 cities, police arrested 138 of more than 1,000 protesters who converged on McDonald's headquarters in suburban Oak Brook, Illinois, for the company's annual shareholders meeting (Resnikoff 2014). The efforts showed signs of impact: following the pay raises in early 2015 by the major retailers previously named, McDonald's said in April it would increase wages at its company-owned locations to at least $1 more than the local minimum wage. The move benefited around 90,000 workers; however, McDonald's directly owns only around 10% of its 14,000 US locations, while the rest are owned by franchisees (Greenhouse 2015).

Since then, the corporate campaign has expanded: in May 2015, thousands more protesters showed up in Oak Brook for McDonald's shareholder meeting at the same time that public pension fund officials in California, Illinois, and New York warned McDonald's and other firms against jeopardizing future growth by engaging in massive share buybacks (Dreier 2015). In January 2016, several U.S. fast food workers traveled to Brussels to support a SEIU-backed coalition of Italian consumer groups in their anti-trust complaint against the company with the European Commission, and in May 2017, SEIU asked attorneys general in California and Illinois to investigate McDonald's for deceptive and unlawful gouging of $3 billion in rent from its franchisees (Larson 2017; Mahdani 2016).

Such tactics draw from the JfJ playbook while aiming at the brand corporate image. In addition, the campaign directly challenged the legal construction of the fissured workplace, in order to reduce the economic insulation of the brands and give them an incentive to negotiate. Beginning in 2012, SEIU filed unfair labor practice charges with the NLRB claiming McDonald's was liable as a "joint employer" along with its franchisees for unlawful retaliation against strikers, and on July 29, 2014, the NLRB's General Counsel agreed and authorized complaints against the corporation and its partners (National Labor Relations Board 2014; Short 2014). Hearings before an administrative law judge began in 2015, and the case received a boost in August when the NLRB ruled in favor of an updated, more comprehensive standard for defining joint employers in the *Browning-Ferris* case involving the Teamsters and a recycling company (Li, Masunaga, and Solomon 2015).

As a target, McDonald's showed potential vulnerabilities. While its stock price reached record highs beginning in 2017, critics said that was inflated by $20.5 billion in stock buybacks from 2014 to 2016. The company experienced three years of steadily falling revenue from $28.1 billion in 2013 to $24.6 billion in 2016, while long-term debt increased from $14.1 billion to $25.9 billion. Perhaps more significantly, from 2013 through 2016, McDonald's customer count fell by more than 10% (Alsin 2017). Nevertheless, the company has showed no signs of yielding to unionization and the campaign has not yet gained recognition in the workplace. Rather, its greatest economic achievements have come through its second strategy: political action on local and state minimum-wage laws.

Raise Up the Wage: A Political Movement

The fast food strikes have been essential to the media attention and popular support for a $15 wage, but the successful campaigns to win local wage increases have relied on a diverse alliance of actors in the labor movement, the community, and government. The first jurisdiction to pass such legislation was SeaTac, Washington, a small, working-class suburb of Seattle and home of the Seattle–Tacoma International Airport. In April 2012, Working Washington, the local affiliate of the SEIU FFE, began to organize subcontracted African American, Asian, East African, Latino, and White workers in and around the airport (Rosenblum 2017: 69). By March 2013, a majority of workers at five of the largest contractors had signed union cards, and, when the employers refused to recognize them, the campaign turned to a local living-wage initiative. Working with the Teamsters and other unions, coalition leaders drafted language to cover the airport and related area travel businesses, mandating a $15 wage, sick leave, requirements to offer part-time workers more hours before hiring new employees, and a private right to sue noncompliant firms in court (Rolf 2016: 107–112; Rosenblum 2017: 110–112). Despite legal challenges, the campaign succeeded in getting the referendum on the ballot, and in November 2013, SeaTac voters passed it by a margin of just over 1% (Rosenblum 2017: 152).

The SeaTac initiative covered a comparatively small number of employees, but together with the fast food strikes, it had a powerful impact on the concurrent city elections in Seattle, where residents experienced widening income inequality and skyrocketing costs of living. The $15 wage issue dominated the municipal races leading to the November election of challenger Ed Murray for mayor and socialist candidate Kshama Sawant for City Council (Rolf 2016: 129–134). Mayor Murray immediately convened a committee of Seattle business, labor, and community leaders, co-chaired by David Rolf, head of the 40,000-member SEIU Healthcare 775NW, which had led the get-out-the-vote effort in SeaTac (Rosenblum 2017: 142). Rolf helped mobilize support from policy experts, labor, and community groups, while independently Sawant began organizing to put an alternative initiative on the November 2014 ballot. In a process that one observer described as an analog of collective bargaining among major local stakeholders, the mayor's committee produced an agreement to phase in $15 over a three- to seven-year period for large and small businesses (Dreier 2015; Meyerson 2014). On May 29, 2014, almost one year exactly after Seattle's first fast food strikes, the City Council voted unanimously for the proposal affecting around 100,000 workers and making Seattle the first major American city to approve a $15 minimum wage (Rolf 2016: 160).

Other cities soon followed, but along paths shaped by their own political environments. In Los Angeles, the movement drew from other, non-SEIU–led labor and community actors, including the Los Angeles Alliance for a New Economy (LAANE) and the politically powerful Los Angeles County Federation of Labor (LACFL). In January 2014, LAANE, LACFL, and the hotel workers union UNITE HERE Local 11 launched a campaign to raise wages for hotel workers in Los Angeles to $15.37. On September 24, the City Council voted 12 to 3 to approve the measure covering at least 40 hotels and up to 13,500 workers (Rainey 2014; Zahniser and Reyes 2014). Less than two weeks later, leaders from LAANE and LACFL stood outside City Hall to call for an increase in the citywide minimum wage to $15. While Los Angeles Mayor Eric Garcetti had previously proposed an increase to $13.25, on May 19, 2015, the councilors voted 14 to 1 to raise the minimum from $9 to $15 by 2020 for as many as 800,000 workers, with annual increases thereafter pegged to inflation (Jamison, Zahniser and Walton 2015; Smith 2014).

In San Francisco, public employees' union SEIU Local 1021 led a coalition to put $15 on the November 2014 ballot (Coté 2014a). After negotiations with business and labor groups and Mayor Ed Lee, the San Francisco Board of

Supervisors unanimously agreed to a compromise initiative that raised the minimum to $15 by July 2018. The announcement came two weeks after the Seattle City Council vote, and, with virtually no organized political opposition, Proposition J won easily in November with 77% of the vote (Coté 2014b; Lagos 2014). Internal rivalries within SEIU, however, threatened to disrupt the effort to take the campaign statewide, despite polls showing 68% support among the electorate. While SEIU Local 1021 led the local wage drives in Northern California, another large SEIU local, United Healthcare West (UHW), began organizing independently in April 2015 for a state ballot initiative (Dayen 2015). Local 1021 and the SEIU state council later filed their own initiative with a faster phase-in to $15, but by early 2016, the SEIU UHW petition, backed by Lieutenant Governor Gavin Newsome and State Controller Betty Yee, had gathered enough signatures to qualify for the November 2016 election. At the end of March, the two coalitions reached a deal with state lawmakers, avoiding a costly political battle. On April 4, Democratic Governor Jerry Brown signed legislation raising the state minimum to $15 by 2022, while allowing the governor to delay increases in the event of state budget or economic crises (Bacon 2016; Green 2016).

New York State displayed yet another path to reform. While cities there do not have authority to set their own minimum wage, the governor can order a special board to review wages in an industry and implement changes without approval by the legislature. Democratic Governor Andrew Cuomo initially opposed raising the minimum to $15, but as the movement gained support he shifted his position (Zillman 2014). In May 2015, Cuomo authorized a fast food wage board composed of members Byron Brown, Mayor of Buffalo; Kevin Ryan, chair of the online retailer Gilt; and Mike Fishman, Secretary–Treasurer of the SEIU international union. In July, the panel recommended an increase for around 180,000 employees of fast food chain restaurants to reach $15 per hour by December 2018 in New York City and July 2021 elsewhere in the state (McGeehan 2015; Zahn 2015). In November, Cuomo announced a $15 minimum for state employees, and the following April he negotiated a budget deal with state legislators to phase in wage hikes along with 12 weeks of paid family leave. The minimum wage would reach $15 at the end of 2018 for businesses with 11 or more employees in New York City, 2019 for those with fewer than 11 employees in New York City, 2021 for the surrounding suburban counties, and subsequently for the rest of the state (McGeehan 2016).

As in the campaign against McDonald's, the minimum-wage initiatives drew on existing action repertoires in the labor movement while extending them in new ways, including further demands for paid leave and scheduling rights, among others (Groover 2016). Moving from the industrial focus on the fast food corporations to the political campaigns for a higher wage, however, carried the movement into a different institutional arena where the actors, rules, resources, and strategies for action can vary considerably. To date, the wage campaigns have been successful in liberal big cities or in states with Democratic governors and legislative support, and they have relied on powerful allies within SEIU and other unions. In other regions, however, the political alignments may be less favorable and the barriers to change more substantial.

CONCLUSION

In just a few short years, the Fight for $15 has achieved extraordinary results. In a bold investment, SEIU spent at least $40 million dollars by 2017 on the campaign, including $10 million in 2016 alone (Greenhouse 2015; Lewis 2017a). The campaign estimates it has raised wages for 19 million workers nationwide, and the walkouts have kept alive the idea of the right to strike at a time when so few unions are prepared to use the tactic. The movement should not be seen in isolation, and the popular momentum has built on synergies with the OUR Walmart strikes and other mobilizations (Curry 2015). SEIU itself has expanded the focus beyond fast food, bringing its campaigns with health aides, adjunct teachers, airport workers, and others into the Fight for $15 and forging alliances with groups such as Black Lives Matter (Greenhouse 2016; Haines Whack 2017).

Nonetheless, the campaign faces strategic problems in both the economic and political arenas. In the economic arena, the legal challenge to the fissured workplace was dealt a blow after Donald Trump won election as United States president in November 2016. The McDonald's case was still at trial when the new Republican majority on the NLRB moved swiftly to overturn the *Browning-Ferris* standard on joint employers in the separate *Hy-Brand* case decision issued in December 2017. With just days left in the trial, in January 2018 NLRB General Counsel and Trump-appointee Peter Robb requested a stay in order to negotiate a settlement with McDonald's. Surprisingly, the following month the NLRB vacated the *Hy-Brand* ruling after its Inspector General reported a conflict of interest for Trump appointee William Emanuel that should have led to his recusal from the case. Nevertheless, in March, the General Counsel and McDonald's proposed a settlement that would give back pay to the fired workers but would not acknowledge joint employer status and would leave the case without a full record or ruling on the issues (DePillis 2018; Scheiber 2018a). In July, Judge Lauren Esposito rejected the settlement, though observers expected the General Counsel to appeal the decision to the NLRB, on which Republican members hold a majority (Scheiber 2018b).

In the workplace, fast food strikers have been threatened with job loss but have not had to maintain durable solidarity over an extended, open-ended strike, and the campaign has been criticized for using the protests in a media "air war" strategy rather than building worker organization on the job (Gupta

2013; Rosenblum 2017). The JfJ approach follows the historic precedents of the coal miners and garment workers of the early 20th-century United States in organizing small workplaces in a highly competitive market (Greenwald 2005), but the fast food industry may not follow the same model. With the janitors, SEIU built on its surviving base and leverage in the industry, but there is no similar history in fast food, and the resources of the brand corporations dwarf those of the building owners and cleaning contractors (Finnegan 2014).

In the political arena, the movement has faced strong countermobilization from business interests, particularly under Republican-dominated state governments. Using models promoted by the American Legislative Exchange Council (ALEC), by July 2017 at least 25 states had passed laws pre-empting cities from adopting higher minimum wages and other employment protections, including measures in Alabama, Iowa, and Missouri, and to take away increases already passed by cities and counties in their states (Chang 2017; National Employment Law Project 2017). In Ohio, Raise Up Cleveland submitted a petition for a $15 minimum wage with 28,000 signatures to the Cleveland City Council in May 2016, but opposition from the councilors delayed a ballot referendum until May 2017. In the meantime, city officials in December asked state legislators to pass a lame duck–session bill to prohibit Ohio cities from raising the minimum above the state level, and within three weeks, Republican Governor John Kasich signed the law, blocking the ballot vote in Cleveland (Atassi 2016; Pelzer 2016).

The political successes of the movement are further tempered by a classic dilemma of the American labor movement: it may win policy gains that benefit a broad range of both union and non-union members, but it is much harder to win reforms that strengthen workers' associational power. The barriers to political success also illustrate the importance of the industrial campaign for collective bargaining rights. If the Fight for $15 could win a national or even regional settlement with McDonald's or any of the brand corporations, it could extend workers' associational power into states where the political alignments are currently less favorable.

Even where the campaign has had legislative success, ensuring compliance with new regulations can be a challenge for overburdened and underfunded local governments. The challenge can provide an opportunity for the movement to demand stronger administration of the laws and to allow community-based organizations to participate officially in "co-enforcement" (Fine 2015; Sanchez 2017). In this way, community organization partners may perform functions similar to a union in the workplace, through investigating and reporting incidents of noncompliance and reaching out to workers, especially immigrants, who may be reluctant to come forward on their own.

Perhaps the greatest concern for the movement, though, is sustainability (Greenhouse 2015; Zahn 2016). The campaign remains dependent on both the financial investment and the organizational and political clout of the 1.9 million–member SEIU, but as yet it has produced no new dues-paying union members in fast food. The union faces enormous challenges of its own, not least a hostile federal government under the administration of President Donald Trump and a widely anticipated Supreme Court decision allowing public sector union bargaining unit members to avoid paying dues. In December 2016, SEIU president Henry announced a 30% cut in the union's budget to preserve needed resources, though the effect on the Fight for $15 is not yet clear (Eidelson 2016a).

In addition, SEIU has contended with internal organizational challenges. In the wake of the #MeToo movement, in late 2017 the union began a public reckoning with longstanding issues of sexual misconduct and abusive behavior among its top campaign staff. By early November, SEIU executive vice president and leading Fight for $15 strategist Scott Courtney and national organizing director Kendall Fells had resigned, and local chapter leaders Mark Raleigh in Detroit and Caleb Jennings in Chicago had been fired. The campaign had already made ending sexual harassment in the fast food industry a key part of its agenda, and, in September 2018, it mobilized strikes in nine major cities demanding that McDonald's do more to prevent sexual harassment on the job (Abrams 2018; Eidelson 2017; Lewis 2017b).

The Fight for $15 has helped win union recognition and contracts for airport workers, among others, and SEIU as a whole gained more than 13,000 members in 2016, a turnaround after five years of decline (Lewis 2017a). At the same time, the campaign is experimenting with new forms of member organization. In June 2017, New York City passed the Fast-Food Worker Empowerment Act, which requires fast food employers to allow employees to authorize payroll deduction of contributions to a qualified nonprofit organization, and upon the law's passage, the New York campaign immediately launched a new nonprofit, Fast Food Justice (Miller 2017). Unlike a union, the nonprofit (like a worker center) cannot engage in collective bargaining with employers, but it can provide services and advocacy for its members or engage in co-enforcement activities. This approach could increase the participation of fast food workers and help fund the movement, but it also poses a question: will the Fight for $15 continue to fight for unionization and collective bargaining rights in fast food, or will it abandon the union goal and seek alternate support through local worker centers?

The Fight for $15 shows the importance of symbolic power, and particularly strike action, in mobilizing workers' grievances over income inequality and low-wage work. In the political arena, the campaign has already succeeded in winning policy gains far beyond initial expectations. The key test of whether it can be transformative nationally, however, will depend on its capacity to convert symbolic power into institutionalized forms of workers' associational power, as in the rise of industrial unionism alongside and shaping the New Deal order, or the upsurge of public sector unions in the wake of the civil rights and women's movements of the 1960s and 1970s. "Since the campaign began, the workers have always had two demands," said one leading organizer. "It's $15 and a union, not $15 or a union" (Zahn 2016). The movement is still in the process of determining exactly what that will mean.

ENDNOTES

[1] Fine (2015) defines worker centers as "local NGOs that organize low-wage workers largely in communities and not primarily at the workplace or for collective bargaining purposes."

REFERENCES

Abrams, Rachel. 2018 (Sep. 18). "McDonald's Workers Across the U.S. Stage #MeToo Protests." *New York Times*. https://nyti.ms/2R27N0a

Allegretto, Sylvia, Marc Doussard, Dave Graham-Squire, Ken Jacobs, Dan Thompson and Jeremy Thompson. 2013. *Fast Food, Poverty Wages: The Public Cost of Low-Wage Jobs in the Fast-Food Industry.* Berkeley, CA, and Urbana, IL: University of California, Berkeley, Center for Labor Research and Education; and University of Illinois at Urbana-Champaign Department of Urban and Regional Planning. http://bit.ly/2GK9QEj

Alsin, Arne. 2017 (Apr. 27). "McDonald's: Burgers, Fries and Stock Buyback." *Forbes*. http://bit.ly/2GKYzUe

Atassi, Leila. 2016 (Sep. 13). "Special Election for Phased-In $15 Minimum Wage Proposal Set for May 2 in Cleveland." *Cleveland.com.* http://bit.ly/2GPMFET

Autor, David. 2010. "The Polarization of Job Opportunities in the U.S. Labor Market: Implications for Employment and Earnings." Washington, DC: Center for American Progress. https://ampr.gs/2EDub8I

Avendaño, Ana, and Jonathan Hiatt. 2012. "Worker Self-Organization in the New Economy: The AFL-CIO's Experience in Movement Building with Community–Labour Partnerships." *Labour, Capital and Society* 45 (1): 66–95.

Bacon, John. 2016 (Apr. 5). "$15 Minimum Wage Coming to New York, Calif." *USA Today*. https://usat.ly/2GPjgKG

Berg, Rebecca. 2012 (Jun. 7). "Bill Pushes for Increase in Wages." *New York Times*, p. B-1.

BerlinRosen. 2017. "Low Wage Work Case Study: Driving Labor's New Frontier." New York, NY: BerlinRosen. http://bit.ly/2EAA0U1

Bernhardt, Annette, Ruth Milkman, Nik Theodore, Douglas Heckathorn, Mirabai Auer, James DeFilippis, Ana Luz Gonzalez, Victor Narro, Jason Perelshteyn, Diana Polson, and Michael Spiller. 2009. "Broken Laws, Unprotected Workers: Violations of Employment and Labor Laws in America's Cities." Chicago, IL; New York, NY; and Los Angeles, CA: Center for Urban Economic Development; National Employment Law Project; UCLA Institute for Research on Labor and Employment. http://bit.ly/2EATp7v

Brown, Jenny. 2013 (Jun. 24). "Fast Food Strikes: What's Cooking?" *LaborNotes*. http://bit.ly/2GP6xYx

Bukowski, Diane. 2014 (Sep. 4). "Detroit Fast Food Workers Block Streets as Part of National Day of Civil Disobedience." *Voice of Detroit.* http://bit.ly/2EBg9UW

Burnett, Jennifer. 2011. "State Minimum Wage Increases Announced for 2012." Lexington, KY: Council of State Governments. http://bit.ly/2EDwAQM

Chang, Clio. 2017 (May 16). "How Republicans Are Blocking Cities from Raising the Minimum Wage." *New Republic*. http://bit.ly/2EzpZGX

Chun, Jennifer. 2009. *Organizing at the Margins: The Symbolic Politics of Labor in South Korea and the United States.* Ithaca, NY: Cornell University Press.

Coté, John. 2014a (Apr. 8). "SEIU Files S.F. Ballot Plan for $15-an-Hour Minimum Wage." *SFGate*. http://bit.ly/2IEdNaj

Coté, John. 2014b (Nov. 4). "Higher Minimum Wage Wins with Big Support in SF and Oakland." *SFGate*. http://bit.ly/2IHLcAP

Curry, Colleen. 2015 (Dec. 21). "The Resurgence of the Labor Movement: The Year in Workers' Power." *Vice News*. http://bit.ly/2EAjun6

Dayen, David. 2015 (Nov. 19). "California Duplicate Minimum Wage Ballot Battle Pits SEIU vs. SEIU." *In These Times*. http://bit.ly/2IHMA6v

DePillis, Lydia. 2018 (Jan. 11). "Trump Appointee May Give McDonald's Break in Landmark Labor Case." *CNN Money*. https://cnnmon.ie/2lrkJOw

Dickson, Alison, Robert Bruno, and Emily Twarog. 2015. "Shift-Work Shuffle: Flexibility and Instability for Chicago's Chicago Fast Food Workforce." Champaign, IL: Project for Middle Class Renewal, School of Labor and Employment Relations, University of Illinois at Urbana-Champaign. http://bit.ly/2EB3ykB

Dreier, Peter. 2015 (May 20). "The Wage War's Two Battlegrounds: The Ballot Box and the Board Room." *Huffington Post*. http://bit.ly/2EA792x

Eidelson, Josh. 2012 (Nov. 29). "In Rare Strike, NYC Fast-Food Workers Walk Out." *Salon*. http://bit.ly/2IKfGCr

Eidelson, Josh. 2013a (Jul. 29). "Fast Food Strikes Intensify in Seven Cities." *Salon*. http://bit.ly/2IH9meF

Eidelson, Josh. 2013b (Aug. 15). "Fast Food Strikes to Massively Expand: 'They're Thinking Much Bigger.'" *Salon*. http://bit.ly/2Jx30zU

Eidelson, Josh. 2016a (Dec. 27). "Fear of Trump Triggers Deep Spending Cuts by Nation's Second-Largest Union." *Bloomberg Businessweek*. https://bloom.bg/2EA8TbG

Eidelson, Josh. 2016b (Mar. 29). "How a $15 Minimum Wage Went from Fringe to Mainstream." *Bloomberg Politics*. https://bloom.bg/2EzQbkM

Eidelson, Josh. 2017 (Nov. 2). "SEIU Ousts Senior Leaders for Abusive Behavior Toward Women." *Bloomberg*. https://bloom.bg/2lqUN5F

Fast Food Forward. 2013. "New York's Hidden Crime Wave: Wage Theft and NYC's Fast Food Workers." New York, NY: Fast Food Forward. http://bit.ly/2EAhFXj

Fine, Janice. 2006. *Worker Centers: Organizing Communities at the Edge of the Dream.* Ithaca, NY: ILR/Cornell University Press.

Fine, Janice. 2015. "Alternative Labour Protection Movements in the United States: Reshaping Industrial Relations?" *International Labour Review* 154 (1): 15–26.

Finnegan, William. 2014 (Sep. 15). "Dignity: Fast-Food Workers and a New Form of Labor Activism." *The New Yorker*. http://bit.ly/2IHbqmV

Franco, Lucas. 2017 (Dec. 11). "Organizing the Precariat: The Fight to Build and Sustain Fast Food Worker Power." *Critical Sociology*. http://bit.ly/2yGcFTB

Freed Wessler, Seth. 2013 (Oct. 16). "Unhappy Meal: Fast-Food Workers Want Unions, Like Their Elders." *Al Jazeera America*. http://bit.ly/2JKSm8U

Green, Emily. 2016 (Jan. 19). "Backers of $15 Minimum Wage Submit Signatures to Get on Ballot." *SFGate*. http://bit.ly/2JIYKxf

Greenhouse, Steven. 2015 (Aug. 19). "How to Get Low-Wage Workers into the Middle Class." *Atlantic*. https://theatln.tc/2JO7WQX

Greenhouse, Steven. 2016 (Nov. 29). "Thousands of Fight for 15 Protesters Rise Up in 340 Cities Across the US." *Guardian*. http://bit.ly/2JMN9xp

Greenwald, Richard. 2005. *The Triangle Fire, the Protocols of Peace, and Industrial Democracy in Progressive Era New York*. Philadelphia, PA: Temple University Press.

Groover, Heidi. 2016 (Sep. 9). "Beginning Next Year, Seattle's Fast Food and Big Box Employees Will Get More Control over Their Work Schedules." *The Stranger*. http://bit.ly/2JMOvZ1

Gupta, Arun. 2013. "Fight for 15 Confidential." *In These Times*. http://bit.ly/2JMgwQl

Haines Whack, Errin. 2017 (Mar. 24). "Black Lives Matter Joining Forces with Minimum Wage Activists for Nationwide Protests." *Chicago Tribune*. https://trib.in/2JKo6Lg

Harris, Paul. 2013 (Apr. 4). "Hundreds of New York Fast Food Workers Go on Strike over Pay." *Guardian*. http://bit.ly/2JNUyfQ

Jamison, Peter, David Zahniser, and Alice Walton. 2015 (May 19). "Los Angeles' Minimum Wage on Track to Go Up to $15 by 2020." *Los Angeles Times*. https://lat.ms/2JJLAA2

Johnston, Katie. 2016 (Mar. 19). "On the Front Line of the Fight for $15." *Boston Globe*. http://bit.ly/2JMDN4s

Kalleberg, Arne. 2011. *Good Jobs, Bad Jobs: The Rise of Polarized and Precarious Employment Systems in the United States, 1970s to 2000s*. New York, NY: Russell Sage Foundation.

Kalleberg, Arne. 2014 (Nov). "Measuring Precarious Work." Working Paper of the EINet Measurement Group. Chapel Hill, NC: University of North Carolina. http://bit.ly/2JKTIk0

Lagos, Marisa. 2014 (Jun. 11). "S.F. to Put $15 Minimum Wage on Ballot." *SF Gate*. http://bit.ly/2JO8RRp

Lambert, Rob, Edward Webster, and Andries Bezuidenhout. 2012. "Global Labour Studies: The Crises and an Emerging Research Agenda." *Labor History* 53 (2): 291–298.

Larson, Eric. 2017 (May 3). "Union Accuses McDonald's of Gouging Franchisees on $3 Billion Rent." *Chicago Tribune*. https://trib.in/2JNUKvA

Lerner, Stephen, Jill Hurst, and Glenn Adler. 2008. "Fighting and Winning in the Outsourced Economy: Justice for Janitors at the University of Miami." In *The Gloves Off Economy: Workplace Standards at the Bottom of America's Labor Market*, edited by Annette Bernhardt, Heather Boushey, Laura Dresser, and Chris Tilly. Champaign, IL: Labor and Employment Relations Association.

Lewis, Cora. 2017a (Mar. 31). "Fighting to Raise the Minimum Wage Isn't Cheap, Union Spending Shows." *BuzzFeed News*. https://bzfd.it/2JM00zN

Lewis, Cora. 2017b (Oct. 23) "A Top Labor Executive Has Resigned After Complaints About His Relationships with Female Staffers." *Buzzfeed News*. https://bzfd.it/2ltxmZ7

Li, Shan, Samantha Masunaga, and Daina Beth Solomon. 2015 (Aug. 28). "NLRB Ruling on Third-Party Employers Could Be a Game Changer for Unions." *Los Angeles Times*. https://lat.ms/2JMPN6j

Luce, Stephanie. 2014. "Living Wages, Minimum Wages, and Low-Wage Workers." In *What Works for Workers? Public Policies and Innovative Strategies for Low-Wage Workers*, edited by Stephanie Luce, Jennifer Luff, Joseph McCartin, and Ruth Milkman. New York, NY: Russell Sage Foundation.

Mahdani, Aamer. 2016 (Jan. 12). "McDonald's Gouging Consumers in EU, Complaint Alleges." *USA Today*. https://usat.ly/2lnMh78

McGeehan, Patrick. 2015 (Jul. 22). "New York Plans $15-an-Hour Minimum Wage for Fast Food Workers." *New York Times*. https://nyti.ms/2JNbVNR

McGeehan, Patrick. 2016 (Apr. 1). "New York's Path to $15 Minimum Wage: Uneven, and Bumpy." *New York Times*. https://nyti.ms/2JMB1fz

McVeigh, Karen. 2013 (Aug. 29). "US Fast-Food Workers Stage Nationwide Strike in Protest at Low Wages." *Guardian*. http://bit.ly/2JJ07vT

Meyerson, Harold. 2014 (May 7). "Seattle's $15 Minimum Wage Agreement: Collective Bargaining Reborn?" *American Prospect*. http://bit.ly/2JNwsSy

Milkman, Ruth. 2006. *L.A. Story: Immigrant Workers and the Future of the U.S. Labor Movement.* New York, NY: Russell Sage Foundation.

Milkman, Ruth, Joshua Bloom, and Vincent Narro, eds. 2010. *Working for Justice: The L.A. Model of Organizing and Advocacy.* Ithaca, NY: Cornell University Press.

Milkman, Ruth, and Ed Ott, eds. 2014. *New Labor in New York: Precarious Workers and the Future of the Labor Movement.* Ithaca, NY: Cornell University Press.

Miller, Justin. 2017 (Jun. 15). "In New York City, Fast-Food Workers May Soon Have a Permanent Voice." *The American Prospect*. http://bit.ly/2ltM5nf

National Employment Law Project. 2013 (Jul. 25). "Going Nowhere Fast: Limited Occupational Mobility in the Fast Food Industry." Data Brief. http://bit.ly/2Mm0MUa

National Employment Law Project. 2017 (Jul. 6). "Fighting Preemption: The Movement for Higher Wages Must Oppose State Efforts to Block Local Minimum Wage Laws." Policy Brief. http://bit.ly/2JM4NBf

National Labor Relations Board. 2014 (Jul. 29). "NLRB Office of the General Counsel Authorizes Complaints Against McDonald's Franchisees and Determines McDonald's, USA, LLC Is a Joint Employer." Washington, DC: NLRB Office of Public Affairs. http://bit.ly/2JMhPPf

Pelzer, Jeremy. 2016 (Dec. 19). "Gov. John Kasich Signs Bill Blocking Cleveland's $15 Minimum Wage Proposal." *Cleveland.com*. http://bit.ly/2JKVth6

Rainey, James. 2014 (Jan. 13). "L.A. Expected to Soon Debate Raising Minimum Wage for Hotel Workers." *Los Angeles Times*. https://lat.ms/2EMCVcF

Resnikoff, Ned. 2014 (May 22). "138 Arrested at McDonald's HQ Protest." *MSNBC*. https://on.msnbc.com/2ENEyqj

Resnikoff, Ned, and Michele Richinick. 2014 (Sep. 4). "Fast Food Strikes Hit 150 US Cities." *MSNBC*. https://on.msnbc.com/2ENEGGj

Rhomberg, Chris. 2012. *The Broken Table: The Detroit Newspaper Strike and the State of American Labor.* New York, NY: Russell Sage Foundation.

Rolf, David. 2016. *The Fight for $15: The Right Wage for a Working America.* New York, NY: The New Press.

Rosenblum, Jonathan. 2017. *Beyond $15: Immigrant Workers, Faith Activists, and the Revival of the Labor Movement.* Boston, MA: Beacon Press.

Ruetschlin, Catherine. 2014. "Fast Food Failure: How CEO-to-Worker Pay Disparity Undermines the Industry and the Overall Economy." New York, NY: Demos. http://bit.ly/2ELkWmQ

Sanchez, Melissa. 2017 (Feb. 8). "Chicago's Lax Enforcement of Minimum Wage Hike Leaves Workers in the Lurch." *Chicago Reporter*. http://bit.ly/2ENHflz

Scheiber, Noam. 2018a (Mar. 19). "Push to Settle McDonald's Case, a Threat to Franchise Model." *New York Times*. https://nyti.ms/2lro3cp

Scheiber, Noam. 2018b (Jul. 17). "Judge Rejects Settlement Over McDonald's Labor Practices." *New York Times*. https://nyti.ms/2xSWYok

Schmitt, John, and Janelle Jones. 2013 (Aug. 13). "Slow Progress for Fast-Food Workers." Washington, DC: Center for Economic Policy Research. http://bit.ly/2ENUh8V

Short, Kevin. 2014 (Jul. 18). "McDonald's Workers Claim They Were Fired for Union Activity." *Huffington Post*. http://bit.ly/2EMMQ1R

Silver, Beverly. 2003. *Forces of Labor: Workers' Movements and Globalization Since 1970*. Cambridge, UK: Cambridge University Press.

Smith, Dakota. 2014 (Oct. 6). "Los Angeles Mayor Eric Garcetti Wants a $13.25 Minimum Wage, but Labor Groups Are Thinking $15 an Hour." *Los Angeles Daily News*. http://bit.ly/2vhTPAb

Speri, Alice. 2014 (Jul. 30). "Fast Food Workers Fight for a Raise, a Union, and Dignity at First National Convention." *Vice News*. http://bit.ly/2vfQLEN

Tung, Irene, Yannet Lathrop, and Paul Sonn. 2015 (Nov. 4). "The Growing Movement for $15." New York, NY: National Employment Law Project. http://bit.ly/2vlJbbY

US Department of Health and Human Services. 2012. "HHS Poverty Guidelines." Washington, DC: US Department of Health and Human Services, Office of the Assistant Secretary for Planning and Evaluation. http://bit.ly/2EKF8Ff

Weil, David. 2014. *The Fissured Workplace: Why Work Became So Bad for So Many and What Can Be Done to Improve It*. Cambridge, MA: Harvard University Press.

Wright, Erik O. 2000. "Working-Class Power, Capitalist-Class Interests, and Class Compromise." *American Journal of Sociology* 105: 957–1002.

Zahn, Max. 2015 (Oct. 15). "Can the Fight for $15 Replicate Its New York Wage Board Victory Around the Country?" *In These Times*. http://bit.ly/2ENM1pk

Zahn, Max. 2016 (May 2). "How Can the Fight for 15 Move from Winning Wage Increases to Winning a Union?" *In These Times*. http://bit.ly/2vgmENu

Zahniser, David, and Emily Alpert Reyes. 2014 (Sep. 24). "L.A. City Council Approves Minimum-Wage Hike for Hotel Workers." *Los Angeles Times* https://lat.ms/2vhUMZh

Zillman, Claire. 2014 (Sep. 4). "Fast-Food Worker Strikes: After Two Years, Is There Anything to Show?" *Fortune*. https://for.tn/2vm82fG

Governing the Market from Below: Setting Labor Standards at the State and Local Levels

KEN JACOBS

Center for Labor Research and Education, University of California Berkeley

As the share of workers in unions has declined, unions and alternative worker organizations have increasingly turned to public policy to legislate labor standards. Thirty-nine cities and 29 states now have minimum-wage standards well above the federal level. Unions and worker organizations have also successfully advocated for state policies concerning paid sick days, worker scheduling, wage theft, paid family leave, and other standards that were traditionally addressed in collective bargaining agreements. They have been extraordinarily successful in passing public policies to benefit workers. Nonetheless, major challenges remain in ensuring enforcement of the newly passed laws and turning the policy successes into sustainable worker organization.

INTRODUCTION

Since the late 1970s, incomes for the bottom half of the American population have stagnated or declined while earnings at the top have soared. In the post–World War II period, wages rose in tandem with productivity and income gains were widely shared, but by the end of the 1970s, the link between wages and productivity was broken (Bivens and Mishel 2015). In the 1980s, the bottom 50% of earners received 20% of national pre-tax national income while the top 1% of earners received 10.7%. By 2014, the income shares were basically reversed, with the top 1% now receiving over 20% of the national income and the bottom 50%, only 12.5% (Piketty, Saez, and Zucman 2016). During this same time period, the share of workers in a union fell from 27.8% in 1970 to 10.8% today. The share of private sector workers who are union members is down to 6.4%, from 24.2% in 1973.[1] The federal minimum wage of $7.25 has lost 25% of its real value from its height in 1968;[2] the federal tipped minimum wage remains at $2.13 an hour.[3]

Strategies to address declining real wages through traditional collective bargaining face significant barriers. Since the 1940s, changes in federal law, unfavorable court rulings, and an industry of anti-union consultants have made organizing difficult under the best of circumstances (Logan 2006; Riddell

1993). Decisions by the Obama administration's National Labor Relations Board (NLRB) opened up some new prospects for union leverage, but those openings are likely to fade quickly with a conservative NLRB and Supreme Court.

Strategies to revitalize labor face other challenges brought about by the changing structure of our economic institutions. Even as capital has become more concentrated, workplaces are more disaggregated/fissured—or aggregated in ways that reduce worker power (Weil 2014). Economists note that much of the increase in wage inequality over the past 20 years is due to growing inequality *between* firms rather than *within* firms (Song et al. 2015). One contributing factor to this trend is the rise in contracting out of services that were once performed by in-house employees. Industries such as building services (janitors and security guards) and air transportation services have seen wages fall sharply as more and more of the positions have been outsourced (Dietz, Hall, and Jacobs 2013; Dube and Kaplan 2010). In low-wage contracted service industries, there is greater pressure on wages resulting from low barriers to entry and labor's high share of the operating expenses. The contractor is the "employer of record"—the party that sets wages and that would engage in any collective bargaining—but the contractor is not the party with the economic power. In manufacturing and warehousing, the use of temporary workers plays a similar role in putting downward pressure on wages while creating additional barriers to organizing and to enforcement of worker protections (Jacobs, Perla, Perry, and Graham-Squire 2016; Kalleberg 2000).

Franchising in the fast food industry reflects another form of "fissuring" in Weil's terminology. While companies like McDonald's Corporation hold the economic power and maintain significant control over franchise operations, each franchise legally operates as a separate independent business with liability for its workforce. This puts tremendous pressure on franchises to keep down labor costs (Rolf 2016a; Weil 2014).

As union density and the reach of collective bargaining has declined, unions and other worker organizations have increasingly turned to using legislative strategies to set new labor standards in order to improve conditions at the bottom end of the labor market. Standards around key issues that were traditionally addressed in collective bargaining agreements—wages, health care, sick leave, and work hours—are becoming enshrined in law.

Fine (2005) argues that worker centers have had much more success in raising wages and improving working conditions through public policy than through organizing strategies designed to put direct economic pressure on employers. Though low-wage workers have little direct bargaining power with multinational companies, Fine argues, they still have political power in a democratic system of one person/one vote. This has allowed organizations of low-wage workers to make the difference in key elections and consequently are able to move cities to pass policies that improve working conditions for their members.

With Republicans in control of both the executive and legislative branches of the US federal government, any near-term policy changes aiming to improve labor standards will likely be state based or at the local level. Urban areas have a greater presence of unions and community-based organizations (CBOs) with the power to win policy changes, as well as electorates more likely to support pro-worker public policy interventions. Worker organizations have also had success in raising wages in more conservative states where they can bring the issue directly to the voters through ballot initiatives. These state and local efforts serve as Supreme Court Justice Louis Brandeis's "laboratories of democracy," where policies can be tested, refined, and expanded to wider geographies.

In this chapter, I will start with a historical background on state and local strategies for establishing labor standards. I will then discuss the rapid expansion of state and local labor standards in the 1990s and again in the past five years following the Fight for $15. Finally, I will discuss the potential for industry wage standards and next steps in going beyond the goal of a $15 minimum wage.

HISTORICAL BACKGROUND

There is a long history of state labor standards regulation in the United States. Kansas passed the first prevailing wage law for construction workers in 1891. Massachusetts adopted the first minimum-wage law in 1912. By 1919, 14 states, Puerto Rico, and the District of Columbia all had their own minimum-wage laws (Nordlund 1997: 13). These early laws only applied to women and minors. In the 1905 *Lochner v. New York* case, the Supreme Court had ruled that labor standards laws covering men were unconstitutional as a violation of liberty of contract. Reformers turned their focus on legislating labor standards for women under the legal theory that their dependence on men created a need for special protections (Zimmerman 1991).

The early state minimum-wage laws took many forms. Most had wage boards that set the minimum wage annually, based on the calculation of a living wage in the state for a single woman. In a few states (Colorado, Massachusetts, and Nebraska), the wage was voluntary and relied on both a calculation of a living wage and employer financial considerations. Three states (Arizona, Arkansas, and Utah) established a flat minimum-wage rate directly in statute; this is the most common method of establishing state minimum wages in the United States today (Nordlund 1997: 13–14).

The Washington, D.C., minimum-wage law was struck down by the Supreme Court in 1923 in *Children's Hospital v. Adkins* on the grounds that, after receiving the right to vote through the 19th Amendment, women no longer needed special protection (Zimmerman 1991). Nevertheless, states continued to enforce existing laws and to enact new ones. Eight more states passed laws; altogether 16 states had mandatory policies in place by 1935 (Nordlund 1997: 26). In 1937, the Supreme Court reversed its earlier position and upheld state minimum-wage laws in *West Coast Hotel Co. v. Parrish* (Grossman 1978).

The Fair Labor Standards Act (FLSA), passed in 1938, largely supplanted state minimum-wage laws, and it covered men as well as women. However, the FLSA excluded agricultural, domestic, and retail workers—positions that comprised half the national workforce and that were far more likely to be held by women and African Americans. Coverage under the FLSA was expanded to 80% of the nonagricultural workforce during the 1960s and 1970 (Reich 2015).

The federal minimum wage reached its peak in real dollars in 1968, at $9.66 an hour in 2016 dollars.[4] But by the end of the 1980s, the real value of the federal minimum wage had fallen by 30%, and states once again began to fill in the gap (Reich 2015). By 1990, 16 states and the District of Columbia had minimum-wage levels higher than the federal government.[5]

THE LIVING-WAGE MOVEMENT TAKES LABOR STANDARDS LOCAL

The modern living-wage movement started in Baltimore in the early 1990s. Pastors associated with Baltimoreans United in Leadership Development (BUILD) were concerned about the surprising number of working people making use of food pantries at the end of each month. Among the low-wage workers in their communities were janitors and school bus drivers working on city contracts. With the support of the American Federation of State, County and Municipal Employees (AFSCME), BUILD created the Solidarity Sponsoring Committee to organize workers across low-wage industries into a community union (Fine 2005).

Any strategy to organize workers on city contracts raises a dilemma: if these private sector workers are successful in forcing contractors to agree to higher wages, the contractor would lose the contract next time it went out to bid because public sector contracting rules require the city to choose the lowest bidder that met the general criteria. BUILD proposed a living-wage law for Baltimore that would require all city contractors to pay a wage rate that was set higher than the state minimum. This would directly improve low-wage workers' earnings while improving conditions for organizing. The living-wage law also reduced the city's incentive to contract various services out.

In the end, the city brought back in house some of the jobs that it had contracted out, which again became public jobs with protections and benefits.

While BUILD's efforts aimed at organizing a community union of low-wage workers in Baltimore was ultimately not successful, the policy succeeded in raising the floor for low-wage contracted service jobs (Fine 2000). It also helped to spark a living-wage movement that quickly spread across the country.

The success in Baltimore helped to open the floodgates to living-wage laws. Within a little over a decade, more than 129 cities, counties, and other local government agencies had passed such laws (National Employment Law Project 2010). The Association of Community Organizations for Reform Now (ACORN) had pursued similar efforts in a number of cities around the country attempting to win wage standards for businesses receiving subsidies from local governments prior to the passage of the law in Baltimore. Learning from the success of BUILD, ACORN began running living-wage campaigns directed at local government contracting with a strategy of building labor–community coalitions (Tilly 2004).[6]

In California, the Los Angeles Alliance for a New Economy (LAANE) took the living-wage concept a step further (Fairris, Runsten, Briones, and Goodheart 2015). In 1997, LAANE developed a law for Los Angeles that set a higher minimum-wage standard not just for city contractors but also for the three regional airports (LAX, Burbank, and Oxnard) as well as development projects receiving a certain level of city subsidies. The Los Angeles living-wage law also went beyond wage setting: firms were required to provide a higher wage if they did not provide health insurance and a minimum number of paid days off. Los Angeles also put in place robust enforcement provisions including protection against retaliation.

With LAANE's leadership, Los Angeles passed the first worker retention ordinance in the country a few years earlier, requiring any new contractor to retain the existing workforce when a contract changed hands. This provided an essential protection for workers in industries where the contractor might change any time the contract comes up for renegotiation. Worker retention rules also give workers more confidence in reporting safety violations because they have less fear that they will lose their jobs if their employer loses the contract as a result.

The living-wage campaigns of LAANE and its California sister organizations affiliated with the Partnership for Working Families were conducted in alliance with union partners, mainly the Hotel and Restaurant Employees Union (now UNITE HERE) and Service Employees International Union (SEIU); a specific goal of these campaigns was to aid union organizing and collective bargaining (Zabin and Martin 1999). In San Jose, for example, Working Partnerships USA successfully advocated for a living-wage law that included labor peace provisions, which helps the city avoid work disruption and costly labor disputes by encouraging neutrality agreements during an organizing drive.

Over time, the laws began to expand both in terms of who was covered and what benefits were provided. Living-wage stipulations have been applied to government service contracts, property leases, subsidies, geographic areas within a city that benefit from public investment, and a growing number of airports. Provisions have included minimum-wage levels, higher wages when health care is not provided, paid time off, training standards, and protections against retaliation in case of employee complaints.

The main limitation of local living-wage laws has always been the relatively small number of workers affected. With the exception of a few cities, most notably Los Angeles, New York, and San Francisco, the number of workers who received wage increases as a result of the laws tended to be small—with as few as 100,000 nationwide in 2002 (Freeman 2005). Enforcement was also spotty, with many cities not putting in sufficient resources or attention to ensure contractors meet the higher standards (Luce 2004).

Perhaps the most important legacy of the living-wage movement was in building a local organizing and policy infrastructure around the country. The organizations and labor–community coalitions built through the living-wage movement were central to the expansion of minimum-wage laws more than a decade later. Organizations such as LAANE, Working Partnerships USA, the Working Families Party, and the National Employment Law Project (NELP), as well as many of the local organizers later affiliated with the Center for Popular Democracy, that were engaged in living-wage campaigns in the late 1990s and early 2000s later played imported roles in winning passage of city and state minimum-wage laws that reach much greater numbers of workers. In some cases, the living-wage movement also built an infrastructure for local wage enforcement that could be built on for enforcement of local minimum-wage laws. Finally, living-wage laws contributed to union organizing and bargaining efforts in multiple cities (Zabin and Martin 1999).

SAN FRANCISCO AND THE TURN TO CITYWIDE LABOR STANDARDS POLICIES

San Francisco is the US city with the most expansive local labor standards regime. Starting in the late 1990s, a shifting coalition of unions and CBOs waged successful campaigns to pass a series of laws to raise labor standards. As in other cities, organizers in San Francisco started by passing laws that applied to city contractors, if on a bigger scale than other cities compared with the size of the workforce. The local coalitions and progressive members of the Board of Supervisors than turned to passing laws that applied to all or most employers operating in the city, significantly expanding the reach of who benefited. These included policies designed to improve wages and benefits, expand access to health care, provide paid sick leave, create more predictable work schedules, reduce discrimination against the formerly incarcerated, promote family-friendly workplace policies, and provide more generous paid parental leave (Reich and Jacobs 2014).

The movement to pass local labor standards policies in San Francisco started with the Equal Benefits Ordinance in 1996, which required firms doing business with the city to extend to employees' domestic partners the same benefits provided to married spouses. While essentially a human rights law rather than a labor standard, the ordinance nonetheless expanded the availability of job-based health coverage to a wider range of workers. Firms were required to provide equal benefits only to those employees whose work was directly related to the contract with San Francisco, but many of the contractors extended the provisions across their entire national workforce. The law, which applied to firms doing business at SFO, survived a legal challenge from United Airlines, Federal Express, and the Air Transport Association, and became a blueprint for the development and passage of subsequent labor standards policies in the city.

The following year, San Francisco passed a "labor peace ordinance" that applied to employers in hotel and restaurant developments where the city had a proprietary interest as a landlord, lender, or loan guarantor. The ordinance required covered employers to enter into card-check agreements upon the request of a labor organization; under card check, an employer agrees to recognize a union if a majority of workers sign authorization cards indicating they want the union to represent them.

In 1998, San Francisco passed a prevailing wage law for janitors working on city contracts. That was followed by prevailing laws covering a wide range of contracted city work including window washing, security, parking lot attending, loading and unloading vehicles on city property, broadcast service work on city property (including the ball park), theatrical work, solid waste hauling, moving services, and trade shows.[7]

The first success in passing a living-wage policy in San Francisco was at the San Francisco International Airport (SFO), which was approved in the context of a multi-union organizing effort at SFO. Turnover rates for some of the contracted jobs at the airport were was 80% per year, which raised concerns about airport safety and security (Reich, Hall, and Jacobs 2003). The Airport Quality Standards Program required permits for contracting firms to operate at the airport and created minimum-wage and training conditions for any firm receiving a permit. At the same time, the Airport Commission also agreed to a labor peace policy for the airport, which led to 2,000 workers organizing and gaining collective bargaining agreements. An estimated one third of the 30,000 workers at SFO received wage increases in April 2000 when the policy went into effect, and employee turnover fell sharply.

Later that year, following an extensive campaign by a labor–community coalition, the Board of Supervisors passed a living-wage policy on city and county contracts. Along with for-profit contracts common in other living-wage laws, it included the city's 12,000 homecare workers organized through SEIU and workers in nonprofit human service agencies, as well as requiring that the higher wage rate be used in calculating the work hour requirements for workers on general assistance. Each of these reflected the concerns and interests of different organizations in the coalition.

Buoyed by the successes in winning labor standards conditions on city contracts, local CBOs and progressive politicians turned their attention to citywide policies. In 2003, San Francisco joined Santa Fe in passing the first citywide minimum-wage laws outside of Washington, D.C. San Francisco set a minimum wage of $8.50 an hour, 26% above the state minimum. The campaign, led by the Chinese Progressive Association and ACORN, placed the issue on the ballot. At the time it was the highest minimum wage in the country, affecting about 54,000 workers—11% of the city's workforce.

Three years later, Young Workers United (YWU) spearheaded the first successful effort in the United States to pass a law requiring paid sick days. As Young Workers United set out to organize workers in fast food and retail establishments in the city, they found that many of their members lacked access to paid sick leave on the job. YWU placed an initiative on the ballot to require businesses operating in the city to provide a minimum number of paid sick days. It passed with 61% of the vote (Lester 2014; Reich and Jacobs 2014).

That same year, a coalition of labor and community organizations ran a campaign to expand access to affordable health care in the San Francisco. The resulting Health Care Security Ordinance had two central components: it created a new health program, Healthy San Francisco, which provides comprehensive health services to uninsured residents of the city, and it required all businesses with 20 or more employees in the city to meet minimum health spending requirements. The requirement was set on a per-worker per-hour basis, with larger firms paying a higher amount than smaller firms. Those firms not directly providing health insurance could meet their obligation by paying into Healthy San Francisco, the city's public option; if they do so, their workers receive a discount on the program's sliding scale enrollment fee.

In a ten-year time span, San Francisco established a robust body of labor standards policies. In 2004, the minimum wage in San Francisco matched the state's at $6.75 an hour; in 2013, the mandated minimum compensation cost for a large firm in that city was $13.31 an hour, including $2.33 in health care spending and $0.43 an hour toward paid sick leave (Reich and Jacobs 2014). As a result of these policies, an estimated 77,500 San Francisco workers (12% of the workforce) received pay increases, 59,000 gained access to paid sick leave, and more than three quarters of San Francisco firms covered by the health law reported improving health benefits in response to the law in a subsequent survey (Colla, Dow, and Dube 2013; Reich, Jacobs, and Dietz 2014).

San Francisco was able to implement these improvements for workers with no measurable negative effect on employment. Between 2001 and 2012, employment trends in San Francisco matched those of the surrounding counties while employment in restaurants—the sector most likely to be affected by the higher wage increases—grew even more in San Francisco (17.7%) than in the surrounding counties (13.2%).

Local organizations in San Francisco continued to build on these successes. In the last three years, San Francisco adopted a policy requiring large retailers to provide workers more predictable schedules, a "ban the box" law prohibiting employers from asking about criminal records prior to offering workers a job, an expanded parental leave policy, and a $15 minimum wage.[8]

Several elements were central to the organizing successes in San Francisco. The city retains a relatively strong labor movement—which was united in support of the standards policies during the time the main laws were passed. It also has a robust network of CBOs. The service unions, which make up the largest share of union membership in the city, have a history of community unionism and deep relationships with CBOs. Of course, San Francisco is not unique among major cities in these ways. The ability to take these issues to the ballot was essential in giving local organizers leverage, even when they negotiated the policies with political leaders. A history of successfully using ballot initiatives to fight the business community also weakened the salience of "job-killer" arguments (Lester 2014). While the business community engaged in a major campaign against the earlier living-wage law, opposition to later efforts was much more muted. When San Francisco went on to pass a $15 minimum wage, the largest tech advocacy organization in the city supported the measure while other business organizations stayed neutral.[9] Once the minimum wage is fully phased in, the effective minimum compensation rate for employees of firms with 20 or more employees will be $17.90 an hour including health spending and paid sick leave.[10]

THE FIGHT FOR $15—RAISING THE BAR

The rise of the Fight for $15 movement radically changed the discussion around state and local labor standards. The demand for $15 an hour altered the perception both of what constitutes a fair wage and what is possible.

The Fight for $15 started when New York Communities for Change began organizing fast food workers in the city with support from SEIU. In November 2012, 200 fast food workers held a one-day strike (Rolf 2016a). The following spring, fast food strikes spread to Chicago, Detroit, Kansas City, Milwaukee, and St. Louis as a result of organizing by SEIU in concert with local coalitions. The demand of the fast food workers was $15 an hour and a union.

The first effort to translate the demand for $15 from rallying cry to public policy took place in the city of SeaTac, home to the Seattle–Tacoma Airport. In 2005, Alaska Airlines fired 500 baggage handlers and outsourced the work to Menzies Aviation. Union jobs that averaged $13.81 an hour and provided benefits were replaced with jobs paying $8.75 an hour with minimal benefits (Dietz, Hall, and Jacobs 2013; Rosenblum 2017). An effort to organize contracted workers at Sea-Tac Airport quickly ran up against the Railway Labor Act (Rosenblum 2017). The union could petition only for an election among all of the contractors' workers nationally, or gain voluntary recognition from the company (which the company refused). In response, the Teamsters and SEIU, along with a large community coalition, made the decision to set basic labor standards via ballot initiative. The 2013 initiative applied to the Sea-Tac Airport and other large tourist-related businesses. It included not only a $15 an hour wage and paid sick days but was also the first measure in the country requiring businesses to offer additional work hours to existing employees before expanding their workforce. The initiative passed by 77 votes (Rolf 2016a).

In 2014, Seattle became the first city to pass an across-the-board $15 minimum-wage law, followed in quick succession by San Francisco and Los Angeles. In 2012, at the time of the first fast food strike, six cities and counties had local minimum-wage laws (Albuquerque; Bernalillo County, New Mexico; San Francisco; San Jose; Santa Fe; and Washington, D.C.), with the highest wage at $10 an hour. Five years later, the total was up to 40 cities and counties (most recently Minneapolis), 21 of which will reach $15 an hour when fully phased in, as shown in Table 1. In 2016, California and New York passed the first $15 an hour state minimum-wage laws. By 2017, 29 states and Washington, D.C. (which collectively include 61%[11] of the national working population) had minimum wages above the federal maximum of $7.25 an hour.[12]

The National Employment Law Project (2016) estimates that the higher state and local minimum-wage laws passed between 2012 and 2016 will increase workers' incomes by $60 billion when fully phased in, benefiting 17 million workers. The new state and local minimum-wage laws in California alone will raise wages for low-wage workers by an estimated $23 billion a year by 2023.[13] This does not take into account two recent increases in the California state minimum wage prior to passage of the most recent law. To put this in perspective, it is greater than the total annual state and federal spending for the largest nonhealth public assistance programs for low-income families in the state (the Earned Income Tax Credit and Temporary Aid to Needy Families cash assistance and food stamps, which totaled $18.2 billion in 2014[14]). While there is a great deal of variation across industries, economists estimate that union workers earn approximately 15% more than their nonunion counterparts after controlling for industry, occupation, and worker demographic characteristics (Mishel 2012; Schmitt 2010). If we assume that holds true in

TABLE 1
State and Local Labor Standards Policies in the United States 1980–2017

	1980	1990	2000	2010	2017
State minimum wage above federal	2	16	10	14	29
Local minimum wage	1*	1*	1*	5	39
Local living-wage ordinances	0	0	51	123	NA
State paid sick days	0	0	0	0	3
Local paid sick days	0	0	0	3	35
State predictable scheduling	0	0	0	0	1
Local predictable scheduling	0	0	0	0	4

*Washington, D.C.

Note: Local minimum wage, paid sick days, and scheduling denote when the law was passed. State minimum wage above the federal is the number of states where the state minimum wage was on average above the federal during the year; declining numbers between 1990 and 2000 are due to increases in the federal minimum wage that went above the minimum in certain state laws.

Minimum Wage
    National Council of State Legislators. "State Minimum Wages: 2017 Minimum Wages by State" (http://bit.ly/2uAzGF6)

    Author's analysis of Vaghul and Zipper, Historical State and Substate Minimum Wage Data Set (http://bit.ly/2pXK7Oy)

    UC Berkeley Center for Labor Research and Education, Inventory of Local Minimum Wage Ordinances (Cities and Counties) (http://bit.ly/2q08kU8)

Living Wage
    National Employment Law Project, "Living Wage Ordinances and Coverage," December 6, 2010 (http://bit.ly/2pUkWwf)

Paid Sick Days
    A Better Balance, "Paid Sick Time Legislative Success" (http://bit.ly/2pWl0LU)

    Katherine Muniz, "Overview of All U.S. State and City Paid Sick Leave Laws" (http://bit.ly/2uKIjgm)

    Workplace Fairness, "State and Local Paid Sick Leave Laws" (http://bit.ly/2uERj6P)

Predictable Scheduling
    Ben-Ishai, Lopez Marchena, and Ziliak Michel (2017); Gorman, Steve. "Oregon Passes First Statewide 'Fair Work Week' Legislation." Reuters, June 29, 2017 (https://reut.rs/2uEpxHP)

California, the total projected wage increase from the $15 minimum-wage laws is equal to or greater than the current total additional wages in the state earned as a result of unionization—albeit less than the increase in compensation for union members if benefits are factored in.[15]

MORE THAN WAGES

Paid Sick Days

The United States is rare among highly developed countries in not mandating any paid sick leave for workers (Heymann, Rho, Schmitt, and Earle 2010). As of 2010, only one third of those in the bottom 25% of the wage distribution and 42% of service workers had access to this benefit (Hill 2013). Without paid sick leave, workers face a financial risk if they take time off work for their own health or to take care of a dependent. Many see no alternative than to work while they are ill because they risk losing income or even their job if they call in sick (Lovell 2014).

In 2006, San Francisco was the first US city to pass a mandated paid sick days ordinance; it was followed by Milwaukee and Washington, D.C., in 2008. Connecticut became the first state to pass such a law in 2011. By the end of 2016, 34 cities and counties as well as four states (California, Connecticut, Massachusetts, and Oregon) had passed paid sick days policies.[16] Following implementation of these laws, the share of workers in the bottom decile with access to paid sick leave rose nationwide from 18% in 2012 to 27% in 2016 (Gould and Schieder 2017).

Fair Scheduling and Part-Time Work

In recent years, fair scheduling in the retail and restaurant industries emerged as a major focus of organizing around local labor standards. Hourly workers in the retail and restaurant industries face a high degree of volatility in their schedules and total work hours. Henly, Fugiel, and Lambert (2014) found that 90% of early-career (ages 26 to 32) food-service workers had fluctuations in their work hours, with an average variation of 68%. More than 10% of workers in the United States are given irregular or on-call shifts, most commonly in the personal service, retail, restaurants, agriculture, and entertainment industries (Golden 2015). An additional 7% have split shifts or rotating schedules. Schedules for retail and restaurant workers may only be available a few days in advance and are often subject to additional last-minute changes. Unpredictable schedules have been found to result in financial insecurity, greater stress, worse health outcomes, and less time with children (Schneider and Harknett 2016). Week-to-week scheduling uncertainty makes it difficult for workers to arrange childcare, establish regular schedules with children, hold down additional jobs, or attend school.

In 2014, San Francisco Jobs With Justice led a campaign to establish the first city policies addressing unpredictable scheduling for workers employed by formula retail establishments. These are defined as chain stores with at least 40 establishments worldwide and 20 employees in San Francisco. The laws mandate premium pay if schedules are not provided two weeks in advance, worker retention if the establishment is sold, on-call pay if workers are not called in, wage parity for part-time workers, and offering of additional hours to current part-time workers before new workers are hired. Predictable scheduling laws have since been passed in the California city of Emeryville, New York, and Seattle. In November 2016, a labor–community coalition in San Jose passed a ballot initiative requiring right of first refusal on additional work shifts for part-time workers. In June 2017, Oregon became the first state to pass a predictable scheduling law.

BEYOND $15

A $15 minimum wage in many areas of the United States meets the self-sufficiency standard for a single individual working full time, but it is still well below what is needed for most families to meet their basic needs (Howell, Fielder, and Luce 2016). Laws regulating standards for employees do not reach workers classified as independent contractors. In this section, I explore further directions in state and local policies to raise the standards and extend the reach of the policies.

Sectoral Wage Setting

In the past several years, there has been a renewed interest in exploring models of industry wage setting in the United States and the potential for using state and local policy to create a framework for new forms of sectoral bargaining or directly set standards on an industry basis (Andrias 2016; Madland 2016; Madland and Rowell 2017). An across-the-board minimum wage covering all workers and industries provides an essential floor but is too blunt an instrument to raise incomes to the level that will meet the full needs for families with children. Industry wage standards can be tailored to the conditions in specific industries and occupations.

Enterprise-based bargaining is an important factor for the relatively low share of workers covered under collective bargaining agreements in the United States compared with other wealthy democracies (Madland 2016; Organisation for Economic Co-operation and Development 2017). When collective bargaining agreements apply at the enterprise level, the resulting differential in labor costs between firms in the same industry puts the unionized enterprises at a competitive disadvantage, creating a strong incentive to resist unionization. This dynamic can be altered with an industry wage-setting strategy.

Industry wage standards can be achieved in a variety of ways. Historically, the main method in the United States was through pattern bargaining in auto, ports, and other high union–density industries. As union density declined in the United States, the power to set industry standards through collective bargaining fell sharply. Some European countries (e.g., Austria, Denmark, and Germany) have industry-wide collective bargaining systems that operate through voluntary employer participation in industry councils. However, these systems have eroded under pressure of European integration and the governing rules of the European Economic Council, which give companies the right to provide time-limited services in other countries using their own workers (Bosch and Weinkopf 2013).

Other wealthy democracies expand the terms of collective contracts across the industry through law. In countries such as Belgium, France, and the Netherlands, the negotiated wage standards are extended across the industry, either automatically or through approval of the labor ministry. The pay scale in the collectively bargained sector is mandated across firms within the industry. Bosch and Weinkopf (2013) note that this creates two minimum wages: the national minimum wage that sets the lower limit, and collectively bargained minimum wages that vary by industry sector and pay grade. Not surprisingly, among the countries analyzed in the paper, the authors find that the percentage of workers who are low-wage workers in countries with industry extensions of negotiated wages is well below that of countries with enterprise-based bargaining or bargaining through voluntary employer organizations.

The concept of wage extenders is not completely alien in the United States. Prevailing wage laws serve this function for construction firms contracting with a public entity. The McNamara-O'Hara Service Contract Act of 1965 similarly extends the prevailing wage in an industry to workers on federal contracts across a wide range of services. Another recent example can be found in Los Angeles, where in 2016, a coalition of labor and tenant organizations successfully passed a ballot initiative setting minimum affordable housing and labor standards for certain residential developments.[17]

Finally, wages can be set for an industry through an industry-specific minimum-wage law. Hotel living-wage policies do this in the California cities of Emeryville, Long Beach, and Los Angeles. Wage standards policies are in place in multiple US airports including Boston, Ft. Lauderdale, Los Angeles, Miami, New York City, Oakland, San Francisco, San Jose, Sea-Tac, and St. Louis.[18] In New York State, a wage board was used to establish a $15 minimum wage for fast food workers. Australia has a very well-developed sectoral minimum-wage system that details minimum-wage settings for 156 industry groups, with multiple occupations and classifications within each industry.[19]

Andrias (2016) argues for the use of wage boards as a form of social bargaining. Wage boards would be made up of worker, industry, and government representatives. Worker organizations would negotiate through the wage board, which would set standards across industry sectors. Unlike a legislated sectoral minimum wage, standards would be set through tripartite bargaining at the industry level. The negotiation process would create a locus for worker organization. Pointing to New York's fast food wage board as a model, workers in the industry could exercise power in the negotiations by holding strikes, turning out en masse for hearings and demonstrations, and engaging in political action. The tripartite nature of the bargaining would help to ensure that agreements were tailored to the specific needs of each industry and to society at large.

These strategies are not mutually exclusive and could be combined. Sectoral wage strategies are especially promising in subcontracted industries where the economic power to increase wages lies higher up the supply chain. Of the various methods to set sectoral standards, wage extenders arguably have the greatest potential to support worker organizing—but are limited to geographies and industries where unions already have significant wage-setting power. Many of the European wage extender laws require a threshold of coverage under the collective bargaining agreement before the standards are extended to the rest of the industry (Organisation for Economic Co-operation and Development 2017).

Broadening the Definition of Employee

A second area for expansion of state and local labor standards is in the definition of employee and, by extension, who is covered under the laws. The gig economy and its implications for labor standards and worker organizing is receiving significant attention in the popular media. There is a widely held belief that the gig economy is expanding rapidly and will soon encompass a high share of the workforce.[20] If true, this would suggest that legislated labor standards will fail to reach large sectors of the workforce and, worse, might incentivize employers to shift work away from employees to gig workers.

Conflicting definitions of who is considered a gig worker have led to very different estimates of the size of the gig economy, ranging from 600,000 to 55 million workers (Bernhardt and Thomason 2017). Recent data on self-employment and tax filings tell a different and more nuanced story. The share of workers reporting that their main job is unincorporated self-employment has been remarkably stable over the past 40 years; it was 6.3% of the workforce in 2016 while an additional 3.7% report they are incorporated self-employed. Tax data give a different picture, with the numbers of 1099s increasing by 42% between 2000 and 2014 (Jackson, Looney, and Ramnath 2017). One possible explanation is that rather than seeing a shift away from W-2 jobs to independent contracting as the main source of income, we are seeing an increase in workers taking on extra part-time work or taking on gig work for short periods of time between other jobs. Gig work could be understood, at least in part, as a response to wage stagnation. Another possible part of the story could be that the new electronic platforms have brought a share of traditional moonlighting work into the formal economy. Bernhardt and Thomason (2017) make the important point that the vast majority of low-wage workers continue to have an employer and thus, labor standards policies are still an important tool for improving wage and benefit standards.

Even if the use of independent contractors is much smaller than discussed in the popular media, the use of independent contractors in many low- and middle-wage industries presents an important challenge for state and local labor standards regimes. Independent contractors are not covered by the FLSA and are excluded from the National Labor Relations Act. Economic strategies by independent contractors through strikes or boycotts to demand higher wages could face legal constraints under anti-trust law.

Union and community-based worker organizations have a range of options for raising labor standards for independent contractors. One option is to expand who is covered by state and local labor standards laws to reach workforces currently treated as independent contractors (National Employment Law Project 2017; Rogers 2016). While some of these may be cases of worker misclassification, expanding the definition of employee under specific state and local labor standards laws would eliminate any legal ambiguity for the purposes of those laws. This could be done through a broad expansion of the definition of employee (e.g., NELP proposes including "independently establishing the price of labor" in the employee test), or through statutorily declaring certain workers as employees (e.g., those who work driving for transportation network companies [TNCs] such as Uber or Lyft).

Another option is to use wage boards, as discussed above, to set minimum labor standards in an industry where workers are treated as independent contractors (whether or not they should be so treated). Seattle went a step further and created a framework for collective bargaining between drivers and TNCs (Madland and Rowell 2017).[21]

CHALLENGES AND LIMITATIONS
Enforcement

One of the central challenges for local labor standards laws is enforcement. Luce (2004) documented the highly uneven enforcement of local living-wage laws, finding that 50% of the laws had minimal—if any—enforcement while only 14% had strong enforcement. Local minimum-wage laws create an additional challenge. While living-wage enforcement could build on existing systems for contract compliance, local governments are starting without a base of existing infrastructure or experience in enforcing across-the-board labor standards policies such as the minimum wage. The challenge is especially great for smaller cities, which typically lack the resources and capacity to build their own enforcement systems. Nonwage labor standards tend to be less familiar to both workers and employers, and they require significant education and outreach as a crucial part of any enforcement effort. Surveys of workers conducted within a few years of implementation of San Francisco's paid sick days and scheduling policies found low worker knowledge of the laws and widespread employer violations (Ben-Ishai, Lopez Marchena, and Ziliak Michel 2017; Lovell 2014).

Effective enforcement of local labor standards policies requires three main elements: strong provisions within the law for enforcement, a proactive enforcement agency, and collaboration with community-based organizations (Koonse, Dietz, and Bernhardt 2015). Most of the new laws name an enforcement agency and include fines, penalties and damages, private right of action, posting requirements, ability to revoke licenses, and protection against retaliation. Some go further, and provide for criminal penalties or the ability to place liens to prevent an employer's assets from disappearing during an investigation. Enforcement agencies will need to, along with other functions, both educate employers and employees about the laws and receive and investigate complaints.

A growing number of cities, including Los Angeles, San Francisco, and Seattle, are contracting with local worker organizations for outreach and education (Koonse, Dietz, and Bernhardt 2015). Worker organizations bring cultural competence and relations of trust in diverse communities. They can play an important role in educating workers about their rights, identifying violations, and building trust between workers and investigators. They may also bring knowledge of specific industries (Fine and Gordon 2010).

State Preemption

Efforts to raise labor standards have been most successful in states and cities where labor has political power and where elected officials are more progressive. Minimum-wage campaigns have also been successful in Republican-controlled states where citizens are able to bypass the legislature and bring the issue directly to the voters through ballot initiatives. States without the right to ballot initiative and where Republicans control the legislature and/or governorship have resisted raising labor standards and are in fact passing laws to take the power away from cities. As of May 2017, 24 states had preemption laws. In some cases, cities never had the authority to regulate wages while in others, such as Alabama, Missouri, and North Carolina, laws were passed more recently in response to the local minimum-wage movement following model legislation promoted by the conservative American Legislative Exchange Council (DuPuis, Langon, McFarland, and Rainwater 2017).

Building Sustainable Organizations

Pursuing public policy strategies can assist, but it does not supplant the need for workers to build self-sustaining organizations. Even as a new nontraditional organization of fast food workers was developed through the Fight for $15, the financial and organizational support from a traditional union, SEIU, was central to their successes (Ginsburg 2017). The threat of a Supreme Court ruling overturning fair-share fees for public sector unions could constrain funding for similar efforts in the future (Walker 2017). Contracting with cities for enforcement is providing a limited source of ongoing funding for workers' centers. Rolf (2016b) sees portable benefit funds as one way to build and sustain membership, on the model of the Ghent system in Scandinavia, where unions play a central role in administering publicly subsidized benefits. Nevertheless, the challenge remains of winning the second half of the workers' demands in the Fight for $15: "$15 and a union."

Care Industries

Childcare, homecare, and services to people with developmental disabilities provide a unique set of challenges in raising minimum wages at the state and local levels. The added difficulty comes in the fact that many of these agencies rely completely or in part on federal, state, or county funding with set reimbursement rates. The governmental body raising the minimum wage may be different than the governmental body responsible for setting these reimbursement rates. Even where they are same, addressing the funding needs may require going beyond our existing minimum-wage strategies. Doing so successfully will require organizing for a greater investment of public funding in these essential services and in some cases, restructuring existing programs or creating new programs to better address the funding needs.

Workers engaged in care work provide vital services for families, seniors, and people with disabilities. The vast majority of the workforce is female, the services are often underfunded, and wages are very low (Professional Healthcare Institute 2016; Whitebook, Howes, and Phillips 2014). This has a significant impact on worker turnover and quality of care (Hewitt and Larson 2007; Howes 2002; Whitebook, Howes, and Phillips 2014). Developing additional strategies to raise labor standards in the care-giving industries is therefore vital for both workers and consumers.

CONCLUSION

The turn toward what Fine (2005) terms "re-governing the market from below" through organizing around state and local labor standards has had real success in improving wages and working conditions for millions of low-wage workers, creating a focus for local organizing and shaping the public debate. In California, the combined value of the increased wages from the new $15 state and local minimum-wage laws is greater than the combined values all of the existing income support programs (EITC, SNAP, WIC, TANF) in the state; it is also equivalent to the estimated union wage premium from collective bargaining across industries. Local organizations are creating and testing new policy models, which are being successfully moved to higher levels of government and other geographic areas.

Re-governing the market from below through raising labor standards does have several important limitations. Building models of sustainable worker organization outside of traditional collective bargaining arrangements remains a challenge. State preemption of local policies and the absence of the right to take issues directly to the voters through ballot initiatives limit the geographical scope of these strategies. Moving the locus of power from the worksite to public bodies cannot substitute for the role of a union in providing voice at work and the direct engagement of workers at their workplace in fighting for dignity on the job.

Finally, the election of Donald Trump is a reminder of how state and local efforts can be dwarfed by actions of the federal government, which is attempting to roll back 50 years of social policy. Progressive cities and states can continue to play an important role in creating models that demonstrate "another world is possible," but more organizing resources will need to be deployed in states and areas within states with the greatest capacity to influence national politics. This will include many states where local labor standards are not legally possible. To organize in those states, strategies will need to be developed that address local conditions.

ACKNOWLEDGMENTS

I wish to acknowledge my colleagues Ian Perry, Sara Thomason, and Gabriel Sanchez for their assistance and Jenifer MacGillvary for her editorial suggestions.

ENDNOTES

[1] Unionstats.com, Union Membership and Coverage Database from the CPS.

[2] Author's calculation using CPI-U to adjust estimates in Schmitt (2012) to 2016.

[3] United States Department of Labor Wage and Hour Division. "Minimum Wages for Tipped Employees," January 1, 2017 (http://bit.ly/2AwfqaZ).

[4] Author's calculation adjusting Schmitt (2012) to 2016 dollars.

[5] Author's analysis of Vaghul and Zipper, "Historical State and Substate Minimum Wage Dataset" (http://bit.ly/2pXK7Oy).

[6] In his analysis of the rapid diffusion of living-wage laws, Martin (2001) found the presence of ACORN was the most important factor in predicting whether a city would pass one.

[7] San Francisco Office of Labor Standards Enforcement, "Prevailing Wage" (http://bit.ly/2OyQkel)

[8] Ibid.

[9] Garafoli, Joe. "S.F. Businesses, Tech Not Blocking Minimum Wage Increase." *San Francisco Chronicle*, August 30, 2014.

[10] Author's calculation. Assumes the health spending requirement increases at the average annual rate for the past ten years of 4.1% a year. Paid sick leave is estimated based on actual utilization following the method in Reich and Jacobs (2014).

[11] Author's calculation using Quarterly Census of Employment and Wages, 2016.

[12] National Council of State Legislators. "State Minimum Wages: 2017 Minimum Wages by State."

[13] Author's calculation using Reich, Allegretto, and Montialoux (2017); Reich, Jacobs, Bernhardt, and Perry (2014); and Reich, Jacobs, and Bernhardt (2015).

[14] Author's calculations using IRS, "SOI Tax Stats—Historic Table 2" (http://bit.ly/2n389Wi); SNAP: US Department of Agriculture Food and Nutrition Service, "Supplemental Nutrition Assistance Program, State Level Annual Data 2014" (http://bit.ly/2n4o6M8); US Department of Health and Human Services Office of Family Assistance, "TANF Financial Data–FY 2014" (http://bit.ly/2AulfFR).

[15] Author's analysis of Current Population Survey, Outgoing Rotation Groups, 2011–2016, normalizing each of the minimum-wage studies to 2016 dollars.

[16] A Better Balance, "Paid Sick Time Legislative Success" (http://bit.ly/2OBELDl); Katherine Muniz, "Overview of All U.S. State and City Paid Sick Leave Laws" (http://bit.ly/2uKIjgm); Workplace Fairness, "State and Local Paid Sick Leave Laws" (http://bit.ly/2uERj6P).

[17] Establishing wage extenders that are closely tied to collectively bargained wages through state and local law raises the prospect of federal pre-emption under the National Labor Relations Act. See *Chamber of Commerce of the United States v. Harvey Bragdon*, US 9th Cir. FindLaw (1995).

[18] Personal communication with Amy Sugimori, SEIU 323BJ, January 16, 2016.

[19] See Australia Fair Work Commission, Modern Awards (http://bit.ly/2AwL0oH).

[20] See, for example, Patrick Gillespie, "Intuit: Gig Economy Is 34% of US Workforce," *CNN Money*, May 24, 2017 (https://cnnmon.ie/2AsXk9H); Lydia Dishman, "How the Gig Economy Will Change in 2017," *Fast Company*, January 5, 2017 (http://bit.ly/2AuFCT4); Elaine Pofelt, "Freelancers Now Make Up 35% of U.S. Workforce," *Forbes*, October 6, 2016 (http://bit.ly/2AwilQS).

[21] The law was enjoined by a federal judge in April 2017. See David Gutman, "Judge Temporarily Blocks Seattle Law Allowing Uber and Lyft Drivers to Unionize," *Seattle Times*, April 4, 2017 (http://bit.ly/2Ax5zS3).

REFERENCES

Andrias, Kate. 2016. "The New Labor Law." *Yale Law Journal* 126 (2). http://bit.ly/2AxJW41

Ben-Ishai, Liz, Emilytricia Lopez Marchena, and Zoe Ziliak Michel. 2017. "Scheduling on the Cutting Edge: Implementation of San Francisco's First-in-the-Nation Fair Scheduling Law." Washington, DC: CLASP, Young Workers United. http://bit.ly/2JdOTzi

Bernhardt, Annette, and Sarah Thomason. 2017. "What Do We Know About Gig Work in California? An Analysis of Independent Contracting." Berkeley, CA: University of California Institute for Labor and the Economy, Center for Labor Research and Education. http://bit.ly/2GtVpEh

Bivens, Josh, and Lawrence Mishel. 2015 (Sep. 2). "Understanding the Historic Divergence Between Productivity and a Typical Worker's Pay: Why It Matters and Why It's Real." Briefing Paper 406. Washington, DC: Economic Policy Institute. http://bit.ly/2JezAGI

Bosch, Gerhard, and Claudia Weinkopf. 2013. "Transnational Labour Markets and National Wage Setting Systems in the EU." *Industrial Relations Journal* 44 (1): 2–19. doi:10.1111/irj.12006

Colla, Carrie H., William H. Dow, and Arindrajit Dube. 2013. "San Francisco's 'Pay or Play' Employer Mandate Expanded Private Coverage by Local Firms and a Public Care Program." *Health Affairs* 32 (1): 69–77. doi:10.1377/hlthaff.2012.0295

Dietz, Miranda, Peter Hall, and Ken Jacobs. 2013. "Course Correction: Reversing Wage Erosion to Restore Good Jobs at American Airports." Berkeley, CA: University of California Institute for Labor and the Economy, Center for Labor Research and Education. http://bit.ly/2Gu009D

Dube, Arindrajit, and Ethan Kaplan. 2010. "Does Outsourcing Reduce Wages in the Low-Wage Service Occupations? Evidence From Janitors and Guards." *Industrial and Labor Relations Review* 63 (2): 287–306.

DuPuis, Nicole, Trevor Langon, Christiana McFarland, and Brooks Rainwater. 2017. "City Rights in an Era of Preemption: A State by State Analysis." Washington, DC: National League of Cities.

Fairris, David, David Runsten, Carolina Briones, and Jessica Goodheart. 2015 (Nov. 12). "Examining the Evidence: The Impact of the Los Angeles Living Wage Ordinance on Workers and Businesses." IRLE Reports. Los Angeles, CA: University of California, Los Angeles. http://bit.ly/2JhjnQU

Fine, Janice. 2000. "Community Unionism in Baltimore and Stamford." *WorkingUSA* 4 (3): 59–85. doi:10.1111/j.1743-4580.2000.00059.x

Fine, Janice. 2005. "Community Unions and the Revival of the American Labor Movement." *Politics & Society* 33 (1): 153–199. doi:10.1177/0032329204272553

Fine, Janice, and Jennifer Gordon. 2010. "Strengthening Labor Standards Enforcement Through Partnerships with Workers' Organizations." *Politics & Society* 38 (4): 552–585. doi:10.1177/0032329210381240

Freeman, Richard. 2005. "Fighting for Other Folks' Wages: The Logic and Illogic of Living Wage Campaigns." *Industrial Relations: A Journal of Economy and Society* 44 (1): 14–31. doi:10.1111/j.0019-8676.2004.00371.x

Ginsburg, Matthew. 2017 (Apr. 26). "Nothing New Under the Sun: 'The New Labor Law' Must Still Grapple with the Traditional Challenges of Firm-Based Organizing and Building Self-Sustainable Worker Organizations." *Yale Law Journal* 126. http://bit.ly/2H6bP2Q

Golden, Lonnie. 2015 (Apr. 9). "Irregular Work Scheduling and Its Consequences." Briefing Paper. Washington, DC: Economic Policy Institute. http://bit.ly/2GuqXtO

Gould, Elise, and Jessica Schieder. 2017 (Jun. 28). "Work Sick or Lose Pay?: The High Cost of Being Sick When You Don't Get Paid Sick Days." Washington, DC: Economic Policy Institute. http://bit.ly/2Gw7DfJ

Grossman, Jonathan. 1978. "Fair Labor Standards Act of 1938: Maximum Struggle for a Minimum Wage." *Monthly Labor Review* 101 (6): 22–30.

Henly, Julia R., Peter J. Fugiel, and Susan J. Lambert. 2014. "Precarious Work Schedules Among Early-Career Employees in the US: A National Snapshot." Chicago, IL: University of Chicago EINet. http://bit.ly/29qNuVT

Hewitt, Amy, and Sheryl Larson. 2007. "The Direct Support Workforce in Community Supports to Individuals with Developmental Disabilities: Issues, Implications, and Promising Practices." *Mental Retardation and Developmental Disabilities Research Reviews* 13 (2): 178–187. doi:10.1002/mrdd.20151.

Heymann, Jody, Hye Jin Rho, John Schmitt, and Alison Earle. 2010. "Ensuring a Healthy and Productive Workforce: Comparing the Generosity of Paid Sick Day and Sick Leave Policies in 22 Countries." *International Journal of Health Services* 40 (1): 1–22. doi:10.2190/ HS.40.1.a

Hill, Heather D. 2013. "Paid Sick Leave and Job Stability." *Work and Occupations* 40 (2): 143–173. doi:10.1177/0730888413480893

Howell, David, Kea Fielder, and Stephanie Luce. 2016. "What's the Right Minimum Wage? Reframing the Debate from 'No Job Loss' to a 'Minimum Living Wage.'" Working Paper 2016-06. Washington, DC: Washington Center for Equitable Growth. http://bit.ly/2GwrkEi

Howes, Candace. 2002. "The Impact of a Large Wage Increase on the Workforce Stability of IHSS Home Care Workers in San Francisco County." Berkeley, CA: University of California Institute for Labor and the Economy, Center for Labor Research and Education. http:// bit.ly/2H8drZR

Jackson, Emilie, Adam Looney, and Shanthi Ramnath. 2017. "The Rise of Alternative Work Arrangements: Evidence and Implications for Tax Filing and Benefit Coverage." Working Paper 114. Washington, DC: US Department of the Treasury, Office of Tax Analysis.

Jacobs, Ken, Zohar Perla, Ian Perry, and Dave Graham-Squire. 2016 (May). "Producing Poverty: The Public Cost of Low-Wage Production Jobs in Manufacturing." Research Brief. Berkeley, CA: University of California Institute for Labor and the Economy, Center for Labor Research and Education. http://bit.ly/2GuZfNw

Kalleberg, Arne L. 2000. "Nonstandard Employment Relations: Part-Time, Temporary and Contract Work." *Annual Review of Sociology* 26 (1): 341–165. doi:10.1146/annu rev.soc.26.1.341

Koonse, Tia, Miranda Dietz, and Annette Bernhardt. 2015 (Oct. 23). "Enforcing City Minimum Wage Laws in California: Best Practices and City–State Partnerships. Berkeley, CA: University of California Institute for Labor and the Economy, Center for Labor Research and Education. http://bit.ly/2H6X147

Lester, Thomas William. 2014. "The Role of History in Redistributional Policy Discourse: Evidence from Living Wage Campaigns in Chicago and San Francisco." *Journal of Urban Affairs* 36 (4): 783–806.

Logan, John. 2006. "The Union Avoidance Industry in the United States." *British Journal of Industrial Relations* 44 (4): 651–675. doi:10.1111/j.1467-8543.2006.00518.x

Lovell, Vicky. 2014. "Universal Paid Sick Leave." In *When Mandates Work: Raising Labor Standards at the Local Level*, edited by Michael Reich, Ken Jacobs, and Miranda Dietz. Berkeley, CA: University of California Press.

Luce, Stephanie. 2004. *Fighting for a Living Wage*. Ithaca, NY: Cornell University Press.

Madland, David. 2016 (Oct. 11). "The Future of Worker Voice and Power." Washington, DC: Center for American Progress. https://ampr.gs/2Gvj4V1

Madland, David, and Alex Rowell. 2017 (May 2). "How State and Local Governments Can Strengthen Worker Power and Raise Wages." Washington, DC: Center for American Progress. https://ampr.gs/2Gw0LPD

Martin, Isaac. 2001. "Dawn of the Living Wage." *Urban Affairs Review* 36 (4): 470–496. doi:10.1177/10780870122184966

Mishel, Lawrence. 2012. "Unions, Inequality, and Faltering Middle-Class Wages." Issue Brief. 342. Washington, DC: Economic Policy Institute. http://bit.ly/2H6r1wO

National Employment Law Project. 2010. "Local Living Wage Ordinances and Coverage." New York, NY: National Employment Law Project. http://bit.ly/2pUkWwf

National Employment Law Project. 2016 (Dec. 8). "Fight for $15: Four Years, $62 Billion." Policy Brief. New York, NY: National Employment Law Project. http://bit.ly/2H8J59Q

National Employment Law Project. 2017 (Jan.). "The On-Demand Economy & State Labor Protections." Policy Brief. New York, NY: National Employment Law Project. http://bit.ly/2GysyPd

Nordlund, Willis J. 1997. *The Quest for a Living Wage*. Westport, CT: Greenwood Press.

Organisation for Economic Co-operation and Development. 2017. "OECD Employment Outlook 2017." Paris, France: Organisation for Economic Co-operation and Development. doi:10.1787/empl_outlook-2017-en

Professional Healthcare Institute. 2016. "U.S. Home Care Workers: Key Facts." PHI Quality Care Through Quality Jobs. Bronx, NY: Professional Healthcare Institute.

Piketty, Thomas, Emmanuel Saez, and Gabriel Zucman. 2016 (Dec. 6). "Economic Growth in the United States: A Tale of Two Countries." Washington, DC: Washington Center for Equitable Growth. http://bit.ly/2Gv5e4R

Reich, Michael. 2015. "The Ups and Downs of Minimum Wage Policy: The Fair Labor Standards Act in Historical Perspective." *Industrial Relations: A Journal of Economy and Society* 54 (4): 538–546. doi:10.1111/irel.12105

Reich, Michael, Sylvia Allegretto, and Claire Montialoux. 2017 (Jan). "Effects of a $15 Minimum Wage in California and Fresno." Policy Brief. Berkeley, CA: University of California Institute for Labor and the Economy, Center for Labor Research and Education. http://bit.ly/2H8uISQ

Reich, Michael, Peter Hall, and Ken Jacobs. 2003 (Mar.). "Living Wages and Economic Performance: The San Francisco Airport Model." Berkeley, CA: University of California, Berkeley Institute of Industrial Relations. http://bit.ly/2GsUW5g

Reich, Michael, and Ken Jacobs. 2014. "When Do Mandates Work?" In *When Mandates Work: Raising Labor Standards at the Local Level*, edited by Michael Reich, Ken Jacobs, and Miranda Dietz, pp. 1–46. Berkeley and Los Angeles, CA: University of California Press.

Reich, Michael, Ken Jacobs, and Annette Bernhardt. 2015 (Mar.). "The Proposed Minimum Wage Law for Los Angeles: Economic Impacts and Policy Options." Policy Brief. Berkeley, CA: University of California Institute for Labor and the Economy, Center for Labor Research and Education. http://bit.ly/2GumKGB

Reich, Michael, Ken Jacobs, Annette Bernhardt, and Ian Perry. 2014 (Aug.). "San Francisco's Proposed City Minimum Wage Law: A Prospective Impact Study." Policy Brief. Berkeley, CA: University of California Institute for Labor and the Economy, Center for Labor Research and Education. http://bit.ly/2H6QtCy

Reich, Michael, Ken Jacobs, and Miranda Dietz. 2014. "Mandates: Lessons Learned and Future Prospects." In *When Mandates Work: Raising Labor Standards at the Local Level*, edited by Michael Reich, Ken Jacobs, and Miranda Dietz, pp. 309–314. Berkeley and Los Angeles, CA: University of California Press.

Riddell, W. Craig. 1993. "Unionization in Canada and the United States: A Tale of Two Countries." In *Small Differences That Matter: Labor Markets and Income Maintenance in Canada and the United States*, edited by David E. Card and Richard B. Freeman, pp. 109–148. National Bureau of Economic Research Comparative Labor Markets Series. Chicago, IL: University of Chicago Press. http://bit.ly/2Gv5BfL

Rogers, Brishen. 2016. "Employment Rights in the Platform Economy: Getting Back to Basics." Social Science Research Network Scholarly Paper ID 2641305. Rochester, NY: Social Science Research Network. http://bit.ly/2H7r1MZ

Rolf, David. 2016a. *The Fight for Fifteen: The Right Wage for a Working America*. New York, NY: The New Press.

Rolf, David. 2016b (Apr. 18). "Toward a 21st-Century Labor Movement." *American Prospect*. http://bit.ly/2H8ZkDF

Rosenblum, Jonathan. 2017. *Beyond $15*. Boston, MA: Beacon Press.

Schmitt, John. 2010 (Feb.). "The Unions of the States." Washington, DC: Center for Economic and Policy Research. http://bit.ly/2Gv6Awx

Schmitt, John. 2012 (Mar.). "The Minimum Wage Is Too Damn Low." Washington, DC: Center for Economic and Policy Research. Issue Brief. http://bit.ly/2H7SI8J

Schneider, Daniel, and Kristen Harknett. 2016 (Sep. 12). "Schedule Instability and Unpredictability and Worker and Family Health and Wellbeing." Working Paper Series. Washington, DC: Washington Center on Equitable Growth. http://bit.ly/2Gvk4bJ

Song, Jae, David J. Price, Fatih Guvenen, Nicholas Bloom, and Till von Wachter. 2015. "Firming Up Inequality." Working Paper 21199. Cambridge, MA: National Bureau of Economic Research. doi:10.3386/w21199

Tilly, Chris. 2004. "Living Wage Laws in the United States: The Dynamics of a Growing Movement." In *Economic and Political Contention in Comparative Perspective*, edited by Kousis, Maria and Tilly, Charles, pp. 143–160. Boulder, CO: Paradigm.

Walker, Naomi. 2017 (May 26). "The Entire Public Sector Is About to Be Put on Trial." Today's Workplace: A Workplace Fairness Blog. http://bit.ly/2GwpQcW

Weil, David. 2014. *The Fissured Workplace*. Cambridge, MA: Harvard University Press.

Whitebook, Marcy, Carollee Howes, and Deborah Phillips. 2014. "Worthy Work, STILL Unlivable Wages: The Early Childhood Workforce 25 Years After the National Child Care Staffing Study." Berkeley, CA: Institute for Research on Labor and Employment, Center for the Study of Child Care Employment. http://bit.ly/2H6ZP19

Zabin, Carol, and Isaac Martin. 1999. "Living Wage Campaigns in the Economic Policy Arena: Four Case Studies from California." Report for the Phoenix Fund for Workers and Communities, The New World Foundation. Berkeley, CA: Center for Labor Research and Education, Institute of Industrial Relations. http://bit.ly/2Hch5Ch

Zimmerman, Joan G. 1991. "The Jurisprudence of Equality: The Women's Minimum Wage, the First Equal Rights Amendment, and *Adkins v. Children's Hospital*, 1905–1923." *Journal of American History* 78 (1): 188–225. doi:10.2307/2078093

Expanding Domestic Worker Rights in the 21st Century: Statewide Campaigns for Domestic Worker Bills of Rights

LINDA BURNHAM
National Domestic Workers Alliance

ANDREA CRISTINA MERCADO
New Florida Majority and New Florida Majority Education Fund

Domestic workers in the United States have explored a wide range of tactics and strategies in their organizing for labor rights. In the late 19th century, washerwomen in Atlanta staged a work stoppage, demanding better pay for their services (Hunter 1997). In 1917, domestic workers who crossed the Mexican border from Juarez to El Paso to work in American homes vigorously protested the daily humiliations inflicted by border-crossing agents, who called their action a riot (Romo 2005). Throughout the 20th century, in addition to millions of acts of individual resistance, workers engaged in joint action to set informal wage floors, refuse demeaning work, develop and share sample contracts, and celebrate the inherent dignity—and necessity—of the work (Nadasen 2015).

The 1935 National Labor Relations Act (NLRA) and the 1932 Fair Labor Standards Act (FLSA) established the legal parameters that frame contemporary domestic worker organizing—and against which that organizing must push. These pieces of legislation, landmark victories for labor organizing, carved domestic workers and farmworkers out of the federal codification of the expansion of the rights of workers to organize and to decent conditions of work. Domestic workers have no federally recognized right to form unions, choose representatives, or bargain collectively. The product of compromise with southern congressmen intent on preserving control over Black labor, one scholar calls the exclusion of domestic workers and farmworkers from the NLRA an "echo of slavery" (Perea 2011). Most domestic workers are also excluded, on a de facto basis, from the protections of federal anti-discrimination law, and they are expressly excluded from OSHA protections. To the extent that legal constraints on organizing and an absence of federal labor protections remain the norm today, those echoes of slavery resound into the 21st century. The exclusion of domestic workers from labor rights and protections at the federal level is mirrored by explicit exclusions in many states.

In addition to the exclusion of domestic workers from collective bargaining rights, the dispersed and disaggregated character of both the workforce and the employers presents a set of organizing hurdles. While enhancing the capacity of individual domestic workers to negotiate for better conditions with their employers is central to the process of workers stepping into their agency, it does not substitute for a bargaining unit and cannot accumulate into legally recognized and enforceable change. This, together with the absence of a corporate entity with which to bargain, has meant that domestic workers have been considered "unorganizable."

The contemporary domestic worker movement takes shape against this legislative and structural backdrop. Beginning in the latter half of the 1990s, local projects and organizations committed to mobilizing and providing services for domestic workers cropped up in immigrant communities across the country. Each group had its own unique character, but all wrestled with how to meet the needs and improve the working conditions of a low-wage, predominantly female, largely immigrant workforce. The vulnerabilities of the workforce rendered it especially subject to labor exploitation and abuse, including sub-minimum wages, wage theft, forced overtime work, no overtime pay, no rest or meal breaks, health and safety hazards, threats and intimidation. As recent news and research have revealed, domestic workers are also susceptible to the far extremes of labor exploitation and human rights violations, including trafficking and semi-enslavement (Hafiz and Paarlberg 2017; Tizon 2017). Finding effective levers to address these conditions has been the core preoccupation of each iteration of domestic worker organizing.

Over the past decade, the domestic worker movement has successfully pursued a strategy of building campaigns to pass legislation at the state level to expand the labor rights of domestic workers. Domestic worker bills of rights have been won in eight states, led by the National Domestic Workers Alliance and its local affiliates, breaking new ground for a long neglected sector of the US labor force.

In 2001, well before the national domestic worker movement took shape, the New York Domestic Workers Justice Coalition, led by Domestic Workers United, launched a citywide campaign to improve working conditions. Two years of coalition building, worker mobilization and winning over key allies on the city council culminated in the passage of Local Law 33 in 2003. The law mandates employment agencies that place domestic workers to provide written statements informing prospective employees and employers of worker rights under New York State and federal law. It requires that agencies inform applicants in writing about the wages, hours, services, and agency fees of each potential position and includes record-keeping and enforcement provisions (Greenhouse 2003). Local Law 33 did not shake up the domestic work industry in a fundamental way, but it was the very first enforceable policy change in nearly 30 years to uphold the employment rights of domestic workers, won through the organizing efforts of domestic workers themselves.

New York's domestic workers were energized by the victory. In short order, they decided to launch a campaign for a statewide Domestic Worker Bill of Rights. They did not anticipate that it would take seven years and countless trips to Albany to wrest a victory from of the state legislature. But on August 31, 2010, Governor Paterson signed the bill. Among other provisions, domestic workers won the right to overtime pay and rest days, as well as explicit protection under New York State human rights and anti-discrimination law (Hobden 2010; New York State Senate 2010; Poo 2010).

Between the New York City win for domestic workers in 2003 and the 2010 statewide victory, domestic worker organizing that had been locally based and dispersed began to cohere nationally. In 2007, at the U.S. Social Forum in Atlanta, 13 organizations came together to form the National Domestic Workers Alliance (NDWA).[1] The alliance created a new container in which organizers could share campaign strategies and lessons. No bill of rights campaigns had been won at the state level at that point, but New York and California were well underway. In the ten years between NDWA's founding and today, domestic worker bills of rights have been won in eight states: New York (2010), California (2013, 2015), Hawaii (2013), Massachusetts (2014), Connecticut (2015), Oregon (2015), Illinois (2016), and Nevada (2017) (see appendix).

Bill of rights campaigns have become a signature strategic initiative of the domestic worker movement. The campaigns have achieved substantive gains for a marginalized segment of the workforce that, traditionally, has had few effective ways to win broadly applicable enforceable rights (Shah and Seville 2012). Domestic workers have been leveraging their collective power to convince states to expand and protect worker rights. The New York campaign provided a general template for the successful campaigns that followed. But domestic workers and organizers in each state contended with distinct sets of political actors and unanticipated challenges. Each campaign forged a unique path to victory. This article examines two of those wins—California and Massachusetts.

CALIFORNIA DOMESTIC WORKER BILL OF RIGHTS CAMPAIGN

In the early 2000s, Latina immigrant women gathered in the meetings rooms of Mujeres Unidas y Activas (MUA), an organization with offices in San Francisco and Oakland, California. MUA offered support group meetings, CPR training, and occupational safety and health trainings to help immigrant women get jobs as nannies, housecleaners, and caregivers. The women, many of whom had experienced domestic violence, needed the jobs to support their families and become economically self-sufficient. Time and time again, they shared stories of abuse at work. The very jobs that were supposed to be pathways to freedom from violence in the home were perpetuating abuse in their lives.

Founded in 1989, MUA had a long track record of developing the leadership of Latina immigrant women. MUA mobilized and engaged the community on issues of immigrant and worker rights, domestic violence, health access, and building women's economic independence. The organization was intent on developing an organizing model and leading campaigns that would grow its membership, building an even stronger bench of immigrant women leaders. In 2003, MUA hired its first community organizer. Together with the Women's Collective of La Raza Centro Legal (La Colectiva) and the Data Center, which had been fighting wage theft cases for many years, MUA embarked on a research project focused on the working conditions of domestic workers in San Francisco. The goal of the survey was to move past anecdotal evidence, gain a more comprehensive understanding of the industry, and identify key issues for potential organizing campaigns. "Behind Closed Doors: Working Conditions of California Household Workers" documents the low pay, wage theft, overwork and health and safety problems endemic to domestic work (Mujeres Unidas y Activas, Women's Collective of La Raza Centro Legal and Data Center 2007). It provided a guide to the many issues to be tackled to bring domestic work up to a reasonable standard.

Meanwhile, in Los Angeles, three other groups were also organizing immigrant women: the Coalition for Humane Immigrant Rights of Los Angeles (CHIRLA), a community organization with deep roots in the Latino community; the Institute of Popular Education of Southern California (IDEPSCA); and the Pilipino Workers Center (PWC). Leaders of the Northern and Southern California organizations began to discuss how the systematic exclusion of domestic workers from labor protections, combined with the cultural devaluation of "women's work," heighten the vulnerability of a largely immigrant and female workforce.

These organizations, together with San Francisco–based People Organized to Win Employment Rights (POWER) and the Graton Day Labor Center, became the core of the long-standing coalition dedicated to winning new labor rights for domestic workers in California. Organizers and member leaders decided that changing state law to remedy the exclusion of domestic workers from labor protections was an important avenue to pursue. Little did they know that they were embarking on a path that would demand more than a decade's commitment. The campaign for labor protections for California's domestic workers unfolded in four main stages:

- The formation of the coalition and the initiation of the campaign for a California Domestic Worker Bill of Rights in 2005 through

Governor Arnold Schwarzenegger's veto of AB 2536 in September 2006 (California State Assembly 2006).

- The coalition's recommitment and introduction of a new bill, AB 889, through Governor Jerry Brown's September 2012 veto (California State Assembly 2011).
- The coalition recommits yet again and introduces AB 241, which clears the state legislature and is signed by Governor Brown in 2013, with a three-year sunset provision requiring reauthorization (California State Assembly 2013).
- The coalition campaigns for and wins permanent labor protections with the passage of SB 1015 in 2016 (California State Senate 2016).

Ultimately, the coalition's campaign to extend labor rights to domestic workers became the longest-running organizing and advocacy drive in the recent history of the domestic worker movement.

The Bill of Rights Campaign Begins

In 2005, domestic workers convened for a statewide gathering, held at the Women's Building in San Francisco. They identified and prioritized the unique problems domestic workers encounter on the job and collectively reviewed the legislative process. The meeting, conducted in English, Spanish and Tagalog, generated a 13-point program. CHIRLA had already reached out to Cindy Montañez, a young woman who had won a seat in the state assembly representing California's heavily Latino 39th assembly district. Montañez, whose mother was a domestic worker, promised to champion the domestic workers' cause. Shortly after the gathering in San Francisco, a small group of domestic workers traveled from across the state to meet with Assemblymember Montañez and discuss what to include in the proposed legislation.

Though domestic workers were eager to right numerous wrongs, Montañez was reluctant to introduce an expansive bill with multiple provisions. Instead, in the 2006 legislative session, she introduced AB 2536, which contained just two provisions: the inclusion of "personal attendants" in overtime laws—with personal attendant defined as a private-pay worker employed to care for a child, an elder, or a person with a physical or mental disability; and the right of household workers to recover liquidated damages from employers who have withheld wages or failed to pay overtime (California State Assembly 2006).

The nascent California Household Workers Coalition (later renamed California Domestic Workers Coalition, CDWC) was committed not only to winning policy change but also to developing the leadership of domestic workers, raising the visibility of domestic work, and advancing the idea that domestic work is as dignified as any other and as deserving of basic labor protections. Legislative change was understood as critical to creating a new legal framework of labor rights and protections and challenging institutional racism and sexism as codified by the state. But, given that noncompliance with existing labor laws is so common in the sector, legislative change was understood to be only one part of a comprehensive strategy for change. This orientation informed choices the coalition made throughout the campaign.

The campaign's most significant hurdle was opposition by the Sacramento-based California Association for Health Services at Home (CAHSAH), advocates for the interests of for-profit agencies that link home health aides and elder caregivers with individuals and families in need of their services. Disability rights advocates, including Disability Rights California, also lobbied against the bill, based on concerns that the legislation would result in people with disabilities and seniors having to pay more for personal attendants. Opposition emerged early in the campaign, was sustained throughout, and was a major factor in campaign setbacks. Dozens of people with disabilities, some assisted by their attendants, were present at the state assembly's labor committee hearing to register their opposition to the Montañez bill. Domestic workers who attended the hearing were shaken and demoralized. Esther Savinon, a long-time care worker disabled by knee problems and failing vision, said, "I don't understand. I gave my life to caring for people. I love the people I have taken care of. Why won't they stand up for us, our equality, and our rights?"

The bill passed the committee, but the mood on the trip back from Sacramento was bleak. The coalition began to research the disability rights advocacy community, reaching out to anyone who could offer perspective and insight. It became very clear that protecting worker rights would require a robust coalition capable of exerting sufficient influence and power to change the law.

Through extensive outreach and one-on-one meetings, the coalition was able to bring labor unions, faith leaders, employers of domestic workers, and people with disabilities on board, expanding well beyond the founding organizations. However, the unrelenting opposition proved to be insurmountable. On the advice of Montañez, domestic workers decided to consent to significant amendments to the bill, ultimately limiting overtime protection to nannies while exempting elder caregivers and attendants to people with physical or mental disabilities. The revised bill made it through both houses of the legislature only to be vetoed by Governor Schwarzenegger (California State Assembly 2006).

Recommitment

When domestic workers gathered in San Francisco's Dolores Park to mourn the defeat and discuss next steps, they took out their frustrations on a Schwarzenegger piñata. Luz Sampedro, a campaign leader, passionately declared, "Governor Schwarzenegger may have vetoed the bill, but he cannot take everything we have learned. We will keep fighting until justice is served." It was a prescient battle cry. Luz had reminded everyone that, in contrast to traditional legislative advocacy, the coalition had invested its time and resources in popular education, a democratic and participatory process, and leadership development.

In doing so, CDWC had, in a short time, developed a cadre of committed leaders and passionate spokespeople. Domestic workers were fully engaged in the campaign and took ownership of it. In addition, through the coalition's work with ethnic media, word was out that domestic workers had rights and strong allies they could turn to for support. The investment in relationship building among the lead organizations and among campaign organizers, the development of the coalition's structure and decision-making process, a commitment to the ongoing development of worker leaders, and sustaining relationships with key allies would be the foundation of the collective effort in the hard years to come. Though they had lost the first round, attention to these values and processes enabled the coalition to weather leadership transitions, stinging defeats, competition for resources, and strategic differences.

Schwarzenegger had refused to sign the significantly watered down version of the domestic worker bill. CDWC realized he would never sign a substantive bill into law and that its resources would be better spent building the coalition, deepening relationships with leaders in the disability rights movement, and expanding the coalition's geographic reach while waiting for the next governor to take office. They took an extended timeout.

While waiting for a more favorable political alignment in Sacramento, the coalition found ways to keep its base of domestic workers organized and focused. It participated in two Bay Area cases, demonstrating support for workers who had been robbed and exploited.

Vilma Serralta, in her late 60s, kept house and cared for a tech investor's child in Atherton, 20 miles south of San Francisco. Her employers lived in a 9,000-square-foot house with an assessed value of $13 million while paying Serralta between $3 and $4 an hour. The case exemplified exactly the kinds of abuses the coalition was working to remedy. Serralta decided to sue her employers for back wages (New America Media 2010; Smith 2008). The pursuit of justice through the courts, led by La Raza Centro Legal, was accompanied by demonstrations on the streets in front of the employer's home, intensive media work, and public education about abuses endemic to the domestic work industry.

Zoraida Peña Canal was lured to the United States from Peru on the promise of decent work and decent pay. Once in Walnut Creek, a Bay Area suburb, her employer confiscated her documents and she was forced to work without pay as a nanny, cook, and cleaner (Salonga 2008). After two years of 15-hour days with no days off, Peña Canal heard a media story about Vilma Serralta's case on the radio. With the support of employees at the school where she dropped off her employers' children, she found the courage to escape the household. Peña Canal decided to take her employers to court as well.

The domestic worker movement in the Bay Area sustained momentum. Serralta reached a settlement for stolen wages. Peña Canal's employer went to trial for labor trafficking and was convicted and sentenced to three years, the first conviction of its kind against an employer of a domestic worker.[2]

In 2010, the coalition partnered with Assemblymembers Manuel Pérez and Tom Ammiano to pass a state resolution recognizing the economic and social contributions domestic workers and their exclusion from labor protections, and resolving that inclusion in state and federal labor law, together with industry-specific protections and labor standards, would be an expression of the dignity and importance of their work (California State Assembly 2010). The resolution was a vehicle to re-engage domestic workers in the legislative process, build relationships in Sacramento, and educate legislators and their staff on domestic worker issues.

New Governor, New Campaign

Hopes rose when Jerry Brown took office in 2011. This was a governor who had championed farmworker rights. Cindy Montañez had lost her bid to become a state senator, so organizers sought a new legislative champion. Assemblymember Tom Ammiano, a respected progressive legislator from San Francisco, had deep relationships with disability rights advocates, together with the combination of experience and political values the coalition was looking for.

The coalition closely studied the New York Domestic Worker Bill of Rights campaign, which had finally registered a win the year before. They decided to push for a more comprehensive set of remedies, understanding that provisions of the bill would inevitably be negotiated out along the way. In addition to overtime compensation, the new bill included provisions for meal and rest breaks, uninterrupted sleep for live-in workers, and workers compensation coverage (California State Assembly 2011).

In spite of Ammiano's relationships with disability rights advocates and numerous conversations address their concerns, a few prominent disability rights organizations swiftly went public with their opposition to the new bill. At the same time, the private homecare companies mobilized by CAHSAH embarked on a smear campaign, dubbing the Domestic Worker Bill of Rights "the babysitter's bill." The California Chamber of Commerce also came out in opposition.

The communications offensive misled legislators and the public to believe that the state would begin regulating a family's relationship with the neighborhood teenager who occasionally watched over the kids. It also raised the fear that disabled people and the elderly who could not afford to pay overtime would be in jeopardy of being institutionalized. Though the coalition had built up a strong network of employers and disability rights leaders to publicly support the bill and had launched a counter-offensive, published op-eds, spoke to dozens of community groups, and gathered signatures of support from hundreds of academics, labor leaders and faith leaders, the bill was unable to withstand the heat. It got stuck in the Senate appropriations committee, where it languished.

California operates on a two-year legislative cycle. When the campaign picked up again in 2012, the coalition made the assessment that the bill would not move forward without a stronger, more consistent presence in Sacramento. The coalition hired a lobbyist who worked on progressive causes to keep the issue in front of legislators and their staff. The coalition began to invest even more resources in communications and media work. Dozens of nannies, housecleaners, and care workers mobilized to every hearing on the bill. Often with their children in tow, they lobbied legislators and shared not only their experiences but also about the policy solutions they had crafted. Regularly turning out hundreds of domestic workers and their allies at the state capitol, in combination with the ongoing presence of a lobbyist, gave the effort a significantly higher profile. The National Domestic Workers Alliance leveraged national relationships to support the campaign. Richard Trumka, president of the AFL-CIO, came to lobby on behalf of the bill—his first time lobbying in Sacramento for any issue. The bill finally made it out of committee and built momentum.

Determined to run a participatory campaign, decisively shaped by the voices and experiences of domestic workers, coalition leaders created a structure to ensure clear decision making by domestic worker leaders on strategy, tactics, and the content of the bill itself. Democratic decision making was logistically complex. Hearings were often scheduled only a few days in advance. Getting to the state capitol from Los Angeles could require an overnight road trip, and many domestic workers feared retaliation if they asked for the day off to participate in the campaign. When concessions were on the table, narrowing the scope of the bill, decisions were especially difficult. And yet domestic workers rose to the occasion. The coalition developed a rapid response system in which each of the organizations with a domestic worker base had at least one organizer and two domestic worker members serve as emergency contacts who were authorized to make collective decisions on changes to the bill. Over time, the workers who participated most consistently became more and more savvy about analyzing who had influence and how it was being exercised and about the relationship between broader movement-building goals and winning in the legislature.

The coalition also learned to seize every opportunity in which domestic workers were part of the public discourse to raise awareness about the issues addressed in the bill. Organizers used the buzz about *The Help,* a 2011 film about midcentury Black domestic workers in the South, and Amy Poehler's Time 100 Gala acceptance speech in which she thanked her nanny, to highlight the dignity and hard work of California's domestic workers.[3] The campaign also developed a strong cultural component. Women like Guillermina Castellanos and Maria Luna wrote songs and composed poems about the fight for labor rights. Domestic workers choreographed dances and performed them in front of the state capitol. The Children's March in January 2012 brought together the children of domestic workers and children cared for by domestic workers to walk side by side around the capitol building. The march affirmed the importance of the workers as economic pillars of their own families and as indispensable caregivers in the homes of their employers.

The coalition won the support of organizations like Senior and Disability Action, which mobilizes and educates seniors and people with disabilities to fight for individual rights and social justice. Numerous disability rights activists were willing express their solidarity with care workers. For example, Nikki Brown-Booker, a family therapist who uses a wheelchair and relies on several personal attendants, became a consistent and powerful proponent of the bill. In partnership with Hand in Hand, a strong chorus of employers mobilized repeatedly to speak out for clear industry standards.

On the legislative front, the bill was amended to, among other things, explicitly exclude from the definition of employee babysitters under the age of 18, workers employed through California's In-Home Support Services, and workers employed by licensed health care facilities. It also excluded from the definition of employers agencies that refer workers to domestic work jobs. The amended bill finally passed the legislature. The coalition was shocked by Governor Brown's veto. It was a hard blow. Hundreds of domestic workers who had mobilized to Sacramento repeatedly and sacrificed their time for long strategy meetings and street outreach were dejected. To highlight the governor's chicken-hearted refusal to stand up for domestic worker rights, live chickens were featured at press conferences in front of state buildings in Los Angeles and San Francisco. Once again, campaign leaders had to get past their disappointment and frustration, take stock of everything they had learned, and commit to reintroducing legislation.

From Defeat to Victory

Moving forward, CDWC developed a robust inside/outside strategy that focused on strategic mobilizations and communications, while also leveraging every relationship with influencers who had the ear of the governor. The coalition got reports that Jerry Brown was being asked about the domestic worker bill at receptions and fundraisers, even in the locker room of his gym.

In a final round of hard negotiations, the coalition agreed both to narrow the bill to overtime protection and to accept a sunset provision (California

State Assembly 2013). Neither of these compromises was easy to swallow, but it was clear that domestic workers could either cap their long campaign with a limited win—or take nothing at all. The legislation required reauthorization in three years. Governor Brown signed the bill on September 26, 2013, with dozens of domestic workers and a new generation of organizers looking on. Emiliana Acopio, a Pilipina care worker in her 70s, was there. She had traveled to Sacramento in support of the bill over 19 times in the course of the campaign. Her face was lit with joy and pride. Against all odds, domestic workers had prevailed in the state with the largest number of domestic workers in the nation and won the right to overtime for nannies and personal attendants.

In the wake of its hard-won victory, the coalition redirected its efforts to public education, worker outreach, and implementation of the law. It maintained and strengthened relationships with the disability rights community, partnered with the UCLA Labor Center to research the impact of the law, and continued organizing and advocacy to win a permanent bill (Waheed et al. 2016). On September 12, 2016, the California Domestic Worker Bill of Rights was signed into law, removing the sunset provision and permanently guaranteeing domestic workers the right to overtime (California State Senate 2016). More than a decade after the initiation of the campaign, the coalition finally rejoiced in a lasting victory.

The California campaign was a means by which hundreds of domestic workers from across the state, many of them undocumented and monolingual in Spanish or Tagalog, learned to decipher and navigate the legislative process. They became skilled spokeswomen about their own experiences and advocates for women too fearful to speak up themselves. Organizers and workers created and sustained long-term relationships among diverse organizations and remained centered on campaign goals despite transitions in personnel and changes at the capitol. Perhaps most important, workers and organizers remained steady in the face of fierce opposition, absorbed lessons from stinging defeats, adjusted and re-adjusted strategies and persevered until victory was in hand. In so doing, they both changed labor law and transformed California's domestic worker movement.

MASSACHUSETTS BILL OF RIGHTS CAMPAIGN

On June 26, 2014, Governor Deval Patrick signed into law a bill granting domestic workers a broader set of rights and protections than they enjoy in any other state. The legislation eliminated provisions in prior law that excluded domestic workers from labor protections, amended labor law to explicitly include domestic workers, and enacted new provisions that address the industry-specific conditions domestic workers face (Commonwealth of Massachusetts 2014). Among other rights and protections, the Massachusetts Domestic Worker Bill of Rights:

- Guarantees a weekly 24-hour rest period and a monthly 48-hour rest period for full-time workers.
- Bars food and lodging deductions for live-in workers that reduce pay below minimum wage and provides that no deductions for meals, rest periods, lodging, or sleeping periods may be made without written consent.
- Clarifies the right of domestic workers to privacy and protects against trafficking, including prohibitions against forced domestic service, monitoring of private conversations, or taking identity or immigration documents.
- Guarantees live-in domestic workers the right to written notice and 30 days' lodging or two weeks' severance pay if terminated without cause.
- Requires that employers keep written pay records and requires a written employment agreement that sets out employment rights and benefits if a domestic worker works more than 16 hours a week for the same employer.
- Brings domestic work under the jurisdiction of the Massachusetts Commission Against Discrimination for claims of sexual or other harassment.
- Protects domestic workers who work under 16 hours a week from employer retaliation for making a wage complaint. These workers had previously been exempted from protection.
- Guarantees eight weeks of maternity leave for the birth or adoption of a child for employees working for the same employer for three months.
- Requires the development of a multilingual outreach program to inform domestic workers and their employers of their rights and responsibilities.

The Massachusetts Domestic Worker Bill of Rights, in addition to encompassing a wider range of provisions than other states, was won in a single two-year legislative session. The bill was introduced in January 2013 and passed fewer than 18 months later. The campaign for the bill was intense, complex, and hard fought, but it did not require the multi-year grind of either the New York or California campaigns. How to account for the unique dynamics of the campaign for domestic worker rights in Massachusetts?

Massachusetts organizers were directly inspired by New York's victory in 2010. Natalicia Tracy, executive director of the Brazilian Immigrant Center, visited with Domestic Workers United staff and members to learn about how they had built the New York Domestic Workers Justice Coalition and their strategic approach to legislators in Albany. Tracy had arrived in Boston from Brazil in 1990. A teenager at the time, she spent two years as a highly exploited, semi-enslaved domestic worker for Brazilian professionals pursuing medical fellowships at Boston's famed medical institutions. After freeing herself from servitude, she continued in domestic work for many years, learning English, raising a family, and ultimately gaining a doctorate in sociology. Tracy had a personal stake in expanding domestic worker rights.

Monique Nguyen, now executive director of MataHari, attended a regional conference of domestic workers held at Barnard College in 2009. It was the first time she witnessed domestic workers "in their light." She talked with workers and organizers from Damayan Migrant Workers, Adhikaar, and Domestic Workers United—groups that were central to the long-running New York campaign. MataHari, which had been founded to provide legal and support services to victims of trafficking, was in the midst of a leadership transition. Nguyen returned to Boston inspired and determined to shift toward an organizing model that centered on developing a membership base of domestic workers capable of campaigning for their rights. Nguyen became the field director for the Massachusetts Domestic Worker Bill of Rights campaign.

The New York bill became law in August 2010. By December of that year, the Brazilian Immigrant Center (now the Brazilian Worker Center), MataHari, the Dominican Development Center, Via Verde, the Women's Institute for Leadership Development, and the Massachusetts Association of Professional Nannies came together to form the Massachusetts Coalition for Domestic Workers (MCDW). In their first year working together, they focused on gathering data about domestic workers in Massachusetts as part an NDWA-initiated research project, the first national survey to study the conditions of domestic workers in the United States (Burnham and Theodore 2012). Apart from gathering crucial data, the survey project served as a training ground for outreach to other workers, as well as a testing ground for diverse organizations with distinct constituencies to work together. Once the survey was completed, the coalition turned its attention to the challenge of creating better conditions for domestic workers by changing public policy. Together they planned a domestic worker conference to provide a space to discuss the problems they encountered on the job—and to propose solutions.

From Wish List to Draft Legislation

More than 100 domestic workers attended the June 16, 2012, conference in Boston. It was the first major event organized by MCDW that brought to-gether the members of the coalition's constituent groups. The conference was conducted in four languages: English, Mandarin, Portuguese, and Spanish. An OSHA representative put up big butcher-paper drawings of the human body and workers affixed Post-it* notes to indicate where they experienced work-related pain. By the end of the day, the drawings were covered in little slips of paper. Workers sat at round tables talking about problematic or exploit-ative work experiences, as well as the measures they would like to see enacted to check employers' power to overwork and abuse their employees. They an-swered the question, "What is just and fair employment for you?" Each table reported back to the whole group, and the day's work was reflected in a comprehensive list of measures that should be taken to improve the working conditions of domestic workers.

The road from a wish list to credible draft legislation is long. MCDW engaged Greater Boston Legal Services (GBLS) to lead them down that road. Monica Halas, lead attorney for GBLS' employment law unit, had just come off a grueling, ultimately successful, ten-year campaign to win employment rights for temp workers in Massachusetts. Though weary from a long legislative battle, Halas was eager to take on the Domestic Worker Bill of Rights. Domestic work was not abstract. Her parents had escaped near-certain death in Eastern Europe at the hands of the Nazis by applying for and getting jobs as a butler and a maid just outside London. Halas had worked on nearly a dozen legislative campaigns. She knew her way around the statehouse, which was brand-new terrain for most of the coalition organizers.

Halas and the GBLS staff combed through Massachusetts state law to find the labor protections from which domestic workers were explicitly excluded, either as a class of workers or because the law applied only to workplaces with multiple employees.

They had in hand the visionary wish list created by domestic workers. They had the New York law and New York's strategic playbook. They had California's pending legislation. And then they stumbled on something they didn't know they had: precedents extending rights to domestic workers enacted in 1970 through the determined advocacy of one Melnea Cass.

Cass was head of the Boston NAACP's Women's Service Club. Among many other things, the club provided support and guidance to Black domestic workers arriving in Boston from the South—women who were part of the great wave of Black migration northward and westward from the post-World War I years through the 1960s. Cass heard firsthand about how commonplace the mistreatment of Black domestic workers was. She pushed through legislation that amounted to the first statewide bill of rights for domestic workers. Included in the legislation, signed by Republican Governor Sargent, were the rights to workers compensation, minimum wage, overtime pay, and unionization. The full story of exactly how Cass accomplished this groundbreaking feat has yet to be told, but 40 years later, MCDW and GBLS found her sturdy shoulders to stand on.

With Cass as inspiration and draft legislation in hand, it was time to find a legislator to act as lead sponsor and carry the bill. MCDW turned to representative Mike Moran. The Brazilian Immigrant Center was in the district Moran represented. His mother had been a domestic worker. Tracy collected the signatures of 200 of Moran's constituents in support of a bill of rights for domestic workers. Moran agreed to sponsor the bill on the condition that he could run it up the flagpole to gauge the opposition. He determined that the bill had a chance at success—but only if the campaign for it was relatively low-key. He was concerned that a high-profile campaign with lots of media coverage and repeated mobilizations and demonstrations at the state capitol would spark entrenched resistance. On the spectrum of US politics, Massachusetts has a liberal reputation. But anti-immigrant sentiment, both among the general public and within the legislature, was a factor to be reckoned with. Because the members of the organizations pushing the legislation were primarily immigrant workers, Moran felt that high-profile advocacy by these organizations would likely tank the bill.

Moran's approach posed a challenge to the coalition. It was not that they distrusted his political instincts. To the contrary, Moran had the respect of his colleagues and of the labor movement. But for the coalition, the campaign for a Massachusetts Domestic Worker Bill of Rights was about more than winning in the legislature. It was also about lifting the voices of domestic workers, developing their leadership, developing their confidence to speak directly to power, and building the membership base of participating organizations across the arc of a complex campaign. How could they do this in the course of a stealth campaign? Working with this conundrum became one of the central dynamics of Massachusetts organizing for domestic worker rights.

Indispensable Allies

With a lead sponsor in place, MCDW turned its attention to building support for the bill. Labor's support was critical, a lesson from both the New York and California campaigns. Fortunately, GBLS is organized, part of United Auto Workers Local 2320 (the National Organization of Legal Services Workers). Halas, who represents the UAW as a vice president on the Massachusetts AFL-CIO executive board, has strong ties to labor. But strong ties alone were not enough. Tracy spent months going to labor breakfasts and union meetings across the state. Over and over again, she explained the conditions of the workforce, the purpose of the legislation, and the importance of endorsements from union locals and labor councils. Ultimately, MCDW got endorsements from 29 different labor organizations, from the Greater Boston Labor Council to the Insulators and Asbestos Workers Local 6. The Massachusetts AFL-CIO promoted the bill as one of its top ten legislative priorities.

Building relations with the disability rights community was also critical to successfully moving the bill, as had become abundantly clear in California. Lydia Edwards, a coalition leader and lawyer who was the director of legal services at the Brazilian Immigrant Center, and who had created the first mediation clinic to resolve disputes between domestic workers and their employers, took on the job of reaching out to the key disability rights organizations. She took the draft legislation to disability rights organizations and activists, listened intently to their concerns, and asked them to review and mark up the bill to make sure their concerns were incorporated into subsequent drafts. The coalition took to heart the disability rights community's motto "Nothing about us, without us." The disability rights community had supported SEIU's unionization of personal care attendants in Massachusetts and, because they were protected by a union contract, the final legislation carves these workers out of the definition of who is a domestic worker. The coalition gained the endorsements of the Disability Law Center and independent living centers across the state, along with the supportive voices of disability rights activists at key junctures in the campaign. In the course of building strong relationships, Edwards became an advocate for disability rights and now sits on the board of trustees of the Boston Center for Independent Living.

Campaigning to Win

Given the commitment to a relatively under-the-radar campaign—no mass mobilizations at the statehouse, no drumbeat of publicity—the coalition looked to other opportunities to focus the organizing energy of workers. Workers testified at in-district events designed to win over state senators and representatives. They lobbied cities and towns to pass municipal declarations endorsing the state bill and local ordinances in support of domestic worker rights. They did outreach and workshops to inform domestic workers about the provisions and progress of the bill. And they spoke at a traveling exhibit of photographic portraits of Brazilian domestic workers, intended to give face and voice to an invisible workforce.

The bill provided the relatively young Massachusetts domestic worker movement with a specific focus for outreach to new workers, identification of "high road" employers, and alliance building with faith-based, civic, labor, and social justice organizations.[4] It established the domestic worker movement in Massachusetts as an integral and effective force on the worker rights landscape.

Bills pile up and die in committee. The coalition was determined that this would not be the fate of the Massachusetts Domestic Worker Bill of Rights. They did the legwork of accumulating sponsors for the bill and organized strong testimony for the Labor and Workforce Development Committee. MCDW met with every member of the committee and, through relentless calls and visits, lined up an impressive roster of co-sponsors.[5]

Meanwhile, Halas and GBLS staff attorneys drafted dozens of versions of the bill, speaking to the questions and concerns of potential supporters while maintaining the core rights and protections for domestic workers. At the committee hearing, four people testified in support of the Domestic Worker Bill of Rights: two domestic workers and two employers, one of the latter an individual with a disability. The stories mattered, as did the countless meetings. The coalition positioned the bill as a broadly popular opportunity to stand for worker rights and civil rights that was also risk free because there was no mobilized opposition. The bill passed out of committee with no "no" votes.

No piece of legislation makes it through the legislative process entirely unscathed, and the bill of rights was no exception. The bill became the unintended temporary hostage to a power struggle between the House and Senate. It endured a spate of ping-ponging and deal making before, in the end, the stand-alone bill passed in the Senate 39 to zero and cleared the House by a wide margin. It was one of the few bills chosen for a governor's signing ceremony, which was attended by workers, organizers, legal advocates, legislators, Boston's mayor, and a raft of supporters who had gone the distance.[6]

An enormous amount of thoughtful strategizing and plain hard work went into the win. MCDW was under considerable pressure to get the legislation passed while a Democratic governor was in office to sign it. Though the coalition suffered from difficult internal dynamics and personality clashes—MDWC burnt out at least one talented coordinator—it was, in the end, a successful instrument of progressive policy change. Many of those most central to the campaign still talk about it in semi-mystical terms: "the stars aligned," "there were magical things that happened." In an era when much of labor is on the defensive or in retreat, the Massachusetts Domestic Worker Bill of Rights broke new ground by creating a far more robust legal framework to protect domestic workers from abusive conditions on the job and broaden the parameters of their rights as workers.

Post Win

The Massachusetts Office of the Attorney General is charged with both enforcing the bill and informing workers and employers of their rights and responsibilities. Their website outlines the law in English, Portuguese, and Spanish; makes it clear that the law applies regardless of immigration status; provides a sample employment agreement, timesheet, and performance review; and directs workers to a hotline to report problematic working conditions.[7]

In June 2017, the Office of the Attorney General recovered $35,000 in back wages and penalties for a live-in domestic who cared for a couple's children. Her employers neglected to comply with the domestic worker law by failing to pay minimum wage, overtime, or vacation pay (Attorney General of Massachusetts 2017). It is highly unlikely that this action would have been undertaken or successfully pursued had the Massachusetts Domestic Worker Bill of Rights not been on the books.

The bill of rights made it through the legislature relatively quickly in part because it was unimpeded by organized employer opposition. Once the bill had passed, though, the au pair industry rallied to try to exempt au pairs from the protections of the bill. Au pairs are young people from abroad, usually young women, who are recruited by agencies and placed with US families to care for their children for one year. They are expected to work up to 45 hours per week. Once food and lodging are deducted, au pairs are paid far below minimum wage, and au pairs have reported being overworked and denied rest days and vacation time (Kopplin 2017). Cultural Care Au Pair, an au pair agency, brought suit in federal court, arguing that the au pair program is a cultural exchange opportunity not an employment program, and that Massachusetts state law covering domestic workers should not take precedence over the provisions of the J-1 visa program administered by the federal government (Woolhouse 2016). This challenge to the bill by the au pair industry—another indication that the bill's provisions constitute a significant gain for workers—was dismissed in federal court.

CONCLUSION

Both the California and Massachusetts campaigns rested on and embodied the broadening of domestic worker organizing from providing support and services to grassroots organizing for policy change. Both campaigns were serious about winning but also determined to implement a model of organizing that strengthened the leadership capacities of domestic workers and built the domestic worker movement. Both wins depended on coalitions that extended beyond domestic workers and garnered the support of organized labor, the disability rights community, and progressive faith-based, feminist, legal, and academic individuals and institutions.

The support of organized labor was critical to both the California and Massachusetts campaigns. Coalition organizers in both states depended on the legislative expertise and relationships that had been accumulated over time by labor leaders, together with the credibility signified by the endorsements of local, statewide, and national unions and federations.

Grassroots lawyering was indispensable to both victories. Beyond their legal skills and commitments to worker justice, the lawyers at Golden Gate University's Women's Employment Rights Clinic and Greater Boston Legal Services were also prepared to respect and engage with processes that required complex, multi-layered democratic decision making. They also assumed the responsibility of extensive and ongoing education in current law, legislative processes, and the potential and limitations of new legislation (Shah 2014).

Both campaigns also elevated culture change as a key element of the organizing. The dignity and value of care and cleaning work was a constant theme, asserted in the voices and through the stories of the workers themselves. The voices of ethical employers spoke both to how important domestic work is to families and communities and to the need to change social norms in relation to the work. Transforming public consciousness and discourse about domestic work informed the communications strategies in both states.

Despite these similarities, the arcs of the two campaigns and the scope of the wins were dramatically different. The California campaign, from the very beginning, encountered headwinds in the form of recalcitrant governors and an organized, determined opposition. That opposition narrowed the range of labor protections the coalition could win and repeatedly forced workers and organizers to recommit and restrategize across the long arc of a campaign that, at some moments, must have seemed unwinnable. Though the domestic worker movement in Massachusetts was less seasoned than that in California, the coalition there was able to exploit more favorable political terrain and faced little organized opposition on its path to victory.

The maturation of the domestic worker movement can, to a substantial degree, be attributed to the strategic decision to pursue policy wins at the state level as a way of both creating the necessary legal framework to protect and expand the labor rights of domestic workers and, at the same time, to increase the capacity of the movement to mobilize, organize, advocate, and shift the narrative about the rights and dignity of low-wage women workers.

In states in which new labor protections have been won, the domestic worker movement faces challenging issues of education and enforcement—educating workers and employers about the rights to which domestic workers are entitled and making sure those rights are enforced by bringing action against those employers who exploit or abuse workers. In states and municipalities where rights have not been expanded, the domestic worker movement faces the challenge of assessing the political terrain and determining whether a policy win is possible. The California and Massachusetts campaigns, different though they were, each added to the power of the domestic worker movement, confirming its ability to make gains for workers despite a national political environment generally hostile to worker rights.

Bill of rights campaigns have carved out new terrain for domestic workers in eight states. They serve as a model for ongoing organizing. The campaigns have won new rights and protections for low-wage workers long overlooked by organized labor. And they have eliminated exclusions from worker protections that are a direct legacy of slavery and racially discriminatory lawmaking. The new laws generated by bill of rights campaigns provide a far sturdier framework to raise the wage floor and improve working conditions for nannies, housecleaners, eldercare givers, and personal attendants in the states in which they have been won.

At the same time, the bill of rights victories demonstrate that organizations outside of the traditional labor movement—what some call "alt-labor"—can play a significant role in mobilizing sectors of workers, focusing their power and winning policy change that improves their conditions on the job. The arc of each statewide campaign differed. Each bill of rights coalition had distinct domestic worker organizations at its center, crafted its own tactics, and encountered distinct political dynamics and personalities in their state legislatures. Each coalition launched their campaigns with high hopes and long lists of wrongs to be righted. The specific measures won vary from relatively narrow to more broad ranging and comprehensive. In every instance, new ground was gained to expand and protect the labor rights of domestic workers.

APPENDIX: STATE BILLS AND PROTECTIONS

California
http://bit.ly/2HPtID2 (legislation passed 9/26/2013, with sunset provision)
http://bit.ly/2HPJoWH (legislation passed 9/12/2016; bill became permanent)

Wages and Overtime Pay
- Requires overtime pay for personal attendants who work more than nine hours per day or more than 45 hours in a workweek.

Enforcement Mechanism
- Claims must be filed with Division of Labor Standards Enforcement.

Connecticut
http://bit.ly/2p9jdlD (legislation passed 6/11/2014)

Discrimination and Harassment
- Eliminates the exclusion of domestic workers under anti-discrimination and harassment protections, thereby extending such protections in workplaces of three or more workers.

Other Protections and Provisions
- Task force to study issues involving domestic workers in the state and make recommendations for legislative initiatives. Report submitted January 13, 2016.

Hawaii
http://bit.ly/2p8YRZp (legislation passed 7/1/2013)

Wages and Overtime Pay
- Closes wage and hour exemptions for domestic service.
- Provides minimum-wage protection and overtime pay after 40 hours of work per week.
- Exempts those working "on a casual basis" and those providing "companionship services for the aged or infirm.

Discrimination and Harassment

- Protects against discrimination/harassment in compensation or terms and conditions of work on the basis of race, sex, sexual orientation, gender identity, age, religion, color, ancestry, disability, or marital status.

Enforcement Mechanism

- Complaints must be filed with the Wage Standards Division of the Department of Labor and Industrial Relations.

Illinois

http://bit.ly/2p8GpjR (legislation passed 8/12/2016)

Wages and Overtime Pay

- Entitles workers to state minimum wage.
- Requires overtime pay after 40 hours of work per week or, for live-in workers, after 44 hours.

Meal Breaks, Rest Breaks, Vacation Time

- Provides for 24 consecutive hours of rest per week. Applies to workers who work for one employer for 20 or more hours per week and to live-in workers.

Discrimination and Harassment

- Includes domestic workers in the definition of employees protected by the Illinois Human Rights Act.
- Provides protection against sexual harassment for one or more workers and discrimination in workplaces of 15 or more, except for pregnancy or physical or mental disability discrimination (workplaces with one or more workers).

Enforcement Mechanism

- Workers have the right to file administrative complaints or civil claims to recover the difference between wages paid and fair wages to which they are entitled.

Massachusetts

http://bit.ly/2CqE2lE (legislation passed 6/26/2014)

Wages and Overtime Pay

- Requires workers be paid at least the state minimum wage, as well as overtime pay after 40 hours of work per week.

- Requires overtime pay for workers who voluntarily agree to work on their days of rest.
- Prohibits employers from deducting costs of food and/or lodging from the wages of live-in workers unless that food and/or lodging is freely chosen.
- Prohibits employers from deducting costs of meals, rest periods, lodging, or sleeping periods without written consent.
- Requires employers to keep written pay records.

Meal Breaks, Rest Breaks, Vacation Time

- Provides for 24 consecutive hours of rest per week and 48 consecutive hours rest per month for workers employed 40 hours or more per week by the same employer.
- Requires 40 hours of sick time per year be provided, as well as a 30-minute unpaid rest break after no more than six consecutive hours of work.
- Workers on duty for fewer than 24 hours must be paid for all meal, rest, and sleeping periods, unless they are free from work duties.
- Workers on duty for 24 hours or more may agree in writing to exclude up to eight hours of meal periods, rest periods, and/or sleep periods from their paid work hours.

Family and Pregnancy Leave

- Includes domestic workers in the state standard of eight weeks of unpaid maternity leave.

Discrimination and Harassment

- Protects against discrimination and harassment for employers (with one or more workers) based on sex, sexual orientation, gender identity, race, color, age, religion, national origin, or disability.

Right to Organize and Protection Against Retaliation

- Provides workers with anti-retaliation protections and allows them to make wage complaints, including those who work fewer than 16 hours per week.

Health and Safety

- Requires that housing for live-in workers meet the state's sanitary code.

Other Protections and Provisions

- Live-in workers who are terminated without cause have the right to written notice and 30 days lodging or two weeks of severance pay.
- Live-in workers have the right to privacy.
- Employers are prohibited from confiscating workers' documents.
- Workers may request a written work evaluation after the first 3 months of work.

- A written employment agreement is required if an employee works more than 16 hours per week.
- Employer must provide notice to worker of all applicable federal and state laws protecting domestic workers.

Enforcement Mechanisms

- Workers have enforcement rights by making claims to the attorney general's office or by taking private action in court.
- Office for Labor and Workforce Development developed a multilingual outreach program to inform domestic workers and employers about their rights.
- Workers may bring discrimination and harassment complaints to the state Commission Against Discrimination.

Nevada

http://bit.ly/2p6HQPy (legislation passed 6/12/2017)

Wages and Overtime Pay

- Entitles workers to state minimum wage.
- Requires overtime pay after 40 hours of work per week or eight hours per day. (Live-in workers are exempted from overtime protection upon written agreement between the worker and the employer.)
- Requires that value of lodging for live-in workers be computed at no more than five times the minimum hourly wage per week. Prohibits employer from deducting for lodging if living in is a condition of employment.
- Sets limits on the amount of wages or compensation that may be withheld to cover the cost of the worker's food. Such compensation may be withheld only with the written consent of the worker.
- Requires employers to keep track of workers' hours and pay.

Meal Breaks, Rest Breaks, Vacation Time

- Provides for 24 consecutive hours of rest per week and 48 consecutive hours of rest per month for workers hired to work for 40 or more hours per week.

Other Protections and Provisions

- Removes the domestic service exemption for child labor.
- Requires a written agreement at the start of employment that includes rate of pay, scope of duties, frequency and method of payment, deductions from wages, if any, and notice of federal and state laws related to domestic employment.

- Workers may request a performance evaluation after three months of employment and annually.
- Live-in workers terminated without cause have the right to notice of termination and 30 days of paid lodging.
- Employers are prohibited from monitoring workers' private communications or taking or holding workers' personal documents.

Enforcement Mechanisms

- Labor commissioner is to adopt regulations to carry out provisions of the law and provide multilingual notice of employment rights.

New York

http://bit.ly/2GPPvsZ (legislation passed 8/31/2010)

Wages and Overtime Pay

- Requires overtime pay after 40 hours of work per week or, for live-in workers, after 44 hours.

Meal Breaks, Rest Breaks, Vacation Time

- Provides for 24 consecutive hours of rest every seven days. If worker agrees to work on rest day, worker is paid at overtime rate.
- Provides three paid days of rest each year after one year of work for same employer.

Unemployment and Workers Compensation

- Amends state workers compensation law to (1) require employers to extend its provisions on disability benefits to workers who work fewer than 40 hours per week, and (2) require employers to provide workers compensation insurance coverage to employees who work 40 or more hours per week.

Discrimination and Harassment

- Creates a special cause of action for workers subjected to harassment based on gender, including sexual harassment or harassment on the basis of race, religion, or national origin.

Right to Organize and Protection Against Retaliation

- Requires New York State to conduct a feasibility study on collective bargaining for domestic workers.
- Prohibits retaliation against workers in response to worker complaints to the employer or the Department of Labor, or for complaining about harassment.

Enforcement Mechanism
- Protections from harassment and/or discrimination, and from retaliation for complaining, are enforced through the state's Division of Human Rights.
- Includes private right of action.

Oregon
http://bit.ly/2p7W1UF (legislation passed 6/17/2015)

Wages and Overtime Pay
- Requires overtime pay after 40 hours of work per week or, for live-in workers, after 44 hours.

Meal Breaks, Rest Breaks, Vacation Time
- Provides for 24 consecutive hours of rest per workweek. If worker agrees to work that day, worker is paid at overtime rate.
- Provides three personal leave days per year if the employee worked at least 30 hours per week during previous year.
- Gives workers a right to meal and rest breaks.
- Provides for eight hours of consecutive rest for live-in workers in a 24-hour period.

Discrimination and Harassment
- Provides protections against harassment and discrimination based on race, color, sex, sexual orientation, religion, age, and marital status.

Right to Organize and Protection Against Retaliation
- Offers protection against retaliation and discrimination with respect to hiring and employment for making an inquiry, reporting a violation, or lodging a complaint.

Health and Safety
- Requires that a living space with adequate conditions for uninterrupted sleep be provided for live-in workers.

Other Protections and Provisions
- Employer may not have possession of the worker's passport.
- Live-in workers have the right to cook their own food.

Enforcement Mechanism
- The Bureau of Labor and Industries enforces civil rights and wage and hour laws.

- The commissioner of the Bureau of Labor and Industries is to adopt regulations for calculating overtime during periods of travel and medical emergencies.

ENDNOTES

[1] The organizations that co-founded the National Domestic Workers Alliance included CASA de Maryland, Casa Latina, Coalition for Humane Immigrant Rights of Los Angeles, Damayan Migrant Workers Association, Domestic Workers United, Haitian Women for Haitian Refugees, La Colectiva de Mujeres, Las Señoras de Santa Maria, Mujeres Unidas y Activas, People Organized to Win Employment Rights, Pilipino Workers Center, Unity Housecleaners Cooperative of the Hempstead Workplace Project, Women Workers Project of CAAAV: Organizing Asian Communities.

[2] In a civil suit, a judge determined that Peña Canal was entitled to two years of back wages at $25 an hour. She is still trying to recover those wages (Correspondence with Rocio Avila, 12/10/2017).

[3] Amy Poehler at Time 100 Gala (https://www.youtube.com/watch?v=zpV6tsvn-WI).

[4] Massachusetts Domestic Worker Bill of Rights supporters (http://bit.ly/2oqsxlu).

[5] Massachusetts Domestic Worker Bill of Rights co-sponsors (http://bit.ly/2osBWJ6).

[6] Massachusetts Domestic Worker Bill of Rights signing ceremony (http://bit.ly/2onFYmg).

[7] Massachusetts Office of the Attorney General on domestic worker rights (http://bit.ly/2ovuKfB).

REFERENCES

Attorney General of Massachusetts. 2017 (Jun. 8) "Couple to Pay More Than $35,000 for Failing to Pay Their Live-in Domestic Worker." http://bit.ly/2GONP31

Burnham, Linda, and Nik Theodore. 2012. *Home Economics: The Invisible and Unregulated World of Domestic Work*. University of Illinois at Chicago: Data Center, National Domestic Workers Alliance, UIC Center for Urban Economic Development.

California State Assembly. 2006. Assembly Bill 2536. Vetoed Aug. 21, 2006. http://bit.ly/2GNpcnf

California State Assembly. 2010. Assembly Concurrent Resolution No. 163, Sep. 7, 2010. http://bit.ly/2GOCNuj

California State Assembly. 2011. Assembly Bill 889, introduced February 11, 2011. http://bit.ly/2HPHEx0

California State Assembly. 2013. Assembly Bill 241, approved Sep. 26, 2013. http://bit.ly/2HPtID2

California State Senate. 2016. Senate Bill 1015, approved Sep. 12, 2016. http://bit.ly/2HPJoWH

Commonwealth of Massachusetts. 2014. "An Act Establishing the Domestic Worker Bill of Rights Chapter 148 of the Acts of 2014, approved June 26, 2014. http://bit.ly/2CqE2lE

Greenhouse, Steven. 2003 (May 15). "New Protections for Nannies Are Approved by Council." *New York Times*. http://nyti.ms/2HScAfR

Hafiz, Sameera, and Michael Paarlberg. 2017. "The Human Trafficking of Domestic Workers in the United States: Findings from the Beyond Survival Campaign." Report. New York, NY; Washington, DC: National Domestic Workers Alliance and Institute for Policy Studies.

Hobden, Claire. 2010. "Winning Fair Labour Standards for Domestic Workers: Lessons Learned from the Campaign for a Domestic Worker Bill of Rights in New York State." Geneva, Switzerland: International Labour Organization. http://bit.ly/2Hp6uCT

Hunter, Tera W. 1997. "'Washing Amazons' and Organized Protest." In *To 'Joy My Freedom: Southern Black Women's Lives and Labors After the Civil War*, edited by Tera W. Hunter, pp. 74–97. Boston, MA: Harvard University Press.

Kopplin, Jack. 2017 (Mar. 27). "They Think We Are Slaves." *Politico*. http://politi.co/2GQ XYfh

Mujeres Unidas y Activas, Women's Collective of La Raza Centro Legal and Data Center. 2007. "Behind Closed Doors: Working Conditions of California Household Workers." Report. San Francisco, CA: Mujeres Unidas y Activas, Women's Collective of La Raza Centro Legal and Data Center. http://bit.ly/2GMlFpm

Nadasen, Premilla. 2015. *Household Workers Unite: The Untold Story of African American Women Who Built a Movement*. Boston, MA: Beacon Press.

New America Media. 2010. "Vilma Serralta: An SF Worker's Victory Fuels Domestic Labor Movement." https://vimeo.com/7078437

New York State Senate. 2010. Senate Bill 2311E. http://bit.ly/2GPPvsZ

Perea, Juan. 2011. "The Echoes of Slavery: Recognizing the Racist Origin of the Agricultural and Domestic Worker Exclusion from the National Labor Relations Act." *Ohio State Law Journal* 72 (1): 95–138. doi:10.2139/ssrn.1646496

Poo, Ai-jen. 2010. "Organizing with Love: Lessons from the New York State Bill of Rights Campaign." Report. Ann Arbor, MI: Center for the Education of Women, University of Michigan. http://bit.ly/2HR3b8q

Romo, David Dorado. 2005. "The Bath Riots: Revolt of the Mexican Amazons at the Santa Fe Bridge." In *Ringside Seat to a Revolution: An Underground Cultural History of El Paso and Juarez*, pp. 223–224. El Paso, TX: Cinco Puntos Press.

Salonga, Robert. 2008 (Nov. 19). "Walnut Creek Real Estate Agent Accused of Forcing Nanny into Indentured Servitude." *Mercury News*. http://bayareane.ws/2Fwe65H

Shah, Hina. 2014 (Apr.). "Grassroots Policy Advocacy and the California Domestic Worker Bill of Rights." Report. Chicago, IL: Sargent Shriver National Center on Poverty Law. http:// bit.ly/2HSArfC

Shah, Hina B., and Marci Seville. 2012. "Domestic Worker Organizing: Building a Contemporary Movement for Dignity and Power." *Albany Law Review* 75: 413.

Smith, Matt. 2008 (Mar. 19). "Working-Class Struggle." *SF Weekly*. http://bit.ly/2HN7nWG

Tizon, Alex. 2017 (Jun.). "My Family's Slave" *The Atlantic*. http://theatln.tc/2HMzyFj

Waheed, Saba, Lucero Herrera, Reyna Orellana, Blake Valenta, and Tia Koonse. 2016. "Profile, Practices and Needs of California's Domestic Work Employers." Report. Los Angeles, CA: UCLA Labor Center. http://bit.ly/2GNmLB8

Woolhouse, Megan. 2016 (Sep. 2). "Au Pair Agency Sues to Get Out from 2015 Mass. Workers Law." *Boston Globe*. http://bit.ly/2GQZuxZ

Section Four:
Working Up the Chain

Worker-Driven Social Responsibility: A Replicable Model for the Protection of Human Rights in Global Supply Chains

Greg Asbed
Coalition of Immokalee Workers

Cathy Albisa
National Economic and Social Rights Initiative

Sean Sellers
Worker-Driven Social Responsibility Network

INTRODUCTION

In a shrinking world of increasingly globalized markets, low-wage workers at the base of corporate supply chains remain isolated, vulnerable, exploited, and abused. Governments, which should be responsible for protecting the rights of those workers, often lack the resources or political will to do so. State-based enforcement agencies and policy frameworks consistently fail to protect workers from dangerous sweatshop conditions and even severe abuses, including forced labor, sexual harassment, and rape, in no small part because those suffering the abuse are largely powerless. Where collective bargaining rights exist and are enforced, unions can provide effective workplace protections. But even when those rights exist in the law, they are ignored in practice for millions of workers, while millions more are excluded from the legal right to form a union altogether.

Corporations, of course, also bear responsibility for ensuring that human rights are respected in their suppliers' operations, but they tend to treat the discovery of abuses in their supply chains as public relations crises to be managed rather than human rights violations to be remedied. Seeking to protect their brands from reputational harm, corporations embrace strategies that profess adherence to fundamental human rights standards but establish no effective mechanisms for enforcing those standards. This approach, known broadly as *corporate social responsibility* (CSR), is characterized by voluntary commitments, broad standards that often merely mirror local law, ineffective or nonexistent monitoring, and the absence of any commitment to or mechanisms for enforcement of the meager standards that do exist (Finnegan 2013; Gordon 2017; Locke 2013; Marosi 2014).

ONE SIZE FITS ALL

Multi-stakeholder initiatives (MSIs) have sought to address the shortcomings in the traditional CSR model by bringing nongovernmental organizations and other institutions into standard-setting and monitoring roles. While they have been successful in setting higher standards and shifting expectations, MSIs have generally failed to secure the commitment necessary to implement sustainable change. This has been reflected in the lack of effective monitoring and—most tragically—enforcement in most MSI efforts (Asbed and Gordon 2014). In Pakistan, both the Ali Enterprise fire that killed nearly 300 workers and the Tazreen fire that killed 112 workers occurred at factories that were certified by MSI monitors (Clifford and Greenhouse 2013; Greenhouse and Walsh 2012; Manik and Yardley 2012). In the United States, the two farms that used workers held against their will in a the prosecution of a particularly brutal slavery operation from 2008 in Florida were certified "socially accountable" by an industry-controlled MSI (Marquis 2017).

CSR and MSIs have failed to address the ongoing human rights crisis in global supply chains in large part because they do not put workers—the very people whose rights are in question and who have the most direct knowledge of the relevant environment—at the center of developing and enforcing solutions to the problem. This failure is evident at all levels of these schemes—in their structure, governance, operation, and allocation of resources—and it is this fundamental design flaw that makes the failure of these systems inevitable. In recent years, however, this bleak portrait has begun to change. Both in the United States and abroad, workers and their organizations have forged effective solutions that ensure the real, verifiable protection of human rights in corporate supply chains. This new paradigm is known as *worker-driven social responsibility* (WSR). This highly flexible model has been tested in some of the most stubbornly exploitative labor environments in the world today—including the agricultural fields of Florida, which were once dubbed "ground zero for modern slavery" by federal prosecutors, and the apparel sweatshops of Bangladesh, the locus of some of this century's most horrific factory fires and building collapses (Bowe 2003). In these oppressive environments, WSR has proven its ability to eliminate long-standing abuses and change workers' lives for the better every day. Consequently, interest in the model is growing beyond these initial sectors.

ORIGINS OF WSR

The concepts and analysis informing the WSR model arose from parallel efforts in agricultural and manufacturing supply chains. The Coalition of Immokalee Workers (CIW) was formed in the early 1990s by farmworkers in Immokalee, Florida, to confront rampant labor abuse in the fields, including frequent sexual assault and, in the most extreme cases, forced labor. Meanwhile, in 1997, North American students and labor unions, in consultation with garment workers and their unions in Central America and Asia, began to develop corporate accountability campaigns to win improvements for workers in the garment industry, where conditions are also horrific and, in some cases, fatal. In analyzing their respective industries, both groups realized that it was the corporations at the top of the chain—not the workers' direct employers—that had the resources and power to improve wages and working conditions.

Florida Agriculture

In 2011, after a decade of organizing in partnership with a national network of student, faith, labor, and community allies, the CIW launched the Fair Food Program (FFP). The FFP was the first comprehensive, fully functional model of the new WSR paradigm. In the case of the FFP, the CIW's Fair Food Agreements (FFAs) leverage the brands' wealth and purchasing power to ensure workers' fundamental human rights in the workplace. The CIW designed the FFP to include multiple redundant mechanisms—including worker-to-worker education, a 24-hour complaint investigation and resolution process, and in-depth field and farm office audits—to ensure that workers not only participate in the monitoring process but in fact drive and inform enforcement of the FFP's standards as the frontline monitors of their own rights.

The FFP emerged from the CIW's successful Campaign for Fair Food. Because farmworkers are excluded from the National Labor Relations Act, the CIW had no access to the traditional collective bargaining process and was obliged during its first decade of existence to pursue a voice on the job through community-wide strikes and other labor actions. By 2000, the CIW had shifted its focus from directly confronting local growers through traditional labor mobilizing tactics to instead holding fast-food brands accountable for conditions in their supply chains. In 2005, the CIW won its first FFA following a four-year boycott of Taco Bell, establishing several fundamental precedents for the emerging paradigm, including

- A binding legal agreement between workers at the bottom of a global supply chain and a retail brand at the top, conditioning the brand's purchases from the workers' employers on human rights compliance in the workplace—even when those rights are not guaranteed by existing law
- The first-ever ongoing payment from a food industry leader to its suppliers dedicated to addressing workers' sub-standard wages
- One-hundred-percent transparency for tomato purchases in Florida, allowing workers to monitor conditions on participating growers' farms and communicate with the buyer when sanctions are required (Asbed and Hitov 2017)

CIW has since incorporated and expanded these principles, including a worker-drafted code of conduct, into 13 subsequent FFAs with corporate buyers.

Over the past six years, the FFP has been implemented across 90% of the Florida tomato industry (approximately 30,000 workers) and currently operates in seven Eastern seaboard states and three crops. The FFP has, without exaggeration, transformed these workplaces. The program has been widely hailed by human rights observers from the United Nations to the Obama administration for its unique success eliminating and preventing slavery, sexual assault, and violence against workers. Less extreme abuses such as wage theft and health and safety violations have become the rare exception rather than the rule, and when they do occur, workers have access to a protected complaint investigation and resolution program that is fair, expeditious, and effective (Fair Food Standards Council 2016; Greenhouse 2014). To date, nearly 2,000 worker complaints have been brought forth under the FFP, and most have been resolved within days and often with systemic reforms that benefit workers beyond the individual who brought forward the complaint (Fair Food Standards Council 2018). This degree of participation is a remarkable achievement given the culture of impunity and retaliation that long reigned in the fields and which still haunts many low-wage industries. The complaint investigation and resolution process has allowed workers to identify bad actors and bad practices and fix them, backed by the purchasing powers of the signatory buyers, gradually but inexorably reshaping the industry from the ground up, complaint by complaint.

Health and safety committees provide another structured channel for worker voice on FFP farms. The program is jointly administered and monitored by the CIW and an independent third-party monitor created specifically for that purpose, the Fair Food Standards Council (FFSC). In addition to staffing the 24-hour FFP complaint line, the FFSC conducts in-depth field and office audits, interviewing thousands of workers and all levels of management, to verify compliance with the code. Recently, the FFP provided the blueprint for the Milk with Dignity program that is being implemented in the Vermont dairy supply chain by another worker-based human rights organization, Migrant Justice (Scheiber 2017). CIW developed the term *worker-driven social responsibility* to refer to this new paradigm (Asbed 2014).

Global Manufacturing

In global garment supply chains, students and the Worker Rights Consortium (WRC), the body created in 2000 by students and universities as an independent monitor of factory conditions, developed and won the right to implement several related models. First, students successfully pressed universities to integrate legally binding labor codes of conduct into their licensing contracts with companies that produced logo apparel, such that apparel companies that failed to respect workers' rights could lose their license and thus their ability to produce university logo apparel. The WRC was given the mandate to assess compliance, and licensees were required to publicly disclose their factory names and locations. While workers were not a party to these agreements, this was an early attempt to create legally binding agreements with financial consequences to protect workers' rights in supply chains. Workers and advocates have used these codes to successfully press for improved conditions—and for new forms of binding agreements between workers and brands, including both bilateral agreements between specific unions and brands and preferential procurement initiatives such as the WRC's Designated Suppliers Program.

The WRC combined lessons learned from its work enforcing apparel industry labor codes, from the CIW's Fair Food Program, and from the early efforts of labor unions to curb sweatshops in the United States to develop with its partners the Accord on Fire and Building Safety in Bangladesh. Union and witness signatories to the 2013 Accord included two global labor unions (IndustriALL and UNI), eight Bangladeshi labor federations (Bangladesh Textile and Garments Workers League; Bangladesh Independent Garments Workers Union Federation; Bangladesh Garments, Textile and Leather Workers Federation; Bangladesh Garment & Industrial Workers Federation; IndustriALL Bangladesh Council; Bangladesh Revolutionary Garments Workers Federation; National Garments Workers Federation; and United Federation of Garments Workers), and four nongovernmental organizations, or NGOs (Worker Rights Consortium, Clean Clothes Campaign, International Labor Rights Forum, and Maquila Solidarity Network). Formed in 1989, the Clean Clothes Campaign (CCC) had seen the failure of voluntary CSR play out in their own efforts with workers and unions around the world. The CCC was, like WRC, developing new approaches to more effectively compel brands to ensure that workers' rights are respected in global garment supply chains.

The second largest exporter of clothing in the world, Bangladesh was also the site of a series of factory fires and building collapses that killed nearly 2,000 workers between 2005 and 2013. The WRC and its partners developed the Accord in 2010. By 2012, despite their proclaimed concern for worker safety, only two brands had agreed to implement the Accord. It was not until the Rana Plaza building collapse in April 2013, the deadliest disaster in the history of the global apparel industry, that brands felt sufficient pressure to join the Accord. As a result, more than 200 companies signed the agreement to make their supplier factories safe. Under the Accord, signatory brands are legally obligated to do the following:

- Require their supplier factories in Bangladesh to undergo fire, building, and electrical inspections conducted by qualified engineers (most of these buildings had never undergone such an inspection before, despite being in operation for many years)

- Publicly disclose the results of those inspections (virtually all brand inspection reports had previously been kept confidential)
- Require suppliers to carry out the renovations and repairs necessary to make their factories safe, pursuant to the inspection results, and provide financial support that allows them to do so (such support can take a variety of forms, including direct payment for renovations, a higher price per piece, upfront payment for goods, or the provision of low-cost loans)
- Maintain purchase orders for at least two years at factories that implement the necessary renovations and operate safely
- Require suppliers to allow worker representatives access to their factories for the purpose of educating workers about workplace safety and their rights
- Terminate business with any factory that fails to comply with the terms of the agreement

As a result, Accord-covered factories have undergone a tremendous transformation. Many factories have installed fire doors and proper fire exits, which were virtually nonexistent in Bangladesh prior to the Accord's implementation, while others have reinforced dangerously weak building structures or finally installed code-compliant electrical wiring. As of February 2018, the Accord reports that more than 90% of remediation has been completed at 726 factories, while 136 factories have completed remediation (Accord 2018). Moreover, for the first time, workers have access to a protected complaint mechanism if they experience retaliation for speaking up about unsafe conditions and are learning about what constitutes a safe workplace (Accord 2017; Associated Press 2017 Brown 2015; James, Miles, Croucher, and Houssart 2018). On the factory floor, the Accord trains and develops joint labor–management safety committees to conduct factory inspections and identify safety hazards, respond to employee complaints about health and safety, review accident reports with an eye toward prevention, and communicate about health and safety goals to the workforce. To date, 846 safety committees are undergoing training, another 196 safety committees have completed training, and nearly 998 all-employee meetings have reached more than 1.3 million workers at Accord factories (Accord 2018). Today, the Accord affords robust implementation of WSR in the garment sector and has led to unprecedented improvements in safety for approximately two million workers.

PRINCIPLES OF WSR

Drawing on the success of the Fair Food Program and the Accord, the Worker-driven Social Responsibility Network was founded in 2015. The objective of the network is to build understanding of the model among a wide range of actors, to provide support and coordination for worker-led efforts to replicate the model, and to create a paradigm shift within the field to establish the model as the baseline for workers' rights programs within global supply chains. Currently, the network's coordinating committee is comprised of the Alliance for Fair Food, Bangladesh Center for Workers Solidarity, Business & Human Rights Resource Centre, Centro de Trabajadores Unidos en la Lucha, Coalition of Immokalee Workers, Migrant Justice, National Economic and Social Rights Initiative, and T'ruah: The Rabbinic Call for Human Rights, and United Students Against Sweatshops. The Worker Rights Consortium and Fair Food Standards Council serve as technical advisors.

Over the past two years, the network has carefully cultivated collaborative practice and strategic alignment among its members, often against a backdrop of complex political terrain and varied experiences in the domestic and international arenas. Additionally, the network has provided extensive on-the-ground technical support for the WSR adaptation effort now taking root in the Vermont dairy industry. Another important early milestone has been the publication of a statement of principles regarding effective programs to protect the rights of workers in global supply chains based on agreements between global corporations and worker organizations. These principles are as follows:

- *Labor rights initiatives must be worker driven.* Workers are the only actors in the supply chain with a vital and abiding interest in ensuring their rights are protected. If, therefore, a program intended to improve their situation is to work, workers and their representative organizations—global, national, or local labor unions; worker-based human rights organizations; or other organizations that genuinely represent workers' interests—must be at the head of the table in creating and implementing the program, including its priorities, design, monitoring, and enforcement. An initiative's labor standards must be based on universal labor and human rights principles, which are embodied in the Universal Declaration of Human Rights and defined by the Conventions of the International Labour Organization.

- *Obligations for global corporations must be binding and enforceable.* Respect for human rights in corporate supply chains cannot be optional or voluntary. Effective enforcement is key to the success of any social responsibility program. Worker organizations must be able to enforce the commitments of brands and retailers as a matter of contractual obligation.

- *Buyers must afford suppliers the financial incentive and capacity to comply.* Corporations at the top of supply chains place constant price pressure on their suppliers, which inexorably translates into downward pressure on wages and labor conditions: the market incentivizes abuse. Corporations must instead be required to incentivize respect for human rights through a price premium, negotiated higher prices, and/or other financial inducements that enable suppliers to afford the additional cost of compliance with the agreed labor standards.

- *Consequences for noncompliant suppliers must be mandatory.* The obligations of global brands and retailers must include the imposition of meaningful, swift, and certain economic consequences for suppliers that violate their workers' human rights, whether or not ending the supplier relationship suits the economic and logistical convenience of the brand or retailer. Only programs that include such economic consequences can ensure protection for workers.

- *Gains for workers must be measurable and timely.* The ability of brands and retailers to obscure the failure of voluntary labor rights initiatives is greatly aided by the absence from these initiatives of the obligation to achieve concrete, measurable outcomes at the workplace level within specific time frames. To ensure accountability, any program designed to correct specific labor rights problems must include objectively measurable outcomes and clear deadlines.

- *Verification of workplace compliance must be rigorous and independent.* Workplace audits—often infrequent and perfunctory and never free of buyer influence—are the exclusive monitoring mechanism in traditional CSR programs and have proven inadequate time and again. Effective verification of supplier compliance is essential and must include the following components: inspectors who have deep knowledge of the relevant industry and labor issues and who operate independently of financial control and influence by buyers or suppliers; in-depth worker interviews, carried out under conditions where workers can speak freely, as a central component of the process; effective worker education that enables workers to function as partners with outside inspectors; and a complaint resolution mechanism free of retaliation that operates independently of buyers and suppliers and in which workers organizations play a central role.

More than 50 leading organizations and individuals from the field of labor and human rights—from the AFL-CIO and Clean Clothes Campaign's International Office to Human Rights Watch and Freedom Network USA, as well as several leading scholars and researchers—have endorsed the WSR statement of principles in a short span of time, demonstrating growing support for this new paradigm of human rights protection.

CONDITIONS FOR WSR

As interest in WSR grows, the network has also begun to reflect on the conditions that are necessary to successfully establish the model on the ground. These factors pertain to the problem, the industry, and the practitioner organization in question. While some of the characteristics discussed are highly resistant to change (e.g., the market structure of a given industry sector), others are more malleable with sufficient time and determination (e.g., the capacity and power of a worker organization). Still others may be addressed with even shorter time horizons and in collaboration with other parties (e.g., the documentation of abuses). Therefore, assessment, or self-assessment, with these criteria should be viewed as a dynamic, iterative process that may help to inform an organization's ongoing strategic choices and paths of development, as well as the eventual design of a WSR campaign and program.

Problem

There are several considerations for assessing whether or WSR is an appropriate strategy given the specific nature of the abuses prompting calls for change. First, there must be credible documentation of the problems facing workers. Third-party documentation of human rights abuses within a supply chain may be demonstrated through a combination of academic and NGO research, media exposés, regulatory agency findings (departments of labor, health, etc.), and successful litigation or criminal prosecutions that spotlight routine or worst-case examples. It is also possible for the practitioner organization to publish firsthand research, though collaborating with an external partner such as a university may improve the credibility of the final product for some audiences.

Additionally, any WSR effort must be tailored to the scope of the problem. Around the world, low-wage workers at the base of corporate supply chains experience similar human rights abuses, which are the result of underlying economic pressures that are similar across countries and industries. At the same time, factors unique to a given sector, location, or specific worker population may result in particular concerns and priorities for workers that must be reflected in program design. Ideally, a WSR agreement would address human rights abuses at a broad regional or global level in order to impact the greatest number of workers. It is possible, however, that there are other factors—such as highly concentrated levels of production, the uniqueness or quality of a product, and logistics considerations such as geographical proximity to consumer markets and delivery timelines—that could strengthen the relative bargaining position of workers in those industries and improve the feasibility of a more delimited solution.

It is important to bear in mind the intense price competition that exists between suppliers, and the consequences this can have when WSR agreements are relatively limited in scope. If a supplier's costs increase because it has implemented improvements mandated by the WSR program, there is a danger that buyers will terminate the supplier and switch to lower-cost suppliers with worse conditions. This is known as "cutting and running." The scope of a WSR agreement should be as broad as possible to prevent this dynamic. The challenge of achieving a living wage in the garment industry is illustrative. Were a garment-producing country to significantly raise wages, buyers would simply shift their purchases to a competing country with lower wages. In this instance, regional or even global approaches, with a WSR program spanning multiple countries, may be optimal for a sustainable solution.

Lastly, a mapping of the landscape should summarize the histories and track records of other worker organizations and supply-chain initiatives in the sector or geographic area. Similarly, if previous attempts have been made to address the problem, it is useful to assess their origin, structure, and outcomes. A comprehensive analysis can be performed by utilizing the principles of WSR as metrics. This assessment can be performed based on media, academic, and NGO reports, the program's own publicly available data (often more revealing for omissions than content), and through firsthand experience that the practitioner organization or others in the field may have with the program. Key to any analysis are two factors: The presence of certain key elements, such as an effective monitoring regime and market consequences for violations; and concrete, measurable outcomes that demonstrate the on-the-ground changes achieved, or not achieved, by the existing initiative.

Industry

There are also specific considerations for assessing whether or not WSR is an appropriate strategy given the specific nature of an industry and supply chain. For example, understanding the structure, layers, and timing of the supply chain, including product and financial flows, is a necessary precondition for designing a WSR program with an enforcement mechanism that applies to both buyers and suppliers. In the case of buyers, the agreement is enforced through legal mechanisms via judicial systems or private arbitration. In the case of suppliers, enforcement is enacted through market consequences, whereby the buyer is legally obligated to cease doing business with any supplier that commits violations and fails to effect remedies. If the product or service is not traceable or cannot be segregated within the supply chain, there must be an alternative method for establishing supply-chain responsibility. There must be an ability to separate bad and good actors within the supply chain so that those that are in compliance with program standards can be rewarded and those that are in violation can be effectively identified and consequences, including market consequences, can be applied.

Relatedly, a similar level of knowledge about end buyers is also required. Corporate accountability campaigns have repeatedly demonstrated that brands are sensitive to public revelations of worker abuse in their supply chains and have proven effective in compelling concrete changes. The bigger the brand's market and cultural footprint, the more susceptible the brand may be to external pressure. A successful WSR program requires the presence of brands that can be effectively pressured through public campaigns to address conditions in the supply chain. It is imperative that the target markets of the brands will be likely to respond favorably to such a campaign. Given that many corporations are vulnerable to this approach, a cottage industry of public relations and crisis management consultants has arisen to help companies navigate these turbulent waters; indeed, CSR and many MSIs are a part of this industry (Deegan 2001). A brand's history, if any, of responding to similar issues or campaigns may reveal its strategic tendencies when responding to human rights issues in its supply chain. Taken together, these factors can help illuminate the likely fit of a WSR approach to any given brand.

Practitioner

Finally, there are also considerations for assessing whether or not a worker organization has the capacity to campaign for and implement WSR. To start, on a practical level, effective application of the WSR model requires deep participation from the worker community. In effect, the WSR model should offer tangible and concrete opportunities for further strengthening of worker organizations. This participation is necessary for such tasks as identifying workplace problems and solutions for an enforceable code of conduct/standard, creating an effective and credible worker education program, evaluating and refining the program's workplace inspection protocols, assisting as needed in the investigation of worker complaints filed under the code/standard, and providing overall strategic direction for the program. Therefore, an organization's ability to engage workers in a participatory and sustainable manner is a necessary condition for it to be able to serve as an effective spearhead for a WSR program. This participation is best channeled through a worker organization—including trade unions, worker-based human rights organizations, or other organizations that genuinely represent workers' interests—that is viewed as accessible, trustworthy, and credible by its members.

Because deep power imbalances exist within corporate supply chains, there is no shortcut or "trick" that will offset the worker organization having insufficient power to secure a WSR agreement. The most reliable way for the worker organization to build that necessary power is through a public campaign driven by a worker–consumer alliance. In the absence of such a campaign and the leverage it provides, it is highly improbable that a worker organization will be able to negotiate a strong agreement with a corporation. Accordingly, it is useful to review the scope, arc, and impact of the organization's previous campaigns. This will establish whether the organization has the experience and capacity to negotiate and enforce settlements stemming from these campaigns. This will also reveal the nature of the organization's relationship to employers. A list of previous partners may provide a window into the organization's milieu and identify active and passive allies, as well as active and passive opponents, for the WSR campaign and program. In the final analysis, an organization must understand or be willing and able to learn negotiating strategies and positioning; have a history of regular planning, persistence, and focus in its campaigning practices; demonstrate an ability to engage and challenge employers strategically (with power but also dialogue); and demonstrate it either has an existing web of strong and willing allies or has the capacity to develop one.

A worker organization's ability to develop effective strategy—a plan of action to achieve an objective within the constraints of limited resources—is necessary for the organization to become a successful WSR practitioner. Exploring the organization's strategy development process will likely intersect with its campaign history and leadership model. While successful outcomes are a clear indicator of effective strategic planning, it is also important to understand the planning process itself, including how key decisions are made and on what timelines. Specifically, it is important to assess whether decisions are made deliberatively and with broad participation within the organization (and even input from key allies) and whether there is follow-through on implementation and accountability to the plan. Additionally, the organization must demonstrate a willingness and capacity to enter into a long-term planning process leading to a focused multi-year campaign, and the ability to accurately assess its internal capacity in relation to its planned activities.

There are also resource access issues to consider. Though the "return of investment" is quite remarkable in terms of WSR's ability to protect workers' rights, these programs cannot be done on the cheap. Even as WSR programs incorporate self-financing mechanisms, such as buyer support payments to underwrite implementation costs and labeling agreements, there will be a need for resources for the worker organization and an independent monitor. Possible sources of funding may include dues, broad-based consumer sponsorship, foundation grants, and a fee for service. If a program generates buyer support payments to underwrite monitoring costs, practitioners must be careful that the overall proportion of funding from this source does not pose the risk of undue influence or introduce potentially compromising dependencies. A diversity of funding streams serves as a necessary check against this risk. Similarly, legal support is necessary for navigating the fine lines required by a corporate accountability campaign as well as for drafting the code/standard and binding

WSR agreements with corporate buyers. If the organization does not have in-house legal counsel, it must evaluate whether external support can be attained and whether that support will be sufficient for and attuned with the identified objectives. In this context, it is important to determine whether there are legal constraints the worker organization could face in pursuing WSR agreements and/or implementing a WSR program.

Finally, the worker organization's external environment must be reasonably conducive. The WSR model requires that workers enjoy sufficient access to their rights of assembly and expression. While organizing is dangerous in many contexts, it is particularly difficult to imagine a WSR program taking root where worker organizations cannot operate above ground in a formal and relatively secure manner. The model may not then be suited the current realities of China, to cite one prominent example, where independent worker organizing is forbidden by the state. However, even in environments as difficult as Bangladesh, the model has proven effective at leveraging sustainable change.

IMPLICATIONS OF WSR

Worker-driven social responsibility has several important implications for the broader field of labor standards enforcement. First, WSR presents a superior alternative, and should therefore displace, CSR and MSI schemes. In the case of WSR, enforcement of program standards is mandatory and binding; in the case of CSR and MSI schemes, enforcement is voluntary and nonbinding. This is particularly relevant when one considers the proliferation of supply chain–focused initiatives that claim to address high-profile problems such as forced labor, child labor, or gender-based violence. Second, WSR provides a redistributive mechanism for addressing the downward price pressure in global supply chains that exacerbates worker abuse and often renders compliance with labor standards virtually impossible. Third, WSR has demonstrated its potential to achieve *fast* and *efficient* remediation in the workplace, which is particularly valuable given the increasingly precarious nature of employment in many low-wage industries; workers cannot afford to wait years for a resolution. Lastly, since WSR is a model for rights protection, it is possible in some contexts that programs could protect workers' right to unionization and collective bargaining.

Additionally, there are areas of interplay between WSR and the state worth mentioning. In an era of resource scarcity, the existence of an effective WSR program in one sector may complement public enforcement by allowing agencies to focus strategically on another sector. The state can also collaborate with WSR programs that uncover abuses that become the basis of criminal complaints, from slavery to sexual assault, again augmenting the effectiveness of the state's resources with the power of workers engaged in the defense of their own rights. Similarly, there may be practices and insights which emerge from WSR programs that can improve the effectiveness of public agencies, such as the importance of a worker-centered enforcement framework that provides relief in case of retaliation. Moreover, the state can support WSR programs through its own procurement practices. Finally, the state could explore strategies that encourage the development of WSR programs by protecting them under law rather than attacking them as they are, in some cases, today. Such topics provide lines of inquiry for future research. In the meantime, we expect ongoing efforts and innovations on the ground to help advance WSR and create more dignified workplaces for the most vulnerable people laboring within global supply chains.

ACKNOWLEDGMENTS

This paper draws from analysis and materials produced by the Worker-driven Social Responsibility Network (www.wsr-network.org). The authors thank Steven Hitov and Gerardo Reyes (Coalition of Immokalee Workers), Scott Nova and Jessica Champagne (Worker Rights Consortium), Theresa Haas (WSR Network), Laura Safer Espinoza (Fair Food Standards Council), Merle Payne (Centro de Trabajadores Unidos en la Lucha), Abel Luna and Brendan O'Neill (Migrant Justice), Rachel Kahn-Troster (T'ruah: The Rabbinic Call for Human Rights), Gregory Regaignon (formerly of Business and Human Rights Resource Centre), and Noelle Damico (Alliance for Fair Food) for shaping this collective analysis and providing feedback on portions of earlier drafts.

REFERENCES

Accord on Fire and Building Safety in Bangladesh. 2017 (Jan. 31). *Annual Report 2015*. Dhaka, Bangladesh: Accord on Fire and Building Safety in Bangladesh.

Accord on Fire and Building Safety in Bangladesh. 2018 (Feb. 28). "Milestones Reached as of 1 February 2018." Dhaka, Bangladesh: Accord on Fire and Building Safety in Bangladesh. http://bit.ly/2u8FNAw

Asbed, Greg. 2014 (Jun. 17). "Worker-Driven Social Responsibility: A New Idea for a New Century." *Huffington Post*. http://bit.ly/2u4EZg2

Asbed, Greg, and Jennifer Gordon. 2014. *The Problem with Multi Stakeholder Initiatives* (Transcript). New York, NY: Open Society Foundations. https://osf.to/2u2UeWy

Asbed, Greg, and Steven Hitov. 2017. "Preventing Forced Labor in Corporate Supply Chains: The Fair Food Program and Worker-Driven Social Responsibility." *Wake Forest Law Review* 52: 497–531.

Associated Press. 2017 (Jun. 29). "World Fashion Brands, Unions Agree to Extend Bangladesh Deal." *ABC News.*

Bowe, John. 2003. (Apr. 21). "Nobodies: Does Slavery Exist in America?" *New Yorker.*

Brown, Garret. 2015 (Oct. 1). "Supply Chain Culture Changing: Real Progress, Challenges in Bangladesh's Garment Industry Safety." *Industrial Safety & Hygiene News.*

Clifford, Stephanie, and Steven Greenhouse. 2013 (Sep. 1). "Fast and Flawed Inspections of Factories Abroad." *New York Times.* https://nyti.ms/2Qso5Pu

Deegan, Denise. 2001. *Managing Activism: A Guide to Dealing with Activists and Pressure Groups.* London, UK: Kogan Page.

Fair Food Standards Council. 2016. *Fair Food Program 2015 Annual Report: Comprehensive, Verifiable and Sustainable Change for Farmworkers and the US Agriculture Industry.* Sarasota, FL: Fair Food Standards Council. http://bit.ly/2u3JgA9

Fair Food Standards Council. 2018 (Feb. 26). Personal interview with Judge Laura Safer Espinoza.

Finnegan, Brian. 2013. *Responsibility Outsourced: Social Audits, Workplace Certification, and Twenty Years of Failure to Protect Worker Rights.* Washington, DC: AFL-CIO. http://bit.ly/2u17Vp7

Gordon, Jennifer. 2017. *The Problem with Corporate Social Responsibility.* New York, NY: Worker-Driven Social Responsibility Network. http://bit.ly/2u32JRs

Greenhouse, Steven. 2014 (Apr. 24). "In Florida Tomato Fields, a Penny Buys Progress." *New York Times.* https://nyti.ms/2QsoWja

Greenhouse, Steven, and Declan Walsh. 2012 (Dec. 7). "Certified Safe, a Factory in Karachi Still Quickly Burned." *New York Times.* https://nyti.ms/2QqFJDb

James, Philip, Lilian Miles, Richard Croucher, and Mark Houssart. 2018 (Jan. 4). "Regulating Factory Safety in the Bangladeshi Garment Industry." *Regulation and Governance.* doi.org/10.1111/rego.12183

Locke, Richard. 2013. *The Promise and Limits of Private Power: Promoting Labor Standards in a Global Economy.* Cambridge, UK: Cambridge University Press.

Manik, Ali Julfikar, and Jim Yardley. 2012 (Dec. 17). "Bangladesh Finds Gross Negligence in Factory Fire." *New York Times.* https://nyti.ms/2MrUTEY

Marosi, Richard. 2014 (Dec. 14). "In Mexico's Fields, Children Toil to Harvest Crops That Make It to American Tables." *Los Angeles Times.* http://bit.ly/2MrVlDa

Marquis, Susan. 2017. *I Am Not a Tractor: How Florida Farmworkers Took on the Fast Food Giants and Won.* Ithaca, NY: Cornell University Press.

Scheiber, Noam. 2017 (Oct. 3). "Ben & Jerry's Strikes Deal to Improve Migrant Dairy Workers' Conditions." *New York Times.* https://nyti.ms/2QsWUE3

CHAPTER 15

Taming Globalization: Raising Labor Standards Across Supply Chains

Nik Theodore
University of Illinois at Chicago

Global economic integration, and the intensifying capital and product flows it has enabled, has called into question existing frameworks of labor protections that rely on national governments to independently regulate their domestic economies. Many government officials are quick to assert that heightened capital mobility creates a regulatory dilemma. Governments must do what they can to attract foreign investment to support business development and spur job creation. But because corporate investors search for jurisdictions where labor and environmental regulations only minimally impinge on business operations, governments are constrained in their efforts to implement and enforce the types of protections that are needed to ensure that the gains from investment benefit domestic labor forces. Officials fear that investors will shun jurisdictions that institute strong labor protections, worrying that this will lead to disinvestment and decline.

The logic of such arguments is flawed, yet this has done little to undermine their authority. Without effective labor protections, the gains from trade overwhelmingly benefit firms and investors, and domestic workforces remain mired in a low-level equilibrium where low wages leave workers unable to climb out of poverty, limiting growth in per capita national incomes and placing a drag on domestic economic performance. The global race to the bottom that has resulted from the false choice between pursuing economic development objectives and instituting strong labor protections has set in motion successive rounds of regulatory undercutting, leading to the degradation of work, an erosion of labor standards, and deepening inequality.

In response to these conditions, nongovernmental organizations have launched a series of innovative initiatives to strengthen labor protections. These initiatives have sought to fill the void created by inadequate government enforcement of labor standards, and they are signs a new global movement is forming to develop strategies that place a floor under wages and working conditions. This chapter examines two approaches for raising labor standards across global supply chains. Focusing on the Asia Floor Wage campaign and the workers' rights campaign at C.J.'s Seafood, this chapter highlights efforts by labor groups to hold powerful corporations accountable for the employment practices of supplier firms. The campaigns featured here are notable because they target supply chains that span political jurisdictions, link product markets, and mobilize labor forces from various countries. Moreover, while they seek to leverage national laws and enforcement mechanisms, the strategies documented here reflect the regional character of production networks, and by doing so, they reconceptualize the terrain for worker organizing, bargaining, and activism. The next section introduces the Asia Floor Wage campaign and examines the challenges of raising standards in the apparel industry. Section two describes the supply-chain organizing campaign among guestworkers at C.J.'s Seafood. The concluding section outlines an agenda for strengthening labor protections and raising workplace standards.

RAISING LABOR STANDARDS ACROSS THE GLOBAL APPAREL INDUSTRY

The apparel industry is the epitome of a globalizing sector. Apparel production systems are highly decentralized, both in terms of the number and location of firms. Apparel production systems also are highly integrated, with commodity chains linking producers and consumers across continents. The globalization of apparel manufacturing has been driven by large retailers, principally those based in the Europe, Japan, and the United States. "The highly concentrated purchasing power of the large retail chains gives them enormous leverage over clothing manufacturers," and they have used this leverage to drive down supplier costs in an effort to boost profits and increase returns to shareholders (Dicken 2015: 466).

With its high labor intensity and low barriers to entry, the apparel industry has been eager to exploit the vast differentials in labor costs that exist between countries (Figure 1). Differentials between production sites in the Global North and South have been widening over the past two decades, and newly industrializing economies have emerged as the key sites of production in this restructuring industry (Werner International 2015). Lured by the creation of special economic zones that lower the costs of doing business; the ready supplies of workers who are employed for a pittance, particularly those who comprise the growing ranks of home-based production in the most informalized segments of the industry; and the weak enforcement of labor protections and the advantages it confers to businesses seeking to boost profits, manufacturers have targeted Asia in their search for low-cost labor (Cowgill and Huynh 2016; Dicken 2015; Ford and Gillan 2016; Kelly 2002). The locus of apparel industry production is now centered in the region, primarily in Bangladesh, Cambodia, China, India, Indonesia, and Sri Lanka.

In governing their distended supply chains, industry leaders have pursued a strategy of regionalization, leading to the rise of "triangle manufacturing" within Asia. Under this system, retailers place orders with lead

FIGURE 1
Hourly Labor Cost, Textile Industry, 2014

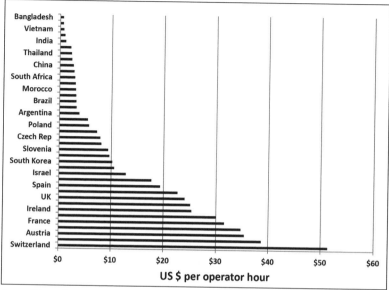

Source: Werner International (2015).

suppliers, which in turn outsource some or all of this production to lower-tier contractors:

> The triangle is completed when the finished goods are shipped directly to the overseas buyer. ... Triangle manufacturing thus changes the status of ... manufacturers [in newly industrializing countries] from established suppliers for US retailers and designers to "'middlemen'" in buyer-driven commodity chains that can include as many as 50 to 60 exporting countries. (Gereffi 1996: 97)

With global supply chains crisscrossing national boundaries, and with international competition for inward investment mounting among the newly industrializing economies, the apparel industry has been able to reap enormous benefits by engaging in global labor arbitrage. Governments have been unable—or unwilling—to effectively monitor and enforce labor protections. This absence of effective mechanisms for protecting workers' rights has led to an entirely predictable result: the widespread deterioration of labor standards.

Strategies to raise wages and strengthen labor protections cannot proceed employer by employer or, for that matter, country by country. The globalization of apparel production systems exposes a flaw in the traditional paradigm for enforcing labor standards, one that relies on lower-income countries to police firm behavior and sanction violators. For newly industrializing countries that are reliant on foreign direct investment, this approach carries with it clear risks of divestment. The threat of firm exit has dissuaded many government officials from fully enforcing employment laws, while heightened competitive pressures among lower-tier apparel suppliers mean that rising costs resulting from labor standards enforcement in one country might result in a shift in production to other countries where standards are less adequately enforced.

The globalization of production also reveals a fundamental weakness in newer, firm-based models of standards enforcement that rely on employer goodwill and voluntaristic actions in the name of corporate social responsibility. The orientation of buyer firms toward their supply-chain networks is one that prioritizes cost minimization and flexibility enhancement—objectives that too often are at odds with the enforcement of worker protections (see Bhattacharjee, Gupta, and Luce 2009; Christopherson and Lillie 2005; Compa and Hinchliffe-Darricarrere 1995; Luce 2009; Werner 2016). In addition, in the context of global sourcing, corporate accountability to distant publics in lower-income countries provides incentives to protect brand reputations that are weak, at best. Furthermore, the multiplication of subcontracting tiers under triangle manufacturing means that it is increasingly difficult for buyer firms to adequately monitor—and sanction—subcontractors that violate labor standards. Firm-based enforcement is a necessary component of a wider enforcement regime, but its limitations render reliance on this approach inadequate to the task of ensuring subcontractor compliance with labor protections (for an assessment of the effectiveness of private regulation of the apparel industry see Esbenshade 2012).

Rather than relying on the altruistic impulses of global corporations, next-generation strategies are needed to safeguard labor standards and ensure corporate social responsibility by institutionalizing labor protections. This requires that standards be applied and enforced throughout supplier networks and across national borders. In other words, it requires a regional approach to standard setting, one that extends protections to workers while also leveling the playing field between countries. The Asia Floor Wage campaign is a one such effort that could alter the prevailing paradigm of labor standards enforcement.

The Asia Floor Wage Campaign

The Asia Floor Wage (AFW) campaign seeks to establish "a new framework for the global economy: one that is based on labor rights and prioritizes the demand for a living wage" (Bhattacharjee, Gupta, and Luce 2009: 72). From the vantage point of global production networks, the regional characteristics of the labor market of a given industry in large part determine the cost structure of its products, with each producing country accounting for a share of average product costs. Within the apparel industry, when workers seek to unionize or otherwise assert their labor rights, employer threats of capital flight, or threats to reallocate production among establishments within a supply chain, are typically confined to Asia—in other words, they are not spread globally. In short, the geography of potential production relocation is primarily regional.

The AFW is founded on the recognition that Asia is home to large labor reserves as well as more than one third of the global working poor. Therefore, the large-scale relocation of labor-intensive apparel production away from Asia is highly improbable, at least until Asian labor supplies are exhausted. These factors suggest that the field of action for the defense of labor rights and protections should be Asia.

Garment workers in Asia, the majority of whom are women, currently earn roughly half of what they require to meet the basic needs (such as for food, water, education, and health care) of themselves and their families. For this reason, the establishment and enforcement of a living-wage standard has been a key demand among workers and labor activists. The demand has been presented to major apparel brands for years, with very little progress beyond rhetorical gestures of support. Trade unions and labor rights organizations across Asia, after years of negotiating with leaders in the apparel industry, collaborated to frame a demand that is both bargainable and deliverable—and that is appropriately targeted given the structure and economics of the industry. The campaign's objectives include (1) raising wages and strengthening labor protections by removing wage differentials as a key source of competition within the apparel industry, (2) strengthening workers' ability to collectively bargain with their employer, and (3) increasing the gains from trade for workers and newly industrializing countries. The AFW does this by setting "a wage that is higher than the poverty-level, national minimum wages in producing countries, and that brings workers within the parameters of a living wage" (Bhattacharjee, Gupta, and Luce 2009: 73).

Setting the Asia Floor Wage

The AFW has been designed using a basic-needs approach to the setting of a living wage based on a basket of goods that includes food and other items.[1] It accounts for national differences in food consumption by establishing a measure of nutritional adequacy based on calories, and it has adopted the Indonesian threshold of 3,000 calories as the benchmark standard. The AFW also takes into account a range of nonfood costs, such as housing, clothing, health care (including maternity care), childcare, education, fuel, transportation, and savings—estimating the cost of these items as a percentage of spending on food items. The resulting wage level is then adjusted assuming a family size of two adults and two children. The AFW is thus set as follows:

- The cost of food is based on a standard caloric intake—3,000 calories per adult (and 1,500 per child).
- The ratio between the cost of food and of other basic needs is 1:1.
- Family size adjustment (two adults and two children) = three consumption units.
- A family is supported by one income, as this is a credible way to account for childcare.
- The wage is earned during each country's legal maximum workweek, though not above 48 hours.
- The wage is a basic wage that excludes overtime and benefits.

The costs associated with food and other basic necessities are calculated in the local currency to establish a monthly minimum-wage requirement for a given country. The concept of purchasing power parity (PPP), the notion that a bundle of goods should cost the same between countries once the exchange rates have been taken into account, is then used to index costs to the US dollar, allowing comparisons to be made across countries. In 2017, the AFW was set at PPP$1,181 per month.

The AFW campaign presented its demands through an international public launch in October 2009. The Asia Floor Wage Alliance (AFWA) wrote letters to nearly 60 brands requesting meetings in order to present the AFW. From 2009 onward, the AFWA has engaged in debates and discussions with brands, as well as several meetings with the International Labor Organization and global labor federations. Over two years, the AFW achieved international credibility and legitimacy and began to be used as a benchmark by some brands and quasi-governmental agencies, and it became a key feature of the global living-wage debate.

The AFW bargaining process targets the leading brands—who are, after all, the firms that govern the buyer-driven global commodity chains that comprise the apparel industry's production networks and that establish the competitive terrain within the industry—to ensure decent wages for workers in the industry. Within the apparel industry, global buyers (brands and major retailers) exert the predominant influence over the organization of production systems by setting prices and determining where production takes place. These practices decisively impact the scope for suppliers to pay a living wage. Scholars have found that brands orchestrate interfirm competition with supply chains, thereby forcing suppliers to provide goods at prices that are below actual production costs, leading firms to recoup these costs by driving down workers' wages (Vaughan-Whitehead 2010). If brands and retailers would share just a fraction of their profits, millions of workers and families could be lifted out of poverty.

Central to the demands of the AFW is the need for concerted efforts by brands and retailers to address the issue of unfair pricing as an important first step toward the implementation of a living wage in the apparel industry. Global sourcing companies pay approximately the same prices to their supplier factories in Asia: around 25% of the retail price. Because apparel workers' wages comprise a very small proportion of the final retail price for clothes—around 1% to 2%—substantial wage raises could be achieved without increasing retail prices.

Since the AFW was unveiled in October 2009, it has gained recognition as a credible benchmark for a living wage in the apparel industry. It has become a point of reference for scholarly living-wage debates, it has been adopted as a living-wage benchmark by the multi-stakeholder forum, the Fair Wear Foundation, and it is a point of reference for brand-level associations such as the Fair Labor Association. In addition, the AFW has been adopted by a few brands as a comparative benchmark for wage analyses.

For its part, the AFWA has developed the Asia Brand Bargaining Group (ABBG), consisting of Asian unions, to enable greater coordination and regional bargaining that complements national priorities and struggles. The ABBG has four common demands for the welfare of garment workers in Asia: a living wage, freedom of association, abolition/regulation of contract labor, and an end to gender-based discrimination. The AFWA has conducted four National People's Tribunals—in Cambodia, India, Indonesia, and Sri Lanka—on the issue of living wages and working conditions in global garment industry supply chains, revealing troubling deficits in labor standards and dangerously low wages. For example, in Cambodia, the mass fainting by women workers was clearly attributed to malnutrition and poverty wages. The juries in all four tribunals have unanimously recommended that living wages need to be paid immediately. In terms of its social impacts, the implementation of the AFW would help decrease the gender gap in pay by raising the wages of lowest-paid workers in the apparel industry. Worldwide, women comprise the vast majority of the garment-manufacturing workforce, and they face systemic obstacles to upward mobility in the sector.

A Regional Approach to Labor Standards

As a policy intervention aimed at reducing poverty by raising wages and strengthening labor protections, the AFW is unique in its emphasis on leveling the playing field across a major apparel-producing region. It does not rely on the governments of newly industrializing countries to operate in a way that is out of step with other economies in the region, and it does not rely on corporate self-regulation, which has proven difficult to maintain in an industry characterized by the decentralization of production. Instead, it proposes to shift the paradigm of labor standards enforcement by instituting a regional policy that is sensitive to conditions within countries while also setting a floor under wages, thereby limiting the downward drag on working standards that is produced by global labor arbitrage.

Crucially, this is an intervention that appears to be viable in terms of garment prices and the dynamics of competition within the industry. Pollin, Burns, and Heintz (2004) have suggested that even substantial increases in the wages of workers engaged in apparel production would result in minor increases in the price of final products, perhaps as little as 1% to 3%. Furthermore, as Weller and Zucconi (2008) have argued, enforcement of labor standards can create a virtuous circle of economic development: rising wages allow low-paid workers to increase their consumption, thereby stimulating domestic demand, which in turn creates jobs locally. In short, increasing the wages for garment workers is a strategy to reduce poverty, redistribute a greater share of the gains from global production to workers in lower-income countries while stimulating local economic development, and institute a more sustainable wage floor while reinforcing the importance of labor protections (Merk 2009). Moreover, there is a possibility that such a strategy could be "scaled up" to include other major garment-producing regions, such as Africa, the Caribbean, Central America, and Eastern Europe, thereby further taking the wages of the lowest-paid workers in the apparel industry out of competition and urging producers in the industry to make in situ investments that improve worker health and safety as well as productivity.

HOLDING RETAILERS AND SUPPLIERS ACCOUNTABLE FOR LABOR STANDARDS

Beginning in the 1980s, a series of changes swept through the retail sector in the United States and elsewhere, forever altering the relationship between retailers and their suppliers. "Big box" stores achieved market dominance, their large sales volumes enabling them to undercut competitors' prices based on increasing economies of scale. Advances in communications technologies allowed order volumes to be more closely calibrated to consumer demand, and large retailers responded by requiring new forms of flexibility, responsiveness, and cost cutting from supplier firms. The advent of just-in-time production and logistics systems as an industry best practice meant that suppliers would have to adapt to the demanding uncertainties of fluctuating consumer markets or risk exclusion from retail supply chains. As retailers' expectations of suppliers came to include not just the timely production and delivery of goods but also cost minimization and improved quality control, the relationships between retailers and firms in their expanding supply chains grew more complex and, paradoxically perhaps, even closer. Large retailers became price-setters in a range of consumer-goods markets, a leadership position that was achieved through the market dominance of the largest retail firms and the influence they now exert over their suppliers.

Walmart, the largest retailer in the world, provides an example of the changes that have been under way in the sector. Walmart maintains ties with approximately 60,000 supplier firms. The company's "Plus One" initiative requires that each of these suppliers reduce product prices, increase quality, or increase speed of delivery year after year. As the pre-eminent retailer, Walmart is able to push such demands through its subcontracting chain, thereby progressively narrowing the margins of its suppliers. Supplier firms have responded by outsourcing production activities, automating manufacturing processes, reducing labor costs by hiring contingent workers, and, in some cases, violating employment and labor laws as a means of maintaining competitiveness and profitability. A report by the National Employment Law Project succinctly summarizes the relationship between Walmart and other large retailers and the spread of substandard labor conditions in US firms:

> Walmart's policy of enforcing ever-lower prices implicates wages and working conditions throughout Walmart's supply chain. … As Walmart and its big-box retail peers have grown, they have achieved a level of dominance that affects—indeed, sometimes dictates—their suppliers' own pricing, profit margins, and operational decisions. (Cho et al. 2012: 6)

The proliferation of subcontracting chains in retail and other sectors presents a challenge to workplace monitoring of labor standards, particularly in highly competitive industries with narrow operating margins because it is here that incentives to violate workplace protections are greatest. Lead firms may indeed be dictating the pricing and operational decisions of their suppliers, yet they also strive to maintain the appearance of an arm's-length relationship with these very same suppliers and the decisions they make. Increasingly, however, workers' rights organizations are bringing pressure to bear on lead firms to demand they use their market power and influence to raise employment standards within supply chains. Arguing that price-setting and other operational decisions within supply chains are driven first and foremost by the demands of lead firms, workers' rights organizations are seeking to hold these firms accountable for violations that occur within the production and logistics spheres. The C.J.'s Seafood campaign of the National Guestworker Alliance (NGA), a US-based workers' rights organization, is an example of an emergent form of supply-chain organizing that seeks to leverage the influence of lead firms to improve working conditions within supplier facilities.

The Campaign at C.J.'s Seafood

C.J.'s Seafood was a supplier to Walmart's Sam's Club division, providing the discount retailer with crawfish tails that had been cooked, peeled, and frozen. C.J.'s Seafood sold approximately 85% of its production output to Walmart. Located in Breaux Bridge, Louisiana, a small city that bills itself as the "crawfish capital of the world," C.J.'s Seafood employed between 50 and 60 workers, many of whom were migrants from northern Mexico. The workers were recruited through the H-2B visa program, a temporary worker program that allows companies in the United States to hire foreign nationals to fill nonagricultural jobs. To be eligible for the program, employers must demonstrate that they face a labor shortage and are unable to hire a sufficient number of US workers to fill jobs, and that in hiring guestworkers, they will not undercut the wages of US workers in similar fields. In fiscal year 2017, the US government authorized the issuance of 66,000 H-2B visas.

C.J.'s Seafood had been meeting its demand for seasonal workers through the H-2B program for many years, hiring guestworkers for periods ranging from a month or two to six months or more. Many workers would return to the company year after year. The work was demanding and the pay was low, but at least employment was consistent and bearable, if only short term. Then a change in company management altered conditions on the shop floor. Workers reported being required to work shifts lasting 16 hours to as many as 24 hours, with no overtime pay; new surveillance equipment was installed to monitor not only the workplace but workers' residences as well; workers were frequently locked in the production facility; and threats of deportation became commonplace, as were threats of physical violence if workers did not comply with a supervisor's orders to work faster (Eidelson 2013). Faced with untenable working conditions and growing uncertainty about whether the company would continue to employ them, a group of workers approached management with a list of modest demands: provide workers an adequate lunch break, remove a supervisor who was threatening workers, and turn off some of the surveillance cameras. The owner refused to comply. Following subsequent threats of violence against workers' families in Mexico by company management, eight of the workers went on strike (Eidelson 2013).

The strike at C.J.'s Seafood was notable for several reasons. First, guestworkers generally are reluctant to report workplace violations out of fear of employer retaliation. Loss of current employment, and with it the ability to legally reside and work in the United States, as well as the risk of being blacklisted by future employers and labor recruiters, has a chilling effect on the willingness of guestworkers to come forward to contest labor standards violations. Yet, in this case, that is exactly what workers did—confronting company management directly, and when unsuccessful in effecting changes in the workplace, seeking the support of NGA and government authorities.

To stabilize the workers' leadership committee at C.J.'s Seafood, NGA successfully secured U visas for workers, a nonimmigrant visa for victims of certain crimes who have suffered mental or physical abuse and are helpful to law enforcement or government officials in the investigation or prosecution of criminal activity. In advocating for the U visa, NGA successfully reframed old-style workplace coercion (threats of retaliation, physical violence, economic hardship) as management's efforts at obstruction of justice through worker intimidation.

Second, the campaign exposed flagrant violations of workplace laws within the Walmart supply chain. The NGA filed complaints against C.J.'s Seafood with the US Department of Labor and the Equal Employment Opportunity Commission. The alliance also notified Walmart of the charges, in part because Walmart's own contracting standards prohibit suppliers from using forced labor or requiring employees to work more than 60 hours in a week. Furthermore, an audit by NGA of US Walmart suppliers that employ guest-workers found that 12 of 18 had been cited by the US Department of Labor for violations related to workplace safety and health conditions or wage and hour practices, had been accused of discrimination and violations of the right to organize, or both (National Guestworker Alliance, no date).

Through NGA, the workers at C.J.'s Seafood launched a broad-based campaign built around worker organizing. In so doing, its activities reached far beyond this particular employer, targeting consumers and forcing Walmart to uphold its stated principles pertaining to corporate social responsibility. The campaign centered on Walmart and its position atop a vast supplier network. Arguing (1) that the company wielded enough influence and authority to ensure labor standards compliance among its suppliers and (2) that Walmart was profiting by awarding supply contracts stipulating operating margins so narrow that they essentially compelled suppliers to violate workplace standards as they strove to meet exacting price and delivery conditions, NGA sought to "move up the value chain" to the business entity that was responsible for structuring competitive conditions for its suppliers. The strike by workers at C.J.'s Seafood was designed to raise public awareness of this problem.

An online petition urging Walmart to terminate its relations with the seafood supplier was launched, receiving 149,750 signatures. The NGA also enlisted the Worker Rights Consortium, a university-based monitoring group, to investigate allegations of workplace violations at C.J.'s Seafood (Worker Rights Consortium 2012). Scott Nova, executive director of the Worker Rights Consortium, summarized the findings of the investigation:

> It's one of the worst workplaces we ever encountered anywhere. … The extreme lengths of the shifts people were required to work, the employer's brazenness in violating wage laws, the extent of the psychological abuse the workers faced and the threats of violence against their families—that combination made it one of the most egregious workplaces we've examined, whether here or overseas." (quoted in Greenhouse 2012)

Finding that the supplier had in fact violated a number of Walmart's own supplier standards, including wage requirements, the retailer suspended its contract with C.J.'s Seafood (Plume 2012).

The US Department of Labor concluded its own investigation and ordered C.J.'s Seafood to pay $214,000 for wage and hour violations, and it levied a

$34,000 fine for safety violations. The department also found that the company had violated laws on the use of temporary foreign workers under the H-2B program by misrepresenting its need for such workers, including the number needed, and by not paying them the required wage. Labor Department officials determined that the company owed $76,608 in back pay to 73 workers for paying less than the minimum wage, not paying overtime for working more than 40 hours in a week, and illegally deducting wages for items required to do the job, including gloves, hairnets, and aprons. The Labor Department also determined that C.J.'s Seafood was liable for an additional $70,014 in liquidated damages, $32,120 in civil damages for overtime violations, and $35,000 for knowingly violating H-2B visa rules (Greenhouse 2012).

The campaign did not end there. A fundamental imbalance of power remained between Walmart and the workers employed by the tens of thousands of suppliers that produce the goods sold by the retailer. Through NGA, workers at C.J.'s Seafood proposed that a forum be created so that workers could bargain directly with Walmart over the contractual terms governing suppliers. They also sought to join other workers in the Walmart supply chain to form a workers' committee that would monitor supplier practices and the contracting process under which they all were employed.

In addition to these proposals, the NGA sought to undermine a key source of employer intimidation and retaliation through the adoption of an anti-forced labor accord. Arguing that employment at workplaces that violate employment standards in itself constitutes a prima facie case of forced labor, in large part because if the extent of worker coercion is so great that employees cannot bring those workplace practices to light (whether because of threats of deportation or other forms of extra-economic coercion, such as the use of law enforcement or immigration authorities to intimidate workers), workers' rights under the 13th Amendment of the US Constitution had been violated. Similar to a code of conduct, the anti-forced labor accord was modeled on the highly regarded Accord on Fire and Building Safety in Bangladesh that stipulates that wherever safety issues are identified, retailers will ensure that repairs are undertaken, that sufficient monies will be made available for the repairs, and that workers at affected factories will continue to be paid a salary during the time that repairs are being made. The anti-forced labor accord instructs suppliers to become signatories; it challenges temporary rehire provisions (which are often used as a form of retaliation and workplace discipline); it contains anti-blacklisting provisions, including calling for the presumptive rehiring of workers for seasonal jobs through a private contract between retailers and NGA; and it puts in place dispute-resolution procedures through a board comprised of US worker and employer advocates.

CONCLUSION: THE SHIFTING GEOGRAPHIES OF LABOR ORGANIZING

Global economic integration is expanding access to new and emerging markets, and the increasing ability of firms to enter into relationships with suppliers operating in these markets has contributed to downward pressures on product prices—and on wages and working conditions. In an increasingly integrated world, countries where low wages are prevalent and labor rights are widely disregarded can be standard setters that negatively impact industry dynamics and employment conditions. They offer mobile capital an escape route when labor unrest erupts or when regulatory measures increase the costs of doing business. In terms of global regulatory standards, they also send market signals, so to speak, to other countries that are considering ways to strengthen labor protections. As a result, low wages and substandard working conditions serve to restrain wage demands in both developed and developing economies.

The problems facing workers in this era of globalization defy simple solutions. In many low-wage industries, workers' bargaining positions have been undermined, and the ability and willingness of national governments to effectively enforce worker protections has been eroded. New sources of leverage will be needed if workers are to realize greater economic gains from globalization.

In this time of global economic uncertainty, the organizing and advocacy efforts of workers' rights organizations represent some of the primary defenses against the downloading of the costs and risks inherent in a volatile economy onto low-wage workforces, and they are an important means through which widening inequalities can be redressed. Transnational strategies are central to these efforts because they attend to two key dimensions of the current global order—the increasing interconnectedness of product markets and the growing interpenetration of labor markets by globalizing production networks. In this context, advocacy to improve labor standards in a given country is necessary but not sufficient. Transnational strategies to create new labor market institutions and norms, and to develop regional approaches to raising labor standards, are urgently needed.

Devising new sources of leverage will require experimentation, and the list of possible strategies is long. This concluding section identifies a few emerging approaches that are being developed by workers' rights organizations, labor unions, and advocacy groups.

Setting Regional Labor Standards

Globalizing production networks extend across jurisdictions, linking countries and spanning regions. The geographical extent of these networks, and with it the ability of lead firms to shift production from country to country, challenges the traditional structure of national employment and labor laws. Reducing the threat of exit that is implicit in global value chains, as well as narrowing the scope for practicing global labor arbitrage, requires regional approaches to standard setting. The Asia Floor Wage is an example of such an approach (Bhattacharjee, Gupta, and Luce 2009; Merk 2009). By instituting living wages across supplier networks, it seeks to set standards across a major apparel-producing region.

Supply-Chain Organizing

It is generally understood that firms in the upper tiers of global supply chains are able to monitor their suppliers and exert pressure on those that are violating labor standards. It is also understood that lead firms benefit from the unscrupulous practices of suppliers that violate labor standards, practices that hold down labor costs, accelerate delivery times from points of production to the marketplace, and provide production flexibilities that allow lead firms to rapidly change product offerings and fluctuate order volumes. In the unequal relationship between lead firms and suppliers, the former outsources risks to the latter, which in turn negatively impacts labor conditions farther down the supply chain. Supply-chain organizing seeks to increase the transparency of contracting and labor practices across production networks, to make employment relationships explicit and subject to enforcement oversight, and to hold lead firms responsible for the practices of supplier firms that violate labor standards, often by extending contractual obligations to supplier firms. In addition to efforts to hold lead firms accountable for supplier practices, supply-chain organizing targets "downstream" links in production networks where worker organizing has been actively dissuaded, providing a means for collective bargaining and for redressing labor standards violations (Quan 2008).

Developing Alternative Forms of Labor Market Intermediation

A variety of labor contractors—recruitment firms, temporary staffing agencies, labor brokers, and other intermediaries—are involved in the recruitment, hiring, and placement of workers in a range of service, manufacturing, agricultural, and construction industries. These intermediaries can be directly involved in setting labor market norms and structuring employment pathways into industries and occupations (Fudge and Strauss 2014; Guevarra 2010; Martin 2017; Tyner 2003). Workers may be employed under a variety of employment arrangements, including as guestworkers, temp workers, contracted labor, pieceworkers, direct-hire employees, and on-call workers. Labor contracting can have significant implications for the enforcement of labor standards. It may (1) obscure employment relationships and reduce accountability by creating uncertainty regarding the entity that is the employer of record under national labor laws; (2) allow worksite employers to establish an arm's-length relationship with their employees, thereby facilitating the misclassification of employees and reducing workers' recourse against employers that violate labor standards; and (3) complicate government enforcement of labor standards, especially when "fly by night" contractors shutter and then reopen operations when enforcement investigations reveal workplace violations.

Alternative staffing agencies operated by nonprofit organizations (Carré, Herranz, and Dorado 2014) and worker centers established by workers' rights groups (Fine 2006; Visser 2017) can inject needed transparency into opaque contingent labor markets. Because they are not governed by profit motives, these labor market intermediaries can devote energies toward improving workers' earnings and monitoring worksite conditions. Worker centers, in particular, can provide a mechanism through which workers can exercise collective decision making and standard setting in contingent labor markets, thereby partially rebalancing power asymmetries in job markets dominated by labor contractors and other employment brokers, or where processes of informalization have undermined labor standards. Through the use of hiring halls, such as those developed to regulate day-labor markets in the United States, worker centers can establish and enforce minimum-wage rates while also regularizing the employment of temporary workers (Theodore 2015; Theodore, Meléndez, and Valenzuela 2009). Such interventions help meet employer demand for contingently employed workers while also placing a floor under wages and working conditions in job markets characterized by rampant violations of labor standards.

Extending Labor Rights to Migrant Workers

Even in cases, such as the United States, where all workers, regardless of citizenship and immigration status, are covered by labor protections, the status of unauthorized migrants exposes them to heightened vulnerabilities, including employer reprisals when they assert their rights. Employers in many low-wage industries exploit undocumented migrants' vulnerabilities, using their precarious status to pay below-market wages and violate basic labor standards (Bernhardt, Spiller, and Theodore 2013; Wills et al. 2010). In addition to compounding the hardships faced by workers, exploitation of migrant workers can have far-reaching impacts on competitive pressures in these industries. As greater numbers of employers pursue low-road employment practices, competitive dynamics can shift, rewarding low-road firms with increasing profits and expanding market share while placing employers that "play by the rules" at a distinct disadvantage. Extending labor rights to all workers, regardless of citizenship—in law and in practice—is a crucial step toward raising the floor on wages and working conditions in low-wage industries and reducing the scope for employer violations of labor standards.

The spatially variegated character of economies is such that any attempt to raise standards for workers will be prosecuted across a highly uneven institutional landscape (see Peck and Theodore 2007; Pike, Rodríguez-Pose, and Tomaney 2014). The reach of governmental regulatory authorities, the strength of worker organizations, the nature and timing of corporate responses to enforcement efforts and organizing campaigns, and the will of government officials to hold businesses accountable for employment practices are among the key factors that will shape the institutional terrain across which the defense of worker protections will be undertaken. This is not simply a question of a north–south binary borne out of the vast differentials in market opportunities and institutional capacities that exist between the privileged economies of the Global North (with their lead firms that typically govern global production networks) and those relatively disadvantaged economies of the South that often are on the receiving end of degraded employment systems. The internationalization of supply chains is remaking connections and conditions in and between economic spaces, and arguably few if any economic zones around the world are left untouched by these processes. Studies of capitalist variegation point to the necessity for analyses of the opportunity structures for pro-worker initiatives to be attentive to the relational geographies of contemporary capitalist formations, both at the macro and micro levels. Corporate exploitation of the profit-making opportunities afforded by uneven development and the unevenness of institutional capacities—conditions that so often are mutually reinforcing—requires that worker protections be rescaled (as the Asia Floor Wage and supply-chain organizing campaigns seek to do), economic rights be extended (the immigration status of workers), and alternative organizations be created to intervene in local labor markets on behalf of workers in precarious and otherwise substandard jobs. Taming globalization through these emergent strategies will be crucial for defending workers' rights and reducing global and domestic inequalities.

ACKNOWLEDGMENTS

Thanks to Anannya Bhattacharjee, Laine Romeo-Alston, JJ Rosenbaum, and Saket Soni for their comments on the arguments presented here. Thanks also to Steven Pitts for his careful reading of an earlier draft of this chapter. Responsibility for errors or omissions remains mine.

ENDNOTES

[1] This section is based on Merk (2009).

REFERENCES

Bernhardt, Annette, Michael W. Spiller, and Nik Theodore. 2013. "Employers Gone Rogue: Explaining Industry Variation in Violations of Workplace Laws." *ILR Review* 66 (4): 808–832.

Bhattacharjee, Anannya, Sarita Gupta, and Stephanie Luce. 2009. "Raising the Floor: The Movement for a Living Wage in Asia." *New Labor Forum* 18 (3): 72–81.

Carré, Francoise, Joaquín Herranz Jr., and Silvia Dorado. 2014. "Alternative Staffing Organizations as Innovations in Labour Market Intermediation." In *Management and Organization of Temporary Agency Work*, edited by Bas Koene, Christina Garsten, and Nathalie Galias, pp. 174–187. New York, NY: Routledge.

Cho, Eunice Hyunhye, Anastasia Christman, Maurice Emsellem, Catherine K. Ruckelshaus, and Rebecca Smith. 2012. *Chain of Greed: How Wal-Mart's Domestic Outsourcing Produces Everyday Low Wages and Poor Working Conditions for Warehouse Workers.* New York, NY: National Employment Law Project.

Christopherson, Susan, and Nathan Lillie. 2005. "Neither Global nor Standard: Corporate Strategies in the New Era of Labor Standards." *Environment and Planning A* 37 (11): 1919–1938.

Compa, Lance, and Tashia Hinchliffe-Darricarrere. 1995. "Enforcing International Labor Rights Through Corporate Codes of Conduct." *Columbia Journal of Transnational Law* 33: 663–689.

Cowgill, Matt, and Phu Huynh. 2016. "Weak Minimum Wage Compliance in Asia's Garment Industry." *Asia–Pacific Garment and Footwear Sector Research Note* 5: 1–8. Bangkok, Thailand: ILO Regional Office for Asia and Pacific.

Dicken, Peter. 2015. *Global Shift: Mapping the Changing Contours of the World Economy,* 7th ed. New York, NY: Guilford Press.

Eidelson, Josh. 2013. "Guest Workers as Bellwether." *Dissent.* http://bit.ly/2DDE2dP

Esbenshade, Jill. 2013. "A Review of Private Regulation: Codes and Monitoring in the Apparel Industry." *Sociology Compass* 6 (7): 541–556.

Fine, Janice. 2006. *Worker Centers: Organizing Workers at the Edge of the Dream.* Ithaca, NY: Cornell University Press.

Ford, Michele, and Michael Gillan. 2016. "Employment Relations and the State in Southeast Asia." *Journal of Industrial Relations* 58 (2): 167–182.

Fudge, Judy, and Kendra Strauss. 2014. *Temporary Work, Agencies, and Unfree Labour: Insecurity in the New World of Work.* London, UK: Routledge.

Gereffi, Gary. 1996. "Commodity Chains and Regional Divisions of Labor in East Asia." *Journal of Asian Business* 12: 75–112.

Greenhouse, Steven. 2012 (Jul. 24). "C.J.'s Seafood Fined for Labor Abuses." *New York Times.* https://nyti.ms/2rXHj4a

Guevarra, Anna Romina. 2010. *Marketing Dreams, Marketing Heroes: The Transnational Labor Brokering of Filipino Workers.* New Brunswick, NJ: Rutgers University Press.

Kelly, Philip F. 2002. "Spaces of Labour Control: Comparative Perspectives from Southeast Asia." *Transactions of the Institute of British Geographers* 27 (4): 395–411.

Luce, Stephanie. 2009. *Raising Wages on a Regional Level: The Asia Floor Wage.* New Delhi, India: Asia Floor Wage Alliance.

Martin, Philip. 2017. *Merchants of Labor: Recruiters and International Labor Migration.* Oxford, UK: Oxford University Press.

Merk, Jeroen. 2009. *Stitching a Decent Wage Across Borders: The Asia Floor Wage Campaign*. New Delhi, India: Asia Floor Wage Alliance.

National Guestworker Alliance (NGA). No date. *Summary of Preliminary Audit of U.S. Walmart Suppliers That Employ Guestworkers*. New Orleans, LA: National Guestworker Alliance.

Peck, Jamie, and Nik Theodore. 2007. "Variegated Capitalism." *Progress in Human Geography* 31 (6): 731–772.

Pike, Andy, Andres Rodríguez-Pose, and John Tomaney. 2014. "Local and Regional Development in the Global North and South." *Progress in Development Studies* 14 (1): 21–30.

Plume, Karl. 2012 (Jun. 30). "Wal-Mart Suspends Louisiana Seafood Supplier." *Chicago Tribune*. http://trib.in/2DD5atx

Pollin, Robert, Justine Burns, and James Heintz. 2004. "Global Apparel Production and Sweatshop Labour: Can Raising Retail Prices Finance Living Wages?" *Cambridge Journal of Economics* 28 (2): 153–171.

Quan, Katie. 2008. "Use of Global Value Chains by Labor Organizers." *Competition & Change* 12 (1): 89–104.

Theodore, Nik. 2015. "Rebuilding the House of Labor: Unions and Worker Centers in the Residential Construction Industry." *WorkingUSA: The Journal of Labor & Society* 18 (1): 59–76.

Theodore, Nik, Edwin Meléndez, and Abel Valenzuela. 2009. "Worker Centers: Defending Labor Standards for Migrant Workers in the Informal Economy." *International Journal of Manpower* 30 (5): 422–436.

Tyner, James A. 2003. "Globalization and the Geography of Labor Recruitment Firms in the Philippines." *Geography Research Forum* 23: 78–95.

Vaughan-Whitehead, Daniel. 2010. Fair Wages: Strengthening Corporate Social Responsibility. Northampton, MA: Edward Elgar.

Visser, M. Anne. 2017. "A Floor to Exploitation? Social Economy Organizations at the Edge of a Restructuring Economy." *Work, Employment and Society* 31 (5) 782–799.

Weller, Christian E., and Stephen Zucconi. 2008. *Labor Rights Can Be Good Trade Policy: An Analysis of U.S. Trade with Less Industrialized Economies with Weak or Strong Labor Rights*. Washington, DC: Center for American Progress.

Werner, Marion. 2016. *Global Displacements: The Making of Uneven Development in the Caribbean*. Oxford, UK: Wiley.

Werner International. 2015. *2014 World Textile Industry Labor Cost Comparison*. Herndon, VA: Werner International.

Wills, Jane, Kavita Datta, Yara Evans, Joanna Herbert, Jon June, and Cathy McIlwaine. 2010. *Global Cities at Work: New Migrant Divisions of Labour*. London, UK: Pluto Press.

Worker Rights Consortium. 2012 (Jun. 20). *Worker Rights Consortium Assessment: C.J.'s Seafood/ Wal-Mart Stores, Inc. (Breaux Bridge, LA). Findings and Recommendations*. Washington, DC: Worker Rights Consortium.

CHAPTER 16

Mobilizing High-Road Employers and Private Sector Strategies: National Domestic Workers Alliance

PALAK SHAH

National Domestic Workers Alliance

Leydis has worked as a nanny for more than 15 years in New York City. She gets up every day at 6 A.M. to get her son ready for school. During the day, she nurtures, protects, and educates her employer's children. Like many domestic workers, Leydis felt her work was important and deserved more respect than she received. But she didn't know what she could do to change the ways she was treated, or that she even had rights.

Then she joined the National Domestic Workers Alliance (NDWA). NDWA creates the space for people like Leydis to step into their leadership, find confidence through connecting with their peers, and receive support as they advocate for respect and fairness. Now she spends her free time leading trainings for other domestic workers, to help them see the sense of power that coming together offers—the power to achieve dignity on the job.

Leydis is one of the millions of nannies, housecleaners, and caregivers who work in our homes—and her story is not unique. When the private home is a workplace, and workers are isolated from their peers, the balance of power is severely skewed. Domestic work is typically characterized by poverty-level wages, without basic employment benefits such as health insurance or sick pay, usually without any tax withholding, no retirement benefits, and little to no control over work schedule. In essence, the workforce we count on to care for our families and homes cannot care for their own families as professionals in this industry.

THE ORIGINAL GIG ECONOMY WORKERS

The domestic work industry, both because it functions in an informal and often "off the books" context and because it has been systematically excluded from basic labor protections, is often compared to the "Wild West." There are no standards or guidelines; one never knows what one might get in terms of employment conditions. As a result, some workers have extremely positive experiences and others are met with human trafficking, sexual assault, and modern-day slavery-type conditions. And everything in between.

These conditions used to be seen as extremely unusual, at the margins and edges of our economy. Today, domestic work serves as a canary in the coal mine to the new economy. The conditions that have always defined domestic work—low wages, long or unpredictable hours, lack of job security and access to benefits—have come to define more segments of the US labor force. As the gig economy grows, more and more of the American workforce faces conditions like those domestic workers have faced for generations.

The movement to win rights and protections for domestic workers, then, becomes almost an "advance team" for the labor movement. New strategies will be needed for the labor movement to continue to be relevant and effective in improving working conditions for increasing numbers of nontraditional or independent workers. Many of the strategies that have been tested by the domestic worker movement can serve as models. Certainly if the labor movement wants to effectively respond to the changing nature of work, it will have to adapt its strategies accordingly.

Cleaning, food and grocery delivery, getting a ride, walking a dog, and performing tasks such as assembling Ikea furniture—these are all gigs that can be ordered on an app with the click of a button and sometimes even completed without the customer having to do any more than that. Platform companies funded by Silicon Valley venture capital connect worker with customer, minimizing the tasks of the customer and reducing the role of the employer. The challenges presented to workers in this new environment are significant and often misunderstood.

Technology has created new means of connecting, finding employment, and matching qualified workers with employment opportunities. While there are many positive associations with this new technology, in too many instances these new opportunities are without the advantages or benefits associated with stable employment, increasing the vulnerability and economic insecurity of the workforce. As technology makes it easy to aggregate people in need of a service and those willing to provide the service, workers find themselves parceling together gig work outside of important protections provided by employee status.

This new generation of workers is assigned to gigs without a manager to assist them when they have questions or problems with the gig. Work hours can be unpredictable and schedules changed last minute, leaving workers vulnerable to loss of income. Fees can be deducted from a paycheck by an algorithm, leaving workers out of pocket and with no clear path for recourse. Workplace safety becomes more difficult to enforce through an app; the gig economy can be particularly dangerous for women, who are disproportionately more vulnerable to violence and abuse.

Workers accrue even more expenses, providing the supplies and equipment they need to complete each job as independent contractors. While the gig economy often attracts workers in need of a flexible schedule, gig economy workers have discovered that the trade-off includes all the other important forms of security that traditional employment offers. Benefits can't be accrued because no one is taking responsibility for being an employer, even when you're working 40 hours or more per week. The customer is shielded by the platform company, the platform company is shielded by the technology, and the technology is shielded by doing only what it was designed to do, in a circular "not my responsibility" way for the actual quality of work—and quality of life for the worker.

The gig economy has been most successful in markets where the extra layer can disproportionately add value. Transport has always struggled with inefficiency. Technology enabled the easy identification of passenger and driver locations in order to match rides for greatest efficiency. The domestic work sector—work done inside homes such as cleaning, childcare, and caregiving—has historically been an informal market, operating behind the closed doors of people's homes. Platform companies have aggregated this workforce at a scale that hasn't existed before now, with apps that can get a cleaner to your home the next day or a babysitter recommended by your community to your home the same day you request them, or that can help you screen a caregiver for your elderly or sick family member. Domestic and care work is now available at the push of a button, and a workforce that has historically been disaggregated and informal is now aggregated and online.

Without question, many of the same challenges exist for domestic workers in the gig economy. However, for our movement, this new aggregation also creates unprecedented opportunities. As a workforce, domestic workers have always faced extraordinary challenges to improving their working conditions. Working behind the closed doors of private residences, usually with a 1:1 worker to employer ratio, domestic workers are not only disaggregated but invisible to most forms of data. There is no registry or place where employment is documented. These and other realities render traditional methods of building worker power, such as collective bargaining, almost irrelevant. The structural challenges of organizing a disaggregated, informal workforce has forced the domestic worker movement to be entrepreneurial and experimental, discovering nontraditional methods to raise standards of work, including leveraging this new tech-based aggregation to both raise standards and organize.

A FRESH LOOK AT OPPORTUNITIES AND THREATS OF THE GIG ECONOMY TO GOOD WORK

The gig economy has grown so rapidly and reached so many sectors that it has now fundamentally changed the way we think about getting what we want. Need a ride somewhere? Reach for your cell phone (or other mobile device) and hail a car just by clicking a button. Had a party on the weekend and don't want to clean your house? Just request a cleaner online, and they can even get the job done while you're out. Need someone to walk your dog? No problem; they'll pick her up before the end of the day. Tasks that once were burdensome are now easily outsourced, quickly and conveniently, by parsing them into gigs and creating marketplaces where they can be allocated to gig workers willing to do the work.

Several factors have contributed to the rapid rise of the gig economy. First, as digital technology advanced, we witnessed the rise of automation; many tasks that required simple calculations or repetition were easily replaced by software. An algorithm can assign a common task to a worker with matching skills, manage work schedules for workers performing many tasks in a day in multiple locations. or process payments from customers, disburse payments to workers, and collect fees. Even collecting job information and requirements from customers can be automated with a responsive Web form.

Second, digital technology gave birth to mobile technology, which created the potential for a degree of efficiency previously impossible. Have a new job request near to where a worker is currently finishing a job? Notify her via the app on her mobile device and have her go directly there when she's done. Need to manage a workforce where the workplace is private homes and there is no central HQ for workers to regroup? Simply coordinate them via the app on their mobile devices, dispatching them to jobs, collecting feedback on completed tasks, and managing all HR requests online. Suddenly, workers can be always available and work from anywhere—and, while the workforce remained disaggregated offline, it was very much aggregated online.

Third, online platforms that serve as marketplaces for gigs are multiplying, and there are now platforms for anything ranging from design work to translation work to buying a home-cooked meal from your neighbor. Online platforms have not only aggregated workforces, they have reduced the startup costs—such as marketing your services—for earning money in various jobs that can be done from home or in someone else's home, creating work opportunities by reducing the barrier to entry. In some cases, the rise of online platforms has shifted a workforce online that previously operated offline only, such as the nannies who usually found work by word of mouth but can now be listed online with recommendations by past clients. In other cases, it has attracted workers to types of work that have a newly reduced barrier to entry such as drivers for transportation network companies such as Uber or Lyft that allow people to earn money using the car and driver's license they already have.

The rise of online platforms has not only changed how we get what we need and want, it's also changing how we think about work. Where does work start and end when we can work from anywhere or when we can log on or off at the click of a button on our phone? Who are we working for when work is assigned by an algorithm for a customer we don't have a direct relationship with? Who is responsible for the safety and well-being of workers when there is no manager or even a phone number to call when a worker needs assistance. When work is flexible, how can a worker be sure she will earn what she needs to pay her bills? Is a worker really "her own boss" when the work is prescribed by the platform company? When no one is responsible for the worker, how are we making sure that the work we are creating is good work?

The future of work is more automated, more flexible, and more mobile but also more vulnerable, less predictable, and with less support for workers. More and more, the future of work is looking like work of the past: piecemeal gigs without the worker protections that were so hard won in the early 20th century. Without intervention, technology will continue us on this path where the worker is inserted into a calculation that connects supply with demand rather than as a person to be invested in and protected—both to benefit business and to benefit society,

Rather than interrupt technology's disruption of work, we should be intervening so that it automates the parts of work that then allow us to work less and live more. We should be using technology to help us maximize our income through efficiency rather than minimize it. We should be using technology to help us work in a way that fits our lifestyle rather than dictates our lifestyle. And we should be using technology to build power among those for whom it has been most difficult and the usual methods ineffective. The future of work will be affected by technology, but how that affects the worker is up to us.

THE TECH-BASED CARE AND CLEANING MARKETPLACE

Domestic work has always been challenged with workplace safety issues, vulnerability to loss of wages, no recourse for issues with employers, and worker isolation. Domestic work via online platforms hasn't solved these problems, and in many cases it has simply added a digital layer to the issue. Some experiences by members of NDWA describe the challenges experienced.

Rachelle started working for an online gig economy platform that connected cleaners with people who need their homes cleaned, after a car accident left her unable to stand for the long periods required for her job in cosmetology. She wanted flexible hours, and some of her customers were kind. But not every customer is kind; one customer told Rachelle that she had to monitor her while she was in her house—to make sure she didn't touch anything—because Rachelle was Black and the customer didn't know her. "I was so uncomfortable, I didn't know what to do with myself. If I walked in or out of the bathroom I had to let her know. If I was taking out the garbage, I had to let her know. It was very uncomfortable."

Despite being subjected to such racism—which would be a clear violation of anti-discrimination laws—Rachelle completed the job so well that the customer asked her if she would come back. Rachelle politely declined. Still, the customer requested her services again via the app, for three more jobs. When Rachelle declined the jobs, she was penalized with a $40 fee by the company for refusing the job. Rachelle reached out to the company to explain her reason for refusing the job and they returned her fee to her—but canceled the remainder of her jobs for that week. Not only was Rachelle not protected from discriminatory treatment in her workplace, she was punished for protecting herself, with real financial consequences.

Another domestic worker, Angela, cleans for a gig economy platform company. While she was attracted to the idea of being her own boss, she was concerned about the risk of entering a stranger's home without knowing anything about them. "You don't know what's waiting for you behind the door," she explains. "We should have something that says that this customer is 'okay' so that we're not going into a situation blind. The company says if you feel unsafe, get out of there quickly and call the cops. Who's to say you can get out of there." Angela's solution has been to keep family members notified of her job locations while she's working, in case something happens. Her safety concerns are amplified by the fact that the platform company she works for is difficult to contact for support: "That's a big thing. If I have a concern, I don't want to constantly communicate through an app. I want to talk to someone with information. There's no physicality."

Alongside these challenges, the digital revolution also presents opportunities. One of the greatest opportunities to the domestic work sector is the chance to cultivate and reach "high-road employers"—employers who believe their employees should work in safe environments, earn a decent living, and have access to support to address their concerns on the job. This is very difficult to implement when a sector operates mostly with 1:1 relationships between employer and worker. But an unprecedented opportunity to establish new norms and improve standards at scale is created by the aggregation that platform companies enable. Rather than implementing new standards with each employer one by one, platforms can implement floors, such as minimum hourly wages, which impact thousands of workers at once. Platforms also have an opportunity to educate employers about fair standards to aspire to, massively decreasing the cost of educating employers when the workforce is disaggregated. There are many employers who use platforms who would willingly take steps to ensure workers have good work if those steps were clear and easy to take, and the aggregation enabled by platforms makes it much easier to communicate those steps and establish new norms and standards, creating "high-road employers" at scale.

SHAPING THE FUTURE: INNOVATION IN ORGANIZING AND RAISING STANDARDS

This strategy of educating employers on the right thing to do—and supporting them to do it—led to the creation of the Good Work Code by NDWA's innovation hub, NWDA Labs. The Good Work Code is a set of eight overarching values that are the foundation of good work:

- Safety
- Stability and flexibility
- Transparency
- Shared prosperity
- Fair pay
- Inclusion and input
- Support and connection
- Growth and development

They were developed in consultation with people working across various gig economy platforms about their experiences and challenges working on the platforms.

With the growth of gig economy work, and the controversy surrounding worker conditions that culminated in multiple lawsuits against gig economy platform companies, it was clear that Silicon Valley needed guidance from labor leaders in creating good work in the online economy. Organizations are testing different approaches to both addressing the threats and seizing the opportunities. NDWA's experience working with domestic workers turned out to be uniquely relevant for addressing the challenges experienced by gig economy workers.

NDWA Labs launched the Good Work Code in November 2015, with 12 online economy companies who endorsed the entire code and committed to improving their practices in at least two of the values or areas of the code. Commitments included implementing a bonus program for workers, exploring ways to offer workers health care benefits, and offering salaried positions to some workers.

While platform companies can span a wide variety of work—from domestic work to legal services—many of these companies are dealing with similar problems. How do you design software to better integrate with workers' schedules? How do you ensure safety when a job has been requested online by a customer who has never been seen? How do you help workers feel less isolated when there is no water cooler to gather around? These are all challenges faced by many platform companies, and sharing solutions with their peers as well as brainstorming challenges together has proven invaluable as they tackle old problems in a new context. Platform companies are learning that not only are worker standards good for workers, they are good for business because the success of the platform company must be connected to the success of the workers who power it. Workers who better understand how the platform works are able to work better on the platform, workers who receive a share in the profits of the platform company are more invested in its success, workers who are able to provide input into the way the platform operates can provide valuable feedback for the platform designers and engineers, and workers who are more connected to their coworkers are more connected to the platform company. As worker marketplaces become more competitive for platforms competing for workers who provide the highest-quality service for customers and create the most value for companies, these worker standards are becoming more important to attract, and retain, the workforce critical to powering the online economy.

The rise of the gig economy also creates opportunities for social movements to partner with private sector companies to work on initiatives that educate their community on ways they can engage to raise worker standards. In 2015, NDWA, Hand in Hand (a domestic employers' network), and Care.com announced the Fair Care Pledge at the Clinton Global Initiative. The Fair Care Pledge is a way for employers to commit to and promote being a fair and respectful employer of a caregiver or domestic workers. The pledge was promoted to the Care.com community and created an important opportunity to raise awareness among families about the obligations of employers to workers. In 2017, NDWA members who work as housecleaners advised Airbnb on a living-wage standard for housecleaners, which was announced to over 300,000 Airbnb hosts. The living-wage standard set a living wage at $25 per hour for independent housecleaners and $15 per hour for those working at companies that cover other expenses. These types of initiatives create the opportunity for mass education about good work standards among employers and consumers on every platform where services are being bought and the structure of work is changing.

NDWA Labs is also developing new tools and products that have the potential to raise standards of work. One product, Alia, helps housecleaners collect contributions from their clients to pay for benefits, including everything from paid time off to a product such as health or dental insurance. Because most of our social safety net has been tethered to traditional, full-time employment, the entire system is jeopardized when work is structured outside the traditional employment framework. For domestic workers, this has long been the case. For gig economy workers, they are quickly learning that the benefits they might have taken for granted in other jobs are not available to them as gig workers. By bringing benefits to independent cleaners—some of the most vulnerable workers in the US economy—

NDWA Labs can tailor a program to a workforce where those benefits are most critically needed, while simultaneously building a product that will benefit the many more workers who are locked out of traditional benefit structures.

NDWA Labs has also created a contract tool called Contracts for Nannies to help nannies and employers come to clear agreement about employment arrangements. Because domestic work arrangements have historically been very informal, domestic workers are vulnerable to terms made in the context of a severe imbalance of power. Without any HR department oversight, employers can create and change employment agreements at will, and even disregard their own agreements without repercussion. By creating a tool that makes it easy for employers and nannies to discuss expectations and each element of employment and by presenting each element in the context of working toward both parties feeling successful in the relationship, workers can feel more empowered in the employment relationship, and potential conflicts can be addressed before they arise. While the worker is still without an HR department to report grievances to, the tool can be effective for worker self-advocacy and for beginning a working relationship on the right foot—addressing needs and concerns up front.

The digital revolution is driving tremendous change in our economy. Advocates and organizers in the labor movement who seek to make life better for working people must also change. Much of this change is unstoppable, but it is also, by definition, malleable. There are real threats to the dignity and security of workers in the future—we must seek both to understand and prepare for those threats. There will also be opportunities to uplift the dignity and value of work and shape the future. But only if we're focused on doing so. Protests and campaigns that target the bad practices of companies remain important strategies that we should never give up. And we must expand the tools in our toolbox for the new era. The same values—dignity and voice at work—that have always been at the heart of the labor movement still hold. Driven by those values, we can innovate new ways to improve the quality of work and the ability of workers to shape the quality of their work and the future of the economy if we orient toward it and challenge ourselves to meet the moment.

CHAPTER 17

Union–Cooperative Alliances: Conditions for Realizing Their Transformational Potential

MINSUN JI

Center for New Directions in Politics and Public Policy,
University of Colorado Denver

Labor unions and worker cooperatives have long shared a similar goal of worker empowerment as both were "integral parts of the same movement during the early growth of the working class under capitalism" (Mellor, Hannah, and Stirling 1988: 17). Both labor unions and cooperatives were designed to "give the common people a larger share in the national income and a greater control of the economy" (Rees 1946: 327) and both aimed to protect "the interests of the common man with limited means against exploitation by intermediaries and privileged class" (Galor 1992). While some radical labor unions critiqued cooperativist goals of reforming the capitalist system by turning workers into capitalists themselves, there still were many synergetic efforts between the two institutions in the early years of industrialism to "achieve mutually desirable goals in a number of areas" (Staples 1954; also cited in Wetzel and Gallagher 1987: 518). For such reasons, Rees, a labor activist in the 1930s, argued that cooperatives gave labor unionists "the other blade of the scissors" (Rees 1946: 327).

However, synergistic cooperation has not always been embraced by labor unions and worker cooperatives. In fact, unions and cooperatives have often departed from each other, building independent movements and organizations of their own, and typically engaging in only limited collaboration as agents of worker empowerment. This typical disconnection is unfortunate for workers facing the challenges of the global economy today because both organizations have weaknesses that mutual alliance might help to address. In terms of their respective weaknesses, the traditional organizing model of labor unions simply doesn't match the decentered, outsourced, and flexible production chains of today's global capitalism, while worker cooperatives face their own challenges of small size, low resources, and little networking with other groups. In terms of their possibly complementary strengths, worker cooperatives are well suited to addressing the growing challenges of union organizing in an informal economy through the cooperative model of organizing precariat workers into small-scale cooperatives, while labor unions are well suited to enlarging the social horizons of cooperative workers by pursuing broad-based political power through collective bargaining, social mobilization, and political advocacy. Considering the potential benefits, is there a way that these two institutions can come together better to advance their ultimately shared goals of worker empowerment and economic justice? Can their respective strengths be synergistically joined?

This chapter explores to what extent a unionized worker cooperative can be a part of a new form of labor movement with potential to address the challenges of neoliberal globalization. The article examines conditions under which unions and worker cooperatives might build alliances with the potential to seed meaningful political–economic changes that go beyond simple improvements in economic outcomes for workers at a particular workplace. Drawing on theoretical and historical analysis, the chapter posits two necessary conditions in order for the two labor organizations to form transformational collaborations. First, worker cooperative members should identify themselves as *workers* rather than as *business owners*. Second, worker cooperatives and labor unions should both align themselves with a stronger sense of political congruence where worker cooperatives and labor unions go beyond a goal of individualistic pursuits of income growth and engage in broader social and political movements as expressions of worker and civic solidarity.

Following this theoretical framework, the article presents a case study of a transformational union–cooperative model in the United States: New Era Windows Cooperative in Chicago. New Era Windows is a rare worker takeover case where a meaningful level of labor militancy accompanied the conversion of a company to a worker cooperative, an unusual model for US union cooperatives. This example is a good case study of a unionized cooperatives led by rank-and-file workers with a militant sense of their social role and power as workers and who share strong political congruence with supportive unions and other community groups in engaging in broader social movements for change. The New Era Windows union–cooperative alliance is a manifestation of the kind of transformational labor mobilization that can emerge when strong social movement unionism undergirds a worker cooperative with a clear sense of worker control.

GLOBALIZATION, THE INFORMAL ECONOMY, AND LABOR UNIONS

According to Neuwirth (2011), the economic activity in the world's informal economy is worth about $10 trillion a year and involves approximately 1.8 billion people. The definition of the informal sector, by Women in Informal Employment Globalizing and Organizing (WIEGO), includes "self-employed, paid workers in informal enterprises, unpaid workers in family businesses, casual workers without fixed employer, subcontract workers linked to informal enterprise and subcontract workers linked to formal enterprise" (Gallin 2001: 537). Informal employment is particularly significant in developing countries, where informal employment patterns are the dominant form of economic activity (Schurman and Eaton 2012).

The explosion of informal employment in the developing world is partly driven by the dramatic growth of the informal manufacturing sector there, due partly to the relocation of first-world manufacturing enterprises into the less formalized developing world. Outsourcing has become more common, as labor intensive and high productivity sectors such as manufacturing have been out-competed by low cost producers (International Labour Organization 2012). According to WIEGO, "more than one-half of nonagricultural employment in most regions of the developing world" is in the informal sector (Vanek et al. 2014: 1–2).

Although the number of informal workers in the United States is somewhat lower than in developing countries, the United States' informal sector is steadily growing. According to data from the Federal Reserve Bank of New York's Survey of Informal Work Participation (with data supplemented by a review of US Bureau of Labor Statistics estimates), 37% of nonretired US adults participate in paid informal work: "When we remove those who engage exclusively in informal renting and selling activities, we find that 20% of the respondents engage in informal work" (Bracha and Burke 2016: 1). US Department of Labor statistics on informal and contingent workers similarly show that 42.6 million workers, or about 30% of the workforce, were self-employed, independent contractors, or contingent/temporary workers at the turn of the decade (Neuner 2013). Also, according to the US Department of Commerce, 2.9 million people as of May 2015 relied on temporary-help services for jobs, accounting for "2.4% of all private sector jobs in the US economy" (Nicholson 2015: 2).

Though such contingent and informal workers earn very low wages and face poor working conditions, labor unions have not been very successful in organizing contingent workers and have been in almost steady decline in both density and coverage for the past half century. Numerous strategies have been adopted to reverse the trend of union decline, ranging "from associate membership arrangements, to labor law reform, to adoption of the 'organizing model' to card check organizing to community organizing, to strategies that have little to do with collective bargaining or workplace representation" (Godard 2009: 82; see also Freeman 2007; Freeman and Rogers 2002). Nevertheless, the reality is that unions have been losing the battle, and membership has been waning for years.

According to the US Bureau of Labor Statistics, the unionization rate of all US workers fell to 10.7% in 2016. The unionization rate for the private sector was a paltry 6.4%, while the public sector unionization rate was at 34.4%.

Unsurprisingly, Rosenfeld, Denice, and Laird (2016) report declining wages as a result of union decline. In the retail sector, union membership fell to 700,000 by 2012, down from 1.2 million in 1983 despite the rapid growth in the retail sector to account for 8. 6% of the GDP in the United States (Luce 2013: 6). However, many of these retail jobs are part time or temporary and are located in often dispersed small shops that don't match the large factory shop floors of old. The traditional way of "organizing shop by shop" in "appropriate units" as defined by the National Labor Relations Board is simply less relevant to a contingent, precarious, and fluid workforce—and unions are suffering as a result.

In short, external conditions such as the rapid explosion of informal workers—and the lack of legal protections for these workers in terms or organizing unions—have made it more difficult for the labor movements to alter their "representational strategies" (Schurman and Eaton 2012). In the preceding historical era of full-time employment in large workplaces, labor unions were a powerful tool to build the "representation/voice" of workers vis-à-vis management and to improve worker livelihood through better pay and benefits. But, in an era of an increasingly informal and contingent workforce, facing increasingly flexible and mobile capital, this traditional view of a collective bargaining union no longer works for many workplaces.

WORKER COOPERATIVE TRENDS IN THE UNITED STATES

According to the United States Federation of Worker Cooperatives (no date), worker cooperatives are defined as "business entities that are owned and controlled by their members, the people who work in them." Since the late 1700s, there have been hundreds of worker cooperatives formed in various industries in the United States, with the cooperative heyday occurring during the days of the Knights of Labor in the 1880s (Jackall and Levin 1986: 35). Worker cooperatives have always grown during times of unusual labor organizing and agitation, such as during the 1880s until the turn of the century, and again during the Depression and early New Deal years of the 1930s. During the 1960s and the 1970s, a time of general social and labor upheaval, there was another wave of hundreds of worker cooperatives and collectives that operated at small scales across the nation (Jackall and Levin 1986: 35; see also Levinson 2014).

Recently, there has been another surge of worker cooperative formation following the economic crisis in 2008, resulting in the creation of at least 80 new ones between 2010 and 2013 (Palmer 2015: 5). The total number of worker cooperatives was estimated at 256 as of 2013, according to a survey by Democracy at Work Institute. These worker cooperatives have 6,300 worker–owners and a median workforce of ten members per worker cooperative, and they have generated a collective annual revenue of $367 million (Palmer 2015: 5). Worker cooperatives have shown diversity in composition: 71% of cooperative members are female and 66% are nonwhite (Palmer 2015: 17). The largest worker cooperatives are in manufacturing, making up 16% all worker cooperatives and retail trade (14%), while the health care sector makes up only 7% of the worker cooperatives (Palmer 2015: 3–4).

In terms of worker cooperative growths, three major actors have played an important role in the development of this recent wave of worker cooperatives. First, in some locales, "anchor institutions" have emerged as important supporters of worker cooperatives because some large institutions in various locales have adopted a mission of supporting worker cooperatives in the local economy. An example is the Evergreen Initiative in Cleveland, where leaders of anchor institutions such as universities, foundations, and notable businesses united to incubate and build out an expanding network of worker cooperatives in 2009 (Alperovitz, Williamson, and Howard 2010; Johnsen 2010). This initiative resulted in more than $11 million being raised to support three worker cooperatives with a goal to create jobs and co-op ownership opportunities for low-income residents in Cleveland (Camou 2016: 8; see also Pinto 2016: 10).

City leaders have been the second actor in developing the recent wave of worker cooperatives. Some major cities such as Cincinnati, Jackson (Mississippi), Madison, New York, Pittsburgh, Reading (Pennsylvania), and Richmond have stepped up to support worker cooperative initiatives as a strategy for job creation (Flanders 2014; Scher 2014; Truthout 2013). New York allocated $3.3 million in 2015 and 2016 to develop worker cooperatives, enacting Local Law 22 in 2015 to encourage worker cooperatives to bid on city contracts (Camou 2016: 14). Madison also passed legislation to allocate $600,000 in city funds over five years (2016–2021) to support worker cooperatives.

Labor unions have been the third actor in developing recent worker cooperatives (Clay 2013; Ji 2016; McFellin 2013). The idea of a union–cooperative alliance resurfaced in particular force after 2009, with the announcement of a collaboration agreement between the United Steelworkers (USW) and Spain's Mondragon network of worker cooperatives (Clay 2013: 2; McFellin 2013; Witherell, Cooper, and Peck 2012). The vision of the USW–Mondragon agreement was to develop a series of worker-owned manufacturing facilities with a commitment to economic democracy shared by both unions and the Mondragon co-ops. The unionized cooperatives envisioned under this partnership are ones in which "worker–owners all own an equal share of the business and have an equal vote in overseeing the business ... one worker, one vote" (Witherell, Cooper, and Peck 2012: 6). In 2011, USW also passed Resolution No. 27, articulating a vision of "Workers' Capital, Industrial Democracy and Worker Ownership" that is to be pursued by creating more union cooperatives as "a profitable and sustainable means to create jobs and invest in our community." And as a result of the partnership between USW and Mondragon, 17 union–cooperative initiatives have been explored in recent

years, such as the Cincinnati Union–Cooperative initiative, which announced
a specific goal of building a stronger labor movement in general (Barker 2015;
Schlachter 2017).

Though progress has been very slow on actually launching new worker
cooperatives in accordance with this union–cooperative model, advocates
continue to believe that the vision offers a promising strategy for organizing workers in an era very hostile to organized labor. The president of the
USW, Leo Gerard, has expressed his optimism for the union–cooperative
model because of the fact that a union–cooperative partnership could begin
in an open environment, which is the opposite of how labor union organizing often gets started in a workplace. "You have to organize in secret," Gerard
noted, regarding typical union organizing. "There are very few places where
you're going to go from an unrepresented workplace and organize right out
in the open. You start off in a hostile environment" (Truthout 2013). Because
union–cooperative organizing is typically so much more open from the
start, and free of the hostility that often comes with organizing a union at
a privately owned workplace, Gerard was hopeful that a unionized cooperative might be a new model for organizing workers without encountering
management or even worker hostility toward a labor union.

McCarthy et al. (2011) have similarly argued that worker cooperatives and
unionization can complement one another. While worker cooperatives share
the union goal of distributing the rewards of capitalism more broadly, unions
can be crucial in enhancing "workplace productivity by providing voice mechanisms" that decrease workplace turnover and in giving workers the "means
and incentives to speak up about ways to improve performance and company
survival" (Doucouliagos and Laroche 2003, cited in McCarthy et al. 2011: 51;
for an older statement of the same vision, see Cornforth 1982; Delmonte 1990;
Eiger 1985). In similar fashion, Schlachter (2017) has argued that unions can
bring a vision of organized, collective bargaining to a cooperative workplace—
a vision in which the organized voice of workers is "a more continuous process
that does not simply begin and end with a contract."

CONDITIONS FOR RADICAL UNION–COOPERATIVE ALLIANCES

Though growing partnerships between unions and worker cooperatives
have promising implications in terms of labor empowerment, these partnerships are not necessarily associated with new forms of progressive labor
action, nor may it be assumed that the power and scope of labor movements
will necessarily grow through such alliances. One problem is the simple
reality that even though the union–cooperative vision is energetically expressed by advocates, and though the number of worker cooperatives since
the economic crisis of 2008 has grown, the fact is that worker cooperatives

are still rare, and very small, in terms of making a significant impact on the economy (Kerr, Kelly, and Bonanno 2016). Worker cooperatives in the United States are small (a median size of ten workers) and are concentrated in low-wage industries like housecleaning, daycare, lawn care, and food services—which means that average wages among cooperatives tend to be low as well. For all its aspirational vision, the USW–Mondragon alliance has yet to find real success in reopening steel mills or other such high-wage manufacturing operations on a union–cooperative model.

But even if union–cooperative advocates were to find more success in launching large cooperatives in high-value economic sectors, they would face other important challenges. Notably, both unions and worker co-ops face deep dilemmas in balancing their practical work as "simply business" against broader aspirations to wage a "battle for socialism" (cited in Prychitko 1989: 3). When the two organizations come together, these dilemmas can be resolved in a way that advances *or* undermines progressive alternatives to capitalism. The result will be contingent on actual strategic and organizational pathways followed by labor activists in response to their local political and economic milieus. Two kinds of available pathways are particularly important in shaping the nature of union cooperative alliances that emerge on the ground: the pathway of *workers or owners?* and the pathway of *shopkeeper or social movement?*

Workers or Owners? Worker-Owned Cooperatives and the Degeneration Thesis

In 1921, the Olympia Veneer plywood cooperative—the nation's first plywood cooperative—began operations in the Pacific Northwest, when 125 workers invested $1,000 each to become worker–owners of their own cooperative, committed to the idea of replacing traditional capitalism with an example of an egalitarian and participatory worker-managed company (Lindenfeld and Wynn 1995; Zwerdling 1978). At Olympia, all staff members, from floor sweepers to plan managers, were paid the same rate. All workers, of whatever rank, received an equal vote in important company decisions. The successful cooperative soon inspired around 30 plywood cooperatives to open across the Pacific Northwest, operating with similar principles. By 1974, eighteen plywood cooperatives were operating in the Northwest, accounting for 12% of all US plywood production (Berman 1982).

However, by the mid-1980s, almost all of these cooperatives had gone out of business, with many of them being bought out by larger, privately owned corporations such as Weyerhaeuser. One of the first to go, decades earlier, was Olympia itself. At Olympia, as the company grew larger in the post-WWII years, the company began to hire nonmember workers when the original founding members left the mill, cashing out substantial equity as they left (Bernstein 1976). At Olympia, like other plywood co-ops, members became increasingly focused on their own economic interests as *business owners*, which were achieved mainly by strictly limiting the circle of new co-op owners and giving new owners less of a stake in the cooperative. Regarding this plywood cooperative, Bernstein argues that "the most basic reason nonowning workers are not brought in as equal partners is that shareowners are reluctant to devalue their stock by adding more shareowners" (Bernstein 1976: 29). For these worker–owners, adding new worker–owners meant "you'd be cutting the melon into thinner slices," so worker–owners began to hire nonowners for part-time or seasonal work, which resulted not only in higher profits for worker–owners but also in growing tensions between worker–owners and nonowners at the workplace.

At the same time, the initial share price that a new member had to pay to become a member of this plywood cooperative became too high for a new worker–owners to afford. The value of shares jumped from an initial $1,000 to $2,000 to a price of $25,000 to $50,000, and thus, *"precisely because they were so successful,"* it became easier to sell shares to outside investors, who were not even co-op owners, rather than selling shares to new worker–owners. "New young workers did not have the money to buy into the co-op, so retiring members found it easier to sell their shares to capitalist lumber companies that wanted to acquire their very profitable business" (Bernstein 1976; Lindenfeld and Wynn 1995). By the 1950s, worker–owners of the small startup of the 1920s were increasingly retiring and cashing out their equity; the larger Weyerhaeuser corporation gained controlling interest, and the cooperative fully converted to a traditional corporation in 1954.

The degeneration story of the Pacific Northwest plywood cooperatives is replicated in other examples. Burley, an Oregon-based worker cooperative founded in the 1970s that made bicycle trailers, ended up failing in 2006 after years of successful cooperative operation based on democratic principles. Although the reason for its failure was partially due to fierce global competition, the major problem for Burley had to do with too rapid growth and the need to hire more workers to keep up with market demand. However, too sudden growth of worker ownership by hiring more worker–owners without appropriate training, and without sufficient time for testing out hired members, became a major problem later on. Normally, Burley had a six-month trial period to test out workers before voting them into full membership, but waiting on a new worker–owner for six months became an obstacle when the company grew rapidly, which put them in urgent need to hire more workers.

As a result of including new worker–owners without appropriate training, Burley started having problems, including growing rifts between original co-op owners and new workers who did not share the same level of commitment to cooperative principles. As these rifts widened and Burley lost some of its original sense of social mission, values of economic self-interest began to drive many worker–owners. For instance, Burley's practice of bringing in new members

> fundamentally altered the cooperative's culture and created rifts that prevented it from effectively responding to market changes. … The membership became more concerned with protecting its dividends, and individuals prioritized the security of their own wealth rather than the general health or mission of the collective. (cited in Semuels 2015)

In the end, Burley failed.

In this way, numerous worker-owned cooperatives have historically lost their original identity as collective social communities and "degenerated into a capitalist firm" (Pencavel 2012: 110)—hiring nonmember employees, selling to a private investor, or adopting a conventional corporate stock ownership structure. In this way, as "a product of capitalist society," worker cooperatives often face a danger of degeneration in terms of any broader goals of social transformation, in that they face pressure to "adopt the same organizational forms and priorities as capitalist businesses in order to survive" (Cornforth 1995: 488).

Adopting those traditional capitalist forms means that degeneration from high-minded social mission principles can occur when worker–owners sell ownership shares to outside investors to make profits or when they introduce a divisive two-class system within the cooperative so that not all workers have equal power or equitable incomes. Degeneration also can occur when cooperatives face competitive pressures to outsource and make operations more efficient, and whenever cooperatives face the reality of accommodating to the existing capitalist system by sacrificing some of their own founding principles (Hochner 1978).

Related to the degeneration thesis, there is a strong tendency of "shopkeeper spirit" developing among cooperative members once a worker cooperative becomes larger. When worker cooperatives are small in scale, democratic principles can be easily maintained. But, as the company becomes competitive and profitable, it becomes a challenge to maintain the co-op principles. In 1922, Malatesta (1922/2015) identified this danger that the "shopkeepers' spirit" would undermine the cooperative challenge to capitalism, while Schoening (2007: 299) more recently reiterated this same danger that "cooperatives come to view themselves as owners, entrepreneurs, and capitalists."

For just these kinds of reasons, many union advocates have long believed that the cooperative form of ownership "would require workers to give up the adversarial role vis-à-vis management and would undercut the traditional union as an organization" (Hochner 1983: 347). Slott (1985: 84) similarly argues that "worker ownership may not necessarily be in the best interests of the labor movement." Once workers gain ownership of a company, Slott (1985: 87) argues, they tend, "over a period of time, to identify less with workers employed by other companies than with the company they now own" (see also Moene and Wallerstein 1993). In similar fashion, and Kruse and Blasi studied employee attitudes and firm performance and found that "ownership status made little or no difference in desired participation or allocation of power" (1997: 129) and that "employee ownership does not magically and automatically improve employee attitudes and behavior whenever it is implemented" (1997: 143).

From this perspective, the most promising strategies of worker empowerment in the face of factory closures or other capitalist inequities don't involve turning workers into employee *owners*; rather, they are to nurture effective resistance at the local level by organizing the rank and file into mobilized *workers* confronting the inequities of individual workplaces and capitalism in general. Stannard (2014) argues that "the movement for worker-owned cooperatives needs organized labor's insistence on the identity and interests of workers as workers." José Orbaiceta, the president of CICOPA, an international organization of industrial and service cooperatives, similarly argues as follows:

> Our concept is that it is the trade unions which represent dependent workers and the cooperative federations which represent the cooperative enterprise, and they can work together because we are all workers, some of whom are in dependent relationships while others own the means of production—but all are workers. (2014: 11)

The emphasis on the characteristic of workers instead of "owners" helps worker cooperatives to develop the radical concept of worker control of the workplace rather than the more conservative notion of participation in management, from the perspective of business owners.

Hunnius, Garson, and Case (1973: 1) explain that "workers' control means democratizing the workplace: the office, the factory, the shop, the company or institution." It means "that a firm's management should be accountable to its employees." More broadly, the notion of workers' control can go beyond workplace concerns; Case defines worker control as "a strategy, a series of demands aimed at extending popular control of the enterprise and the economy" (1973: 444). Gorz also understands worker control in this far-ranging, radical sense, arguing that worker control means "the capability of the workers to take control of the process of production and to organize the working process as they think best" (1973: 339).

For real worker ownership, it is not enough to simply allow workers to buy substantial shares of stock ownership in a company, which might result in worker ownership but not likely result in a change in management philosophy to reflect a labor-managed firm. Mandel (1973) argues that the benefit of workers' control over the product of their own work is that it contributes to the well-being of workers while also decreasing their alienation from the work process and product (Azzellini 2015; Gorz 1982; Marcuse 2015; Wolff 2012). Some have called this a process of "dealienation," in which worker control becomes an important factor in restoring dignity and satisfaction in work itself (Gorz 1982: 409).

These far-reaching and radical ideals of building a transformational cooperative by fostering workers with a deep commitment to comprehensive democratic control of the workplace, and with the personality characteristics and professional skills to actualize that commitment, have always meant that the actual size and scope of radical worker cooperatives in practice has been quite limited. Building a worker cooperative with deep commitment to democratic practice among all worker–owners, and filled with members with congruent political and economic ideologies of equality and de-alienation from work, requires careful selection processes and long mentoring of new worker–owners. It is unrealistic to expect that such a demanding and lengthy worker-cultivation process could result in a large enough worker-cooperative sector with the potential to measurably transform the broader political–economic system. The dilemma seems to be that worker cooperatives can either cultivate radically transformational worker–owners (and thus be small and hard to replicate) or they can adopt more traditional forms of "shopkeeper" cooperativism, following normal business practices (and thus grow in size and become more economically sustainable). This is exactly the dilemma that the degeneration thesis recognizes explicitly and that certainly remains a challenge to union–cooperative advocates.

Shopkeepers or Social Movement?

Another factor to achieving a radical union–cooperative model is that both union and cooperative leaders in this partnership should share a congruent commitment to political activism to achieve social change, which goes beyond the "shopkeepers'" goal of enhancing workers' income through co-op ownership. Both worker cooperatives and labor unions have a dual roles as economic entities and as social–political institutions. While a labor union is an economic organization seeking to enhance workers' wages, a worker cooperative also has an economic role to improve the income of cooperative members. While a labor union defends workers against employers through the collective bargaining mechanism, a worker cooperative seeks to secure better income for its members through the employee ownership mechanism that delivers all business income and profits directly to workers themselves. These are well-recognized economic roles of both institutions. However, when either labor unions or worker cooperatives focus only on these economic roles, broader goals of community and social change—and the broader role of unions and cooperatives as agents of political–economic change—may be undermined. Zamagni and Zamagni explain the dilemma as follows:

> The cooperative is a genuine, two-faced Janus. It combines two distinct if not conflicting dimensions: the economic dimension of an enterprise that operates within the market and accepts its logic; and the social dimension of an institution that pursues meta-economic aims and produces positive externalities for other agents and for the entire community. This dual nature is what makes the cooperatives difficult to explain and so hard to govern. (2010: 1)

Facing this dual nature, worker co-ops often must consider the path of an efficient, business-like approach because, in the end, worker cooperatives are economic organizations that need to survive in the capitalist system and therefore must operate like any other business—that is, seeking to build profits through efficient business practices. As "a product of capitalist society," the goal of the cooperative is simply to operate an efficient business so as to "improve the income of members as part of the private enterprise system" (Abrahamsen 1976: 11). However, worker cooperatives also have transformational potential because of their concerns for a sustainable and equitable community and because of their commitment to workplace democracy as part of a radical critique of capitalism (Clay 2013; Engler 2010; Malleson 2014; Restakis 2010). From this perspective, economic democracy through a worker cooperative becomes one way to practice political democracy and build a "broader social democracy" (Bernard 2008–2009).

Though many co-ops naturally have such broader social and political goals, worker co-ops often find it difficult to build new forms of competitive businesses while also staying connected to broader political goals. In their focus on operating a successful business, for example, worker cooperatives typically are "disassociated from the labor movement" (Hochner et al. 1988: 16). It is often challenging for cooperatives to be efficient economic entities and provide "a high living standard for their members" while also participating in progressive campaigns and advancing "egalitarian and participatory values" across their community (Lawrence 2001). Pointing out this dilemma, Zamagni and Zamagni (2010: 1) argue that "whenever one of these aspects is sacrificed to the other, the cooperative is denatured, losing its identity" (see also Esim and Katajamaki 2017). In this regard, achieving a balance between their economic role (individual income gains) and their social role (communality) has been a challenge for many cooperatives.

Labor unions share a similar dilemma of having a dual role of enhancing union members' income and benefits, while also seeking to build a more equitable and just society more generally. When a labor union emphasizes its economic role to enhance the wages of its members only, scholars describe it as conservative "business unionism." In this business unionism model, collective bargaining focuses only on winning benefits for dues-paying union members (avoiding broader community concerns), and the union works like a business enterprise, "effectively selling their members services for a fee. … Much like insurance companies, they act as vendors of certain important employment protections" (DeMartino 2004: 34), delivering the goods to paying union members and leaving the broader capitalist system unchallenged.

However, if a labor union goes beyond seeking a better wage for only its members, then there is a potential to build a stronger labor movement. Though Marx was critical of many labor unions' conservative tendency to adopt forms of business unionism, he also argued that trade unions could be "important as an organized means to promote the abolition of the very system of wage labour" (cited in Dridzo 1935: 17). In this logic, labor unions can fight for the entire working class as a revolutionary organization, though such a stance will necessarily entail adversarial relations between unions and employers and might distract unions from winning incrementally better collective bargaining agreements with individual employers (Kelly 1998).

When both labor unions and worker cooperatives share a goal of broad-based political activism, they may be better able to create new sources of transformational power for workers. Many (Dean 2013; Ranis 2014; Wright 2014) are optimistic about the recent growth of worker cooperatives, regarding them as tool to catalyze a more effective labor movement. Curl (2009, 2010) and many others have argued that the current worker cooperative movement has characteristics of a social justice movement because the worker cooperative movement is best characterized not as an isolated number of individual cooperatives but as a collective movement, united through cooperative associations with self-defined goals of broader social transformation.

Through collective associations of cooperatives, and by joining directly with unions in labor organizing campaigns, worker cooperatives may develop a more well-articulated commitment to their "social change" roles. In his study of worker cooperatives in the United States, Ciplet points to such possibilities and emphasizes that "the worker cooperative activists should embrace cooperative principles for the movement, and strategically engage in the tensions of building a democratic movement in the context of global capitalism" (2007: 3). This social change perspective is advocated by a wide range of union–cooperative activists and scholars, who argue that cooperatives can only maintain their transformational "values and culture through ongoing connections to social movements" (Langmead 2017: 82; see also Levinson 2014).

In short, union–cooperative collaboration is fraught with many ontological and organizational dilemmas, and how those dilemmas (owners or workers? shopkeepers or social movement activists?) are resolved leads to substantially different organizing outcomes on the ground (Ji 2016). Thus, the question of how a labor union and a worker cooperative should come together so as to best advance their transformational potential requires both organizations to find a common thread of solidarity in standing as *worker* organizations first and foremost. To best realize the transformational potential of allying with a labor union, therefore, worker cooperative members should identify as *workers* instead of *owners*. At the same time, both worker cooperatives and unions both are in need of emphasizing their social and political roles that go beyond the limitations inherent in "becoming simply a 'collective egoist' concerned only with the well-being of its membership" (Schweickart 2011: 70). When broad social and political movement goals are shared by both labor unions and worker cooperatives who emphasize the importance of political organizing, their collaboration can build a stronger labor and social movement. It all depends on whether or not labor unions and worker cooperatives "limit themselves to their real function as defenders of the immediate interests of their members or are animated and influenced by the anarchist spirit, which makes the ideas stronger than sectional interest" (Malatesta 1922/2015: 110).

A CASE STUDY IN UNION–COOPERATIVE COLLABORATION: THE NEW ERA WINDOWS COOPERATIVE

This case study highlights the story of the New Era Windows union–cooperative collaboration that emerged in Chicago when a direct-action window factory takeover by workers on the shop floor catalyzed an alliance between the United Electrical, Radio and Machine Workers Union (UE) and a self-started workers cooperative. Although cases of worker takeover in the United States are rare, the takeover of Chicago's New Era Windows represent an approach where workers became critical in taking over the factory in order to save jobs and to create a democratic ownership structure.

In December 2008, after decades of successful operation selling vinyl replacement windows and patio doors since 1965, the owner of Chicago's Republic Windows and Doors, Richard Gillman, declared bankruptcy and shut down the operation with only three days of notice to workers. Unionized workers were told their jobs were immediately terminated, with no back pay or severance pay, and with immediate termination of medical benefits. At the same time, the company continued to operate at a profit, and owners of the family business were busy planning new window factories in other regions—and hiring non-unionized temp workers through low-wage labor agencies. The owners also ended up in court fighting allegations of financial fraud in their allegations of bankruptcy.

In response to the crisis, and without prior authorization by their national union, 270 Republic Windows workers decided to occupy their factory floor in December 2008. As workers mobilized on their own to gain control of the factory, the UE came to their aid; a massive unionized sit-down strike captured the attention of Chicago and the nation for six days. Republic Windows workers had been with the UE Local 1000 since 2004 after rejecting a preceding alliance with a different union, the Central States Joint Board (CSJB), which workers found to be "conservative, undemocratic and corrupt" (Wright 2014: 204). Before their switch to an alliance with the more radical UE union, Republic Windows workers had actually launched a wild strike against the CSJB union in 2002 to show discontent with their union representation; with the window company that employed them; and with the police, who encouraged strikebreakers to cross the picket line (Wright 2014: 205).

After the factory occupation by workers in 2008 and the ensuing legal troubles for the factory owner, a bankruptcy court judge ruled that a different company out of California (Serious Energy) "could purchase the plant's assets and employ the 260 workers involved in the occupation of the factory" (Ranis 2016: 115). Serious Energy soon took over the factory with a promise to rehire all the workers. However, that company didn't keep its promise and in fact only rehired 30 workers, leaving hundreds without jobs (Ranis 2014: 65). Even with such dramatic labor-shedding practices to save money, ineffective management and constant changes in company leadership eventually led to declining profits for Serious Energy, and a second factory closure notice was announced in February 2012. When no one emerged to purchase the factory after 90 days, workers finally decided to take over the company directly, resulting in a 12-hour sit-in strike (Lavender 2012; Ranis 2014: 65).

Facing severe economic problems and facing growing labor militancy, the owners of Serious Energy decided to transfer ownership directly to workers, giving workers time to raise the capital necessary to purchase factory equipment. But finding secure capital to purchase factory equipment was not an easy task for workers, confirming a Federation of Protestant Welfare Agencies (FPWA) report in 2015, which concluded that worker cooperatives typically face financing troubles because of "lack of financials to support the loan application, insufficient collateral, and the requirement of a personal guarantee" (Jaffe 2015). However, a nonprofit organization that provides investment capital to worker cooperatives (The Working World) emerged at the critical moment and provided Republic Windows workers with the entire capital package needed ($665,000) to purchase the equipment and to convert their company into a worker cooperative (Jaffe 2015; Lydersen 2013a; Ranis 2016).

To cut the cost of operation, workers relocated to a smaller place and restarted their business as the New Era Windows Cooperative in May 2013 (Lydersen 2013b; Ranis 2016: 115). The reason for the downsizing of the worker cooperative was that the majority of workers who were workers at Republic Windows left when the company closed the doors on them—most of them felt they had to search for new jobs immediately. Also, the majority of workers were rather skeptical about a worker cooperative because the majority did not have any knowledge regarding how worker cooperatives operated or how a cooperative might be in the economic interests of workers (Martin 2014). Initially, 25 workers were committed to the worker cooperative, paying their buy-in fee of $2,000. But by the time that the company reopened, there were only 16 worker–owners and one associate member who had seen the vision through to completion (Martin 2014).

While New Era Windows didn't generate profits for the first two years, its annual gross revenue grew to $500,000 in 2014 and doubled to $1 million in 2015, with 23 cooperative members and two staff (van Gelder 2015, 2017; also http://bit.ly/2GIj0k8). In 2016, the New Era Windows Cooperative also received a settlement of $295,000 from a bankruptcy court, which found that Republic Windows failed to negotiate with the union over the closing of the factory in 2008. As a result, workers received two weeks of back pay (Lydersen 2016; Ranis 2016).

This financial payout, together with healthy and growing annual revenues, has allowed New Era Windows to survive as a worker cooperative, with a horizontal governing structure in which workers run the entire business by themselves without outside owners or management directing operations in any way. Helping this model succeed, the UE union has been an important ally in developing and sustaining this worker cooperative. The workers at New Era Windows retained their union membership with UE and established a union contract that "covers work rules, grievances, and mediation in case of conflict" (Jaffe 2015). At the same time, UE is responsible for educating and training workers regarding business operations, leadership strategies, and business marketing techniques such as various social media strategies (Fried 2014).

Direct Action and Total Participation by Workers Not Owners

Novkovic, Prokopowicz, and Stocki make a case for "the application of the total participation approach," which is defined as the idea that "individuals decide to participate in the life of an organization of their own will and that they act for a common goal" (2012: 8; see also Stocki, Prokopowicz, and Zmuda 2010; Zamagni and Zamagni 2010). This total participation approach well summarizes the strategy of New Era Windows workers, where co-op members "actively engaged in the processes, structures and strategy of their organizations" (Novkovic, Prokopowicz, and Stocki 2012: 8–9) and demonstrated a commitment to "labour as action" rather than "labour as toil" (Novkovic, Prokopowicz, and Stocki 2012: 8). This emphasis on the total participation of workers in sustaining an effective worker cooperative is echoed in the study by Kruse and Blasi, which finds that "employee attitudes are better under employee ownership only if perceived worker influence or participation in decisions is higher" (1997: 129).

The unionized worker–owners of New Era Windows remain represented by UE, which has been "democratized to become more responsive to the needs of the rank and file and [which is] less prone to be incorporated by the employers with whom they negotiate" (DeMartino 2000: 32). Whereas typical American unions have been mostly run by professional staff, and therefore worker ownership campaigns have often not been well supported by union leadership (Early 2008; Tillman and Cummings 1999), the UE has maintained "rank-and-file unionism" to ensure that members run their union, set all the policies of the union, and make all decisions at the local level. The UE was actually one of the first members of the Congress for Industrial Organizations (CIO)—a relatively radical arm of the US labor movement in the 1930s and 1940s, and the UE became the CIO's third largest affiliate, with 500,000 members (Early 2008: 33; Wright 2014: 206). However, the UE was expelled from the CIO in 1949 owing to its union radicalism.

Although the UE has faced substantial declines in membership in the past few decades, especially severe from the loss of manufacturing jobs in the 1970s and the 1980s, it has continued to maintain its radicalism and its commitment to rank-and-file leadership as the key to organizing. Upchurch, Croucher, and Flynn argue that the problem of many labor unions in the era of neoliberal globalization lies in their "unwillingness, hesitation, or limited commitment" to "mount attacks and fight back, combined with rank-and-file workers' lack of confidence to act independently" (2012: 91).

However, UE's case is different because it has consistently emphasized a bottom-up organizing strategy to develop working-class consciousness of all workers. UE members are the ones who select "local officers, stewards, negotiators, and delegates to national conventions" and they also choose "when to strike and to end a strike, when to accept a contract, and what terms to demand and how to use local dues" (Wright 2014: 206).

Richard Bensinger, director of the AFL-CIO Organizing Institute, describes the importance of such rank-and-file leadership in bringing a more comprehensive movement philosophy to the union world: "We need more staff, and unions need to hire more organizers. But I think unless the fight is owned by the membership, and unless union leaders give ownership to the membership, it won't succeed" (cited in Robinson 2002: 125). This call to action is what Moody calls a "rank-and-file strategy," which argues that organizers should orient themselves toward mobilizing the strata of worker activists at the base of unions, who are the most engaged in shop-floor militancy and resistance to management, rather than "attempt to gain influence by sidling up to the incumbent bureaucracy or its alleged progressive wing" (2014: 115; see also Early 2009: 241).

It is natural that large labor unions, over time, form "hierarchical and bureaucratic structure with their own specialized personnel" and that this structure provides union officials with "authority and power over the rank and file" (Darlington and Upchurch 2012: 83). But this kind of structure tends to isolate union leaders from the rank-and-file base and, thus, labor unions fall into the trap of being bureaucratic organizations with enervated organizing initiatives because they see themselves only as a business agent that provides members various services in return for membership fees.

In workplace takeovers like New Era Windows, however, rank-and-file workers and their union representatives have turned away from such tendencies toward "business unionism" and instead have built up a culture of leadership development and mobilization of workers. In a personal interview, UE Local 1000 organizer Leah Fried (2014) reflects the view that

> this plant takeover could happen because leadership of workers was already in place, even before taking over the plant. I am doubtful if this kind of worker takeover would happen to other unions unless there is strong worker leadership coming from the bottom. Having a rank-and-file culture within the union is critical in making this kind of worker takeover possible.

In short, the New Era Windows Cooperative is an example of how strong rank-and-file leadership by co-op members, demonstrating strong "worker consciousness" (rather than simple pursuit of an "owner's" equity gains), and in partnership with a similarly radicalized and class-conscious labor union like UE, can foster a radicalized union–cooperative organization.

Political Congruence

Upchurch, Croucher, and Flynn argue that political congruence is "shared political values and vision … similar values, norms, and expectations," which are vital in order to achieve "trade union renewal" (2012: 865). The collaboration between the UE and New Era Windows has shown just this sort of strong political congruence, evidencing a strong commitment to broader social change goals. When the unionized workers of New Era Windows took to the factory floor and forged a new model of unionized worker ownership, they weren't just substituting one group of owners for another. When workers launched a six-day strike to occupy the factory, UE tied the issue of the economic crisis and the very expensive bank bailout to the challenge of closing of the local window factory in order to create a broader sense of community outrage and political protest—not only against the individual owner of Republic Windows and Doors, but also against larger systemic problem. Six-day worker strikes occurred around the same time that large banks received the $700 billion federal bailout of the Wall Street, in which Bank of America received $25 billion in taxpayer funds. Because Bank of America refused to renew loans to Republic

Windows, which contributed to an abrupt closing, workers could mobilize broader protests under the slogan of "you got bailed out, we got sold out" (United Electrical, Radio and Machine Workers of America 2016). As a result of massive public protests, Bank of America eventually agreed to pay a $1.75 million settlement to the UE, and workers received the payment of lost wages and $6,000 each in severance pay (United Electrical, Radio and Machine Workers of America 2016).

In this light, the birth of New Era Windows Cooperative is aligned with the goal of offering the local community a different model of how to run a company with concern for broader social health. The Working World website describes the story as follows.

> In many ways, this is not the story of a few workers, but of all of America. The old window factory was closed despite being profitable, its workers sent into unemployment despite their immense potential.
>
> As we watch our once proud workforce dismantled and impoverished by forces and motivations not of their own, we ask if these crises present opportunities. The workers of New Era want to succeed not just for themselves, but for their country, to show that downsizing does not have to be the end of the story, that there is way forward if we take our fate into our own hands. The possibilities that are emerging within the walls of this new factory have potential to flower across the country. (The Working World, no date)

This effort to frame actions as a response to the broader neoliberal globalization contexts is also well matched by the UE union, which has actively engaged in organizing in various regions to transform the condition of workers, not only through collective bargaining but also through "worker control over workplaces, community institutions, and the policies of the federal government itself" (Fields 2017). With this kind of broad social change horizon, the UE union has helped workers to look beyond their own workplace and become active in a broader range of initiatives to "sustain community" across their region—a form of wider-ranging political engagement that addresses community challenges while also enhancing their own cooperative's success. The president of UE Local 1000, Armando Robles, describes how:

> Our workers have been very active with the union for the past four years, and we learned of many social struggles. The option of worker ownership was not available in the beginning. But, when the second owner failed, we thought that we could be our own bosses, and we were ready because we have been receiving so much education for the past four years. (Robles 2014)

Similarly, one worker–leader at New Era Windows describes how worker involvement with broader social and political struggles is necessary to address both the individual challenges of the window factory and larger economic challenges facing the entire community. "There should be governmental help to keep factories open and allow the workers to try to keep their jobs," says this worker. "When there is no government help, at least there should be social help, community help, anything. The loss to a community is overwhelming when a whole factory closes" (Flanders 2013). Standing with New Era co-op owners against such dangers, the UE union is increasingly proactive about supporting union–cooperative models such as the New Era Windows model. For example, Leah Fried argued that UE passed a resolution at a national convention in 2014, committing the union to fostering more union–cooperative alliances s nationwide by helping educate workers, providing mutual support for existing partnerships, and seeking to unionize those cooperatives (Fried 2014).

In this way, militant direct action by rank-and-file workers at New Era Windows Cooperative demonstrates a collective expression of workers' consciousness that goes beyond the pursuit of income gains by individualistic workers. "It's not just about profits," claimed one worker–leader at New Era Windows Cooperative. "It's about sustaining communities, keeping jobs in places where people need them" (Flanders 2013).

CONCLUSION

The case of New Era Windows union–cooperative alliance illustrates how the current florescence of union–cooperative collaboration may presage a "new direction for the labor movement" (Alperovitz 2012)—an era of union–labor collaboration in which labor unions find common ground with the radical notion of worker control embedded in worker cooperatives. A key factor bringing these two institutions back together is the recent articulation of an increasingly harsh political–economic system in which organized labor unions are finding limited room to secure gains for their members. Confronted by increasingly harsh world of global capitalism, unions and cooperatives are rediscovering their old common principles.

We can predict that some of these emerging union–cooperative alliances will pursue accommodating paths of "business unionism" and "business cooperativism," but others will pursue paths seeking a broader and more transformational challenge to the extant political–economic order. We can also identify some of the necessary conditions for buwilding union–cooperative alliances with these more radical potentials. Two of these conditions are that worker-cooperative members should identify as *workers* rather than *owners*, and a second condition is that both union and co-op members should share politically congruent goals of engaging social movements for broad community change. When union activists stay within the boundaries of workers' economic self-interest (business unionism) or when cooperative members display only a "shopkeeper spirit" (business cooperativism), a union–cooperative partnership will be very unlikely to move forward with progressive social movement characteristics.

However, when both organizations build from the foundation that they are both workers' organizations striving toward better working conditions across the general community and seeking to create workplace democracy and broad social reform, more radical partnerships can emerge. Rob Witherell of USW argues as follows:

> Solidarity may sound like an old, foreign word to many in the United States, conjuring up images of old black-and-white photographs during the Great Depression of the 1930s. But solidarity means supporting each other, helping each other. It may be an ancient idea, but it is one that is critical to achieving a better future. (2013: 267)

Regardless of such high hopes for labor solidarity, it must be admitted that the economic scale and impact of unionized worker cooperatives today remain very small. Even as worker cooperatives blossom across the globe, with a model of decentralized, small-scale employee ownership that responds well to the growth of the precariat in the increasingly informal global economy, these small businesses still lack mass numbers, organizational power, and—most important—adequate access to capital resources to finance worker-owned cooperatives. As the case of New Era Windows shows, however, unions can play a critical role in solidifying community support, developing worker leadership, negotiating with banks for financing, or providing financing of their own (Flanders 2012).

Uniting labor union political, technical, and financial muscle with the grassroots innovations and growing membership numbers of worker cooperatives is the kind of partnership that some call broad-minded "social unionism" or "stakeholder unionism" (Biyanwila 2008; Clawson 2003; DeMartino 2004; Lambert 2002; Moody 1997; Waterman 2005) in which labor activists do not restrict themselves to struggles to involving workers at specific worksites. Instead, labor activists conceive of themselves as a broader alliance of people committed to similar economic and social goals, including both union members and circles of co-op owners and members of the broader community as well.

As these new and more inclusive forms of social movement unionism emerge, in response to the profound challenges of the neoliberal global era, we mays be witnessing a revitalized labor movement through new alliances between unions and worker cooperatives. Although these alliances may take significant time to bring scale and to impact the broader economy, the potential is real. What we are witnessing are serious efforts for unions and worker cooperatives to rediscover their common roots in shared commitments, and the enhanced power of each through alliance. In realizing the full potential of such alliances, however, it is vital to get the first principles right: workers—not owners; broad political horizons—not business unionism.

REFERENCES

Abrahamsen, Martin A. 1976. *Cooperative Business Enterprise*. New York, NY: McGraw-Hill.

Alperovitz, Gar. 2012 (Mar. 26). "The New 'Union Co-Op' Model." Personal website. http://bit.ly/2GIBBMF

Alperovitz, Gar, Thad Williamson, and Ted Howard. 2010 (Feb. 11). "The Cleveland Model." *The Nation*. http://bit.ly/2GIjWoE

Azzellini, Dario. 2015. *An Alternative Labour History: Worker Control and Workplace Democracy*. London, UK: Zed Books.

Barker, Kristin. 2015 (Mar.). Executive director, Cincinnati Union Co-Op Initiative. Interview with author.

Berman, Katrina V. 1982. "The Worker-Owned Plywood Cooperatives." In *Workplace Democracy and Social Change*, edited by Frank Lindenfeld and Joyce Rothschild-Whitt. Boston, MA: Porter Sargent.

Bernard, Elaine. 2008–2009. "The Power to Change Things: Labor Rights as Human Rights." *Our Times* 27 (6): 20–25.

Bernstein, Paul. 1976. *Workplace Democratization: Its Internal Dynamics*. Kent, OH: Kent State University Press.

Biyanwila, Janaka. 2008. *Re-Empowering Labour: Knowledge, Ontology and Counter-Hegemony*. Hawthorn, Victoria: The Australian Sociological Association.

Bracha, Anat, and Mary A. Burke. 2016. "Who Counts as Employed? Informal Work, Employment Status, and Labor Market Slack." Working Papers Nos. 16–29. Boston, MA: Federal Reserve Bank of Boston.

Camou, Michelle. 2016. "Cities Developing Worker Co-Ops: Efforts in Ten Cities." Medina, OH: Imagined Economy Project. http://bit.ly/2uDt0Gx

Case, John. 1973. "Workers' Control: Toward a North American Movement." In *Workers' Control: A Reader on Labor and Social Change*, edited by Gerry Hunnius, G. David Garson, and John Case, pp. 438–468. New York, NY: Random House.

Ciplet, David. 2007. "Beyond the Boss: Building the U.S. Worker Cooperative Movement in the Context of Global Capitalism." MA Thesis. School for International Training, Brattleboro, VT.

Clawson, Dan. 2003. *The Next Upsurge: Labor and the New Social Movements*. Ithaca, NY: Cornell University Press.

Clay, John. 2013 (Jul. 4). "Can Union Co-Ops Help Save Democracy?" *Truthout*. http://bit.ly/2uzUbSv

Cornforth, Chris. 1982. "Trade Unions and Producer Co-Operatives." *Economic and Industrial Democracy* (3): 17–30.

Cornforth, Chris. 1995. "Patterns of Cooperative Management: Beyond the Degeneration Thesis." *Economic and Industrial Democracy* 16: (4): 487–523.

Curl, John. 2009. *For All the People: Uncovering the Hidden History of Cooperation, Cooperative Movements, and Communalism in America*. Oakland CA: PM Press.

Curl, John. 2010. "The Cooperative Movement in Century 21." *Affinities: A Journal of Radical Theory, Culture and Action* 4 (1): 12–29.

Darlington, Ralph, and Martin Upchurch. 2012. "A Reappraisal of the Rank-and-File Versus Bureaucracy Debate." *Capital & Class* 36 (1): 77–95.

Dean, Amy. 2013. "Why Unions Are Going into the Co-Op Business." *Yes Magazine*. http://bit.ly/2uzGH9o

Delmonte, Toni. 1990. "In Defense of Union Involvement in Worker Ownership." *The Public Interest*. Spring: 14–30.

DeMartino, George. 2000. "U.S. Labor Faces an Identity Crisis." In *Political Economy and Contemporary Capitalism: Radical Perspectives on Economic Theory and Policy*, edited by Ron Baiman, Heather Boushey, and Dawn Saunders. Armonk, NY: M.E. Sharpe.

DeMartino, George. 2004. "Organizing the Service Sector from 'Labor' to 'Stakeholder Unionism.'" In *The Institutionalist Tradition in Labor Economics*, edited by Dell P. Champlin and Janet T. Knoedler. Armonk, NY: M.E. Sharpe.

Doucouliagos, Christos, and Patrice Laroche. 2003. "What Do Unions Do to Productivity? A Meta-Analysis." *Industrial Relations* 42 (4): 650–691.

Dridzo, Solomon Abramovich. 1935. *Marx and the Trade Unions*. New York, NY: International Publishers.

Early, Steve. 2008. "Remaking Labor—From the Top-Down? Bottom-Up? or Both?—Review of *L.A. Story: Immigrant Workers and the Future of the U.S. Labor Movement* and *U.S. Labor in Trouble and Transition: The Failure from Above and the Promise of Revival from Below*. *Working USA: The Journal of Labor and Society* 11:1. http://bit.ly/2uFOBhE

Early, Steve. 2009. *Embedded with Organized Labor: Journalistic Reflections on the Class War at Home*. New York, NY: Monthly Review Press.

Eiger, Norman. 1985. "Changing Views of U.S. Labor Unions Toward Worker Ownership and Control of Capital." *Labor Studies Journal* 10 (2): 99–122.

Engler, Allan. 2010. *Economic Democracy: The Working-Class Alternative to Capitalism*. Halifax, NS: Fernwood Publishing.

Esim, Simel, and Waltteri Katajamaki. 2017. "Rediscovering Worker Cooperatives in a Changing World of Work." IUS/Labor 1/2017. Geneva, Switzerland: International Labour Organization. http://bit.ly/2uDo18A

Fields, David. 2017. "New Book by James Young: *Union Power—The United Electrical Workers in Erie, Pennsylvania*." *Radical Political Economy*. http://bit.ly/2uwE5c8

Flanders, Laura. 2012 (Mar. 1). "Republic Windows Workers Consider Employee-Owned Co-Op." *The Nation*. http://bit.ly/2GIhgYa

Flanders, Laura. 2013 (May 9). "Worker-Owned Window Factory Opens for Business." *Yes Magazine*. http://bit.ly/2GIhUoy

Flanders, Laura. 2014. "How America's Largest Worker Owned Co-Op Lifts People out of Poverty." *Yes Magazine*. http://bit.ly/2wBs047

Freeman, Richard. 2007 (Feb. 22). "Do Workers Still Want Unions? More Than Ever." EPI Briefing Paper No. 182. Washington, DC: Economic Policy Institute.

Freeman, Richard, and Joel Rogers. 2002. "Open Source Unionism: Beyond Exclusive Collective Bargaining." *Working USA: The Journal of Labor and Society* 7 (2): 3–4.

Fried, Leah. 2014 (Mar.). International representative for the United Electrical, Radio and Machine Workers of America. Interview with author.

Gallin, Dan 2001. "Propositions on Trade Unions and Informal Employment in Times of Globalization." *Antipode* 33 (3): 521–549.

Galor, Zvi. 1992. "Trade Union Enterprises: A New Approach to the Problem of the Relationship Between the Trade Unions and Cooperatives." Kfar Saba, Israel: The International Institute of Leadership. https://bit.ly/2J7Bn0c

Godard, John. 2009. "The Exceptional Decline of the American Labor Movement." *Industrial & Labor Relations Review* 63 (1–2): 82–108.

Gorz, Andre. 1973. "Workers' Control Is More Than Just That." In *Workers' Control: A Reader on Labor and Social Change*, edited by Gerry Hunnius, G. David Garson, and John Case, pp. 325–343. New York, NY: Random House/Vintage.

Gorz, Andre. 1982. Gorz, Andre. 1982. *Farewell to the Working Class*. Translated by Michael Sonenscher. Boston, MA: South End Press.

Hochner, Arthur. 1978. *Worker Ownership and the Theory of Participation*. Ph.D. Dissertation. Cambridge, MA: Harvard University.

Hochner, Arthur. 1983. "Worker Ownership, Community Ownership, and Labor Unions: Two Examples." *Economic and Industrial Democracy* 4: 345–369.

Hochner, Arthur, Cherlyn S. Granrose, Judith Goode, Eileen Appelbaum, and Elaine Simon. 1988. "Using Worker Participation and Buyouts to Save Jobs." In *Job-Saving Strategies: Worker Buyouts and QWL*, pp. 1–12. Kalamazoo, MI: W.E. Upjohn Institute for Employment Research.

Hunnius, Gerry, G. David Garson, and John Case, eds. 1973. *Workers' Control: A Reader on Labor and Social Change*. New York, NY: Random House/Vintage.

International Labour Organization. 2012 (Jul. 6). Cooperatives: Resilient to Crises, Key to Sustainable Growth. http://bit.ly/2LRkiHX

Jackall, Robert, and Henry M. Levin, eds. 1986. *Worker Cooperatives in America*. Berkeley, CA: University of California Press.

Jaffe, Sarah. 2015 (Jan. 13). "Can Worker Cooperatives Alleviate Income Inequality?" *Al Jazeera*. http://bit.ly/2uDzPHW

Ji, Minsun. 2016. "Revolution or Reform? Union–Worker Cooperative Relations in the United States and Korea." *Labor Studies Journal* 41 (4): 355–376.

Johnsen, Michael. 2010. "Network of Cooperatives Gets Organized in New York City: Low-Income and Immigrant Workers Well-Represented." *Grassroots Economic Organizing Newsletter* II (5). http://geo.coop/node/435

Kelly, John. 1998. *Rethinking Industrial Relations: Mobilization, Collectivism and Long Waves*. Abingdon, UK: Routledge.

Kerr, Camille, Marjorie Kelly, Jessica Bonanno. 2016. *Taking Employee Ownership to Scale*. Oakland, CA: Democracy at Work Institute.

Kruse, Douglas, and Joseph Blasi. 1997. "Employee Ownership, Employee Attitudes, and Firm Performance: A Review of the Evidence." In *Handbook of Human Resource Management*, edited by David Lewin and Daniel J.B. Mitchell, pp. 113–151. Greenwich, CT: JAI Press.

Lambert, Rob. 2002. "Labor Movement Renewal in the Era of Globalization: Union Responses in the South." In *Global Unions? Theory and Strategies of Organized Labour in the Global Political Economy*, edited by Jeffrey Harrod and Robert O'Brien, pp. 185–203. London, UK, and New York, NY: Routledge.

Langmead, Kiri. 2017. "Challenging the Degeneration Thesis: The Role of Democracy in Worker Cooperatives?" *Journal of Entrepreneurial and Organizational Diversity* 5 (1): 79–98.

Lavender, George. 2012. "Republic Windows Opens New Era for Coops in Chicago." *Race, Poverty & the Environment* 19 (2): 49–50. http://bit.ly/2uBAsC2

Lawrence, John. 2001. "Democratic Worker Co-Ops and the Struggle for Economic Democracy." *Grassroots Economic Organizing.* http://bit.ly/2MmaMNo

Levinson, Ariana R. 2014. "Founding Worker Cooperatives: Social Movement Theory and the Law." *Nevada Law Journal* 14 (2): 322–363.

Lindenfeld, Frank, and Pamela Wynn. 1995. "Why Do Some Worker Co-Ops Succeed and Others Fail?" *Grassroots Economic Organizing.* http://bit.ly/2uDBfSM

Luce, Stephanie. 2013 (Oct.). "Global Retail Report." UNI Global Union. http://bit.ly/2uygQyB

Lydersen, Kari. 2013a (Dec. 18). "As One Window Closes in Chicago, Another One Opens." *In These Times.* http://bit.ly/2uCbz93

Lydersen, Kari. 2013b (May 9). "A New Era for Worker Ownership, 5 Years in the Making." *In These Times.* http://bit.ly/2uAgwzo

Lydersen, Kari. 2016 (Jan. 25). "Chicago Window Workers Who Occupied Their Factory in 2008 Win New Bankruptcy Payout." *In These Times.* http://bit.ly/2uArcOB

Malatesta, Errico. 1922/2015. *Life and Ideas: The Anarchist Writings of Errico Malatesta,* edited by Vernon Richards. Oakland, CA: P.M. Press.

Malleson, Tom. 2014. *After Occupy: Economic Democracy for the 21st Century.* New York, NY: Oxford University.

Mandel, E. 1973. "Workers' Control and Workers' Councils." *International, The Theoretical Review of the International Marxist Group* 2 (1): 1–17. British Section of the United Secretariat of the Fourth International. http://bit.ly/2LPiorh

Marcuse, Peter. 2015. "Cooperatives on the Path to Socialism." *Monthly Review* 66 (9). http://bit.ly/2uwRsZS

Martin, Brendan. 2014 (Jun.). Executive director, The Working World. Interview with author.

McCarthy, John E., Paula Voos, Adrienne E. Eaton, Douglas L. Kruse, and Joseph R. Blasi. 2011. "Solidarity and Sharing: Unions and Shared Capitalism." In *Employee Ownership and Shared Capitalism: New Directions in Research,* edited by Edward Carberry. Champaign, IL: Labor and Employment Relations Association.

McFellin, Atlee. 2013. "Labor Unions in the New Economy." *Common Dreams.* http://bit.ly/2uIRgXV

Mellor, Mary, Janet Hannah, and John Stirling. 1988. *Worker Cooperatives in Theory and Practice.* Milton Keynes, UK: Open University Press.

Moene, Karl, and Michael Wallerstein. 1993. "Unions Versus Cooperatives." Reprint Series No. 443. Oslo, Norway: Department of Economics, University of DSLO.

Moody, Kim. 1997. *Workers in a Lean World: Unions in the International Economy.* London, UK: Verso.

Moody, Kim. 2014. *In Solidarity: Essays on Working-Class Organization in the United States.* Chicago, IL: Haymarket Books.

Neuner, Jeremy. 2013. "40% of America's Workforce Will be Freelancers by 2020." *Quartz.* http://bit.ly/2uBB3ng

Neuwirth, Robert. 2011. *Stealth of Nations: The Global Rise of the Informal Economy.* New York, NY: Anchor Books.

Nicholson, Jessica R. 2015. "Temporary Help Workers in the U.S. Labor Market." ESA Issue Brief #03-15. Washington, DC: US Department of Commerce.

Novkovic, Sonja, Piotr Prokopowicz, and Ryszard Stocki. 2012. "Staying True to Co-Operative Identity: Diagnosing Worker Co-Operatives for Adherence to Their Values." In *Advances in the Economic Analysis of Participatory and Labor-Managed Firms*, edited by Alex Bryson. Bingley, UK: Emerald Group.

Orbaiceta, José. 2014. "Trade Unions and Cooperatives: The Experience of CICOPA-Mercosur." Geneva, Switzerland: International Labour Organization. http://bit.ly/2uy0PJ6

Palmer, Tim. 2015. "U.S. Worker Cooperatives: A State of the Sector." Research Publication Series. Oakland, CA: The Democracy at Work Institute.

Pencavel, John. 2012 (Oct.). "Worker Cooperatives and Democratic Governance." IZA Discussion Paper No. 6932. Institute of Labor Economics. http://bit.ly/2uB4rd9

Pinto, Sanjay. 2016 (Mar.). "Ours to Share: How Worker-Ownership Can Change the American Economy." New York, NY: Surdna Foundation. http://bit.ly/2uBvlSj

Prychitko, David. 1989. "The Political Economy of Workers' Self-Management: A Market Process Critique." Ph.D. Dissertation. George Mason University, Fairfax, VA.

Ranis, Peter. 2014. "Promoting Cooperatives by the Use of Eminent Domain: Argentina and the United States." *Socialism and Democracy* 28 (1): 51–69.

Ranis, Peter. 2016. *Cooperatives Confront Capitalism: Challenging the Neoliberal Economy.* London, UK: Zed Books.

Rees, Albert. 1946. "Labor and the Co-Operatives: What's Wrong?" *The Antioch Review* 6 (3): 327–340.

Restakis, John. 2010. *Humanizing the Economy: Co-Operatives in the Age of Capital.* Gabriola Island, BC: New Society Publishers.

Robinson, Ian. 2002. "Does Neoliberal Restructuring Promote Social Movement Unionism? US Developments in Comparative Perspective." In *Unions in a Globalized Environment: Changing Borders, Organizational Boundaries and Social Roles*, edited by B. Nissen. Armonk, NY: M.E. Sharpe.

Robles, Armando. 2014 (Mar.). President, United Electrical, Radio and Machine Workers of America Local 1000. Interview with author.

Rosenfeld, Jake, Patrick Denice, and Jennifer Laird. 2016. "Union Decline Lowers Wages of Nonunion Workers." Washington, DC: Economic Policy Institute.

Scher, Abby. 2014 (Jun. 21). "Leveling the Playing Field for Worker Cooperatives." *Truthout.* http://bit.ly/2uAzBBr

Schlachter, Laura. 2017. "Stronger Together? The USW–Mondragon Union Co-Op Model." *Labor Studies Journal* 42 (2): 124–147.

Schoening, Joel. 2007. "Democracy Derailed: Cooperative Values Confront Market Demands at a Worker Owned Firm." Ph.D. Dissertation. University of Oregon, Eugene, OR.

Schurman, Susan J., and Adrienne E. Eaton. 2012. "Trade Union Organizing in the Informal Economy: A Review of the Literature on Organizing in Africa, Asia, Latin America, North America and Western, Central and Eastern Europe." Washington, DC: Solidarity Center. http://bit.ly/2uEUrzy

Schweickart, David. 2011. *After Capitalism (New Critical Theory).* Lanham, MD: Rowman & Littlefield.

Semuels, Alana. 2015 (Jul. 8). "Getting Rid of Bosses." *The Atlantic.* https://theatln.tc/2uBUKex

Slott, Mike. 1985. "Debate: The Case Against Worker Ownership." *Cornell University ILR School Labor Research Review* 1 (6): 83–97. http://bit.ly/2uEVBuU

Stannard, Matt. 2014 (Jul. 5). "Organized Labor, Public Banks and the Grassroots: Keys to a Worker-Owned Economy." *Occupy.com.* http://bit.ly/2GsUIar

Staples, Ralph. S. 1954 (Dec.). "Problems of Employee Relationship in the Co-Operative Movement." *The Canadian Unionist.*

Stocki, R., P. Prokopowicz, and G. Zmuda. 2010. "Total Participation in Management. Critical Management Practice." Published in Polish by Wolters Kluwer in 2008 under the title *Pełna Partycypacja w Zarządzaniu.* Translated by Wyższa Szkoła Biznesu, National Louis University, Krakow.

The Working World. No date. "New Era Windows." http://bit.ly/2GL6eRU

Tillman, Ray, and Michael Cummings, eds. 1999. *The Transformation of U.S. Unions: Voices, Visions, and Strategies from the Grassroots.* New York, NY: Lynne Reinner.

Truthout. 2013 (May 24). "Can Unions and Cooperatives Join Forces? An Interview with United Steelworkers President Leo Gerard." http://bit.ly/2uzsvgI

United Electrical, Radio and Machine Workers of America. 2016 (Jan. 21). "Another Back Pay Win for Republic Windows Workers, Result of 2008 Plant Occupation. http://bit.ly/2GKNqSC

United States Federation of Worker Cooperatives. No date. "What Is a Worker Cooperative?" http://bit.ly/2uC0Z1Z

Upchurch, Martin, Richard Croucher, and Matt Flynn. 2012. "Political Congruence and Trade Union Renewal." *Work, Employment and Society* 26 (5): 857–868.

Vanek, Joann, Martha Alter Chen, Francoise Carre, James Heintz, and Ralf Hussmanns. 2014. "Statistics on the Informal Economy: Definitions, Regional Estimates & Challenges." WIEGO Working Paper No. 2. Cambridge, MA. Women in Informal Employment Globalizing and Organizing. http://bit.ly/2wCiDRE

van Gelder, Sarah. 2015 (Oct. 9). "Three Years Ago, These Chicago Workers Took Over a Window Factory. Today, They're Thriving." *Yes Magazine.* http://bit.ly/2uEQD1k

van Gelder, Sarah. 2017. *The Revolution Where You Live: Stories from a 12,000 Mile Journey Through a New America.* Oakland, CA: Berrett-Koehler.

Waterman, Peter. 2005. "Labour and New Social Movements in a Globalizing World System: The Future of the Past." *Labor History* 46 (2): 195–207.

Wetzel, Kurt, and Daniel Gallagher. 1987. "A Conceptual Analysis of Labour Relations in Cooperatives." *Economic and Industrial Democracy* 8: 517-540.

Witherell, Rob. 2013. "An Emerging Solidarity: Worker Cooperatives, Unions, and the New Union Cooperative Model in the United States." *International Journal of Labour Research* 5 (2): 251–268.

Witherell, Rob, Chris Cooper, and Michael Peck. 2012. "Sustainable Jobs, Sustainable Communities: The Union Co-Op Model." United Steelworkers. http://bit.ly/2wBrzqJ

Wolff, Richard. 2012. *Democracy at Work: A Cure for Capitalism.* Chicago, IL: Haymarket Books.

Wright, Chris. 2014. *Worker Cooperatives and Revolution: History and Possibilities in the United States.* Bradenton, FL: Booklocker.com.

Zamagni, Stefano, and Vera Zamagni. 2010. *Cooperative Enterprise: Facing the Challenge of Globalization.* Cheltenham, UK: Edward Elgar.

Zwerdling, Daniel. 1978. *Democracy at Work.* Washington, DC: Association for Self-Management.

About the Contributors

Cathy Albisa is executive director of the National Economic and Social Rights Initiative (NESRI). She is a constitutional and human rights lawyer and co-founded NESRI in order to build legitimacy for human rights in general, and economic and social rights in particular, in the United States. She is committed to a community-centered and participatory human rights approach that is locally anchored but universal and global in its vision. She clerked for the Honorable Mitchell Cohen in the District of New Jersey. She received a B.A. from the University of Miami and a J.D. from Columbia Law School.

Greg Asbed, a 2017 MacArthur Fellow, is a co-founder of the Coalition of Immokalee Workers, the Fair Food Program (FFP), and the Worker-Driven Social Responsibility model, a breakthrough approach to verifiable corporate accountability recognized by observers from the United Nations to the White House for its unique effectiveness in combating forced labor, sexual violence, and other gross human rights violations in agriculture. He spearheads the development of the FFP's market-based enforcement mechanisms, rights standards, and worker education processes. He has a B.S. from Brown University and an M.A. from Johns Hopkins School for Advanced International Studies.

Xóchitl Bada is an associate professor of Latin American and Latino Studies at the University of Illinois at Chicago. Her research interests include migrant access to political and social rights, migrant organizing strategies, and transnational labor advocacy mobilization in North America. Her recent research has appeared in the journals *Population, Space, and Place* and *Forced Migration Review*. Her book, *Mexican Hometown Associations in Chicagoacán: From Local to Transnational Civic Engagement* demonstrates how and why emergent forms of citizen participation practiced by Mexican hometown associations engage simultaneously with political elites in Mexico and the United States.

Jacob Barnes is a doctoral student in the Rutgers School of Management and Labor Relations. His research interests include precarious work, employee misclassification, and nontraditional labor organizations. Before that, he was a research specialist at the Worker Institute at Cornell University, studying such topics as the New York State Arts & Entertainment Workforce, growing alliances between labor unions and nontraditional labor organizations, and nascent unionization efforts in the video game production industry. He holds a bachelor's degree from the Cornell School of Industrial and Labor Relations, with minors in business and inequality studies.

Joseph C. Bazler is a Ph.D. candidate in international and comparative labor at Cornell University's School of Industrial and Labor Relations (ILR). His research focuses on questions of community unionism and care work, with a particular focus on teachers' unions in Buenos Aires, Argentina. He earned an M.S. from the ILR School, an M.A. from the University of Chicago, and a B.A. from Bellarmine University.

Linda Burnham is senior advisor at the National Domestic Workers Alliance and co-author of *Home Economics: The Invisible and Unregulated World of Domestic Work*. She has worked for decades as an activist, writer, and strategist focused on women's rights and racial justice. She co-founded the Women of Color Resource Center, where she served as executive director for 18 years. Burnham has published numerous articles on African American women, African American politics, and feminist theory in a wide range of periodicals and anthologies. "Gender and the Black Jobs Crisis" appeared in the June 2016 issue of the journal *Souls*.

Austin Case earned a juris doctor degree from the University of California Davis School of Law and a master's in industrial and labor relations from Cornell University's School of Industrial and Labor Relations in 2017. Before attending law school, he was a research analyst for UNITE HERE Local 5 in Honolulu.

Els de Graauw is an associate professor of political science at Baruch College, the City University of New York. Her research centers on the nexus of immigration and immigrant integration, civil society organizations, urban and suburban politics, and public policy. She is the author of *Making Immigrant Rights Real: Nonprofits and the Politics of Integration in San Francisco*. She earned her Ph.D. in political science from the University of California Berkeley.

Janice Fine holds a Ph.D. in political science from the Massachusetts Institute of Technology and is an associate professor of labor studies and employment relations at the School of Management and Labor Relations, Rutgers University, and director of research and strategy at the Center for Innovation in Worker Organization, where she leads the work on membership-building and distributed leadership practices and strengthening labor standards enforcement. Fine is the author of the book *Worker Centers: Organizing Communities at the Edge of the Dream*. Before becoming a professor, she worked as an organizer for more than 20 years.

Leslie C. Gates is an associate professor and director of graduate studies at Binghamton University's Department of Sociology. She recently served as chair of the American Sociological Association's Section on Political Economy of the World-System (PEWS). Her work and teaching employ both quantitative and qualitative techniques to analyze empirical evidence. Her interests include worker advocacy efforts and the relationship between corporate power and politics. She is the author of the book *Electing Chávez: The Business of Anti-Neoliberal Politics in Venezuela*.

Shannon Gleeson earned her Ph.D. in sociology and demography from the University of California Berkeley in 2008. She joined the faculty of the Cornell University's School of Industrial and Labor Relations in 2014, after six years on the faculty of the Latin American and Latino Studies Department at the University of California Santa Cruz. Her books include *Precarious Claims: The Promise and Failure of Workplace Protections in the United States* and *Conflicting Commitments: The Politics of Enforcing Immigrant Worker Rights in San Jose and Houston*

Kati L. Griffith is an associate professor of labor and employment law and chair of the Labor Relations, Law, and History Department at Cornell University's School of Industrial and Labor Relations. She is a research fellow affiliated with New York University's Center for Labor and Employment Law and Cornell University's Institute for the Social Sciences. She is a co-author (along with Michael Harper and Samuel Estreicher) of the textbook *Labor Law: Cases, Materials, and Problems,* 8th edition. Her research and teaching focus on labor and employment law, immigration policy, and legal issues affecting low-wage workforces.

Hahrie Han is the Anton Vonk Professor of Political Science at the University of California Santa Barbara. She specializes in the study of civic and political participation, collective action, organizing, and social change, particularly as it pertains to social policy, environmental issues, and democratic revitalization. She has published three books: *How Organizations Develop Activists: Civic Associations and Leadership in the 21st Century, Groundbreakers: How Obama's 2.2 Million Volunteers Transformed Campaigning in America*, and *Moved to Action: Motivation, Participation, and Inequality in American Politics*. Her award-winning work has been published in the *American Political Science Review, American Sociological Review, American Journal of Sociology*, and numerous other outlets.

Ken Jacobs is the chair of the UC Berkeley Labor Center, where he has worked since 2002. His areas of research include low-wage work, labor standards policies, and health care coverage. Recent work includes economic impact studies of proposed minimum wage laws for the cities of Seattle, Los Angeles, and San Jose and analyses of the public cost of low-wage work. Jacobs was a co-editor of *When Mandates Work: Raising Labor Standards at the Local Level*, an edited volume on the impacts of labor standards policies in San Francisco.

Andrea Cristina Mercado is the daughter of immigrants from South America, and she has been organizing in immigrant communities and communities of color for over a decade. She is one of the co-founders of the National Domestic Workers Alliance and led the California Domestic Worker Coalition, a statewide effort to include domestic workers in labor laws. Mercado served as director of campaigns for the National Domestic Workers Alliance for five years, where she led nationally recognized campaigns for immigrant and worker rights such as We Belong Together, and the 100 women/100-mile pilgrimage for migrant dignity. She is now the executive director of New Florida Majority and the New Florida Majority Education Fund, an organization building the independent political power of marginalized communities for racial, economic, and climate justice.

Minsun Ji is the director of the Center for New Directions in Politics and Public Policy in the Political Science Department at the University of Colorado Denver. She was the founder and long-time executive director of a worker center in Denver, El Centro Humanitario para los Trabajadores (Humanitarian Center for Workers), organizing immigrant day laborers and domestic workers. She was also a labor activist in her native country, South Korea. She received her Ph.D. from the Josef Korbel School of International Studies at the University of Denver. Her special interests in research include international political economy, worker cooperatives, social movements, labor politics of different countries, and solidarity economy.

Jonathan L. Kim graduated from Cornell University's School of Industrial and Labor Relations in 2017, minoring in law and society. He worked for the Worker Institute at Cornell as an undergraduate research fellow, conducting research on worker center funding sources. He presented his research at Harvard's Engaged Scholarship and Undergraduate Research Conference and SUNY's Undergraduate Research Conference. After graduation, he joined Capital One as a business analyst.

Jane McAlevey is an organizer, author, and scholar. Her first book, *Raising Expectations (and Raising Hell)*, was named Most Valuable Book of 2012 by *The Nation* magazine. Her second book, *No Shortcuts: Organizing for Power in the New Gilded Age*, was released late in 2016. She is a regular commentator on radio and television. She continues to work as an organizer on union campaigns, lead contract negotiations, and train and develop organizers. She spent the past two years as a postdoctoral researcher at Harvard Law School, and she is presently writing her third book—*Striking Back*—about organizing, power, and strategy.

Joseph A. McCartin is executive director of the Kalmanovitz Initiative for Labor and the Working Poor and a professor of history at Georgetown University, where he teaches courses on US labor, social, and political history. Among his books are *Labor's Great War: The Struggle for Industrial Democracy and the Origins of Modern American Labor Relations, Collision Course: Ronald Reagan, the Air Traffic Controllers, and the Strike That Changed America*, and *Labor in America: A History*, 9th edition, co-authored with Melvyn Dubofsky.

Zane Mokhiber is a research assistant at the Economic Policy Institute (EPI) in Washington, D.C. He supports the research of EPI's economists on topics such as wages, labor markets, inequality, trade and manufacturing, and economic growth. Prior to joining EPI, Mokhiber worked for the Worker Institute at Cornell University as an undergraduate research fellow and was supported by the Rawlings Cornell Presidential Research Scholars program.

Victor Narro is a nationally known expert on the workplace rights of immigrant workers. He is project director for the UCLA Labor Center. He is a core faculty member of the UCLA Department of Labor and Workplace Studies. He is also a lecturer in law at the UCLA School of Law. In addition to writing many law review and journal articles, Narro is co-author of *Broken Laws, Unprotected Workers: Violations of Employment and Labor Laws in America's Cities*, and *Wage Theft and Workplace Violations in Los Angeles* and co-editor of *Working for Justice: The L.A. Model of Organizing and Advocacy*. He is also author of *Living Peace: Connecting Your Spirituality with Your Work for Justice*.

Steven C. Pitts came to the UC Berkeley Labor Center in August 2001. He received his Ph.D. in economics with an emphasis on urban economics from the University of Houston in 1994. At the Labor Center, Pitts focuses on issues of job quality and Black workers. In this arena, he has published reports on employment issues in the Black community, initiated a Black union leadership school, and shaped projects designed to build solidarity between Black and Latino immigrant workers. He co-founded the National Black Worker Center Project. He is currently developing a new project focused on the intersection of mass incarceration, work, and unions.

Ai-jen Poo is director of the National Domestic Workers Alliance and co-director of the Caring Across Generations campaign. She has been organizing immigrant women workers for over two decades, forging pathways to sustainable, quality jobs for the caregiving workforce and ensuring access to affordable childcare and eldercare for all working families. She is a 2014 MacArthur Fellow and was named one of *Fortune* magazine's World's 50 Greatest Leaders for 2015. She is the author of *The Age of Dignity: Preparing for the Elder Boom in a Changing America.*

Chris Rhomberg is an associate professor of sociology at Fordham University. His research has focused on historical and contemporary issues of labor, race, urban development, and politics in the United States. He is the author of *The Broken Table: The Detroit Newspaper Strike and the State of American Labor* and *No There There: Race, Class and Political Community in Oakland.* He is past chair of the American Sociological Association's Section on Labor and Labor Movements, and he is a member of the National Writers Union/UAW 1981.

Sean Sellers is director of strategic partnerships at the Worker-Driven Social Responsibility Network. Since 2003, he has supported the Coalition of Immokalee Workers' efforts to improve farm labor conditions in several capacities, first as national co-coordinator of the Student/Farmworker Alliance and then as a W.K. Kellogg Foundation Food & Society Fellow. In 2011, his work pivoted to implementation of the Coalition of Immokalee Workers' Fair Food Program across the US East Coast tomato industry as a founding staff member of the Fair Food Standards Council. He has a B.S. and an M.A. from the University of Texas at Austin.

Palak Shah is the social innovations director of the National Domestic Workers Alliance (NDWA) and the founding director of Fair Care Labs, the innovation arm of the domestic worker movement. Shah leads NDWA's national strategy on raising market norms and standards, partnering with the private sector and building scalable and sustainable business ventures. NDWA is the nation's leading organization working for power, respect, and fair labor standards for the 2.5 million nannies, housekeepers, and eldercare givers in the United States.

Erica Smiley is co-executive director of Jobs With Justice. Before that, she performed many roles at Jobs With Justice, including organizing director, campaign director, and senior field organizer for the southern region. She has authored several articles highlighting some of the organization's most exciting developments in the *New Labor Forum, Dissent, Class, Race and Corporate Power,* and other publications. She serves on the board of the Highlander Research and Education Center based in Tennessee and is on the leadership council of the Workers Defense Project in Texas. In the past, Smiley has organized with community groups and unions such as the Tenants and Workers Support Committee (now Tenants and Workers United) in Virginia and SEIU

Local 500 in Baltimore. She was national field director of Choice USA (now United for Reproductive and Gender Equity—URGE), where she received the Young Women of Achievement Award in 2004, before joining the staff of Jobs With Justice in 2005.

Marilyn Sneiderman directs the Center for Innovation in Worker Organization at Rutgers' School of Management and Labor Relations. She has 30 years of experience in labor, community, faith-based, immigrant, and racial justice organizing, as well as extensive experience in managing large staffs and managing intensive organizational change work. For ten years, Sneiderman directed the national AFL-CIO's Department of Field Mobilization, where she helped launch the national Union Cities initiative. The campaign focused on increasing the capacity to support and win organizing, political, and policy campaigns throughout the United States. Working with the AFL-CIO's international unions, state federations, and central labor councils, the program was designed to unite community, union, religious, and civil/immigrant rights groups in building local movements to fight for social and economic justice.

Aaron C. Sparks joined Elon University as an assistant professor of political science in the fall of 2018. He earned a B.S. in biology from Westmont College, a master's in public administration from Penn State Harrisburg, and an M.A. and Ph.D. in political science from the University of California Santa Barbara. His research interests center around the politics of environmental policy, and he is particularly interested in understanding how people form their beliefs and attitudes on environmental issues and how those attitudes shape their behavior.

Nik Theodore is a professor of urban planning and policy and associate dean for faculty affairs and research in the College of Urban Planning and Public Affairs, University of Illinois at Chicago. His current research focuses on urban informal economies, low-wage labor markets, and worker organizing in the United States and South Africa. He is author (with Jamie Peck) of *Fast Policy: Experimental Statecraft at the Thresholds of Neoliberalism.*

Kyoung-Hee Yu focuses her research on how work and employment experiences are impacted by and can motivate institutional and organizational change. Her recent research has examined the influence of commitments to social causes—such as social and environmental justice—on the employment relationship. Her research also addresses the impact of international migration on individual migrants and collective action, as well as implications for diversity and inclusion in organizations. Yu is the recipient of a US–Korea Fulbright Fellowship. She served as book review editor and editorial board member of the journal *Organization Studies* and is currently on the advisory board of the *Journal of Industrial Relations*. Her papers have been recognized by the American Sociological Association (Best Student Paper, Labor and Labor Movements Section), the Labor and Employment Relations Association (Best Dissertation Award Runner-Up), the Academy of Management (Best Paper Runner-Up, Careers Division), and the Australian and New Zealand Academy of Management (Best Paper, Critical Management Studies Division).

IT
TAKES
WORK
TO SHAPE
OUR
FUTURE.

ILR School

ilr.cornell.edu

A *Better* WAY TO →→→→→→→ WORK

Kaiser Permanente and the Coalition of Kaiser Permanente Unions thank all our workers, managers and physicians for 21 years of partnership.

Affordable, quality care. It started in California's shipyards and steel mills during World War II, serving working men and women on the home front. Today we continue this history of service to our community with skilled, union caregivers.

Today Kaiser Permanente is America's largest nonprofit health care delivery organization. And our Labor Management Partnership is the largest, longest-running and most successful such partnership in the country. Together we create award-winning results for our members, patients and workforce.

 KAISER PERMANENTE®   LMPartnership.org   COALITION OF KAISER PERMANENTE UNIONS

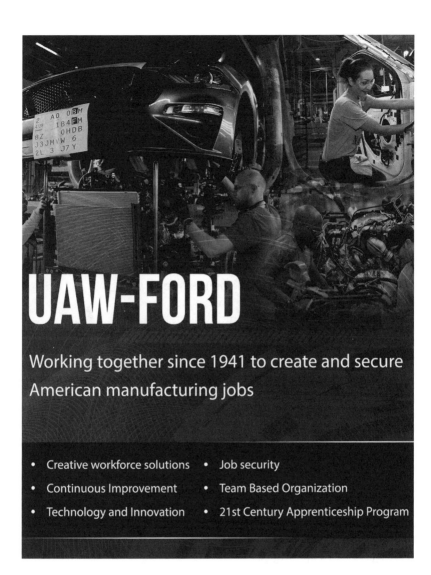

UAW-FORD

Working together since 1941 to create and secure
American manufacturing jobs

- Creative workforce solutions
- Continuous Improvement
- Technology and Innovation
- Job security
- Team Based Organization
- 21st Century Apprenticeship Program

RORY L. GAMBLE
Vice President, UAW Ford Department

BILL DIRKSEN
Vice President, Ford Motor Company

LERA Officers, 2018–2019

President
Kris Rondeau
AFSCME

President-Elect
Dennis Dabney
Kaiser Permanente

Past President
Harry Katz
Cornell University

Secretary–Treasurer
Ryan Lamare
University of Illinois at Urbana-Champaign

Editor-in-Chief
Ariel Avgar
Cornell University

National Chapter Advisory Council Chair
William Canak
Middle Tennessee State University (ret.)

Legal Counsel
Steven B. Rynecki

LERA Executive Board Members

Sylvia Allegretto, Center on Wage & Employment Dynamics

John Amman, IATSE Local 600

Annette Bernhardt, University of California, Berkeley

Matthew Bodah, University of Rhode Island

Ezio Borchini, George Washington University

John Budd, University of Minnesota

Paul Clark, Penn State University

Bill Dirksen, Ford Motor Company

Virginia Doellgast, Cornell University

Jonathan Donehower, Kaiser Permanente

Adrienne Eaton, Rutgers University

Cyndi Furseth, Portland General Electric

Michele Hoyman, University of North Carolina at Chapel Hill

Brad Markell, AFL-CIO

Daniel Marschall, Working for America Institute

Sheila Mayberry, Arbitrator and Mediator

Jim Pruitt, Kaiser Permanente

David Weil, Brandeis University

Jeffrey Wheeler, Georgetown University